LIVING LAW

This collection of essays is the first edited volume in the English language which is entirely dedicated to the work of Eugen Ehrlich. Eugen Ehrlich (1862–1922) was an eminent Austrian legal theorist and professor of Roman law. He is considered by many as one of the 'founding fathers' of modern sociology of law. Although the importance of his work (including his concept of 'living law') is widely recognised, Ehrlich has not yet received the serious international attention he deserves. Therefore, this collection of essays is aimed at 'reconsidering' Eugen Ehrlich by bringing together an interdisciplinary group of leading international experts to discuss both the historical and theoretical context of his work and its relevance for contemporary law and society scholarship.

This book has been divided into four parts. Part I of this volume paints a lively picture of the Bukovina, in south-eastern Europe, where Ehrlich was born in 1862. Moreover, it considers the political and academic atmosphere at the end of the nineteenth century. Part II discusses the main concepts and ideas of Ehrlich's sociology of law and considers the reception of Ehrlich's work in the German-speaking world, in the United States and in Japan. Part III of this volume is concerned with the work of Ehrlich in relation to that of some his contemporaries, including Roscoe Pound, Hans Kelsen and Cornelis van Vollenhoven. Part IV focuses on the relevance of Ehrlich's work for current socio-legal studies.

This volume provides both an introduction to the important and innovative scholarship of Eugen Ehrlich as well as a starting point for further reading and discussion.

Oñati International Series in Law and Society

A SERIES PUBLISHED FOR THE OÑATI INSTITUTE
FOR THE SOCIOLOGY OF LAW

General Editors

Johannes Feest　　　　　　　　　　　　Judy Fudge

Founding Editors

William LF Felstiner　　　　　　　　　　Johannes Feest

Board of General Editors

Rosemary Hunter, University of Kent, United Kingdom
Carlos Lugo, Hostos Law School, Puerto Rico
David Nelken, Macerata University, Italy
Jacek Kurczewski, Warsaw University, Poland
Marie Claire Foblets, Leuven University, Belgium
Roderick Macdonald, McGill University, Canada

Titles in this Series

Social Dynamics of Crime and Control: New Theories for a World in Transition edited by Susanne Karstedt and Kai Bussmann

Criminal Policy in Transition edited by Andrew Rutherford and Penny Green

Making Law for Families edited by Mavis Maclean

Poverty and the Law edited by Peter Robson and Asbjørn Kjønstad

Adapting Legal Cultures edited by Johannes Feest and David Nelken

Rethinking Law Society and Governance: Foucault's Bequest edited by Gary Wickham and George Pavlich

Rules and Networks edited by Richard Appelbaum, Bill Felstiner and Volkmar Gessner

Women in the World's Legal Professions edited by Ulrike Schultz and Gisela Shaw

Healing the Wounds edited by Marie-Claire Foblets and Trutz von Trotha

Imaginary Boundaries of Justice edited by Ronnie Lippens

Family Law and Family Values edited by Mavis Maclean

Contemporary Issues in the Semiotics of Law edited by Anne Wagner, Tracey Summerfield and Farid Benavides Vanegas

The Geography of Law: Landscapes, Identity and Regulation edited by Bill Taylor

Theory and Method in Socio-Legal Research edited by Reza Banakar and Max Travers

Luhmann on Law and Politics edited by Michael King and Chris Thornhill

Precarious Work, Women and the New Economy: The Challenge to Legal Norms edited by Judy Fudge and Rosemary Owens

Juvenile Law Violators, Human Rights, and the Development of New Juvenile Justice Systems edited by Eric L Jensen and Jørgen Jepsen

The Language Question in Europe and Diverse Societies: Political, Legal and Social Perspectives edited by Dario Castiglione and Chris Longman

European Ways of Law: Towards A European Sociology of Law edited by Volkmar Gessner and David Nelken

Crafting Transnational Policing: Police Capacity-Building and Global Policing Reform edited by Andrew Goldsmith and James Sheptycki

Constitutional Politics in the Middle East: With special reference to Turkey, Iraq, Iran and Afghanistan edited by Saïd Amir Arjomand

Parenting after Partnering: Containing Conflict after Separation edited by Mavis Maclean

Responsible Business: Self-Governance and Law in Transnational Economic Transactions edited by Olaf Dilling, Martin Herberg and Gerd Winter

Rethinking Equality Projects in Law edited by Rosemary Hunter

Living Law
Reconsidering Eugen Ehrlich

Edited by
Marc Hertogh

Oñati International Series in Law and Society

A SERIES PUBLISHED FOR THE OÑATI INSTITUTE
FOR THE SOCIOLOGY OF LAW

·HART·
PUBLISHING

OXFORD AND PORTLAND OREGON
2009

Published in North America (US and Canada) by
Hart Publishing
c/o International Specialized Book Services
920 NE 58th Avenue, Suite 300
Portland, OR 97213-3786
USA
Tel: +1 503 287 3093 or toll-free: (1) 800 944 6190
Fax: +1 503 280 8832
E-mail: orders@isbs.com
Website: www.isbs.com

© Oñati IISL 2009

All rights reserved. No part of this publication may be reproduced, stored in a retrieval system, or transmitted, in any form or by any means, without the prior permission of Hart Publishing, or as expressly permitted by law or under the terms agreed with the appropriate reprographic rights organisation. Enquiries concerning reproduction which may not be covered by the above should be addressed to Hart Publishing at the address below.

Hart Publishing Ltd, Worcester Place, Oxford, OX1 2JW
Telephone: +44 (0)1865 517530 Fax: +44 (0)1865 510710
E-mail: mail@hartpub.co.uk
Website: http://www.hartpub.co.uk

British Library Cataloguing in Publication Data
Data Available

ISBN: 978-1-84113-897-8 (hardback)
ISBN: 978-1-84113-898-5 (paperback)

Typeset by Compuscript, Shannon
Printed and bound in Great Britain by
the MPG Books Group

Acknowledgements

The history of this volume started in 2004, when Marc Galanter and I decided to organise a panel on the life and work of Eugen Ehrlich at the Law and Society Association Annual Meeting in Chicago. The lively discussions at this event led to the idea to publish a collection of essays which would be entirely dedicated to Ehrlich's sociology of law. In May 2006, we organised a very stimulating and enjoyable two-day workshop on 'Living Law: Rediscovering Eugen Ehrlich' at the International Institute for the Sociology of Law (IISL) in Oñati, Spain, with a group of leading international scholars. The results are published in this book.

I would like to thank Marc Galanter for his advice and encouragement in setting up this project. I am also grateful to the participants of this workshop who, besides the contributors to this volume and several master students, included Bernie Trujillo (who replaced Marc Galanter) and Martin Krygier. Their creativity and commitment made this volume possible. I would also like to thank Malen Gordoa Mendizabal and the other staff members of the Oñati Institute, who were the perfect hosts for this workshop and contributed a great deal to its success. Finally, I wish to thank the General Editor of the Oñati International Series in Law and Society, Johannes Feest, and two anonymous reviewers for their comments and assistance in preparing the manuscript for publication.

Marc Hertogh

Contents

Acknowledgements vii
List of Contributors xi

1. From 'Men of Files' to 'Men of the Senses': A Brief
   Characterisation of Eugen Ehrlich's Sociology of Law 1
   Marc Hertogh

Part I: Eugen Ehrlich: Life, Work and Context 19

2. Governing in the Vernacular: Eugen Ehrlich
   and Late Habsburg Ethnography 21
   Monica Eppinger

3. Venus in Czernowitz: Sacher-Masoch, Ehrlich
   and the *Fin-de-siècle* Crisis of Legal Reason 49
   Assaf Likhovski

Part II: Ehrlich's Sociology of Law 73

4. Ehrlich at the Edge of Empire: Centres and Peripheries
   in Legal Studies 75
   Roger Cotterrell

5. Eugen Ehrlich's Linking of Sociology and Jurisprudence
   and the Reception of his Work in Japan 95
   Stefan Vogl

Part III: Ehrlich and his Contemporaries 125

6. Facts and Norms: The Unfinished Debate between
   Eugen Ehrlich and Hans Kelsen 127
   Bart van Klink

7. Pounding on Ehrlich. Again? 157
   Salif Nimaga

8. The Social Life of Living Law in Indonesia 177
   Franz and Keebet von Benda-Beckmann

Part IV: Ehrlich and Contemporary Socio-legal Studies 199

  9. Naturalism and Agency in the Living Law 201
     Jeremy Webber

 10. World Society, Nation State and Living Law
     in the Twenty-first Century... 223
     Klaus A Ziegert

 11. Ehrlich's Legacies: Back to the Future in the Sociology
     of Law?... 237
     David Nelken

Index... 273

List of Contributors

Roger Cotterrell Professor of Legal Theory, Department of Law, Queen Mary, University of London, United Kingdom.

Monica Eppinger Doctoral Candidate, Department of Anthropology, University of California at Berkeley, United States.

Marc Hertogh Professor of Socio-Legal Studies, Faculty of Law, University of Groningen, the Netherlands.

Assaf Likhovski Associate Professor of Law, Faculty of Law, Tel Aviv University, Israel.

David Nelken Distinguished Professor of Legal Institutions and Social Change, University of Macerata, Italy.

Salif Nimaga Doctoral Candidate, Faculty of Law, Freie Universität Berlin, Germany.

Bart van Klink Associate Professor, Faculty of Law, Tilburg University, the Netherlands.

Stefan Vogl Lecturer, Kansai University, Japan.

Franz von Benda-Beckmann Professor of Legal Anthropology, Max Planck Institute for Social Anthropology, Halle, Germany.

Keebet von Benda-Beckmann Professor of Legal Anthropology, Max Planck Institute for Social Anthropology, Halle, Germany.

Jeremy Webber Professor of Law and Canada Research Chair in Law and Society, Faculty of Law, University of Victoria, Canada.

Klaus A Ziegert Associate Professor, Faculty of Law, University of Sydney, Australia.

1

From 'Men of Files' to 'Men of the Senses': A Brief Characterisation of Eugen Ehrlich's Sociology of Law

MARC HERTOGH

BACKGROUND

THE YEAR 2006 marked the 70th anniversary of Eugen Ehrlich's pioneering work *Fundamental Principles of the Sociology of Law* (1936),[1] which was originally published in German in 1913.[2] To commemorate this special occasion, a two-day workshop was held at the International Institute for the Sociology of Law (IISL) in Oñati, Spain, in the spring of 2006. Eugen Ehrlich (1862–1922) was an eminent Austrian legal theorist and professor of Roman law, as well as the founder of the Institute (Seminar) for Living Law. He is considered by many as one of the 'founding fathers' of modern sociology of law. Although the importance of his work (including his concept of 'living law') is widely recognised, Ehrlich has not yet received the serious international attention he deserves. Or, as another observer put it, 'many, if not most, sociologists of law today would be hard pressed if asked how their work was related to Ehrlich's foundation of the sociology of law'.[3] Over the years, there have been several important publications about Ehrlich's work, many of which were initiated by Manfred Rehbinder.[4] Most of these books were, however, published in

---

[1] E Ehrlich, *Fundamental Principles of the Sociology Law* (Cambridge, Mass, Harvard University Press, 1936); and E Ehrlich, *Fundamental Principles of the Sociology of Law* (New Brunswick/London, Transaction Publishers, 2002).
[2] E Ehrlich, *Grundlegung der Soziologie des Rechts* (Berlin, Duncker & Humblot, 1913).
[3] KA Ziegert, 'Introduction to the Transaction Edition' in Ehrlich (2002), above n 2, xix.
[4] See, eg M Rehbinder, *Die Begründung der Rechtssoziologie durch Eugen Ehrlich* (Berlin, Duncker & Humblot, 1967); E Ehrlich (hrsg. von M Rehbinder), *Recht und Leben: Gesammelte Schriften zur Rechtstatsachenforschung und zur Freirechtslehre* (Berlin, Duncker & Humblot, 1967); E Ehrlich (hrsg. von M Rehbinder), *Gezetz und lebendes Recht: vermischte kleinere Schriften* (Berlin, Duncker & Humblot, 1986); and H Kelsen and E Ehrlich, *Rechtssoziologie und Rechtswissenschaft. Eine Kontroverse (1915/1917)* (Baden-Baden, Nomos Verlagsgesellschaft, 2003).

2 *Marc Hertogh*

German and are not widely known to an international audience. Moreover, Ehrlich is frequently mentioned in text books on law and society, but there are still only a few examples in which his work is being discussed in greater detail. Therefore, this workshop was aimed at 'reconsidering' Eugen Ehrlich by bringing together an interdisciplinary group of leading international experts to discuss both the historical and theoretical context of his work and its relevance for contemporary law and society scholarship. This collection of essays, the first edited volume in the English language which is entirely dedicated to the work of Ehrlich, builds on the papers that were presented at this workshop.

The life and work of Ehrlich will be discussed in greater detail in the various essays of this volume. By way of introduction, this chapter offers a brief characterisation of Ehrlich's sociology of law.

OPINIO NECESSITATIS

Many scholars either like or hate Ehrlich's work or, to make things more complicated, both like and dislike his work at the same time. Why does Ehrlich's work often provoke such strong and contradictory reactions? Rather than taking on his complete writings, this introduction focuses on one specific aspect of his work, consisting of passages in *Fundamental Principles* where Ehrlich introduces his approach to differentiate between legal and other social norms. Here we will refer to this as the '*opinio necessitatis*-problem'. Although this particular element of his work did not receive much attention in previous introductions,[5] here it will be argued that it offers a good illustration of both the strengths and weaknesses of Ehrlich's work.[6]

Different Norms and Different Feelings

In a chapter entitled 'The State and the Law', Ehrlich takes issue with those lawyers who hold that only rules and regulations which are directly connected with (or recognised by) the state legislature or with state courts can be considered 'law'. Ehrlich strongly disagrees with this view, not on (normative) grounds of legal dogmatics, but because he feels that this conception of law does not correspond with the practice of law as he sees it. In this chapter, Ehrlich discusses a number of historical examples, including the Roman household and the English medieval manor, in which legal activities are not directly connected with the state or a state court. From this he concludes: 'The view that law is created by the state will not bear

---

[5] Ziegert (2002), above n 3; and R Pound, 'Introduction' in Ehrlich (2002), above n 1.
[6] See also the chapters by Cotterrell, Vogl, Van Klink and Nimaga in this volume.

the test of historical analysis' (p 160)[7] and therefore should be dismissed as 'scientifically untentable' (p 163). According to Ehrlich, this limited view on law has had an important negative effect on the development of the discipline of law:

> By confining the attention of the investigator to the state, to tribunals, to statutes, and to procedure, this concept of law has condemned the science of law to the poverty under which it has been suffering most terribly down to the present day. Its further development presupposes liberation from these shackles and a study of the legal norm not only in its connection with the state but also in its social connection (p 164).

This eventually leads Ehrlich to formulate his by now famous alternative concept of the 'living law': 'the law which dominates life itself even though it has not been posited in legal propositions' (p 493). The 'living law' is not directly linked to the state but to the inner orderings of various social groups or associations instead.

After Ehrlich has disconnected the law from the state, he continues by saying that the legal norm 'has always been found in the company of other social norms' (p 164). Nevertheless, he argues, there is 'an unmistakable difference between [the legal norm] and the non-legal norms'. Since Ehrlich rejects the idea that all legal norms are connected with the state, he needs an alternative criterion which can be used to identify the legal norm.

He starts by saying that this may seem an important theoretical puzzle, but in practice nearly anyone will be in a position to tell 'without hesitation' whether a given norm is a legal norm or whether it belongs to, for example, the sphere of religion or morality. Therefore, Ehrlich argues in a crucial passage that the question as to the difference between the legal and the non-legal norm 'is a question not of social science but of social psychology' (p 165). In his view, the emotional value attached to a norm contains important clues:

> The various classes of norms release various overtones of feeling (*Gefühlstöne*), and we react to the transgression of different norms with different feelings (p 165).

Whereas a violation of law leads to a feeling of revolt (*Empörung*), the violation of a law of morality leads to a feeling of indignation (*Entrüstung*). Moreover, an indecency corresponds with the feeling of disgust (*Ärgernis*), tactlessness with a feeling of disapproval (*Mißbilligung*), an offence against etiquette with ridicule (*Lächerlichkeit*) and, lastly, those who do not follow the same fashion cause a critical feeling of superiority (*kritischen Ablehnung*)

---

[7] Unless indicated otherwise, all references to Ehrlich in this essay refer to Ehrlich (2002), above n 1.

among true fashion-followers. Ehrlich claims that these differences will also be helpful in identifying the legal norm:

> Peculiar to the legal norm is the reaction for which the jurists of the Continental common law have coined the term *opinio necessitatis*. This is the characteristic feature which enables one to identify the legal norm (p 165).

In his view, the legal norm regulates a matter 'which, at least in the opinion of the group within which it has its origin, is of great importance, of basic significance (p 167).

The way in which Ehrlich treats the *opinio necessitatis*-problem is characterised by: (i) a lucid and polemical style; (ii) an emphasis on methodological innovation; (iii) multiple and contradictory interpretations to which his ideas have given rise; and (iv) the continuity with important contemporary socio-legal research.

Lucid and Polemical

One of the unique features of Ehrlich's writing that attracts attention is to be found in the openness and directness of his style. Although Ehrlich wrote his book nearly a century ago, in a time and context which were considerably different from ours, the text has suffered surprisingly little from the passage of time. This is even more clearly reflected in the original German version. Notwithstanding the serious subject matter, his tone is generally fresh and lively. Moreover, it is clear from the brief discussion of the *opinion neccessitatis*-problem that Ehrlich favours a confrontational and polemical approach. In his view, the position that law is always connected with the state is not only wrong, but also 'scientifically untenable'. Moreover, this has left the discipline of law in a state of 'poverty'.

These features are not only present in the discussion on the *opinio necessitatis*-problem, but in the rest of Ehrlich's work as well. According to the translator of the German edition, for instance, 'Ehrlich's style is simple and direct, and his sentences are somewhat loosely strung together'.[8] Furthermore, in the introduction of the most recent English edition, Ziegert highlights the 'unfashionable simplicity' of Ehrlich's work, which is 'free of both legal and sociological jargon'.[9] Some scholars, however, consider Ehrlich's distinctive style as one of his biggest weaknesses. It is not only lucid and provocative, but also rather essayistic. Ginsberg, in one of the first reviews of the English edition, noted that as a result this book was 'not the systematic exposition of the sociology of law which the title suggests', but rather 'a series of independent essays' which are 'loosely linked' and

---

[8] WLM, 'Translator's Preface' in Ehrlich (2002), above n 1, lvi.
[9] Ziegert, above n 3, xx.

unsystematically presented.[10] In a later review, Partridge takes a similar position and argues that it is difficult to 'nail down' Ehrlich because he persists in 'claiming more than he is willing to defend'. 'Whenever he puts a card on the table you can be sure that within a few pages he will have snatched it away again.'[11] And lastly, Cotterrell has argued that Ehrlich's concept of 'living law' was 'a concept devised solely for polemical purposes' which invites 'inquiries of seemingly boundless scope' and makes it not very useful as a guide for research.[12]

Methodological Innovation

A second feature of the way in which Ehrlich approaches the *opinio necessitatis*-problem is that, in the perennial debate on 'what is law?', he introduces a completely new methodology. Rather than studying court decisions, legal documents or the theoretical literature, he promotes the 'liberation from these shackles' (p 164) and suggests that we should instead focus on various 'overtones of feelings' (p 165) that are associated with the various groups of norms.

This, too, is an important general quality of Ehrlich's work. In the first chapter of *Fundamental Principles*, he condemns the fact that the discipline of law of the time was only concerned with solving practical legal problems. Instead, he insists on developing an 'independent science of law', not to serve practical ends, but which is aimed at 'pure knowledge' and is concerned 'not with words but with facts' (p 4). For Ehrlich, this also meant methodological innovation. Ultimately, Ehrlich claims, there are no 'antitheses' between science and art.

> For this reason every independent investigator must create his own method, just as every creative artist must create his own technique (p 472).

For him, 'method is as infinite as science itself' (p 506) and legal scholars should learn from other disciplines. In 1912, in a famous key address at the 'Annual Meeting of the German Lawyers Association' on legal education, this led him to advocate a radical change in the legal curriculum, so that young lawyers would also be taught in sociology, psychology and economics.[13] Ehrlich hoped that this would contribute to a transformation of lawyers from 'Men of Files' (*Aktenmenschen*) to 'Men of the Senses'

---

[10] M Ginsberg, 'Review "Fundamental Principles of the Sociology of Law"' (1937) *Modern Law Review* 169 at 169.
[11] PH Partridge, 'Ehrlich's Sociology of Law' (1961) 39 *Australasian Journal of Philosophy* 201 at 211.
[12] R Cotterrell, *The Sociology of Law: An Introduction* (London, Butterworths, 1992) 34.
[13] The full (translated) title of the address is: 'What Can be Done to Enhance the Insight of Lawyers in Psychological, Economic and Sociological Issues', *Transactions of the 31st Annual Meeting of the German Lawyers' Association*, 1912.

(*Mensch der Sinne*).[14] Methodological innovation could help with these efforts and would produce better lawyers:

> If one were to ask me which quality I would value most in a lawyer, I would not refer to his 'historical sense', nor his sparkling dialectics or his sharp wit, but instead I would say: what I value most are his eyes, to see, and his ears, to listen.[15]

Multiple Interpretations

Both his essayistic style and the emphasis on methodological innovation mean that Ehrlich's work is characterised by a number of serious 'gaps', which leave room for multiple interpretations and misunderstandings. Thus far, the literature on Ehrlich has focused on one particular version of the *opinio necessitatis*-problem. Yet his work also contains important clues for a second, alternative, version.

Ever since Ehrlich first published his ideas on *opinion necessitatis*, these were not taken very seriously. The mocking reaction of Kelsen is indicative of most commentaries in Ehrlich's time: 'Among the many attempts to determine the essence of law this one is certainly the most curious.'[16] Likewise, Rehbinder, who is an expert on Ehrlich's work and who usually writes very favourably of him, considers the *opinio necessesitatis*-discussion to be the most problematic element of Ehrlich's work.[17] More recent commentators share this critique. Nelken, for instance, calls Ehrlich's emphasis on various overtones of feelings a 'not altogether happy solution'[18] and according to Tamanaha, it is 'difficult to apply and incapable of providing a reliable distinction between legal and non-legal norms'.[19]

Underlying most of these critical reactions is the assumption that Ehrlich's *opinio necessitatis*-solution should be interpreted as a fundamental, normative principle in reaction to the jurisprudential question of 'what is law?' After all, Ehrlich claims he has identified 'essential characteristics of law' (p 167). Focusing on people's emotions (with the help of social psychology) is, however, not very helpful in answering this question, these critics argue. Moreover, how should a judge ever decide a case on the basis of this criterion?

---

[14] E Ehrlich, 'Die Erforschung des Lebendes Rechts' in E Ehrlich, *Recht und Leben: Gesammelte Schriften zur Rechtstatsachenforschung und zur Freirechtslehre* (Berlin, Dunker & Humblot, 1967 [1911]) 25 (my translation, MH).
[15] Ehrlich, *ibid*, 23 (my translation, MH).
[16] H Kelsen, 'Eine Grundlegung der Rechtssoziologie' (1915) 39 *Archiv für soziale Gesetzgebung und Statistik* 861 (my translation, MH).
[17] M Rehbinder, *Die Begründung der Rechtssoziologie durch Eugen Ehrlich* (Berlin, Duncker & Humblot, 1967) 39.
[18] D Nelken, 'Law in Action or Living Law? Back to the Beginning in Sociology of Law' (1984) 4 *Legal Studies* 157 at 163.
[19] BZ Tamanaha, 'An Analytical Map of Social Scientific Approaches to the Concept of Law' (1995) 25 *Oxford Journal of Legal Studies* 501 at 505.

Yet, there is also an alternative, and perhaps more favourable, way to interpret the *opinio necessitatis*-discussion. First, it should be noted that Ehrlich appears very reluctant to address the specific characteristics of the legal norm. He also emphasises that, 'in view of the present state of the science of the law', it is difficult 'to indicate precisely' where the legal norm differs from other norms (p 164). Moreover, before he unfolds his ideas, he adds: '[T]he object of the discussion that follows is rather to define the problem than to offer a solution' (p 164, my emphasis). He immediately adds another cautious remark:

> The sociological science of the law ... will not be able to state the difference between law and morals in *a brief simple formula* in the manner of the juristic science that has hitherto been current. Only a thorough examination of the psychic and social facts, which at the present time have not even been gathered, can shed light upon this difficult question (p 167, emphasis added).

Secondly, Ehrlich has repeatedly argued that he is not interested in making normative (legal dogmatic) claims about what should count as law (for instance, in a court of law). Instead, he claims his work to be entirely aimed at describing and analysing what people themselves consider as 'living law'. In his view, sociology of law is a science of law, 'excluding any practical application either in jurisprudence or in legal policy',[20] '[t]he question itself how law should be, goes beyond the reach of sociology'.[21] In a rather similar way, Pound, in his introduction to the English translation of Ehrlich's book, argues that contrary to legal science of the nineteenth century, 'in the twentieth century, the problem seems to be, first not what law *is*, but what law *does* ... '.[22] (Living) 'law' in a sociological sense then refers to those rules that people live by, but is not identical to 'law' in a legal sense. As a result, what Ehrlich has to say about the *opinio necessitatis*-problem is not meant as a 'brief single formula' to solve the jurisprudential problem of 'What is law?' (or as a basis for deciding court cases), but instead offers a novel research approach to analyse people's 'legal consciousness' and to see which norms they consider important in their daily lives.

Thirdly, most critics emphasise Ehrlich's reference to 'social psychology', but it is not entirely clear what he means by this. What is clear, however, is that Ehrlich repeatedly explains that the only way to analyse the living law is by 'observing life attentively, to ask people and to note down their replies' (p 498). Moreover, on the final pages of *Fundamental*

---

[20] E Ehrlich, 'Soziologie des Rechts' in M Rehbinder (ed), *Gezetz und lebendes Recht: vermischte kleinere Schriften* (Berlin, Ducker & Humblot, 1986) 179 (translation by Vogl, in this volume).
[21] Ehrlich, *ibid*, 180.
[22] Pound, above n 4, lxi (emphasis added).

Principles, he discusses something which we would now describe as experiments in social psychology. Ehrlich is, however, very critical about this approach because a person in such an experiment knows that the situation is fictitious and will therefore not show any important emotions (p 506). From this we can conclude, as Rottleuthner does, that the *opinio necessitatis*-approach should be considered a predominantly 'behavioural definition' of (legal) norms, which is restricted to 'observable behaviour'.[23] Likewise, Nelken argues that Ehrlich avoids the 'necessity for psychological introspection' by choosing norms 'which have a parallel form in existing legal systems'.[24] In this way, Ehrlich's 'social psychology' is part of his wider sociological approach to law and not much different from the rest of his empirical work. Ehrlich's approach is perhaps somewhat similar to the way in which Macaulay has looked at how businessmen react to a breach of contract in order to identify the group norms of the business community.[25]

These competing interpretations of Ehrlich are not limited to the *opinio necessitatis*-problem. In the literature, there are similar multiple understandings of, for example, Ehrlich's concept of 'living law' and the role of the state in his sociology of law. To some readers, this flexibility in interpreting important elements of Ehrlich's work adds to the attractiveness of his work. It makes it relatively easy to use as a source of new insight. Others, however, consider the same feature a great weakness and would probably argue that the 'sponge-like' character of his work makes it less useful for further research.

Continuity with Contemporary Studies

A final feature of the *opinio necessatis*-discussion by Ehrlich is the great degree of continuity that it shows with similar concerns in contemporary research. First, the idea that law is not necessarily connected with the state is also reflected in the current literature on legal pluralism.[26] More recently, this argument is supported by the increasing number of studies that focus on law in an international or transnational context.[27] Secondly, the idea that people's feelings and reactions are important in analysing the social significance of law and other social norms is echoed in other studies as well.

---

[23] H Rottleuthner, 'A Purified Sociology of Law: Niklas Luhmann on the Autonomy of the Legal System' (1989) 23 *Law & Society Review* 779 at 787.
[24] Nelken, above n 15, 163.
[25] S Macaulay, 'Non-Contractual Relations in Business: A Preliminary Study' (1963) 28 *American Sociological Review* 55.
[26] See, eg A Griffiths, 'Legal Pluralism' in R Banakar and M Travers (eds), *An Introduction to Law and Social Theory* (Oxford, Hart Publishing, 2002).
[27] See, eg W Twining, 'A Post-Westphalian Conception of Law' (2003) 37 *Law & Society Review* 199.

We find interesting parallels between Ehrlich's 'living law' and Petrazycki's concept of 'intuitive law', which was also devised in the same period. However, in contrast to Ehrlich's interest in the social norms of associations and their collective legal experience, Petrazycki focused more on the individual's experience of legal phenomenon.[28] There is also an interesting connection with studies of 'procedural justice', which strongly relies on ideas of social psychology.[29] Finally, Ehrlich's suggestion that people's feelings and emotions are an important indicator of the social significance of law and legal institutions has found strong empirical support in recent legal consciousness studies.[30]

Again, this continuity with contemporary studies is not only limited to the issue of *opinion necessatis*. There are also many other elements of Ehrlich's work that are directly or indirectly linked with more recent debates.

As will be demonstrated in the various individual essays of this collection, these four characteristics of the *opinio necessitatis*-problem—his style, his interest in methodological innovation, the fact that his work allows for multiple interpretations and the continuity with contemporary research—play an important role throughout Ehrlich's work.

OVERVIEW OF THE BOOK

In the spirit of Ehrlich's work, this collection of essays has a rather open and exploratory character. Rather than focusing on one central interpretation of Ehrlich or the application of a standardised theoretical framework, the authors were asked to 'reconsider' one of four different elements of Ehrlich's work, each from their own perspective. In this approach, it is unavoidable that the authors will sometimes use the same passages of Ehrlich's classical writings. Moreover, the authors will present a plurality of interpretations of these passages. Sometimes, their interpretations of Ehrlich will reveal a considerable degree of overlap, but in other cases these interpretations are mutually exclusive.

This book has been divided into four parts. The first part considers the life and work of Eugen Ehrlich, with special reference to its historical and geographical context. The second part discusses Ehrlich's sociology of law. The third part considers Ehrlich's work in relation to some of his contemporaries. The fourth part discusses the relevance of Ehrlich for contemporary socio-legal research.

---

[28] R Banakar, 'Sociological Jurisprudence' in Banakar and Travers, above n 23, 33.
[29] See, eg J Thibaut and L Walker, *Procedural Justice* (Mahwah, NJ Erlbaum, 1975).
[30] See, eg M Hertogh, 'A "European" Conception of Legal Consciousness: Rediscovering Eugen Ehrlich' (2004) 31 *Journal of Law and Society* 455; and S Silbey, 'After Legal Consciousness' (2005) 1 *Annual Review of Law and Social Science* 323.

10   *Marc Hertogh*

Part I: Eugen Ehrlich, Life, Work and Context

It is often argued that Ehrlich's work is closely connected to the specific characteristics of the Austrian-Hungarian Empire of his day. The first part of the collection of essays explores this assumption in greater detail. The chapters in this part of the book paint a lively picture of Bukovina, in southeastern Europe, and of its capital Czernowitz (today Cernovitsi in Ukraine), where Ehrlich was born in 1862. Moreover, it discusses the political and academic atmosphere at the end of the nineteenth century in relation to Ehrlich's work and some of his contemporaries.

In the opening chapter, Monica Eppinger studies the personal background of Ehrlich. Eppinger observes that, while his ideas are acknowledged for their influences, Ehrlich himself is largely unknown. Little is available in English about his life or intellectual formation. Moreover, he is virtually unmentioned in the history of Bukovina or Ukraine, although he is undoubtedly the most internationally influential legal scholar either has produced. Despite these obstacles, this chapter paints an interesting and detailed picture of Ehrlich's career against the background of the Slavic hinterlands of the Habsburg empire around the turn of the twentieth century.

In her chapter, Eppinger relates her study of Ehrlich's biography to the life and work of Bronislaw Malinowski, who became known as a founder of method in British social anthropology. Eppinger notes that there is no reason to believe that Ehrlich and Malinowski knew of each other or each other's work, and yet the questions that interested them and the steps they advocated to answer them are strikingly reminiscent of each other. Ehrlich's legal science, with the help of ethnography, incorporates contemporary practice as an authoritative source to complement formal law. The result is a program for 'governing in the vernacular', a contribution to the administration of a pluralistic society and to understanding law and society beyond the boundaries of formalism.

Assaf Likhovski in his chapter explores the relationship between Ehrlich's work and other *fin de siècle* thinkers in order to gain a better understanding of the intellectual and cultural context from which Ehrlich's thoughts emerged. The starting point of his chapter is the concept of law found in *Venus in Furs*, a novella published by the Austrian writer Leopold von Sacher-Masoch in 1870. Masoch's notions of law have been briefly analysed by Gilles Deleuze, but Deleuze's analysis ignored the relationship of Masoch's work to general trends in late nineteenth-century legal thought, trends that ultimately produced Ehrlich's sociology of law.

Likhovski argues that one can read both Masoch's and Ehrlich's works as expressions of a general 'crisis of reason', evident in many areas of *fin de siècle* European culture, and specifically as part of a crisis of liberal legal thought. His chapter examines several themes present in both Masoch's and Ehrlich's work, such as the critique of the concept of free will, the contrast between 'public' state sanctions and 'private' honour and the problems associated with the textual representations of reality. It concludes by expanding the frame of reference, pointing to the similar themes found in other literary and artistic products of *fin de siècle* culture.

Part II: Ehrlich's Sociology of Law

The second part of the book contains two chapters which focus on Ehrlich's sociology of law. The aim here is to present some of the main concepts and ideas of Ehrlich's work, including his concept of the 'living law', 'norms for decision' and 'social associations'. The chapters will also consider some of the strengths and weaknesses of the way in which Ehrlich tried to combine sociology and jurisprudence. Following up on the previous chapters, the authors in this part of the book will situate Ehrlich's work within its specific context. In this discussion, the authors will also look at the reception of Ehrlich's sociology of law in the German speaking world, in the United States and in Japan.

The chapter by Roger Cotterrell is about marginality and centrality in social and intellectual life. It examines what is known about the conditions in which Ehrlich worked, and his relation both to the professional legal communities of his time and to the diverse populations of Bukovina (and Austria-Hungary more generally). Drawing on this material, Cotterrell discusses various perceptions of legal 'insiders' and 'outsiders' which have informed legal philosophy and sociology of law. The chapter draws conclusions from this discussion that bear on the significance of legal pluralism in legal theory and on efforts to specify a workable concept of law to serve as the focus of sociology of law.

In his essay, Cotterrell attempts to look at Ehrlich's sociology of law not as a product of marginality, but in terms of an interplay of marginality and centrality, which reflects both Ehrlich's own personal and professional situation and the consistent strategy of his sociology of law. His argument is that this dialectical relationship accounts not only for the most valuable contribution of his sociology of law—its full-frontal challenge to juristic certainties about what legal inquiries encompass and how they are to be pursued—but also for its most serious, most frequently criticised weakness: the vagueness of its concept of law.

Stefan Vogl in his chapter argues that Ehrlich's sociology of law has often been regarded in the German-speaking world as a threat to jurisprudence. In contrast, American jurists appreciated Ehrlich's sociology of law as 'sociological jurisprudence' (Roscoe Pound) or 'realistic jurisprudence' (Karl Llewellyn) and in Japan it is said to rank among the classics of jurisprudence. Vogl attempts to show that Ehrlich made a clear distinction between the sociology of law and jurisprudence, by comparing his purely

12 Marc Hertogh

empirical-scientific approach to law in his *Fundamental Principles* with his partly normative-practical approach in his *Juristische Logik*. Hence, Vogl argues, it becomes apparent that the kind of critique in the tradition of Kelsen, based on an isolated misinterpretation of the *Fundamental Principles*, insinuating normative-practical intentions to Ehrlich's sociology of law is misplaced.

Ehrlich's sociology of law neither aspired to replace jurisprudence nor to interfere with its genuine evaluative tasks. Vogl claims that Ehrlich's intentions were much more modest, but nevertheless revolutionary for jurisprudence. He only wanted to force jurisprudence to deal with social reality as it is, ie established by empirical-scientific methods and not distorted by preformed legal concepts based on the everyday knowledge of jurists. This would lead the decision-making process of jurisprudence away from merely interpreting the 'words' of the law to dealing with the conflicting interests explicitly expressed, hidden behind, or not even encompassed by existing norms.

Part III: Ehrlich and His Contemporaries

The third part of this collection of essays discusses the work of Ehrlich in relation to that of some his contemporaries. This discussion includes both one of Ehrlich's most famous critics, Hans Kelsen, as well as one of his biggest proponents, Roscoe Pound. Moreover, there are several interesting parallels between Ehrlich's concept of 'living law' and that of the Dutch scholar Cornelis van Vollenhoven, whose work has been particularly influential in the Dutch East Indies and later in Indonesia.

Bart van Klink's chapter focuses on the polemic between Ehrlich and Kelsen. In his highly critical review of Ehrlich's *Grundlegung der Soziologie des Rechts*, Kelsen accuses Ehrlich of confusing facts and norms in his conception of law. According to Kelsen, Ehrlich seems to waver between an *empirical* conception of law, in which law is a fact, an observable regularity that is subject to the laws of causality, on the one hand, and a *normative* conception of law, in which law is a norm that evades empirical observation and causal explanation, on the other. Unwilling to write a counter-criticism, Ehrlich refrains from engaging himself fully in this fundamental debate; he claims only to want to correct some factual errors in Kelsen's representation of his work.

In his chapter, Van Klink aims to continue this unfinished debate. He considers whether Kelsen is right in claiming that facts and norms are blurred in Ehrlich's conception of law and, more principally, whether facts and norms can or should be separated strictly. Van Klink argues that if such a separation is impossible and/or undesirable, Kelsen's distinction between a solely empirical sociology of law and a 'pure' science of law becomes untenable. By giving up a rigid fact-norm distinction, Van Klink notes that one has to rethink the relation between the sociology of law and the science of law and between the working of law and its validity.

Salif Nimaga's chapter focuses on the comparison between Ehrlich and the work of Roscoe Pound. Although this comparison had a strong influence on the reception of Ehrlich's work in the Anglo-American world, Nimaga demonstrates in this chapter that some of the presumed analogies between both scholars are in fact misleading.

Nimaga observes that in too readily comparing Ehrlich's 'living law' to Pound's 'law in action', important subtleties get lost. In Ehrlich's original terminology, there are three main analytical concepts: legal norms, norms for decision and legal propositions. As a result, 'living law'—at least in conceptual terms—only plays a marginal role in Ehrlich's work. Also, Nimaga notes that the concept of 'law in action' is derivative and always depending on the 'law in the books'. This is the main difference with Ehrlich's approach, whose legal norms exist without any dependency on the prior activity of a legal staff—be it in legislative, executive or judicative form.

In their chapter, Franz and Keebet Von Benda-Beckmann turn their attention to Indonesia. While Ehrlich had developed his concept of 'living law' in contrast to conventional legal doctrines and theories, in Indonesia, 'living law' was incorporated into legislative texts and court judgments, in which it became the decisive ground and justification for establishing court jurisdiction and substantive inheritance law.

This chapter shows that the living law which made such an amazing career in Indonesia was not Ehrlich's but the 'living law' of the Dutch scholar Cornelis van Vollenhoven (1874–1933), who used it regularly, and more or less in the same time period as Ehrlich. Nothing points to the two authors being familiar with each other's work. Yet, as Franz and Keebet Von Benda-Beckmann observe, their understanding of law was rather similar. Also similar were the legal conditions which led them to talk in terms of living law as the 'really relevant law for people' and as the subject to which a social (and legal) science of law ought to direct its attention. In Ehrlich's case, these conditions were formed by the complex plural legal conditions in the Austro-Hungarian Empire; in Van Vollenhoven's case, it was the complexity of law in the colony of the Dutch East Indies.

Part IV: Ehrlich and Contemporary Socio-Legal Studies

The final part of the book moves away from the past and focuses on the future. The aim here is to consider the relevance of Ehrlich's work for contemporary socio-legal studies.

Jeremy Webber in his chapter argues that many approaches to the 'living law' tend to 'naturalise' law, treating it as though it were ingrained in human interaction, emerging spontaneously in unified, coherent and uncontroversial form. According to Webber, these approaches tend to occlude disagreement over social norms; they minimise the role of deliberate human decision-making in the creation of norms; and they take those norms as being implicit in conduct.

Webber aims to demonstrate that this is too simple, and indeed hides the central characteristic of all (living) law: the establishment by emphatically social means of a collective standard of conduct despite the continued presence of individual disagreement. With special reference to Ehrlich's work, this chapter describes this naturalising tendency, and will suggest a more adequate way of considering how the law is developed against the backdrop of particular practices, in a manner that takes better account of human agency in the creation of norms.

In his chapter, Klaus A Ziegert revisits the controversy of statist legal theory versus a sociological theory of law and state, with the benefit of the hindsight of 100 years of further development of law and state since Ehrlich made his famous analysis and in view of a world which perhaps has not changed all that much since then. With that focus on twenty-first-century world society in mind, he aims to re-examine Ehrlich's constructs of society and law, especially in defining the role and function of the state for ordering world society. Here, Ehrlich's findings will be compared with the writing of his near contemporary Herbert Spencer, who appears to have been an important source for Ehrlich, especially in respect to a social science which is informed by evolution theory.

According to Ziegert, the main reason why Ehrlich wanted to lay the ground for a theory of law sociologically was his vision of a universal theory of law. Ehrlich arrived at this view by his conviction that the unity of law was constituted by society and not by law. In this radical call for a general sociological theory of law, Ziegert argues, we can find the connection to a modern general theory of world society and its law. Contrary to the criticisms that Ehrlich's neglect of state omnipotence in his sociological theory of law was a serious flaw in his theory, disqualifying it from twenty-first-century consumption, Ziegert concludes, this is one of the fundaments on which the robustness of Ehrlich's sociological theory of law rests.

David Nelken concludes this collection of essays. In his chapter, Nelken enquires into the point of reconsidering Ehrlich. He distinguishes between trying to get Ehrlich's ideas right and asking whether they are right, or between putting Ehrlich in his context and getting him out of it. He explains that his aim will be the second of these alternatives, to trace Ehrlich's legacies—and in particular the way in which he has and continues to influence various areas of the sociology of law.

Nelken first examines three types of study, which he calls *law beyond the law*, *law without the state* and *order without law*. Here, references to Ehrlich tend to be relatively brief; his ideas are used mainly as 'authority' or as a reminder of aspects of law in society that have been neglected or forgotten. Following this, he goes on to discuss authors who offer more radical re-readings of Ehrlich in the light of more recent sociological approaches inspired by Luhmann and his autopoietic theory. Nelken concludes with some considerations about Ehrlich's continuing relevance as shown by the different ways in which his writings have been drawn on.

RECONSIDERING EUGEN EHRLICH; RECONSIDERING LAW AND SOCIETY

The different chapters in this volume highlight both some of the biggest strengths and weaknesses of Ehrlich's work. In general, they underscore one of the earliest critiques on Ehrlich—that important weaknesses of his work include: its essayistic character; its use of vague concepts and explanations; and the many overlaps between descriptive and normative analysis.[31] In particular, several essays in this volume criticise the vagueness of Ehrlich's concept of law and the way in which he seeks to differentiate between law and other social norms (for instance, by applying the *opinio-necessitatis* test) (Cotterrell, Van Klink, Nimaga, Webber). Moreover, several authors discuss the way in which Ehrlich tried to link sociology with jurisprudence. While some recognise the importance of this 'revolutionary' approach (Vogl, Cotterrell), others are much more critical of this 'unlucky interdisciplinarity'[32] (Van Klink, Webber).

An 'Instrumental' and a 'Constitutive' Perspective

In a number of different ways, the essays in this volume also emphasise the importance of Ehrlich's work for the sociology of law. First, in the literature, Ehrlich's work is generally appreciated for the way in which it has contributed to a better understanding of the (in)effectiveness of law in promoting social order. Ehrlich showed that much legislation, which did not correspond with local understandings of the living law, was 'dead law'. In this way, Ehrlich's sociology of law contained important clues to make legal norms work in society and his work provided a strong argument against the 'light switch' model of legal positivism, which assumes that law has social effects because it exists and that legal propositions have a social effect in their own right.[33] This element of his work is also reflected in many of the essays in this volume.

---

[31] J Kraft (1930), cited in Rehbinder (1967), above n 3, 102.
[32] KA Ziegert, 'The Sociology behind Eugen Ehrlich's Sociology of Law' (1979) 7 *International Journal of the Sociology of Law* 11 at 11.
[33] Ziegert (2002), above n 3, xxxii.

16 Marc Hertogh

Yet, in addition to this common 'instrumental' interpretation of Ehrlich's work, this volume also emphasises a second, and less developed, element of his sociology of law. Perhaps this can best be described as the 'constitutive' element of Ehrlich's work. In addition to the focus on 'what law does *to* society', Ehrlich was also among the first scholars to emphasise 'what law tells us *about* society'.[34] For Ehlich, law was just another way of understanding society (Eppinger). His interest in the local 'living law', for instance, not only allowed him to analyse the (in)effectiveness of the 'state law' from Vienna, but also helped him to understand daily life in Bukovina in terms of numerous 'social associations', each with their own 'inner order'. Much in the same way, the different (legal) approaches to 'living law' in continental Europe and Japan illustrate important differences in the social structure and the role of legal authorities in both societies (Vogl). Similarly, the relation between living (adat) law, state law and Islamic law reveals important characteristics of Indonesian society (Von Benda-Beckmann). Furthermore, just as the law at the end of the nineteenth century reflects the 'crisis of reason' in *fin de siècle* European culture (Likhovski), the law at the beginning of the twenty-first century may reflect the emergence of a 'global human society' (Ziegert).

It is this 'constitutive' element of Ehrlich's sociology of law which makes the jurist become a sociological observer of legal processes, while it makes the sociologist dig deeply into legal doctrine and juristic thought to see how these inform social relations (Cotterrell). Finally, this feature of Ehrlich's work not only contributed considerably to the study of law and society of his own time, but it also suggests a new and exciting research agenda for the study of law and society in the future.

Picturing Eugen Ehrlich

Despite his status as one of the 'founding fathers' of contemporary sociology of law, there are only two—rather fuzzy—photographs of Ehrlich available.[35] In a way, this collection of essays is much more revealing. They show that Ehrlich is a man with many different faces. Among other things, he is characterised as 'an Austro-German jurist in the centre of a sophisticated legal world' as well as a 'participant observer of imperial provinciality and multiculturalism', as both a 'visionary foundation-layer for enlightened

---

[34] See S Silbey, 'Everyday Life and the Constitution of Legality' in M Jacobs and N Hanrahan (eds), *The Blackwell Companion to the Sociology of Culture* (Malden, MA, Blackwell Publishing, 2005) 334. As important examples of this second approach, she refers to Durkheim, Weber and Oliver Wendell Holmes, but curiously enough she does not mention Ehrlich here.

[35] See E Ehrlich, *Grundlegung der Soziologie des Rechts* (4. Aulage) (Berlin, Duncker & Humblot, 1989); and Rehbinder (1967), above n 3.

administration' and a 'righteous critic of state fetishism', and as a 'radical jurist' as well as a 'modest sociologist'. The purpose of this volume is not, however, to present a single definitive portrait of Ehrlich. After all, the process of interpreting the message of a 'founding father' is never ending (Nelken). Instead, the reader of this volume is invited to paint his or her own picture of Eugen Ehrlich and his sociology of law.

Part I

Eugen Ehrlich: Life, Work and Context

2

Governing in the Vernacular: Eugen Ehrlich and Late Habsburg Ethnography

MONICA EPPINGER

INTRODUCTION

EUGEN EHRLICH'S LEGACY in Anglophone scholarship presents us with a conundrum. Legal scholars recognise Ehrlich's work as having decisive effects on the course of twentieth-century American jurisprudence. US legal historians cite his contributions to the Free School[1] that exerted a dispositive influence on the inception of Legal Realism and the creation of whole new bodies of US law; critical legal studies scholars[2] and legal anthropologists[3] still credit his understanding of 'living law' in their work on the limits of formal law. While Ehrlich's ideas are acknowledged for their influences, his claims themselves are rarely probed and the man himself is largely unknown. We are left with little to evaluate the competing interpretations of his legacy. Which version—visionary foundation-layer for enlightened administration or righteous critic of state fetishism—is more true to Ehrlich's project? Anglophone scholarship offers few answers. Beyond habitual genuflection by the meticulous legal academic and brief, rare citation by the specialised historian,[4] Ehrlich is a cipher. Little is available in English-language sources about his life or intellectual

---

[1] See, eg J Whitman, book review of *François Gény e la scienza giurdica del Novecento* (March 1995) 67 *The Journal of Modern History* 176.

[2] See, eg D Kennedy, 'Two Globalizations of Law and Legal Thought: 1850–1968' 36 *Suffolk University Law Review* 631 at 648–9.

[3] See, eg L Nader, *The Life of the Law* (Berkeley, University of California Press, 2002) 136 (hereinafter: Nader, *Life*). See also L Nader, 'The Anthropological Study of Law' (December 1965) in *The Ethnography of Law* (special issue of *American Anthropologist*, L Nader (ed), 67 *American Anthropologist* 6).

[4] See, eg B Hett, 'The "Captain of Koepenick" and the Transformation of German Criminal Justice, 1819–1914' (2003) 36 *Central European Jurisprudence* 1.

formation.[5] He is virtually unmentioned in the history of Bukovina or Ukraine, although he is undoubtedly the most internationally influential legal scholar either has produced. This is particularly surprising, given how seriously legal scholars took Ehrlich's advice to examine the social movement behind a legal thinker in order to understand what is going on and possible causes.[6] A background contention of this chapter is that this gap in our understanding of Ehrlich's life leaves us vulnerable to misreading or missing some points in his work.

How much do we know of Ehrlich's setting and personal history? The bare facts do not reveal much. Ehrlich was born in Chernivtsi, the capital of Bukovina in Austria (now Ukraine). He trained at the University of Vienna in law and served as a docent there until returning to Chernivtsi as professor of Roman law in 1898. He was made rector of the university in 1906 and died in 1922.

Ehrlich's program gives us a point of entry to examine his principal ideas more closely. In a talk to the Juridical Society of Vienna in 1903, Ehrlich lays out a new vision for what law is and how legal science should proceed. Ehrlich contrasts a 'dynamic conception of law'—which legal science until then was ill-equipped to fathom—with the 'traditional, dogmatic conception' of a bounded set of legal rules governed by formal logic and sophisticated doctrine.[7] To understand law in its dynamic conception, Ehrlich suggests that we turn to three sources: decisions of the courts (mindful that every decision is the result of a number of factors, only one of which is the text of a legal rule); actual legal transactions that have not had to resort to courts or government agencies for adjudication; and, most importantly, the 'facts of daily life, apart from their legal aspect'. 'In reality life creates primarily its own rules', apart from the rules of law.[8] Legal scholars should undertake investigations of real life and furnish them back to the courts to inform judicial decisions.[9] In this program, Ehrlich sets up a new challenge for legal science that demands new equipment.[10]

---

[5] Notable exceptions are A Likhovski, 'Czernowitz, Lincoln, Jerusalem, and the Comparative History of American Jurisprudence' (2003) 4 *Theoretical Inquiries in Law* 621; and B Weiler, 'E Pluribus Unum? The Kakanian Intellectual and the Question of Cultural Pluralism', MS of paper presented at the conference, "The Contours of Legitimacy in Central Europe: New Approaches in Graduate Studies", at St Anthony's College Oxford, available at <http://users.ox.ac.uk/~oaces/conference/papers/Bernd_Weiler.pdf> accessed 22 July 2008.

[6] E Ehrlich, 'Judicial Freedom of Decision: Its Principles and Objects' (a translation of Ehrlich's 'Freie Rechtsfindung und freie Rechtswissenschaft' (Leipzig, 1903)) in E Bruncken and L Register (trs), *The Science of Legal Method: Selected Essays by Various Authors* (New York, Macmillan, 1921) 78 (hereinafter: Ehrlich, 'Judicial Freedom').

[7] Ibid 78.

[8] Ibid 78–80.

[9] Ibid 83.

[10] This term comes from Paul Rabinow. See P Rabinow, *Anthropos Today: Reflections on Modern Equipment* (Princeton, NJ, Princeton University Press, 2003).

When he searched for adequate equipment, Ehrlich found a technology increasingly common in his milieu, the Slavic hinterlands of the Habsburg empire around the turn of the twentieth century.[11] The tool was ethnography.[12] Ehrlich did not invent this method of inquiry—it was already practised throughout central Europe—but he did use it in new ways. In this chapter, I examine the practice of ethnography as an artifact. In trying to learn more about Ehrlich's intellectual formation, ethnography focuses our attention on where he came from, as a tool specific to Ehrlich's time and location, and on where he ends up, as a tool that transformed him and his discipline. I propose that ethnography was one answer to a certain set of problems formulated in the late Habsburg period. This chapter, then, explores Ehrlich's work, specifically his methodological program using ethnography for making legal decisions. I will take up, in turn, what ethnography meant in his time; a survey of the late Habsburg landscape in which ethnography was conceived as a means for solving practical problems; and finally some modest proposals for further work.

THE DESCRIPTIVE VERSUS NORMATIVE REGISTER IN FIN-DE-SIÈCLE ETHNOGRAPHY

Ethnography is a familiar term to us, but we should not assume too much; its meaning has undergone considerable slippage since Ehrlich's time. It is worth examining, briefly, how ethnography was understood in Austria-Hungary at the turn of the century.

Ethnography was meant first as a descriptive genre. Critical thinkers dating back to Kant have marked a categorical difference between a descriptive work and a normative work. Ehrlich articulated his view of this demarcation in the critique of Montesquieu's *L'Esprit des Lois* that he wrote for Justice Holmes. The French term *devoir* permits an elision between the meaning of 'ought' and 'is', he says, signifying 'both what ought to be and what must be'. Montesquieu mostly uses *devoir* in the former meaning, but he was influenced enough by natural law beliefs 'as not to draw a sharp line between the law that ought to be and the law that is',

---

[11] This should not be read as the start of an argument for environmental or social determinism nor, necessarily, a claim for uniqueness. It is rather an effort to explore the particulars of Ehrlich's context.

[12] Ethnographers from Bukovina and Galicia working at the same time as Ehrlich did as a publishing jurist include the team working out of L'viv (or, in Austrian or Yiddish, Lemberg), of Xv Volkov, M Zubritskiy, M Russov, M Litvinova-Bartush, A Veretelnyk, M Shishkevych, V Domanitzkiy, Ol Radakov, M Dikarev; famed folklorist V Hnatiuk; folklorist and writer Sh Aleykum; ethnographer of legal affairs S Dniestrzanski; and, overlapping with the last decade of Ehrlich's career, B Malinowski.

which Ehrlich denounces as vagueness.[13] Ehrlich intended his ethnography to be a record of what people are actually doing, rather than a prescription for what they should be doing.

He points us to several peers, most of them Austro-Hungarian, who in his view have taken up the same agenda as he has. Bogošič, a Croat, drew up a questionnaire (of more than 800 questions!), the answers to which form the basis of a work on southern Slavs (*Zbornik Sadašnih Pravnih Običaja Južnih Slovena*). Bobčev adopted Bogošič's method and produced a collection of Bulgarian customary law, *Sbornik na Blgarski Juriditski Obitschai*.[14] They ventured into the countryside like nineteenth-century Romantic folklorists, collecting legal custom instead of fairytales. The survey method was also taken up by *fin-de-siècle* British anthropology: witness members of the 1896 Torres Straights expedition clambering ashore to query a small number of informants from a given list of questions.[15] This hit-and-run methodology could yield staggering amounts of data in a short period of time. We will examine later how Ehrlich distinguishes his work from theirs and how his work transforms the method. This initial look at least gives us a glimpse of the starting point of ethnography when Ehrlich took it up. The ethnographer was collector and describer; his work involved collecting data through surveys, usually in rural areas, and writing it up into detailed descriptions.

BEYOND IS VERSUS OUGHT

That said, we should be aware that Ehrlich and his central European peers regarded ethnography as potentially more active than we would be prone to. Even if a description was not delivered in a normative register, Ehrlich and his contemporaries understood that description under some circumstances could be creative—a form of performative speech.[16] Here is how. In late Habsburg Austria, ethnography was used as a synonym, in some instances, for ethnicity or ethnic group.[17] Within an empire where certain rights were, by definition, group rights (meaning that recognition of some rights depended on a certain kind of legal recognition of the group), discerning,

---

[13] E Ehrlich, 'Montesquieu and Sociological Jurisprudence' (April 1916) 29 *Harvard Law Review* 582 at 583 (hereinafter: Ehrlich, 'Montesquieu').

[14] E Ehrlich, *Fundamental Principles of the Sociology of Law*, W Moll (tr) (New York, Russell and Russell, 1962 (1913)) 464–5 (hereinafter: Ehrlich, *Fundamental Principles*). The other peer Ehrlich cites is a Spaniard, Costa, who used direct observation to produce a compendium of legal relations in real life.

[15] For one ethnography resulting from such an expedition, see W Rivers, *The Todas* (New York, Macmillan, 1906).

[16] For an explanation of performative speech, see JL Austin, *How to Do Things with Words* (Cambridge, MA, Harvard University Press, 1962).

[17] T Snyder, personal communication, 17 April 2006.

naming, describing a social group in a certain way could be part of building an argument for group recognition.[18] Description could be a political act or have political consequences. 'Ethnicity' and 'nation' were both terms for politically aspirant groups. Turn-of-the-century Ukrainian nationalist Ivan Franko called for an independent country within what he and his generation called 'ethnographic' borders.[19] The Ivan Frankos, the Theodor Herzls, of Austria-Hungary understood that ethnography, creating a written record of an ethnos, could serve to etch ethnos in consciousness, map it onto territory, inscribe it in history. This logic was later borne out in the entry into international law of the right of a people to self-determination and the emergence of Habsburg successor states based on claims of ethnicity and nationality—a Bulgaria, a Poland, eventually an Israel, a Ukraine. Habsburg political organisation set the stage for nation-state successors by according legal recognition of certain rights based on inclusion in or exclusion from a group that had established some precursor claims. Over time, ethnography was a way to stake a claim as a 'people', to build an argument for self-determination. That came after the war (World War I), of course: a central Europe of nation-states was beyond Ehrlich's historical horizon and, as far as we can discern, was nowhere in the realm of his expectations. To understand some of the impetus for ethnography before the war, we need to look at the Austria-Hungary that preceded. We start with a most local institution, the university in Ehrlich's hometown where he taught and did most of his research into living law, and then we move on to his native province and the empire into which it fit.

THE ETHNOGRAPHER

Ehrlich's Bukovina and Vienna's Ehrlich

Bukovina

The University of Czernowitz, where Ehrlich would become professor in the law school and then rector, came into being as part of a wave of Liberal state institution-building in the 1870s.[20] A member of Bukovina crown

---

[18] This kind of power of description is not unknown in the US legal system. Jeremy King, for example, compares Habsburg group classifications and their effects with a similar process in contemporary US affirmative action law. See, eg J King, 'Group Rights in Liberal Austria: the Dilemma of Classificatory Procedure' (November 2005) (MS).

[19] T Snyder, *The Reconstruction of Nations: Poland, Ukraine, Lithuania, Belarus 1569–1999* (New Haven, CT, Yale University Press, 2003).

[20] After they won a parliamentary majority, Liberals displaced the army from its parade grounds in the centre of Vienna and on the site erected buildings of the University of Vienna (built 1873–84) that Ehrlich attended, as well as the house of the Austrian Parliament (built 1874–83).

land parliament, Constantin Tomaszczuk, led the campaign to convince Vienna to fund a university in Czernowitz. He argued that the monarchy would be well served by a university in its eastern borderlands as an instrument of unity through enlightenment, prestige associated with German-language science and learning, and common enculturation. A university in Czernowitz, Tomaszczuk argued, 'could be an intellectual fortress, which will secure the unity and integrity of the monarchy much better than bastions lined with cannons'.[21] Two Austro-Hungarian universities, Tomaszczuk's alma mater the University of Lemberg (L'viv) and the University of Cracow, had recently (in 1870–71) been 'polonised'. Slavicism seemed provincial and separatist; the empire needed non-Slavic alternatives in the East. With the help of Baron Gheorghe Hurmuzaki, who led his fellow Romanian aristocrats in Bukovina's *Landtag* to support the plan,[22] Tomaszczuk's initiative succeeded. The Austrian Government converted an existing theological institute into the Franz Josef University of Czernowitz, consisting of three sections (*fakultäten*): theology; philosophy, philology and natural sciences; and law and political economy. It opened on 4 October 1875.

The Imperial Charter for the University explicitly recognised the pluralistic population the university would serve, as well as the transcendent ideals of learning and Austrian citizenship it hoped to inculcate. It read:

> As the German, so the Romanian and the Slav gladly quenches his thirst and draws strength from the fountain of German science; this in greater measure will offer him the means to retain and nurture his individuality; but it will also be an inducement to work and strive together toward the happiness and glory of our beloved fatherland, Austria.[23]

Reading these words today, we must remind ourselves that 'Germany' was a nascent project, having just formed as a unified country in 1871. 'German science' might here refer to affiliation with a certain Western Enlightenment discourse, expressed in German tongue, or common cause with a learned elite of Vienna and other Habsburg cities. It did not refer to a science produced on the territory of a long-standing German political entity. Hegemony was conveyed in the 'science' at least as much as in the 'German'.

---

[21] Constantin Tomaszczuk, quoted in R Wagner, *Vom Moldauwappen zum Doppeladler: Ausgewählte Beiträge zur Geschichgte der Bukowina* (Augsburg, Hormann-Verlag, 1991) 282, cited by I Livezeanu, *Cultural Politics in Greater Romania* (Ithaca, Cornell University Press, 1995) 228. The author cited, Rudolf Wagner, was a student at the University of Czernowitz from 1930 to 1932. Livezeanu, *ibid* 228.

[22] I Livezeanu, *Cultural Politics in Greater Romania* (Ithaca, Cornell University Press, 1995), citing Wagner.

[23] M Popescu-Spineni, *Instituţii de înaltă cultură* (Vălenii-de-Munte, Datina românească, 1932) 175–76, 178, cited in Livezeanu, above n 22, 228.

Tomaszczuk, named first rector of the new university, indicated this dual supranational orientation towards political and moral affiliation in his inaugural speech. A Liberal presumption of equality of men underwrites his assertion of the capacity of education for 'levelling up'. 'German science has a claim to universality', he said. 'And because German education has a universal importance, non-German sons of Bukovina also strive for this German university.' As if to confirm that 'German science' referred to a form of learned discourse or to the elite that produced it instead of a product of 'Germany', Tomaszczuk went on to embrace plurality and advocate openness. 'Beware to the nation which has to be afraid of the influence of foreign cultures. This nation is signing its own death certificate.' His reaffirmation,

> We are not only Poles, Germans, Romanians, we are in the first place human beings, with roots in the same soil out of which we draw our common strength, and by this I mean our Austria ...

contains elements of a transcendent call to humanism, an appeal to empire loyalty and a naming of even narrower ethnic identities. Clearly, collective identity and personal loyalties were objects of interest or anxiety; his attention marks them as emergent and contested. After we look at the social world of Bukovina and the political currents that defined the Austria that encompassed it, we may return to consider whether we agree with his conclusion that '[t]he university in Czernowitz is an authentic Austrian concept'.[24]

Even before the university was founded, the Chernivtsi[25] of Ehrlich's childhood was ruled by a Catholic dynasty, host to an eastern Orthodox seminary and home to a significant Jewish community. As provincial capital, it was the centre of its own regional hinterland (where Ehrlich chose to conduct his first ethnographic research). Vis-a-vis the wider world, the city lay on the frontier of three highly developed *oecumenes* (Russian, Austrian and Romanian), ruled by three different dynastic traditions and divided between mutually unintelligible language families (Slavic, Germanic and Romance).[26] Traders, translators and other specialists in border hustling were native species.[27] Moreover, Chernivtsi was a post on centuries-old

---

[24] Tomaszczuk, quoted in Wagner, above n 21, 282, cited by Livezeanu, above n 22, 229.

[25] A note of explanation on place names is due here. Part of the Austrian heritage is a toleration of a plethora of toponyms for a single place in the many dialects of a region. To name Ehrlich's hometown, Czernowitz is the Germanisation of the Ukrainian Chernivtsi and the Romanian Cernăuți. Because Ukrainian speakers were a plurality of the province's population at the time, I will refer to it by the Ukrainian name, Chernvitsi, unless naming a specific Austrian institution like the university, in which case I will use Czernowitz.

[26] Of course, before Austrian rule, this area had at times been part of the borderlands contested with Turkey. Assaf Likhovski has concentrated on the formative influence of location and frontier on Ehrlich's work (Likhosvski, above n 5).

[27] For an insightful description of a present-day Bukovina border city dynamic, see D Blank, 'Fairytale Cynicism in the Kingdom of Plastic Bags: Powerlessness of Place in a Ukrainian Border Town' (autumn 2004) 5(3) *Ethnography*.

riparian trade routes connecting north-eastern Europe to the Black Sea, and from there to the Caucasus, Ottoman lands and beyond, bringing even more remote and exotic peoples and professions into contact and residence. As a result, Bukovina was a miniature of the cohabitating 'compact populations' of the pluralistic empire. In this, Ehrlich enjoyed a typically Austrian childhood milieu. It is difficult to assess how quiet or remote its residents perceived Bukovina to be, but at least it was cosmopolitan. Ehrlich himself noted the diversity of community traditions thriving in this small province, counting Armenians, Germans, Jews, Russians, Ukrainians, Slovaks, Hungarians and Gypsies among those bringing different ways of life to Bukovina society.[28]

This was no different for Austria as a whole. By the 1910 census, Germans constituted less than 25 per cent of the monarchy's population; the rest belonged to 'minority populations'.[29] Notably, Austria and Bukovina did not cultivate an ideology of a 'melting pot'. As the Polish-Austrian subject and anthropology graduate student Bronislaw Malinowski wrote to his British dissertation adviser: 'There is no such blooming thing as an "Austrian"—it is a pure fiction'. Happily, thought Malinowski, Austria was 'a confederation of fairly autonomous peoples'.[30] This is not to overly romanticise the situation. Assimilation became an aspiration for some, and by the turn of the twentieth century, Vienna had the highest conversion rate of Jews to Christianity in Europe.[31] One can, however, note the effects of an imperial policy of toleration. Communities within one locale maintained distinct practices, even languages, from each other, and the period during which Ehrlich published all of his significant writings was one of rising ethnic identification and political nationalism within the empire. Self-consciousness about group identity and curiosity about other groups were remarkable. Take, for example, the content of a series of

---

[28] E Ehrlich, 'Das lebende Recht der Völker der Bukovina' in E Ehrlich and M Rehbinder (eds), *Recht und Leben: Gesammelt Schriften zur Rechtstatsachenforschung und zur Frierechtslehre* (Berlin, Duncker and Humblot, 1967 (1913)) 43.

[29] R Kann, *The Multinational Empire: Nationalism and National Reform in the Habsburg Monarchy 1848–1914, Vol. II Empire Reform* (New York, Columbia University Press, 1950) 299–307. Note that in the 1910 census, individuals were not asked their nationality but which language they spoke and which confession they belonged to. Also problematic, not all languages that were spoken in the realm could be selected as a mother tongue, only those that were recognised as 'national languages' in the terms of art XIX of the 1867 Constitution. This ruled out Yiddish; most Yiddish-speaking Jews from Galicia chose Polish and most from Bukovina chose German. This clarification adapted from Weiler, above n 5.

[30] Malinowski's letter to Seligman (1914) quoted in R Firth, 'Malinowski as Scientist and as Man' in R Firth (ed), *Man and Culture: An Evaluation of the Work of Bronislaw Malinowski* (London, Routledge & Kegan Paul, 1957) 13.

[31] D Edmonds and J Eidinow, *Wittgenstein's Poker* (New York, HarperCollins Publishers, 2001) 94.

for-pay adult-education courses offered by the Chernivtsi Historical Society in 1912. The syllabus included:

> ... world history; Ukrainian history; history of the formation of state, region, and community; ... geography of the world and Ukraine; anthropology and ethnography (about types and life ways of people); history of culture (and discovery); ... history of religion; Ukrainian language and literature; ... cooperation.[32]

Themes of national consciousness, curiosity about others and concerns about how to live together in a cosmopolitan mix were clearly not exclusive to Ehrlich and the law school.

Over the last decades of the nineteenth century, as the growth of capitalism and pursuit of Liberal political reforms reshaped the Austrian landscape, ethnicities and confessions responded differently to changing opportunity structures. The experience of Jews, often the limit case for European Liberal reforms seeking to replace status-based economics and politics with a free competition of equal individuals, may be looked at to measure Chernivtsi's climate for national minorities. Despite marked anti-Semitism in Vienna by the 1890s,[33] Chernivtsi remained relatively hospitable to Jews. In the last decades before the First World War, Chernivtsi had several Jewish mayors[34] and—in part because of the law school led by Ehrlich—by 1914, 86 per cent of the town's lawyers were Jewish.[35]

Now that we have delineated and taken measure of Bukovina's pluralism, we must take a further step to slip into a Bukovinian mindset: we must play with the categories, for the categories themselves produced fluidity, arbitrage and slippage. Identities were assumed, lost, cultivated; groups were imagined, resented, taken pride in, historicised, credited and discredited. Witness Ehrlich's own story: born a Chernivtsi Jew, a native speaker of Polish, he became a convert to Catholicism, educated and educating in German. What do we call such a person? Certainly without error we can call him a Bukovinian and an Austrian. (Of course, the meanings of those terms too were emergent, changing over the course of Ehrlich's life.) What does this mean for his work?

I propose that this milieu fundamentally informed Ehrlich's conception of society (and, we shall see later, of law). 'Pluralist' was not an adjective that

---

[32] 'Из Наших Товарств [From our Societies]' in 3 *Нова Буковина* [*Nova Bukovina*] (Chernivtsi, 18 January 1912) 3.

[33] JW Boyer, *Political Radicalism in Late Imperial Vienna: Origins of the Christian Social Movement, 1848–1897* (Chicago, Chicago University Press, 1981); and C Schorske, *Fin-de-Siecle Vienna: Politics and Culture* (New York, Knopf, 1979).

[34] W McCagg, *A History of Habsburg Jews, 1670–1918* (Bloomington, IN, Indiana University Press, 1989) 172–3, cited in Livezeanu, above n 22, 55.

[35] H Sternberg, 'Zur Geschichte der Juden in Czernowitz' in H Gould (ed), *Geschichte der Juden in der Bukovina*, vol 2 (Tel Aviv, Olamenu, 1962) 46, cited in Livezeanu, above n 22, 55.

might or might not modify 'society'. Instead, pluralism for Ehrlich was an inherent quality of society:

> Society is the sum total of the human associations that have mutual relations with one another. And these associations that constitute human society are very heterogeneous.[36]

A person belongs to many associations simultaneously; membership overlaps and changes. Moreover, the 'interdependence of all elements of social life is assumed'.[37] Unlike, say, holism of British social anthropology of the time, Ehrlich's holism does not necessarily rely on a metaphor of a 'social structure', an internally consistent mechanism that could be described synchronically. For Ehrlich:

> ... the social order is not fixed and unchangeable ... It is in constant flux. Old institutions disappear, new ones come into existence, and those which remain change their content constantly.[38]

A living organism, not a fixed structure, is the image that comes to mind. To understand society, the sociologist must pay attention to the particularities of these many human associations. Bukovina's pluralism suggested, then, not only a particular conception of society, but a particular method of apprehending and studying it. Ethnography, for the Bukovinian Ehrlich, becomes not just a means of recording a series of folkways, but a method for understanding a sum total constantly in flux.

Vienna: Liberal Order in the Era of Ausgleich

The last decades of the Habsburg empire in which Ehrlich lived and worked were a period of compressed political change. A rise and decline of Liberalism, which in other parts of Europe took decades to articulate into political philosophy and political organisation, were squeezed into a span of roughly a quarter of a century in late Habsburg Austria. At the same time, a grand compromise (*Ausgleich*) with Hungary and 'little compromises'[39] with other constituent parts of Austria organised Austria-Hungary into an agglomeration of polities, each with their own

---

[36] Ehrlich, *Fundamental Principles*, above n 14, 26.

[37] Ehrlich, 'Montesquieu', above n 13, 586.

[38] E Ehrlich, 'The Sociology of Law' (December 1922) 36 *Harvard Law Review* 130 at 139. We find a bridge between the two in SF Nadel. Nadel, like Malinowski, was an Austrian by birth and upbringing who became a central figure in British social anthropology, but he stayed in Vienna longer into his adulthood and his thinking was more in Ehrlich's line: more attuned to complex relations, the artificiality of boundaries and change over time. See, eg SF Nadel, *Black Byzantium: the Kingdom of Nupe in Nigeria* (London, Oxford University Press Publisher for the International Institute of African Languages and Cultures, 1942).

[39] Jeremy King alerted me to this late Habsburg phenomenon. See, eg King, above n 18. See also J King, 'Group Rights in Liberal Austria: Dilemmas of Equality' (April 2006) (MS).

system of traditional rights.[40] Where *Ausgleich* politics sought to preserve local traditions of noble privilege within the order of the empire, Liberalism worked from an assumption of a shared human nature justifying claims for equal political rights and an equal capacity for economic success given equal opportunity. The core tenets of Austrian Liberalism were that 'the freedom and worth of the human being are the highest values'.[41] A cornerstone of the Liberal ideology was an Enlightenment belief that each person was a blank slate, theoretically equally capable, who could be raised to a common level through education. This version of *laissez-faire* had a progressive cast, seeking to replace privilege or charity as the basis of access to economic opportunity. In the last half-century before the First World War, Austria-Hungary's political reorganisations addressed the recurrent question: local noble privilege or universal equal rights? Throughout Ehrlich's life, accommodations to these two movements and tensions between them produced a different kind of state and innovative technologies of governance unlike anything in Europe. A few examples from its political history and technologies of governance may suffice to convey a sense of this peculiar empire.

Between 1860 and 1867, a series of pressures led to a remaking of the Austrian political order, with several fundamental changes incorporating local representation under a constitutional monarchy. The Constitutional Law (Diploma) of 1860 reinstated the old constitutions belonging to the different lands of the monarchy and gave legislative power to the provincial Diets. The Diploma was a concession of 'state-right' (a body of privileges which maintained a nation's independence while acceding to Habsburg rule) to the conservative aristocracy of different crown lands attached to their 'local liberties' and hostile to 'German centralism'.[42] The Patent of 1861 established a parliament, the *Reichsrat*, at Vienna, with members nominated by the provincial Diets until an 1873 law provided for direct elections. The *Ausgleich* with Hungary in 1867 recognised the Hungarian parliament and nobility as co-equal with the Austrian, with Franz Josef head of both. Within the emerging system, each province maintained its own political structure and indigenous nobility with attendant privileges. Franz Josef was simultaneously emperor of one crown land, king of another and

---

[40] Considering a longer time horizon, one of Kann's theses is that Austria-Hungary became an 'empire' somewhat by a series of accidents, not military or commercial conquest; within, what spread was not homogenous law, but an overarching respect for local custom. R Kann, *A History of the Habsburg Empire, 1526–1918* (Berkeley, University of California Press, 1974).

[41] This description of the core tenets of Austrian Liberalism was formulated to describe Ukrainian Austrian Liberal Myhhailo Drahomanov. I Rudnytsky, 'Drahomanov as Political Theorist' in P Rudnytsky (ed), *Essays in Modern Ukrainian History* (Edmonton, Canadian Institute of Ukrainian Studies, 1987) 205.

[42] J Bérenger, *A History of the Habsburg Empire 1700–1918* (Harlow, Addison Wesley, 1990) 210.

archduke of yet another, his different titles reflecting the variety of polities he simultaneously headed.

In its peculiar history, as an accidental empire, and in its peculiar means of self-preservation, by striking constitutional compromises (first in the Diploma and then in a series of *Ausgleichs*) with the polities of its heartland, Austria-Hungary by the early 1900s was a genre of state distinct from its European contemporaries. The common term 'empire' disguises deep differences: the relationship between ruler, ruled and territory did not follow patterns seen elsewhere in Europe. Austria-Hungary did not seek overseas colonies, was constituted only of geographically contiguous lands and ruled its territories neither by overt military force nor by 'indirect rule'. One reference explains it thus. There was Hungary, and then:

> The rest of the empire was a casual agglomeration without even a clear description. Technically it was known as 'the kingdoms and lands represented in the Reichsrat [parliament]' ... These confusions had a simple cause: the empire of Austria with its various fragments was the dynastic possession of the House of Habsburg, not a state with any common consciousness or purpose.[43]

In exchange for confirming the *Ausgleich* with Hungary, the Liberals won a series of concessions from the Emperor towards securing the rights of individuals,[44] creating an impartial judiciary and guaranteeing freedom of belief and education. In the non-Hungarian provinces, then, the Austrian Constitution of 1867 gave Austria a Liberal regime. The right to vote was granted to non-noble Austrian men, but under a weighted voting system in which voting males directly elected 72 of 425 members of the *Reichsrat*. The remaining members were designated to other *curia* (electoral bodies or voting blocks): great estate owners were allotted a certain number of members of parliament, chambers of commerce others, and rural districts, others. Each provincial elected assembly consisted of similar blocks of seats, to which members were elected by their *curia*. While the division into *curia* by forms of property ownership or types of residential locale might have compounded the pluralism of a polyethnic empire, in fact not uncommonly they were associated with ethnicity. For example, in Galicia, large estate owners were almost exclusively 'Polish' (and in Bukovina, Polish or Romanian), meaning that if a family of another ethnicity, say Ukrainian, managed to gain land-owning status, it would adopt Polish language and religion and become Polish. In some cases, crown land *Landtag* elections may have even served to strengthen

---

[43] 'Austria-Hungary' in *Encyclopedia Britanica Micropedia* (15th edn, London, Encyclopedia Britanica, 2002) 720.

[44] Art 2, Fundamental Law [of Austria] 142, regarding the General Rights of Citizens. (Article 2 read: 'All citizens are equal before the law.')

ethnic identities and loyalties, to mobilise voting blocks. The 'compact populations' of the empire may to some extent have been the result of dispersed populations that compacted themselves: in 1910, one-quarter of the inhabitants of Austria (6,350,000 people) had changed their political district.[45] Records do not show clearly how many stayed in place but changed ethnicity.

Curia is one of many terms for expressing group identities in Austria-Hungary, leaving us to grope towards understanding and translation. Take, for example, turn-of-the-century political theorist Mykhailo Drahomanov's explanation that 'the Jews in Ukraine represent [simultaneously] a nation, a religion, and a social class', where 'social class' (the Ukrainian *сословие* (*soslovie*)), the later historian Rudnytsky tells us, translates literally as 'estate', which is one of the translations offered for *curia*.[46] The measures for trying to manage pre-existing systems of privileges and the *curia* they mark within the legal order of the empire may have informed Ehrlich's understanding of the human associations that, in his theory, form a social order. One can imagine the analogy at work. Nobles enjoyed privileges, special bodies of customary rights recognised by the *Ausgleich* constitutions and laws. Non-nobles did not enjoy the nobles' advantages and special recognition by the state, but the alternative was not the null set; it was clear that non-nobles too had their discernable bodies of custom and particular sets of rights arising from their legal relations.[47] Ehrlich sets out to investigate them and proposes their incorporation into the legal order through judicial and administrative decision-making.

The occasional (but not automatic) association of ethnicity with economic identity, such as that which we see in some of the *curia*, was clear to Ehrlich. In a 1909 work based on research in Roman law, Ehrlich argues that the legal capacity of an individual and his or her position in the economic order are always related.[48] Likewise, in his early ethnography, a literal investigation into the practices of ethnic groups, he found some of these ethnic-professional affiliations at work in generating bodies of

---

[45] R Wischenbart, 'Vienna in 1910: A City Without Viennese' in SE Bonner and FP Wagner (eds), *Vienna: The World of Yesterday, 1889–1914* (Atlantic Highlands, NJ, Humanities Press International, 1997) 37.

[46] M Drahomanov, 'Evreiski vopros na Ukraine' ('The Jewish Question in Ukraine') in *Sobranie politicheskikh sochinenii 2* (*Collection of Political Essays 2*) 534, quoted in I Rudnytsky, 'Mykhailo Drahomanov and Ukrainian-Jewish Relations' in P Rudnytsky (ed), *Essays in Modern Ukrainian History* (Edmonton, Canadian Institute of Ukrainian Studies, 1987) 286. Description of voting rights and the parliamentary system under the 1867 Constitution may be found in J Bérenger, above n 42, 209–89.

[47] Ehrlich points to an example of a non-noble body of rights in the customary-law research of Dzniestrzanksi among the *bojken* clan of Ukrainians in Galicia. Ehrlich, *Fundamental Principles*, above n 14, 499.

[48] E Ehrlich, *Die Rechtsfähigkeit* (*Legal Capacity*) (1909), in the collection of F Kobler, *Das Rechts* (*The Law*).

legal relations. For example, in his first work among the rural Ruthenians (Ukrainians) and Romanians of Bukovina, he discovered that there was:

> ... [a] numerous priesthood, which is made up for the most part of the same families in which this office is usually hereditary, and this priesthood, spread over a wide territory, forms a nation within a nation, which has its own traditions and its own customs.[49]

As he encounters them, Ehrlich treats such professional groups as one of the human associations to be studied for their legal practices; this insight and methodological inclusion marks a significant point of departure from other ethnographers of his day, the Bogošičs and the Bobčsevs. Ehrlich considered both ethnic and professional groups the objects of legal ethnography, treating the two categories as practically analytical equals.

Ethnic groups then were a complicated category, in ethnography and within the law of the empire. For all of its carve-outs for local bodies of tradition, there was a limit to the structural parity given to ethnic groups under the 1867 Constitution. Peoples that had not previously in history had a named, recognised state did not possess any 'state-right' and constituted 'non-native groups' in Austria and Hungary.[50] Both Ukrainians and Jews, two of the three most numerous populations in Bukovina, were so classified. Just as the *curia* coalesced into disciplined voting blocks in the *Reichsrat*—like the famous *Polenklub* of Polish Galician estate owners—political alliances grew up between the 'non-native' groups. After universal suffrage in 1906, incidentally the year that Ehrlich became rector in Chernivtsi, cooperative Jewish-Ukrainian voting pacts yielded electoral successes in the Bukovina *Reichsrat* elections for both Jews and Ukranians.

A lack of 'state-right' by no means amounted to complete neglect or exclusion by the Austrian state. Language offers many examples. The 1867 Constitution made clear guarantees about the right to receive state services in one's native language, even for those who were linguistic minorities in a subregion.[51] For example, children were to be educated in publicly funded schools in their mother tongue, if feasible, according to an 1869 federal law.[52]

---

[49] E Ehrlich, 'Professor Ehrlich's Czernowitz Seminar of Living Law', presented by W Page, *Proceedings of the Fourteenth Annual Meeting of the Association of American Law Schools* (Chicago, Association of American Law Schools, 1914) 58–9 (hereinafter: Ehrlich, 'Seminar').

[50] Bérenger, above n 42, 216. A group could thus legally be 'non-native' without losing a consensus acknowledgement that its linguistic or historical forebears predated other known groups in a given region. 'Earliest known' could still mean 'non-native'.

[51] Art 19, Fundamental Law [of Austria] 142. (Article 19 read: 'All nations [*Volksstämme*] of the state are equal in their rights, and each nation has the inviolable right to preserve and to promote its nationality [*Nationalität*] and language. For all languages whose use is customary in a land, the state recognizes equality of rights in schools, government institutions, and public life. In those crownlands inhabited by more than one nation, public institutions of education shall enable each of the nations to be educated in its language, without being compelled to learn a second language of the land.')

[52] King, above n 18, 3.

Perhaps even more indicative of a bottom-up economy of knowledge in the empire, army officers were to speak the language spoken by a majority of their troops.[53]

New ideas of balance, conscious of ethnicity but not based on traditional privileges, also came into play. For example, different nationalities on local governing boards were balanced to create proportionate representation.[54] State-based efforts are not the full story, either. People of the empire cultivated other means for regularising friendly contact between ethnicities. Austrian Social Democrat Karl Renner, a native of Bohemia, recalled in his autobiography that his family, like many German peasant families, took part in a tradition of *Kinderwechsel*, or children's exchange. German children would spend a year living with a Czech family and attending a Czech school, and vice versa. The Czech boys who stayed with his family 'called my parents "Vater" and "Mutter", just as our lads did the Czech parents "Otec" and "Matka"'.[55] The children and families who took part, he reminisces, remained life-long friends.

These examples show how Austria-Hungary differed from other models of empire that tried to unite and rule through homogeneity. The important point for our purposes is the space that the empire's official policies allowed for identity to remain unsettled. In its accommodations to a variety of languages and practices in its own heartland, the Habsburg House did not foreclose certain conditions of possibility[56] for variance among political elites. This is very different from other European states of the time seeking to unite through extension of symbolic systems of the metropolis. In contrast to them and to the totalitarian regimes that later took its place, one would be tempted to call Austria-Hungary a 'fragmentarian' state. The Habsburg dynasty did not insist on a common tongue, try to spread one national origin myth or forge a single national identity. Nor did it use law as a starting point for identity as, say, US governments did. Its concern was with loyalty to the Habsburg House, not to the Austrian Constitution. Emperor Franz Josef permitted the maintenance of separate traditions, different levels of political engagement by *curia* and a variety of forms of economic engagement, using difference to leverage voting in the parliament.[57]

---

[53] I Deák, *Beyond Nationalism: A Social and Political History of the Habsburg Officer Corps, 1848–1918* (New York, Oxford University Press, 1990).

[54] For example, national representation on school boards was closely watched (and frequently challenged). See J King, above n 18.

[55] K Renner, *An der Wende Zweier Zeiten* (Vienna, Danubia-Verlag, 1946) 46.

[56] I am indebted to Alexei Yurchak for directing me to conditions of possibility as a focus of inquiry.

[57] This point raises serious problems for Likhovski's application of a Turner frontier hypothesis to understanding Chernivtsi and Ehrlich (Likhovski, above n 5). Law and its relation to empire are quite different in his Austrian and US cases. As one example of the differing approaches to governing disparate cultures on the frontier, Austria tried neither to confine the 'other' in reservations nor to contain or exterminate them via cavalry campaigns.

Nationalism and ethnic identities were increasingly powerful concerns and practices were cultivated to manage inter-ethnic relations. I suggest that ethnography was one way of making sense of this milieu and, in Ehrlich's program, one of many experimental proposals for operationalising toleration that marked this period.

The Supranational Notable and Operationalising Toleration

At the same time that nationalism was rising, a new figure emerged in late Habsburg Austria defined by expertise rather than origin. A civil service and army were recruited and educated to administer the empire. Cross-cutting associations—the army, the state bureaucracy, commerce—provided home, trajectories, circuits of exchange categorically different from the previous milieus more closely tied to native place or group. Liberal reforms, changing subjects into citizens, reinforced some of the cross-cutting categories, demanding duties to the state and recognising rights, indifferent to origin. As state institutions extended their reach, experience beyond the local began to extend to lower classes. Take, for example, participation in the army. Universal conscription was introduced in 1868. One Ukrainian nationalist newspaper listed the conscription statistics for the province in 1910 as having in significant numbers Ukrainians, Romanians, Jews, Germans, Poles, Hungarians, Czechs and Slovaks.[58] Conscription imposed duties on all, but also gave openings. As status privileges spread to office-holders, the meaning of ethnicity to others changed as well.[59]

Bérenger tells us that the last decades of the nineteenth century gave rise to a 'human type', the 'Austrian notable' who had received an education in law or a military academy and made his career in the administration

---

[58] The relative numbers are listed for 1900 and 1910, respectively, as Ukrainians ('Ruthenians'), 297,798 and 305,101; Romanians ('Wallachians'), 229,018 and 273,254; Jews, 96,150 and 102,919; Germans, 63,336 and 65,935; Poles, 26,857 and 36,205; Hungarians ('Madryars' or Magyars), Czechs, Slovaks, and others, 596 and 1005. 'Конскрипція на Буковині' ['Conscription in Bukovina'], 9 *Нова Буковина* [*Nova Bukovina*] (Chernivtsi, 2 February 1912) 1.

[59] Deák, for example, explains changes related to a specific communicative practice, duelling. Prior to the Liberal reforms, a gentile man might offer an insult to a Jew on the street, knowing that a Jew's status meant that one could ignore a demand for satisfaction in a duel. Army officers not only could demand satisfaction, they were obliged to by the Austrian officer corps' honour code, and other officers were obliged to support each other's right to demand satisfaction. ['It is against the army's notion of honor to refuse chivalrous satisfaction (*ritterliche Genugtuung*) to a person simply because he belongs to another nation or religious community.'] *A Guide for Reserve Officers* (1915), commenting on the case of a German nationalist military academy student who lost his rank in the army after refusing satisfaction to a Jewish student who challenged him to a duel, cited in I Deák, *Jewish Soldiers in Austro-Hungarian Society* (New York, Leo Baeck Institute, 1990) 21. As the army incorporated more Jewish officers (by 1897, every fifth reserve officer was a Jew) (Deák, *ibid*, 17), there was an increasing chance that a Jewish man one met on the street would be a reserve officer and able to demand satisfaction. The incidence of provocative insults to randomly met Jews dropped.

or the army. 'While acknowledging his ancestry, he felt first and foremost a servant of the state and of the dynasty.' Language and the affiliations it connotes play a role: the Austrian notable was not ethnic German, but 'partially Germanised'.[60] Henri Gobard's model distinguishing different types of languages is useful here. Gobard distinguishes the vernacular, a maternal or territorial language, from the 'vehicular', an urban language of commerce or bureaucratic transmission (as German was in Habsburg Austria).[61] We might add scholarship to the domains of vehicular language. One striking phenomenon of late Habsburg Austria is the rise of a supranational figure, working for fluency in the vehicular language, at the same time that participation in the everyday affairs of state was reworked to accommodate vernacular languages of the participating nationalities.

Ehrlich certainly fits the description of the Austrian notable. What is peculiar is his self-consciousness. He understands that lawyers, notaries and judges constituted themselves in social formations that could be studied with the same methods that others applied only to 'ethnic groups' and 'natives'. Here we recall the broad scope of his 1903 proposal, where the subjects of his study include judges and document producers with the everyday producers of 'real life' who should be investigated.

From Free School to User Theory of Rights

Responding to the Multi-national Empire and Constitutional Democracy

As we saw in Tomaszczuk's vision for the University of Czernowitz, some concepts and organisational methods inspired by the multi-national empire in themselves served as a common purpose and touchstone for Austrian identity. Plurality was taken for granted as the base from which Austrian citizens came, and not necessarily as a centripetal force that threatened the unity of the empire. This is the point of departure for Ehrlich's own ideas on how law works.

Ehrlich took up the perennial question of the age of codification, what to do with 'gaps' in the Code. Ehrlich claimed intellectual lineage with a branch of the 'Free School of Law' following François Gény, who had proposed that gaps should be filled by a 'free decision of the judge', subject to the judge's understanding of social utility, his innate sense of justice and the subject of the dispute (in Gény's words, 'the nature of the thing'). The judge

---

[60] Bérenger, above n 42, 228.
[61] Gobard's other types are referential language, entailing cultural reference; and mythic language, caught up in a transcendent spiritual or religious practice (as Latin was in Austrian Catholicism). Henri Gobard cited in G Deleuze and F Guattari, *Kafka: Towards a Minor Literature*, D Polen (tr) (Minneapolis, University of Minnesota Press, 1986 (1975)) 23.

and his intent replace the legislator and his, as the key figure in juristic analysis and in the practical matter of filling gaps. (Ehrlich took the state's description of separation of powers less literally than Gény, understanding that executive branch administrators could take decisions interpreting regulations that served as the functional equivalent of judicial decisions, but his analytical tack was the same as Gény's.) As Ehrlich notes:

> [T]he significance of law in the daily life of a people depends far more on the persons charged with its administration than on the principles according to which it is administered.[62]

Where would one look for sources of law to deal with gaps in the Code? The alternative to the written for Ehrlich is not orality as much as it is custom. Ehrlich had started his career as a classics scholar writing on Roman customary law, and later we see the formative influence of ethnography on his developing theory of what 'custom' is. Looking at the details of daily life, Ehrlich came to the conclusion that by definition humans in society produced social order through regular practices, which in turn gave rise to binding norms. Recall that for Ehrlich, a social association is:

> ... [a] plurality of human beings who, in their relations with one another, recognize certain rules of conduct as binding, and, generally at least, actually regulate their conduct according to them.[63]

The 'inner order' of associations is determined by what Ehrlich calls 'legal norms', not to be confused with legal propositions. The legal proposition is the 'precise, universally binding formulation of the legal precept in a book of statutes or in a law book'. The 'legal norm' by contrast does not necessarily depend on spoken or written communication for its expression: it is 'the legal command, reduced to practice, as it obtains in a definite association, perhaps of very small size, even without any formulation in words'.[64] Ehrlich worried that legal authorities increasingly slighted customary legal norms in the era of codification. Introductory textbooks assure us that:

> ... customary law is of equal force with written law. Yet, if one looks at the actual practice rather than the verbal expression, one will soon come to the conclusion that treatises, manuals, essays, and decisions proceed from an assumption—never, of course, openly confessed—that there really is no law except statutory law.[65]

The thrust of Ehrlich's argument here is key: associations of human beings are formed when individuals recognise certain rules of conduct as binding. Ehrlich calls these rules of conduct 'law'. Law is by definition a part of

---

[62] Ehrlich, 'Judicial Freedom', above n 6, 48.
[63] Ehrlich, *Fundamental Principles*, above n 14, 39.
[64] Ehrlich, *ibid*, 38.
[65] Ehrlich, 'Judicial Freedom', above n 6, 50.

human associations. Since Ehrlich has already told us that a society is the sum total of associations of human beings, legal pluralism must be an inherent quality of society. Law, then, necessarily takes the form that Bakhtin would call heteroglossia[66] and what later anthropologists would, in various ways, call legal pluralism. Ehrlich illuminates for us the basic social fact of legal pluralism and further gives us a methodology for tapping into those rich resources as a source of law for state decision-makers. What he neglects to cover is an inevitable product of legal pluralism: conflicts of laws. He does not describe for us what happens when a person, case or collective is simultaneously subject to more than one normative order that conflicts with one another, nor instructs us how a decision-maker should choose between them or reconcile conflicts. This problem is left for the future. It is not a surprise, then, that conflicts-of-laws doctrine is the area taken up as the first major area of US legal reform by Legal Realists (and becomes, perhaps, the source of its greatest cynicism).

Ehrlich was not concerned with homogenising or pluralising.[67] A note here is in order on space and time, territory and history, in Ehrlich's work. Ehrlich critiques codes not only in their reach across space, but (perhaps more strongly) in their reach across time, not with regard to their heavy hand as much as to their dead hand:

> Accordingly, our codes are uniformly adapted to a time much earlier than their own, and all the juristic technique in the world would be unable to extract the actual law of the present from it, for the simple reason that it is not contained therein. But the territory within which our codes are valid is so vast, the legal relations with which they deal are so incomparably richer, more subject to changes than they ever have been ... To attempt to imprison the law of a time or of a people within the sections of a code is about as reasonable as to attempt to confine a stream within a pond.[68]

Weiler argues that the persistent question of Austrian governance was 'from the many, one' or 'out of one, many', and that Ehrlich advocated the latter.[69] However, as Ehrlich's work proceeded, I think he argued rather for legal decisions that reflect social reality. His argument for an

---

[66] For a discussion of heteroglossia and dialogism, see M Bakhtin, 'Discourse in the Novel' in M Holquist (ed), C Emerson and M Holquist (trs), *The Dialogic Imagination: Four Essays by M.M. Bakhtin* (Austin, TX, University of Texas Press, 1981 (1934–45)) 259–422, particularly at 270–75.

[67] Likhovski, looking into the generative conditions for anti-formalist movements, tells us that Ehrlich's Chernivtsi was like Pound's Lincoln, Nebraska: a provincial town on the frontier of empire, where different cultures clashed and the legal culture of the centre had only a tenuous hold (Likhovski, above n 5, 622). Ehrlich by contrast conveys the sense that we get of Austria-Hungary from other contemporary sources: not an empire using law as a centripetal force, but an agglomeration of rich cultures used by the emperor to forge and manipulate alliances to maintain loyalty to the dynasty (Ehrlich, *Fundamental Principles*, above n 14, 487–8).

[68] Ehrlich, *ibid*, 487–8.

[69] Weiler, above n 5.

understanding of law as heteroglossia reflects empirical findings, not a political preference.

It is important to note how this conception of law departs from the Free School. Although Ehrlich does not frame his conception of law as a rejection of the Free School's, we are no longer talking about stuff to fill gaps in the Code. We are talking about multiple legal discourses that carry on constantly and independently of the Code, which Ehrlich proposes judges and decision-makers call on as sources of information about existing law when the decision-maker encounters a gap in law that happens to be written down already. Without fanfare, Ehrlich reframes the Free School discussion of 'gaps' into an account of legal pluralism.

To say that law is more than commands of the state at this point would be redundant. Forestalling some formalist critics, in his inaugural address as rector in 1906, Ehrlich reported conclusions about customary law from his long research into Roman legal history, but as its title shows, he framed it for the contemporary argument. In *Die Tatsache des Gewohnheitrechts* (The Fact of Customary Law), he concludes that:

> ... when the classical Roman jurists speak of *ius civile* they mean Roman customary law; but when they quite generally speak of *mores* or *consuetudo*, they do not.[70]

This address seems a carefully calculated attempt to head off critics who would argue that going beyond the state for a definition of law means that just anything could be classified as 'law'. Ehrlich anticipates that argument and inoculates his model against it by demarcating an inside and an outside of Roman customary law. To some extent, though, it cannot be avoided that demarcation is in tension with the holism that underwrites his conception of society and law. The boundary problems that orality, custom and ultimately ethnography raise are still with us.

The radical innovation that Ehrlich proposes to the Free School is that the judge's sense of what to do in an instant case be predominantly informed by careful study of current practice in the domain in controversy. If a case involves suit for damages of spoiled milk from a milk-seller to a buyer, find out what community standards for evaluating milk quality and apportioning risk are, and apply them. Again, it is not that Ehrlich seeks to create many social groups or to streamline them; he assumes that they exist and proposes a means for incorporating their standards into legal decisions. After Nader, who, analysing the development of the common law in the United States, elaborates a 'user theory of law',[71] I would call Ehrlich's

---

[70] Ehrlich, *Fundamental Principles*, above n 14, 441.
[71] L Nader, 'A User Theory of Legal Change as Applied to Gender' in *The Nebraska Symposium on Motivation: The Law as a Behavioural Instrument* 1–33; and L Nader, *Life*, above n 3, 49.

approach to addressing gaps a 'user theory of rights'. Like Jhering, he does not believe that rights are metaphysical entities to be found as a part of human make-up, nor are they principles to be deduced and constructed from a code. Unlike Jhering, whose purposive jurisprudence would pose as a primary question for a judge filling a gap, 'What outcome do we want?', Ehrlich would ask, 'What are people doing?'. We understand, then, how the question of methodology becomes central to Ehrlich's program. Ethnography is required for the judge to learn what current practice is. Ehrlich starts his "Seminar in Living Law" to teach law students how to study the details of real life and to enlist them in investigations.

Once discovered by German-reading American legal scholars inspired by the Free School, Ehrlich's work enjoyed rapid dissemination in the United States. *The Free Finding of Law and Free Legal Science* (1903) and *Fundamental Principles of the Sociology of Law* (1913) in particular sparked their imagination. News of his efforts to put these insights to work in a systematic ethnographic enterprise to inform legal content, in his "Seminar in Living Law" at the University of Czernowitz, provoked great interest. Ehrlich was invited to address the influential Association of American Law Schools in Chicago in December 1914, but the difficulties of wartime travel precluded his attending. An explanation of his seminar, both its methodology and some preliminary results, were presented *in absentia*.[72]

In Two Places at Once

I argue above that, while Ehrlich's methodology, ethnography, was a radical proposal in the Free School's discussion of how judges should make their decisions, it was less striking in the late Habsburg context. A confluence of factors—an emperor tolerant of difference within a frame of dynastic loyalty, Liberal political reforms, rising national consciousness—led to many experiments in operationalising toleration within the structures of governmental organisation and practice across the empire. Pluralism was not only protected; arguably, given the electoral and imperial politics around the new parliamentary democracies in the crown lands, plurality may even have been cultivated.

Ehrlich carved out for himself a position that Nader has described as 'the double marginal',[73] which became a defining position of twentieth-century ethnographers. Ehrlich developed a methodology based on duration in a time of hit-and-run survey work, conducting his fieldwork right where he

---

[72] For a summary, see Ehrlich, Seminar, above n 49.
[73] L Nader, personal communication, October 2003.

had spent most of his life, but also insistently plunged into international scholarly discourse. Immersion in the local was as fundamental to his work as his commitment to the cross-cutting associations that defined his professional identity. Though a specialist in the local, he became part of a group of supranational notables, working in the vernacular, but transmitting in the vehicular.

ETHNOGRAPHY (REPRISE): THE NEW ETHNOGRAPHIC METHOD

What, then, did ethnography come to mean for the Ehrlich of late Hapsburg Bukovina? There are several important ways in which he differs from his contemporaries.

Experience as Method and Science

Ehrlich argues that social order and social institutions, although not tangible, are susceptible to sense perception.[74] Every investigator must devise the method that suits his or her own individuality, but 'whatever method or technique it may be, its starting point will always be that which the external world presents to the human mind'.[75] Experience is the basis for Ehrlich's empiricism and a central justification for ethnography as a means of inquiry. As opposed to other sciences based on observation, however, the investigator is not remote from his or her subjects beyond class or professional separations inherent in their milieu. It is the immediacy of perception, the direct experience that makes the work empirical. This kind of ethnography depends on experience as method.

This reliance on experience as a basis for empiricism shows us that although Ehrlich reacted against the 'legal science' practised in the nineteenth century, he does not discard science as discipline and aspiration, but rather thinks through a particular meaning for science. Ehrlich calls for developing both practical and theoretical legal science. Although famous for his promotion of a practical science of law incorporating insights from in situ observation of the 'living law' into judicial decisions, his less famous promotion of a theoretical science of law was no less central to his program for research, teaching and conduct of law. The two are intimately connected for Ehrlich. A theoretical science for Ehrlich is marked by systematicity and deduction based on empirical observation.

> Only after a concrete observation is finished does the scientist ask himself whether the principles which he has deduced from the specific observation hold true

[74] Ehrlich, *Fundamental Principles*, above n 14, 131.
[75] *Ibid* 472.

generally; and he can determine this fact only by a series of concrete observations. The same is true for the legal investigator.[76]

Observation, Ehrlich thought, should also be used as part of the method for formulating a problem for research. Montesquieu claimed that he 'laid down principles and saw particular cases yield to them of themselves'. Ehrlich adds:

> That is seemingly the genuine scholastic method, beginning with principles and progressing to particular cases by logical ratiocination. But in reality the principles Montesquieu starts with are not conceived *a priori*. They are all derived from facts he collected, scrutinized, and turned over in his mind during the twenty years he was engaged in his work.[77]

We have discussed how, in Habsburg use, ethnography could be used interchangeably with ethnicity and indicated a descriptive genre. The latter remains the predominant meaning of 'ethnography' in current parlance: one writes an ethnography. As we saw, for other social scientists at the turn of the century, ethnography could also indicate the additional practice of gathering data: one collected ethnographic material. Here, Ehrlich sees the limit that distinguishes his work from his contemporaries. He gathered social facts like Bogošič, Bobčev, Costa and other ethnographers, but, he emphasises, they did not develop their observations into a systematic body of statements, a sociology. Bogošič, for example, 'supplied us with invaluable material' in writing up a codification of Montenegran property law based not merely on the small number of legal propositions, but 'chiefly on the concrete legal relations and legal institutions'. In writing with the object not of a historical understanding but of that which is in existence, today, Bogošič produced a 'recognized masterpiece'. However, nonetheless, 'it would be a vain endeavour to look for general thoughts in his works'.[78] The only peer whom Ehrlich thinks has taken on the same kind of project, of close ethnographic observation used as the basis for study of patterns and generalisations, was the Austrian-Ukrainian ethnographer Dniestrzanski in his *Customary Law and the Social Associations*.[79] In his work, Ehrlich recognised the germs of a number of thoughts like those he was presenting in *Fundamental Principles in the Sociology of Law*. Data-gathering is not enough. Ethnography also meant a mode of analysing data: one thought through ethnography. Ethnography serves as epistemology.

---

[76] Ehrlich, 'Seminar', above n 49, 59.
[77] Ehrlich, 'Montesquieu', above n 13, 587.
[78] Ehrlich, *Fundamental Principles*, above n 14, 465–6.
[79] S Dniestrzanski, *Das Gewohnheitsrecht und die sozialen Verbände* (*Customary Law and the Social Associations*) (Czernowitz, 1905), cited in Ehrlich, *Fundamental Principles*, above n 14, 465 and 499.

The Humanities and the Place of the Translator

Ethnography as epistemology requires a certain sort of food for thought. Vienna's other new social sciences, like psychology, agreed that what was understood as 'artistic sensibility' is part of good social science.[80] Ehrlich firmly located his ethnographic work at the intersection of science and art.

> Every true work of science is a work of art, and the man who is not an artist is a poor man of science. Production of a work of science requires the same qualifications as production of a work of art.[81]

He understood this to have methodological implications. As artists:

> ... every independent investigator must create his own method, just as every creative artist must create his own technique ... For the mind which thinks and works independently will ever be seeking new methods and new techniques which correspond to his individuality.[82]

While Ehrlich here acknowledges the role of creativity in scientific inquiry, that is not to confuse scholarly work with creation or individuality with authorship. Rather, implicit throughout Ehrlich's project is a central purpose: ethnography itself was to be an act of translation. He emerged from Austrian pluralism with a goal not of homogeneity, but of communication. In Ehrlich's program, the natives' own legal documents, practices, customs would be translated from the vernacular into the vehicular language of bureaucratic administration of justice.

Ethnography is translation in another respect. The ethnographer is not correctly understood as the author of ethnography; rather it is the subjects, the group of humans under study, who have produced the content. The ethnographer is transcriber, except that in most cases the target reader is one who does not understand the vocabulary of practice being presented. If the ethnographer has made the switch to a methodology of the humanities, adopting the natives' own terms and ideas for understanding practice from within, the analysis he or she produces is not mere reproduction, still unintelligible to the alien reader. Instead, the ethnographer is translator of that which a collective has authored, as Ehrlich has taught us, as a body of custom. Here is where we see the old story of tool-use retold: the tool was fashioned and eventually the tool refashioned the tool-bearers. In Ehrlich's case, ethnography transforms his work from legal theory to social science, but instead of a grand science of eternal truths, one of emergent tales of

---

[80] See also Malinowski, *Argonauts of the Western Pacific* (Prospect Heights, IL, Waveland Press, 1984 (1922)) 18.
[81] Ehrlich, *Fundamental Principles*, above n 14, 472.
[82] *Ibid*.

the particular. Ethnography can transform the ethnographer from master scientist into translator of the vernacular.

EPILOGUE AND CONCLUSION

Epilogue

There is a tension to this day in ethnography between an Enlightenment commitment to human universals and a Romantic commitment to particulars. Ehrlich's program for a sociological jurisprudence, like many Austrian experiments in governance, sought to integrate the particular into the whole. However, Ehrlich's laboratory of a legal science and the pluralistic empire it served succumb to the former.

On 22 October 1918, a Romanian propaganda organ *Glasul Bucovinei* (Bukovina's Voice) began to appear in Chernivtsi. Its editorial board attacked Bukovina's 'Austrian' pluralist tradition and urged Romanian-speakers to unite. On 17 October 1918, a Romanian National Council had formed in Vienna in response to the emperor's manifesto calling for the federalisation of Austria based on nationalities. In his last imperial audience, the president of the council informed Franz Josef that the Romanians would vote against a reformed monarchy, the equivalent to a declaration of ethnic Romanian secession. On 27 October 1918, a Constituent Assembly of the Romanians of Bukovina met in Chernivtsi and voted for the union of Bukovina with other 'Romanian lands'. These moves carried ominous overtones: already in prewar Romania, a struggle for national self-definition against the pluralism and toleration of Austria across the border had resulted in part in an understanding that 'to be Romanian became synonymous with being an anti-Semite'.[83] At a 'General Congress' in Chernivtsi boycotted by Ukrainians and Jews, Romanian, German and Polish delegates voted unanimously for the union of Bukovina with Romania. The ambitions of France at the Paris negotiations at the end of the War, eager to reward Romania as a perceived ally and to establish it as a buffer state, aligned with those of Romanian chauvinists. Bukovina was incorporated into Romania in January 1919.[84]

That same month, a new Romanian administrator, Ion Nistor (who had been one of the underground editors of *Glasul Bucovinei*), took the rectorship of the University of Czernowitz (the post Ehrlich had held at the beginning of his reform program in 1906). Nistor declared in his first speech as rector that he sought to purge the province and the university of a despised

---

[83] Livezeanu, above n 22, 12.
[84] This information on the Romanian takeover of Bukovina summarised from Livezeanu, above n 22, 57–9.

species, *homo bukovinensis*, the name he gave to a creature that tolerated the mishmash of communities and thrived under pluralism. Ehrlich, like all but three faculty members of the two secular departments of the university, was an Austrian who did not speak Romanian. The student body was also mixed. The last figures from before the First World War, the 1913–14 school year, give a total of 1,198 students at the university, including: 401 Jews, 310 Romanians, 303 Ukrainians, 86 Polish and 57 Germans.[85] Nistor 'invited' non-Romanians on the faculty to use Bukovina's new official language, 'failing which they would have to leave'. Only four Austrian professors consented to these conditions and remained. Decree 4091 of 23 September 1919 formally transformed the Austrian University of Czernowitz into the Romanian University of Cernăuţi.[86]

Withdrawing to Vienna offered scant respite. As Wittgenstein wrote to Bertrand Russell in 1918 upon returning home to Vienna from the Italian prisoner-of-war camp in which he spent the last nine months of the war, 'The city is starving'.[87] The conditions of Ehrlich's last years are murky. It is said Ehrlich died on 22 May 1922 in Vienna, although Pound thought it was 1 April.[88]

CONCLUSION

What are ethnography and a human science good for? In the spirit of modernism, one would be tempted to issue a ringing conclusion. One could issue a call to the new science, an empirical science using experience as the method of data collection and basis for analysis. Ethnography could yield hypotheses tested by local observation and challenge hypotheses alien to experience. Ethnography depends on the notion that understanding of human experience can transcend context. Ehrlich emphasised that we could learn about the plurality in which we live, but implicitly he also argued that it should inform a more comprehensive science of law that could claim broader insights about human ordering. This commitment affirms that we can learn from each other about ourselves. With ethnography as a tool, one is uniquely equipped to advocate for the species. Go forth, make science!

However … it would also be true to Ehrlich to give a more modest answer. This is what I mean by modesty. Ehrlich's legal science differs from

---

[85] F Riedl, 'Die Universität Czernowitz, 1875–1920: Ein Blick auf ihr Wesen und Ihre Entwicklung Beziehungen zu Ost- und Mitteldeutschland' 2 *Mitteldeutsche Vorträge* (1971) 19, cited in Livezeanu, above n 22, 231.
[86] Livezeanu, above n 22, 231.
[87] L Wittgenstein, GH von Wright (ed), *Letters to Russell, Keynes, and Moore* (Oxford, Basil Blackwell, 1974).
[88] R Pound, obituary note on Eugen Ehrlich as preface to Ehrlich's 'The Sociology of Law' (December 1922) 36 *Harvard Law Review* 129, 129.

his contemporaries in social science and even from many of his fellow jurists' legal theory. For him, law is simply a way of discussing that which arises from normal human conduct, another way of describing society as current practice. The late Habsburg political structure left room for local traditions and political orders, and does not convey a sense of lack regarding those spaces where the law of empire did not intrude. This seems to be Ehrlich's sense as well. Let the worker bees buzz and bumble between their sections of the hive, let them do their work of building, repairing, filling in, carrying away. You could speak of 'gaps' and, while not incorrect, it would seem a strange characterisation of a honeycomb that is defined as much by its empty spaces as by its connectors. Such, for Ehrlich, is an understanding of society and law.

Ehrlich's program seems less totalising and more contemporary and useful to us. Ehrlich's work involved going out and talking to individuals—peasants, priests, notaries, traders, businessmen—understanding in each modest strand of legal relations that 'society' is nothing more grand, nor less, than that. Modest, yes, but still ambitious, clear, close to the ground, empirical. Ehrlich's work takes his fellow citizens seriously enough to pay attention to their details and, as a social scientist recognising their practice as already law, his legal reform program gives them authority to create law.

Ehrlich does not use ethnography to create a new set of eternal truths, a new mythic language that one must master in order to establish authority in law. He is not blind to power relations based on knowledge, but he offers an alternative to acquiescence or rebellion. Instead, Ehrlich takes on the work of translating the vernacular into the vehicular language of state administration. His program could be read as a blueprint for governing in the vernacular. The ethnographer, as translator, is a key link, but does not claim to produce law or to know the right answers. His proposals rest on observations of the law that others are already practising.

This is a different kind of authoritative discourse, different from existing science and law. Ethnography in Ehrlich's hands does not furnish bricks to build a grand edifice, but the components for a simple mirror. The technology does not fix the image in place; in fact, it is chosen because it reflects the contemporary, the emergent. The ethnographer holds it up so that we see the scientific claim, the legal authority, is the prosaic, changing image of ourselves and our fellow persons in the mirror.

3

Venus in Czernowitz: Sacher-Masoch, Ehrlich and the Fin-de-siècle Crisis of Legal Reason

ASSAF LIKHOVSKI[1]

The artist ... does not produce his work of art from his inner self; he can but give shape to that which society furnishes him with.[2]

There is no antithesis between science and art. Every true work of science is a work of art.[3]

INTRODUCTION

HERR LEOPOLD VON Sacher-Masoch agrees on his word of honor to be the slave of Frau von Pistor and unconditionally fulfill her every wish and every order for a period of six months ... Fanny Pistor in return, promises to wear fur as often as practical and especially when being cruel ... This contract is confirmed by the signatures of the participants. Taking effect on 8 December 1869 [signed] Fanny Pistor Baddanow, Sir Leopold von Sacher-Masoch.[4]

This contract, formally sealing the relationship between Austrian writer, Leopold Sacher-Masoch, and his lover, Fanny Pistor, also became (in modified

---

[1] I would like to thank Yishai Blank, Gila Haimovic, Yossi Harpaz, Roy Kreitner, Shai Lavi, Itamar Mann, Menachem Mautner, Adar Ortal, the participants of the *Rediscovering Eugen Ehrlich* conference, especially Marc Hertogh, and two anonymous reviewers for their comments and assistance.
[2] E Ehrlich, *Fundamental Principles of the Sociology of Law*, Walter L Moll (tr) (New York, Transaction, 2002) 208.
[3] Ibid 472.
[4] L Sacher-Masoch, *Venus in Furs*, J Neugroschel (tr) (New York, Penguin Books, 2000) 121–2. Fanny Pistor's name is spelt 'Bogdanow' by O'Pecko and 'Baganov' in the Zone Books edition of the novella. See M O'Pecko, 'Leopold von Sacher-Masoch' in DG Daviau (ed), *Major Figures of Nineteenth-Century Austrian Literature* (Riverside CA, Ariadne Press, 1998) 472 and 481; and G Deleuze and L Sacher-Masoch, *Masochism: Coldness and Cruelty by Gilles Deleuze/Venus in Furs by Leopold von Sacher-Masoch* (New York, Zone Books, 1991) 278.

form) the core of Masoch's novella, *Venus in Furs*, published in 1870. The book tells the story of a love affair between Masoch's literary alter-ego, Severin von Kusiemski, and his mistress, Wanda von Dunajew.[5] This contract will also serve as the starting point of this chapter, the goal of which is to use *Venus in Furs* to highlight a number of themes found in Eugen Ehrlich's sociology of law.

Masoch's work has enjoyed tremendous scholarly interest in recent decades.[6] It has been studied by historians of gender, cultural historians, literary theorists, psychologists and philosophers. The interest in Masoch, it seems, stems in part from the fact that he provides interesting insights on a number of important themes in late-nineteenth-century culture.[7] However, despite the fact that Masoch studied law and despite the important role that law plays in Venus in Furs, Masoch's work still awaits analysis by historians of legal thought and jurisprudence. Even in cases when the role of law in Masoch's work was mentioned, for example, in the influential discussion of Masoch's notion of law in Gilles Deleuze's *Coldness and Cruelty*, interest in law is subordinated to an interest in other topics (psychology, in Deleuze's case).

For historians of modern legal thought, Masoch's curious use of contracts in his real-life relationships and in his fictional works raises a number of interesting questions: Why did Masoch base his relationships on a contract? How was this use related to the growing importance of contractual relationships and to the centrality of the notion of free will in nineteenth-century European culture? How did the paradoxical use of contract to create a status-based relationship relate to contemporary theories of legal evolution? Did Masoch's conception of sovereignty reflect common nineteenth-century understandings of the term? In this chapter, I take Masoch's interest in law seriously. I analyse *Venus in Furs* in order to point to some jurisprudential themes found in it, rather than reading the novella merely as a literary text on the nature of a peculiar kind of love. I do so in order to gain a better understanding of the cultural context from which Eugen Ehrlich's sociology of law emerged.

Ehrlich was Masoch's younger contemporary and his academic career peaked several years after Masoch's death. However, they did share a common background, and this common background was the reason for my initial interest in juxtaposing their work. Both Masoch and Ehrlich were born in the eastern backwater of the Austro-Hungarian Empire, Masoch in Lemberg

---

[5] Sacher-Masoch, *Venus in Furs* 73. Some scholars have claimed that the contract was fictitious. See M O' Pecko, 'Leopold von Sacher-Masoch' 481.

[6] See, eg SR Stewart, *Sublime Surrender: Male Masochism at the Fin de Siècle* (Ithaca, Cornell University Press, 1998).

[7] See, eg O'Pecko, 'Leopold von Sacher-Masoch' 484–5; JW Burrow, *The Crisis of Reason* (New Haven, Yale University Press, 2000) 174 and 242; J Kucich, 'Melancholy Magic: Masochism, Stevenson, Anti-Imperialism' (2001) 56 *Nineteenth Century Literature* 364; and VL Lewis, 'Afterword' in L Sacher-Masoch, *Jewish Life: Tales from Nineteenth Century Europe*, VL Lewis (tr) (Riverside CA, Ariadne, 2002) 205 and 208.

(now L'viv), the capital of the province of Galicia, and Ehrlich 200 kilometres to the south, in Czernowitz (now Chernivtsi), the capital of Bukovina. Both remained connected to their provincial birthplaces throughout their lives: Masoch using his native Galicia and its heterogeneous ethnic society as a source of much of his literary work; and Ehrlich returning to Bukovina to spend most of his academic career at the University of Czernowitz.[8] Both Masoch and Ehrlich were trained in law, although Masoch later became a *privatdozent* in history and then a professional writer.[9] In an earlier piece on Ehrlich, I argued that Ehrlich's work (as well as the work of other innovative late-nineteenth-century legal thinkers) did not emerge in a vacuum. Instead, it was a product of their specific geographic location on the frontier of empires, places characterised by their ethnic and cultural heterogeneity.[10] Was the geographical and social proximity of Masoch's and Ehrlich's birthplaces also reflected in some way in shared ideas they had about the law?

In this article, I argue that one can indeed find in Masoch's and Ehrlich's works similar ideas about law. This was not necessarily the result of the geographical proximity of their birthplaces. Ehrlich and Masoch were expressing, each in his own particular way, a more general theme prevalent in *fin-de-siècle* European culture, the 'crisis of reason' (to use John Burrow's term). The 'crisis of reason' was a fascination—evident across many areas of human activity, be they scientific, literary or artistic—with the non-rational aspects of human life.[11] Specifically, I argue that the ideas produced by Masoch and Ehrlich can be seen as an *avant-garde* attack on formalist legal science, seeking to undermine the rationalist and positivist assumptions on which it was based and which dominated continental and Anglo-American legal thought in the mid-nineteenth century.

Nineteenth-century legal formalism assumed that law was a gapless geometric-like system in which specific rules could be abstractly deduced from general propositions. Formalism saw the legal order as emanating from an all-powerful state headed by a sovereign. It championed the autonomy of legal knowledge and sought an alliance with liberal ideology and its main organising concept—free will. Anti-formalist conceptions of law, which emerged in both the continental and Anglo-American world in the late nineteenth and early twentieth centuries, called into question some or all of these notions.[12]

---

[8] See A Likhovski, 'Czernowitz, Lincoln and Jerusalem and the Comparative History of American Legal Thought' (2003) 4 *Theoretical Inquiries in Law* 621.

[9] See G Lenzer, 'On Masochism: A Contribution to the History of a Fantasy and Its Theory' (1975) 1 *Signs* 277. On Masoch's education, see also O'Pecko, 'Leopold von Sacher-Masoch' 473.

[10] Likhovski, 'Czernowitz'.

[11] JW Burrow, *The Crisis of Reason* (New Haven, Yale University Press, 2000).

[12] See, eg D Kennedy, 'Two Globalizations of Law and Legal Thought: 1850–1968' (2003) 36 *Suffolk University Law Review* 631.

The similarity between Masoch's and Ehrlich's ideas about the law, I shall argue, was an expression of a wider interest in the non-rational aspects of law and legal knowledge evident in the works of other important figures in late-nineteenth- and early-twentieth-century culture, for example, Franz Kafka. My intention is therefore to read *Venus in Furs* together with Ehrlich's sociology of law, pointing to a number of similar themes that appeared in the works of both authors.[13]

The aim of this exercise is archaeological (to use a Foucauldian term). It seeks to uncover a set of assumptions and concerns shared by thinkers working in very different fields at a given point in time, rather than tracing the emergence of a specific concept or idea over a long period of time.[14] As a quasi-archaeological project, this chapter does not seek to trace 'influence'. I have not come across any indication that Ehrlich ever read Masoch's work and, even if he did, my intention is not to discover how Masoch may have influenced Ehrlich. My aim, instead, is to describe some common ideas which Masoch and Ehrlich (as well as many other late-nineteenth-century intellectuals) shared.

By comparing disparate thinkers working in different genres and showing affinities in their thought, I wish to demonstrate that the intellectual history of legal thought in general, and the history of the emergence of the sociology of law as an academic discipline at the end of the nineteenth century in particular, must be written from a broad perspective which considers not only legal scholars, but the wider intellectual and cultural context in which they operated. Instead of a vertical history of the sociology of law which views this history as an autonomous entity, describing it as a relay race in which forerunners or heroes of this sub-discipline, such as Ehrlich or Max Weber, created the ideas that were later elaborated by modern law and society scholars, I suggest a horizontal history in which thinkers such as Ehrlich are viewed as embedded in their specific historical time and place, emphasising their relationship to broader themes prevalent in the culture of their period.

---

[13] Similarity, it is important to note, is a relative concept. There was a huge difference between the ideologies of Stalin and Tito, but if one compares both of them to, say, Adam Smith, one will find that Stalin's and Tito's thought was quite similar. In the same way, Ehrlich's thought can be compared to other thinkers in ways which will emphasise either difference or similarity. See, eg D Nelken, 'Law in Action or Living Law? Back to the Beginning in the Sociology of Law' (1984) 4 *Legal Studies* 157; M Hertogh, 'A "European" Conception of Legal Consciousness: Rediscovering Eugen Ehrlich' (2004) 31 *Journal of Law and Society* 457 at 473; (emphasising the difference between Ehrlich's thought and that of other legal thinkers); K Ziegert, 'The Sociology behind Eugen Ehrlich's Sociology of Law' (1979) 7 *International Journal of the Sociology of Law* 225 at 233; and Likhovski, 'Czernowitz' (emphasising similarities). See also K Ziegert, 'A Note on Eugen Ehrlich and the Production of Legal Knowledge' (1998) 20 *Sydney Law Review* 108 at 112 and 121.

[14] A truly Foucauldian archaeology would not examine two thinkers, but a whole discursive community. Such an endeavour is impossible within the limited confines of this article.

The discussion proceeds as follows. The first part of the article provides a brief outline of *Venus in Furs* and the role of law in that novella. It then discusses Gilles Deleuze's analysis of Masoch's use of law. The second part compares Masoch's and Ehrlich's concept of law (as outlined in Ehrlich's major work, *Fundamental Principles of the Sociology of Law*). Specifically, this part focuses on four themes found in the work of both writers: the critique of the concept of free will; the contrast between state sanctions and honour; the use of the exotic as a source of knowledge; and the problems associated with the textual representation of reality. The conclusion discusses a few additional products of *fin-de-siècle* culture in which similar ideas appear.

THE PLEASURES OF LAW

Masoch's *Venus in Furs*

Venus in Furs, part of a cycle of six novellas on the nature of love published by Masoch in 1870, tells the story of Severin von Kusiemski, a young Galician nobleman, and his love affair with his cruel mistress, Wanda von Dunajew.[15] The story has often been read as a thinly veiled autobiography of Masoch and, indeed, some of its details, such as the contract signed by the heroes, may have echoed episodes from Masoch's own life.[16]

In the novella, Severin recounts the history of his affair with Wanda. He meets her in a small Carpathian resort. He falls in love and asks that she enslave him, begging her to torture him. She consents, and draws up a contract in which Severin undertakes to serve her for as long as she so desires. Severin does not sign the contract immediately, but he perceives it nevertheless as binding. Following this, the couple leaves the Carpathian resort for Italy. Severin travels there as Wanda's servant under an assumed name—Gregor. They arrive in Florence and rent a villa. Now Wanda produces the contract of enslavement and another document, a suicide note supposedly written by Severin, which will allow her to kill him at her whim. Severin signs the documents. Once he does, a long period of humiliation follows in which Wanda mistreats and abuses him. Finally, Wanda abandons Severin and he returns to his Galician estate, healed of his desire to become the slave of a domineering woman.[17]

---

[15] On the place of *Venus in Furs* in Masoch's wider literary *oeuvre*, see M O'Pecko, 'Afterword' in L Sacher-Masoch, *Love: The Legacy of Cain*, MT O'Pecko (tr) (Riverside CA, Ariadne Press, 2003) 181.
[16] Sacher-Masoch, *Venus in Furs* xx.
[17] Sacher-Masoch, *Venus in Furs* 119. See also O'Pecko, 'Leopold von Sacher-Masoch' 476–7 and 481.

Law plays a major part in the novella, providing the foundation for the masochist relationship which is its theme: 'I seriously want to be your slave', Severin tells Wanda:

> I want your power over me to be sanctified by law, I want my life to be in your hands, I want nothing in this world to be able to protect me or save me from you. Oh, what voluptuousness to feel dependent entirely on your whim, your mood, a flick of your finger ...[18]

Following these words, Wanda draws up a contract binding Severin by his 'oath and word of honor to be her slave as long as she desired it'. Severin objects that the contract only includes obligations for him, and Wanda agrees to add an obligation on her part—that she 'must always appear in fur'. The signing of the contract is postponed since Wanda believes it should be signed 'in the right place', adding that she desires:

> ... a slave with no will of his own, a slave who is put into my hands not by the law, not by my privilege or brutal violence, but solely by the power of my beauty and my being.

Severin swoons, 'unable to think clearly or make a free decision', he cries out that he wants to be completely at Wanda's mercy, 'with no qualification, with no restriction' on her power, to surrender to her 'despotism unconditionally'.[19]

When the couple reaches Italy, Wanda produces the contract together with the suicide note. The contract states that:

> Herr Severin von Kusiemski ... renounces all rights as lover [of Wanda]; he then commits himself, on his word of honor as a man and nobleman, to being henceforth the *slave* of Frau von Dunajew until such time as she herself restores his freedom.
>
> As the slave of Frau von Dunajew he is to have the name of Gregor, unconditionally fulfill each of her wishes, obey each of her orders, show submissiveness to his Mistress and view any sign of her favor as extraordinary grace.
>
> Not only may Frau von Dunajew punish her slave as she sees fit ... but she also has the right to mistreat him at whim or merely as a pastime ... and she even has the right to kill him if she so wishes ... He is her absolute property ...
>
> For her part, Frau von Dunajew promises as his Mistress to appear in fur as frequently as possible, especially when she is being cruel to her slave.[20]

Deleuze's Coldness and Cruelty

Despite the fact that law plays an important role in *Venus in Furs*, its use by Masoch has not received the attention it deserves. One rare exception

[18] Ibid 50.
[19] Ibid 51–3.
[20] Ibid 73.

to this statement is found in *Coldness and Cruelty*, an essay written by the French philosopher, Gilles Deleuze.[21] Deleuze's ultimate goal in this essay, however, is not to understand Masoch's conception of law. Instead, Deleuze's main aim is to undermine the belief that a unified sadomasochist syndrome existed. Sadism and masochism, Deleuze argues, are not two aspects of the same phenomenon. Masochism does not share a complementary and dialectical unity with sadism.[22]

Deleuze's analysis of law in his essay contrasts the role of law in sadism and masochism. 'The sadist', Deleuze says, 'is in need of institutions, the masochist of contractual relations'. The sadist thinks in terms of possession of his or her victim, the masochist in terms of contractual alliance.[23] The language of the sadist is based on imperatives, while the language of the masochist is based on persuasion.[24] Contract, argues Deleuze, 'represents the ideal form of the [masochist] love-relationship and its necessary precondition'. Its use in the relationship relies on the idea of the 'jurists of antiquity' that slavery itself is based on contract. The contract represents free consent. It is reciprocal and is not meant to affect third parties. It is limited in time and does not alter inalienable rights. Finally, contract creates law, but once law exists, it binds, suspends and immobilises its creators (a theme which is, in itself, a major aspect of masochism).[25]

However, argues Deleuze, the masochist does not blindly submit to law. In fact, the masochist's use of law should be understood as a critique of it. Blind obedience is utilised to expose the absurdity of law. The masochist is an anti-formalist who, by adhering strictly and absurdly to the form of the law and by reversing the conventional legal order, seeks to undermine this very order. Thus, for example, the conventional view of the role of legal punishment is the prevention of the satisfaction of desire. In the masochist's world, however, punishment is transformed from a tool to prevent the satisfaction of desire to a precondition to pleasure—being punished becomes part of a ritual meant to elicit sexual gratification.[26] The 'excess of zeal' which the masochistic contract displays is a metaphor for a whole system

---

[21] The essay was reprinted in *Masochism: Coldness and Cruelty by Gilles Deleuze/Venus in Furs by Leopold von Sacher-Masoch* (New York, Zone Books, 1991) 9–138. Following Deleuze, a few other scholars attempted to analyse Masoch's use of law, but these works were mostly written by literary theorists who were less interested in the possible relationship between Masoch's ideas and the history of nineteenth-century jurisprudence. See, eg JK Noyes, *The Mastery of Submission: Inventions of Masochism* (Ithaca, Cornell, 1997) 70–73; A Koschorke, 'Mastery and Slavery: A Masochist Falls Asleep Reading Hegel' (2001) 116 *MLN* 551; K Yau, 'Spacing and Timing: Contract and Mise-en-Scene in Fiction by Balzac, Sacher-Masoch and Lu Xun' (2000) 14 *Textual Practice* 81; and N Bentley, 'The Strange Career of Love and Slavery' (2005) 17 *American Literary History* 460.
[22] *Masochism: Coldness and Cruelty* 11.
[23] Ibid 20–21.
[24] Ibid 23 and 35.
[25] Ibid 75–8.
[26] Ibid 87–9.

of reversals upon which the masochistic relationship is built and, first and foremost, the reversal of the traditional roles of men and women.[27] The contract serves as the basis of the relationship, but is ultimately replaced by law, which itself is superseded by myth and ritual.[28]

Deleuze's analysis of law in *Venus in Furs* is interesting, but it lacks a historical context. Masoch's work should not only be compared, as Deleuze compares it, to the work of the Marquis de Sade, whose works reflect eighteenth- rather than the nineteenth-century culture. Instead, the novella can also be read as reflecting Masoch's specific assimilation of notions of law prevalent at the time in European culture. Instead of comparing Sade and Masoch, the eighteenth and nineteenth centuries, one can locate Masoch within the intellectual context of his time, comparing his work to that of his contemporaries or near contemporaries. Such a comparison is the topic of the next section.

EHRLICH IN FURS

In this section I analyse several themes common to Masoch's *Venus in Furs* and Ehrlich's *Fundamental Principles of the Sociology of Law*. The four themes that will be discussed are examples, merely meant to show the affinity between the works of the two men. I believe that these themes were shared by a much broader stratum of thinkers in late-nineteenth-century Europe.[29]

Undermining Free Will and State Sovereignty

Free will was the major organising concept of nineteenth-century legal thought.[30] This notion was full of contradictions, and much of the energy of nineteenth-century thinkers, in Europe and North America, was spent trying to resolve these contradictions. Thus, many nineteenth-century legal scholars devoted a good deal of time trying to differentiate between contractual labour and slavery.[31] In Europe, liberal thinkers like Henry Maine turned contract, and the notion of free will associated with it, into the

---

[27] *Ibid* 92.
[28] *Ibid* 102 and 130.
[29] On the relationship of Ehrlich's thought to that of other continental legal thinkers, see eg K Ziegert, 'The Sociology' 226–7.
[30] See, eg PS Atiyah, *The Rise and Fall of Freedom of Contract* (Oxford, Clarendon, 1979); and Kennedy, 'Two Globalizations' 637.
[31] See, eg AD Stanley, *From Bondage to Contract: Wage Labor, Marriage, and the Market in the Age of Slave Emancipation* (New York, Cambridge University Press, 1998); and R Steinfeld, *Coercion, Contract, and Free Labor in the Nineteenth Century* (New York, Cambridge University Press, 2001). See also P Tuitt, *Race, Law, Resistance* (London, Glasshouse, 2004) 15 (on the role of the figure of the slave in the creation of modern law).

major source of the distinction between ancient and modern societies, discussing the evolutionary movement from 'status to contract'.[32] Even non-liberal thinkers such as Friedrich Engels accepted the distinction between status and contract, coercion and free will, in their critique of bourgeois society. Thus, Engels berated bourgeois labour and marriage contracts precisely because he viewed them as acts of bad faith that assumed false equality between the parties, concealing inequality and domination and reinventing coercive servitude in a modern guise.[33] However, the notion of free will proved elusive. As the nineteenth century progressed, the idea of free will, and indeed the larger idea of a stable self of which free will was merely one manifestation, was subjected to growing attacks by psychology, psychoanalysis and philosophy. These attacks gradually eroded the belief that a stable self and independent free will did indeed exist.[34]

The notion of free will was also a recurrent theme in *Venus in Furs*. One of the major questions that the novella raises has to do with the paradoxical possibility of using free will in order to totally lose it.[35] Severin's most burning desire is to be Wanda's slave 'with no will of my own! To be your absolute property with which you can do as you please ...'[36] He therefore enters into a contract with her that allows him to fulfil this desire, turning himself into her slave and even authorising Wanda to take his life at her will. The absurdity of such a contract (which is, of course, unenforceable) turns it from a legal artifact into a sexual fetish. Pleasure is derived from de-familiarisation: using the ordinary, boring, bourgeois business contract in the intimate sphere, thus turning it into something totally different and strange (and therefore erotic)—a contract for domination and gender role-reversal.

This transgression of law into the intimate sphere is, of course, not something that Masoch invented. There were certainly historical precedents, such as the medieval courts of love, which Peter Goodrich has recently analysed.[37] However, the meaning of the love-law encounter is not fixed or static. The interaction of law and love in the medieval French context had a different meaning from its interaction in Masoch's work. True, the medieval culture of courtly love (of which Goodrich's court of love was merely a part)

---

[32] H Maine, *Ancient Law* (new edn, London, John Murray, 1930) 182; and Burrow, *Crisis* 113–24.
[33] F Engels, *The Origins of the Family, Private Property and the State* (1st edn, 1884, New York, International Press, 7th Printing, 1964). See also Bentley, 'The Strange Career' 471–4.
[34] Burrow, *Crisis* 160–69.
[35] Every contract involves the loss of some measure of freedom. The difference between an ordinary modern contract and a contract establishing a relationship of slavery is that in the latter case the loss is total.
[36] Sacher-Masoch, *Venus in Furs* 49.
[37] P Goodrich, *Law in the Courts of Love* (London, Routledge, 1996) 1–5 and 29–71.

certainly inspired Masoch's work.[38] However, Masoch did not replicate the medieval tradition; instead, he used it in new and original ways.[39]

Apart from any erotic meaning that the contract may have, it also exposes the paradox inherent in the notion of free will itself. As Albrecht Koschorke has noted:

> ... just as for Hobbes, human beings living in a state of nature submit to their sovereign in a single, irrevocable legal act ... the masochist solemnly submits to his chosen mistress ... and as with Hobbes, Sacher-Masoch's contracts suffer from a threshold paradox: they institute autonomous subjects who have nothing more urgent to do than abandon their autonomy.[40]

By exploring the boundaries of free will, the places where will is exercised in order to limit and bind itself, Masoch's contracts undermined the sober, liberal conception of free will. The nineteenth-century theory of contract, based on the assumption that the parties to the contract are equal, was thus turned upside down, establishing a mutual recognition of inequality.[41] Masoch's contract served to remind his readers of the old notions of status which existed beneath the thin veneer of modern liberal law. Instead of accepting Henry Maine's distinction between old slavery-based status societies and modern free-will-based ones, Masoch's story made a mockery of this distinction.[42]

The problems associated with the notion of free will were also a major theme in Ehrlich's work. Ehrlich was always interested in exploring the boundaries of this concept. Already in *Die stillschweigende Willenserklärung*, published in 1893, he attempted to deal with the problems associated with the gap between internal will and its external (and legally recognised) modes of expression.[43] The problems associated with free will were also a major theme in *Fundamental Principles of the Sociology of Law*.[44] In this book, Ehrlich expanded his discussion, focusing not merely on the problem of how to legally recognise internal will, but also discussing the very same paradox that Masoch's contracts exposed: free will is not something that people desire. In fact, they often have no use for it.[45] Thus, in his discussion of social and state sanctions, Ehrlich explained that state coercion is not

---

[38] For a classical description of the culture of courtly love, see J Huizinga, *The Autumn of the Middle Ages*, RJ Paton and U Mammitzch (trs) (Chicago, University of Chicago Press, 1996).

[39] For a contrary argument, see S Žižek, *The Metastases of Enjoyment* (London, Verso, 1994) 89.

[40] Koschorke, 'Mastery and Slavery' 560.

[41] Bentley, 'The Strange Career' 476.

[42] Bentley, 'The Strange Career' 478–9. An alternative reading might argue that by using free will in order to deny it, Masoch was actually affirming its all-encompassing power.

[43] E Ehrlich, *Die stillschweigende Willenserklärung* (Berlin, Carl Heymann, 1893).

[44] See Ehrlich, *Fundamental Principles* 187 and 494.

[45] This is also the major theme of E Fromm, *Fear of Freedom* (London, Routledge, 2001).

the real reason why people obey the law. The real reason is the individual's desire not to think and act independently:

> He who obeys a command is spared the arduous labor of doing his own thinking, and the still more arduous labor of making his own decision. Liberty and independence are ideals of the poet, the artist, and the thinker only. The average man is a philistine, without much appreciation of these things. He loves that to which he has become habituated, the instinctive, and hates nothing more than intellectual exertion.

This, he continued:

> ... is the reason why women become enthusiastic over men of strong will. The latter make their decisions for them, and do not even give the thought of resistance opportunity to arise. For all the trouble and pains that they are thereby freed from, they are sincerely grateful to their husbands.[46]

Elsewhere, Ehrlich mentioned Bentham's concept of greatest happiness to the greatest number, noting that:

> ... the 'greatest number' are happiest when they are led by strong men who forge their fates for them ... when their individuality is merged in a community, or even when they serve a master who provides for the day, and in the evening protects them from privation and misery.[47]

Severin's observations that the only choice that man has is to be 'woman's tyrant or [her] slave' and his talk about 'the bliss of being the slave of a beautiful female tyrant who ruthlessly tramples us underfoot', were thus echoed by Ehrlich.[48]

Of course, there is a difference between Masoch's celebration of the loss of will and Ehrlich's elitist association of this desire only with the 'average man' and with women. In Ehrlich we find none of the erotic mystique that Masoch attached to the desire for submission. In addition, while Masoch's reaction to the paradox of free will was to parody it by taking it to extremes in his fictional contracts, Ehrlich's reaction was more sober, merely pointing to the fact that it was not universally desired. Yet both Masoch and Ehrlich shared the same scepticism about the ideal of free will and its applicability to actual human relations.

Ehrlich's critique of individual free will had another aspect. Unlike Henry Maine's bright-line dichotomy between status and contract, which identified contract with modernity, Ehrlich's description of the history of contract emphasised that slavery and contract were born intertwined. Basing his description of the history of contract on Roman law, Ehrlich noted that the law of contracts had two roots, both violent. One root was barter and the other was submission. Barter 'did not arise from friendly intercourse between neighbors',

---

[46] Ehrlich, *Fundamental Principles* 78.
[47] *Ibid* 210.
[48] Sacher-Masoch, *Venus in Furs* 10 and 14.

but out of piracy.[49] Submission, that is, the 'subjection to the domination of another' could be found in Roman contracts for the 'sale of one's own person'. A man who was in need 'surrenders himself as a slave to the wealthy lord, who [takes] the man into custody for the advance and lets the latter work for him'.[50] Contract was thus born not in opposition to status, but instead as a part of a relationship of slavery, with 'self-surrender into the possession of another'.[51] Such a use of will to extinguish itself did not disappear in later years. Contract and servitude remained intertwined in feudal society as well.[52]

The centrality of the notion of will in nineteenth-century legal thought found its expression in yet another concept—the positivist Austinian definition of law as the expression of the will of the sovereign. This concept too was critiqued in the work of both Masoch and Ehrlich. A major theme in *Venus in Furs* is border-crossings of various sorts. Such border-crossing also appears in the novella in a literal sense. The story begins in Galicia, but moves to Italy, as part of an explicit rejection of the ability of the sovereign to impose his norms on the lovers. When Severin tells Wanda that he wants to be her slave, 'with no will of my own', she replies that this is a 'golden fantasy that can never come true ... because slavery doesn't exist in our country'. However, Severin does not give up: 'Let's go to a country where [slavery] still exists', he says, 'to the Orient, to Turkey', thus escaping the will of the Austrian sovereign.[53] The lovers do not ultimately go to Turkey. Instead, they move to Italy, but this does not matter. They do not seek to replace one state with another. Their aim is to create a private, small-scale slave state of their own. When Severin suggests they go to Turkey, Wanda rejects this, saying, 'I want to be alone in having a slave'—unwilling to share her sovereign role with anybody else, including the state.[54]

This anti-statist notion, the idea that the state cannot really influence the norms created in an individual relationship, was also a major theme in Ehrlich's work. In his book, Ehrlich attacked the idea that law is based on the positivist conception of the will of the sovereign as expressed in legislation. Instead, Ehrlich sought to replace the focus on state legislation with the notion of living law which arises spontaneously and apart from the state.[55] The prevailing school of jurisprudence, he said:

... which sees in every legal proposition only the expression of the 'will of the lawgiver' altogether fails to recognize the important part of society in its creation.[56]

---

[49] Ehrlich, *Fundamental Principles* 105.
[50] *Ibid* 106.
[51] *Ibid* 116 and 219.
[52] *Ibid* 32–3.
[53] Sacher-Masoch, *Venus in Furs* 49 and 50.
[54] *Ibid* 52. See also Bentley, 'The Strange Career' 477.
[55] See, eg M Rheinstein, 'Sociology of Law, Apropos Moll's Translation of Eugen Ehrlich's *Grundlegung der Soziologie des Recht*' (1938) 48 *International Journal of Ethics* 232 at 234; and Nelken, 'Law in Action or Living Law?' 167 at 174.
[56] Ehrlich, *Fundamental Principles* 213.

Indeed, if there is a central theme in Ehrlich's work, it is rejection of the identification of law with the state.[57] Law for Ehrlich is not a top-down phenomenon. It does not exist in general rules created by the legislator and then applied by judges to specific cases. Instead, each village, each lord creates his own law. Similarly, there is no general law of contract. Each contract creates it own legal universe, its own small-scale state.[58] In suggesting a bottom-up rather than a top-down approach to the formation of law, Ehrlich was following the German Historical School, which argued that law was first and foremost customary law created by the people and not the sovereign. However, unlike the Historical School, Ehrlich did not believe in a uniform law reflecting the *volksgeist*. His description of the way in which law is formed was based on the idea of countless individual associations, each creating its own unique set of legal rules. In this sense, the little state that Severin and Wanda tried to establish for themselves would perfectly fit Ehrlich's vision of the law.

Ultimately, one can see both Masoch's and Ehrlich's work as expressions of the late-nineteenth-century 'crisis of reason'—the pessimistic and neo-romantic fascination with the darker and irrational sides of humanity, combined with a skeptic approach to the idea of human progress and perfectibility.[59] This pessimistic notion was certainly evident in Masoch's literary works, but I would argue that even a legal scholar like Ehrlich shared its basic assumptions, chiefly the assumption about the importance of non-rational elements in human life and society.

In the work of both authors, the crisis of reason was manifested in their approach to the notion of free will. In Masoch's case, the notion of free will was taken to its absurd limit. Ehrlich can be viewed as representing a different type of critique of free will, one in which the critic is no longer content with exposing the paradoxical nature of this notion, but also attempts to replace individual will with communal alternatives. This approach was not found only in Ehrlich's work. It was also apparent in the late nineteenth-century interest in various pre-modern, sub-state forms of association (the *Mark*, the *Mir*, the guild).[60] Like many other late-nineteenth-century thinkers, both Masoch and Ehrlich may be viewed as trying to rediscover various forms of association which existed in the space between the individual and the state, both seeking these associations in reaction to the flattening urge of modern liberal ideology.

Replacing State Sanctions with Honour

Masoch's story is based on the rejection of the Austinian notion of law not only because Severin seeks to enthrone his own private sovereign—Wanda—who

[57] Ibid lix.
[58] Ibid 29, 31 and 38.
[59] See, eg Burrow, *Crisis* 60–67.
[60] Ibid 113–24.

wields the power of life and death over him. The story also undermines the Austinian notion of state sanctions as the basis of compliance with law. Severin fulfils his unenforceable contract with Wanda not because of his fear of state sanctions, but because in breaching it he would lose his honour. After one of the ritual humiliation scenes in *Venus in Furs*, Wanda offers to free Severin, telling him that he is 'a coward, a liar and not a man of [his] word'. Severin then prostrates himself at her feet and begins to cry, telling her that he wants to be her slave. She disdainfully calls him a dog and promises to kick him. But he refuses to leave. 'I could flee', he says, 'but didn't want to, and I tolerated everything the instant she threatened to give me my freedom'.[61] When Severin tries to avoid going to Italy as Wanda's slave, she says:

> ... you as a man of honor must above all keep your word, your oath to follow me as a slave wherever I order you and to obey any and all of my commands.[62]

He of course obeys. The basis of his compliance is not the private contract that he signed with Wanda, but the power of his word alone. Thus, when Wanda tells Severin during the first contractual scene in the novella that 'you are not my slave as yet, you haven't signed the contract as yet. You're still free, you can leave me at any time', Severin does not seize the opportunity.[63] Later, when the contract is signed, he tries to flee, but now he cannot. After Wanda begins an affair with another man, Severin sends her a letter in which he claims that her adulterous behavior has freed him. Now that she is 'about to turn common' he is no longer bound by his word to be her slave and he is therefore leaving her. However, even now he cannot release himself because 'she had my pledge, my word of honor'.[64]

Severin's compulsion to uphold his agreement with Wanda was obviously based on desire, but it was also rhetorically justified by reference to his 'word of honor'. This is just the sort of compulsion that, for Ehrlich, formed the basis of law, rather than the threat of state sanctions which was viewed as the basis of compliance by nineteenth-century positivist thinkers. Promises, Ehrlich argued, were enforceable not because of sanctions but because of social norms:

> ... to a person ... whose conception of law is that of a rule of conduct, compulsion by threat of penalty as well as of compulsory execution becomes a secondary matter. To him the scene of all human life is not the court room ... the thought of compulsion by the courts does not even enter the minds of men.[65]

---

[61] Sacher-Masoch, *Venus in Furs* 57.
[62] *Ibid* 60.
[63] *Ibid* 66.
[64] *Ibid* 105.
[65] R Pound, 'Introduction' in Ehrlich, *Fundamental Principles* lxvii; and Ehrlich, *Fundamental Principles* 21 and 64–5. A similar notion appeared in the work of Leon Petrażycki. See HW Babb (tr), *Law and Morality: Leon Petrażycki* (Cambridge, Harvard University Press, 1955) 35–40.

Social norms, 'whether they be norms of morality, of ethical custom, of honor', use non-legal sanctions, but these sanctions are far more powerful than legal ones:

> Many a man pays his gambling debts although he fails to pay his tailor, fights a duel with the person who challenges him, contemptuous of the criminal law, but blindly obedient to the social sanction.[66]

Unenforceable contracts are still law, because society sustains these social sanctions. Thus, says Ehrlich, as if speaking specifically of Severin's contract:

> ... we can see every day that void, forbidden, punishable marriages ... relations of domination and possession ... are actually being sustained; that even slavery, thinly disguised, flourishes in spite of abolition and amenability to punishment ...[67]

Using the Exotic as a Source of Knowledge

A major theme in modern thought is the interest in delineating the difference between 'barbarism' and 'civilisation'.[68] Sometimes (beginning perhaps with Rousseau) the barbarism/civilisation dichotomy was turned upside down and true knowledge was sought in the barbarism pole of the dichotomy. In the late-nineteenth-century German context, one can find an echo of this idea in the attempt to reject or reform the liberal individualist notion of society by going back to the old communal models (in the work of scholars like Tönnies or Gierke). However, the romantic fascination with the barbaric was augmented in the late nineteenth century by an additional idea, also originating in romantic thought, of the importance of excess, of the need to explore experience to the limit, to use the exotic and the bizarre in order to gain a better understanding of the normal.[69] The exotic (or primitive) was not merely seen as interesting. Its study was also deemed essential for the discovery of truth, which now became based on 'sober research into the primitive history of society and law', in Henry Maine's words, as opposed to the abstract, unempirical eighteenth-century mode of knowledge which was based on arid arm-chair speculation.[70] The barbarism/civilisation dichotomy was often used to describe the relationship of Europe with non-European societies, but it also informed an inter-European distinction, in which Eastern Europe and its people were often identified with the 'barbarism' side of the dichotomy.[71]

---

[66] Ehrlich, *Fundamental Principles* 22–3. See also *ibid* 64–5.
[67] *Ibid* 196.
[68] See, eg Engels, *The Origins of the Family*.
[69] Burrow, *Crisis* 174 and 178–90.
[70] Maine, *Ancient Law* 3.
[71] L Wolff, *Inventing Eastern Europe* (Stanford, Stanford University Press, 1994) 4, 13, 308, 318 and 357; and O'Pecko 'Leopold von Sacher-Masoch' 483.

Interest in the exotic, and more specifically in the Eastern European exotic, was a major theme of Masoch's work. It is found, for example, in the attention he paid in his work to depicting the customs and manners of East European Jews.[72] Indeed, one can describe Masoch's whole *oeuvre* as an attempt to write a universal tale (about 'the history of cruelty in love') using as a database the 'inexhaustible ... stories and customs' of the people of the Austro-Hungarian empire, whether they were Galician, Hungarian, Polish, German or Jewish.[73]

In *Venus in Furs* too, the non-European orient (Turkey) and the European orient (especially Russia) played an important role. The whip Wanda buys in the bazaar to punish Severin is of the sort 'used on rebellious slaves in Russia'.[74] The novella abounds with references to Russian princes, Cossacks and 'Cracovian customes'. It is populated by Russian despots, such as Catherine the Great.[75] The barbarism/civilisation, East/West dichotomy is superimposed on a number of other dichotomies: female/male, passion/thought, nature/culture, upper class/lower class. For example, when Wanda seeks to explain feminine nature to Severin, she says that:

> ... despite all the progress of civilization, women have remained exactly as they emerged from the hand of Nature. A woman has the character of a *savage*, who acts loyal or disloyal, generous or gruesome, depending on whatever impulse happens to rule him at the moment. In all times, only deep and earnest formation has created the moral character. Thus, a man, no matter how selfish, how malevolent he may be, always follows principles, while a woman always follows only impulses.[76]

Ehrlich, like many other late-nineteenth-century sociologists, also used the barbarism/civilisation dichotomy.[77] Ehrlich often talked about the dichotomy between the 'civilized nations of the earth' and the 'the savage and the barbarous nations'.[78] He distinguished between modern European societies and societies which were 'outside the pale of European civilization'.[79] He used an evolutionary conception of social organisation.[80] He turned to Henry Maine's notions of law as embodying stages of development relying

---

[72] See Sacher-Masoch, *Jewish Life*. See also Sacher-Masoch, *Venus in Furs* xii-xiii; D Biale, 'Masochism and Philosemitism: The Strange Case of Leopold von Sacher-Masoch' (1982) 17 *Journal of Contemporary History* 305; and I Massey, 'Sacher-Masoch, Talmudist' (1992) 7 *Aschkenas-Zeitschrift für Geschichte und Kultur der Juden* 341.
[73] *Masochism* 38; *Venus in Furs* xv.
[74] Sacher-Masoch, *Venus in Furs* x–xi and 39.
[75] Ibid 53–4, 60, 62, 63, 75 and 83–4.
[76] Ibid 47–8.
[77] See generally, Burrow, *Crisis* 75.
[78] Ehrlich, *Fundamental Principles* 26 and 27.
[79] Ehrlich, *Fundamental Principles* 79.
[80] Ehrlich, *Fundamental Principles* 26–38 and 113 (evolutionary development of norms of inheritance among the Romans, Germanic people and the Slavs).

on ancient texts such as the Icelandic sagas or Tacitus' *Germania* to discover early stages of legal development.[81]

The dichotomy between civilisation and barbarism was accompanied in Ehrlich's work by the idea that truth may be found not in the civilised (or 'modern'), but in the barbaric. The essence of Ehrlich's sociological project was to take the peasant customs of Eastern Europe seriously and use them to understand law generally. He collected these customs not because of an antiquarian interest in the exotic or as part of a romantic-nationalist project seeking to reveal the 'spirit' of national law, as his German or Slav predecessors did.[82] Instead, Ehrlich (like Masoch) turned to these customs as exemplifying universal truths about human nature, without attempting to use them for nationalist purposes. This search for universal truth in the primitive and barbaric was not unique. It is found in many other manifestations of modern culture of the time, in anthropology, psychology, literature and the arts.[83]

Piercing the 'Thin Surface' of the Legal Text

Masoch's interest in role-playing, border-crossing and gender-blurring has often been noted by scholars.[84] His world is one of shifting identities in which the self and others are 'mere appearances, endlessly elusive and unfixed'.[85] It is also a world turned upside down, where the conventions of nineteenth-century bourgeois morality do not have a hold: women dominate men, pain becomes pleasure, opposites mix.[86] As we have seen, Masoch's work also shows an interest in the creation of individual counter-realities, small worlds whose rules are dictated by the action of their all-powerful creator rather than by the state.

Inversions and border-blurring are also found in the contract upon which Severin's relations are based. First, the very use of the contract in the relationship blurs the border between the public and private. Regular family relationships are not based on contract.[87] The contract in *Venus in Furs* is thus not meant to be real. It is used as a ritual object, creating a kind of virtual bondage to complement the actual physical bondage which also figures in the relationship between Severin and Wanda. Just as masochists get their pleasure from being tied up, so the contract serves as an imaginary tying up, and willingly submitting to it is done as part of the ritual.

---

[81] *Ibid* 30–31.
[82] On Ehrlich's methodology and its relations to the methodology of the Historical School, see, eg Ziegert, 'The Sociology' 237–8 and 269 fn 47.
[83] See, eg M Torgovnick, *Gone Primitive: Savage Intellects, Modern Lives* (Chicago, University of Chicago Press, 1990); and Noyes, *The Mastery of Submission* 53, 55 and 68.
[84] Lenzer, 'On Masochism' 310.
[85] *Venus in Furs* xiv–xv; Lenzer, 'On Masochism' 320; and Kucich, 'Melancholy Magic' 367.
[86] Sacher-Masoch, *Venus in Furs* 42. See generally Stewart, *Sublime Surrender* 2.
[87] Ehrlich, *Fundamental Principles* 117.

However, the contract is used for border-blurring in another sense as well. The contract itself is not what it seems. It does not reflect the real terms of the relationship between Severin and Wanda. Severin is Wanda's slave, but in fact he is the real master of the relationship, which is scripted and directed exactly according to his own wishes. As Koschorke notes, the slave-master relationship is really dialectical—although the masochist styles himself as the victim of the contract, 'behind the set he is in fact the director'.[88] Severin is supposedly dominated by Wanda, but in reality he 'forms her, dresses her for the part and prompts the harsh words she addresses to him'.[89]

The insight encapsulated in Masoch's use of contract is that a contract may have more than one meaning. It can represent reality in a certain way, but this representation may be false. It can thus hide more than it reveals. This was also Ehrlich's approach to legal texts in general and to contracts in particular. Real relationships, Ehrlich argued, cannot be understood only on the basis of formal legal texts.[90] First, legal provisions are not sufficient. For example, if one is to understand the life of urban medieval communities:

> ... one must not confine oneself to a study of the legal propositions, but must study it in the deeds of grant, the charters, the land registers, the records of the guilds, the city books, the regulation of the guilds ... the inner order of the human associations.[91]

However, Ehrlich noted, even this is not enough:

> The value of the document would be greatly over-estimated if one should think that one could, without more ado, read the living law from it ... [T]here is much in the document that is simply traditional; this part is copied from a form book by the person who drafts the document, but it never reaches the consciousness of the parties.[92]

Ehrlich argued that we cannot know about life by reading the provisions of legal codes. He first attempted to discover life by reading court decisions. However, he later realised that these decisions do not give a real picture of 'legal life' because only a small part of life is brought before them, and an unrepresentative part, because (for example) one cannot learn about modern families by looking at the dysfunctional families whose affairs are decided by the courts.[93] His answer was therefore to turn to the modern business document in order to understand 'living law'. As he said, 'the living law must be sought in marriage contracts, in contracts of purchase ... and not in sections of the codes'.[94] The contract is the source of our understanding of the relationship, its summary. He notes that 'the most important source

---

[88] Koschorke, 'Mastery and Slavery' 560.
[89] *Masochism: Coldness and Cruelty* 22.
[90] See generally, Ziegert, 'A Note' 119.
[91] Ehrlich, *Fundamental Principles* 34.
[92] *Ibid* 496–8.
[93] *Ibid* 494 and 495.
[94] *Ibid* 495.

of knowledge of the living law is the modern legal document'.[95] However, even these documents, he ultimately concluded, may not be sufficient if we really want to learn about the relationship between the parties, since many of the provisions found in them are not meant to be taken seriously.

The disjunction between texts and reality is indeed a major theme in Ehrlich's work. One can see it, for example, in his discussion of family law. As Ehrlich observed:

> ... the family law of the Austrian Civil Code, as is well known, is extremely individualistic, perhaps the most individualistic in present day Europe ... In Bukovina, however, although it is a part of Austria, and although the Civil Code is in force there as well as in the other parts of Austria, the power of the father is an extremely serious matter. The Rumanian peasant, perhaps the only true Roman of our day, exercises a *patria potestas*, which seems strikingly familiar to the student of Roman law.[96]

He later noted that this was not something which was unique to Bukovina. Similar things could be said about the disjunction between the Austrian Code and the norms governing the family life of the 'German peasantry in Austria',[97] and indeed about the disjunction between positive law and actual family life in every other European country.[98] Ehrlich therefore concludes that:

> ... the basic social institutions, the various legal associations, especially marriage, the family, the clan, the commune, the guild, the relations of domination and of possession, inheritance, and legal transactions, have come into being either altogether or to a great extent independently of the state. The center of gravity of legal development therefore from time immemorial has not lain in the activity of the state but in society itself, and must be sought there at the present time.[99]

One should therefore study the 'old law' that 'lives under the thin surface of modern statute law'.[100] For example:

> Bogišić has discovered the ancient Sadruga, one of the most primitive of human organizations of mankind, within the very territory within which the Austrian Civil Code is in force. In another remote corner of Austria, in eastern Galicia, Dniestrzanski ... has found a mercantile partnership comprising the entire Ruthenian tribe of *Bojken*, and having a remarkable form of organization, which of course is quite foreign to the Austrian Statutes.

Furthermore, Ehrlich himself discovered such peasant-family-communities in eastern Galicia and Bukovina.[101]

---

[95] *Ibid* 493.
[96] *Ibid* 369–70.
[97] *Ibid* 490.
[98] *Ibid* 491.
[99] *Ibid* 390.
[100] *Ibid* 498.
[101] *Ibid* 499.

Ehrlich sought to show that the real law of Bukovina had nothing to do with the civil code, just as Masoch tried to show that the actual norms governing the relationship between men and women had nothing to do with the bourgeois image of the family as an equal partnership based on love and not on domination. Both Masoch and Ehrlich shared an approach which argued that the methodology of human sciences (and of the arts) should be based not on analysis, but on inner understanding through lived experience using 'life' rather than sterile texts in order to know the world.[102] *Venus in Furs* can be read as a scientific essay on the role of domination in love. Ehrlich's sociology of law was based on the (partial) replacement of legal texts with an anthropological study of peasant customs, although Ehrlich still believed that certain unofficial legal texts could be used as an important source of legal knowledge.

CONCLUSION

Both Masoch's *Venus in Furs* and Ehrlich's *Fundamental Principles* contain anti-formalist conceptions of law, born perhaps as a reaction to the excessive formalism of the state law of the Austro-Hungarian empire, a place which Ehrlich described as a 'paradise of the narrowest sort of worship of the letter [of the law]'.[103] In both works, one finds questions about the notion of free will and state sovereignty. Both authors seek to show that honour rather than the fear of state sanctions is the real reason why people obey norms. Both display fascination with the exotic and a belief that it should be studied as a source for the discovery of universal truths and both reveal a suspicion of legal texts, emphasising that these have multiple layers of meaning and that there is a reality which is hidden rather than revealed by them. Such ideas were not unique. They were echoed in many other products of *fin-de-siècle* culture.

Masochism was a major theme in late-nineteenth-century culture.[104] It was especially evident in the culture of Austro-Hungary and its successor states.[105] It appeared in the works of Franz Kafka in Prague, in the stories of Bruno Schulz, perhaps the most important Polish writer of the interwar period (who lived in the Galician town of Drohobytsch, 60 kilometres south of Lemberg), and even in the work of the SY Agnon, the leading Hebrew

---

[102] On Ehrlich's conception of knowledge as based on experience and not theory, see WM Johnston, *The Austrian Mind* (Berkeley, University of California Press, 1983) 91. See also Burrow, *Crisis* 88, 174 and 238–9. On Masoch, see, eg Masoch, *Venus in Furs* 10; and O'Pecko, 'Afterword' in *Love: the Legacy of Cain* 181–2.

[103] Ehrlich, *Fundamental Principles* 470.

[104] See, eg B Dijkstra, *Idols of Perversity: Fantasies of Feminine Evil in Fin de Siècle Culture* (Oxford, Oxford University Press, 1986) 371–2 and 375–6.

[105] However, see MC Finke, 'Sacher-Masoch, Turgenev, and other Russians' in M Finke and C Niekerk (eds), *One Hundred Years of Masochism* (Amsterdam, Rodopi, 2000) 119–21 (associating it with nineteenth-century Russia).

Gustav Klimt, Jurisprudence (1903–7).

novelist of the twentieth century (who was born in another small Galician town, Butschatsch, midway between Lemberg and Czernowitz).[106] Often, masochist-like themes could be found in close proximity to critiques of law, for example, in Kafka's 1919 story, 'In the Penal Colony'.[107] Howver, the link was not confined to literature. Another expression of the phenomenon, I would like to argue, is found in Gustav Klimt's painting, *Jurisprudence*, created between 1903 and 1907.

Like any great work of art, *Jurisprudence* has a variety of meanings and one can analyse it in a number of ways. At first glance, the painting merely depicts the Greek myth about the triumph of state law, as told in Aeschylus' *Oresteia*. Thus, the bottom part of the painting shows the state of private vengeance before the creation of the law—the figure of the naked man is Orestes and the women who surround him are the furies, put to sleep by

---

[106] See, eg MM Anderson, *Kafka's Clothes* 136–8. On Schulz, see SD Chrostowska, '"Masochistic Art of Fantasy": The Literary Works of Bruno Schulz in the Context of Modern Masochism' (2004) 55 *Russian Literature* 469. On masochistic themes in Agnon, see, eg SY Agnon, *Shira*, Z Shapiro (tr) (Syracuse NY, Syracuse University Press, 1996) 108–14.

[107] See M Norris, 'Sadism and Masochism in Two Kafka Stories: "In der Strafkolonie" and "Ein Hungerkünstler"' (1978) 93 *MLN* 430.

Apollo. The upper part of the painting may refer to Orestes' acquittal at the Areopagos in Athens.

However, there are additional themes present in the painting. Thus, some scholars have argued that the painting (and its related paintings, *Philosophy* and *Medicine*) expressed the decline of the optimistic, liberal-bourgeois culture of the mid-nineteenth century and its replacement by a pessimistic anti-rationalist *fin-de-siècle* culture.[108] Others saw the painting as being about 'the miseries of punishment that flow from judgment'.[109] In a previous article, I argued that one can also interpret the painting as being about the gap between the conception of law as a formal, rational and geometric entity promising clarity and certainty, on the one hand, and the understanding that real-life law is messy, chaotic and irrational, on the other; that it is about the distinction between 'law in the books' and 'law in action'.[110]

While I consider all of these interpretations to be correct in some sense, I would like to end this article by adding another possible layer of meaning to Klimt's *Jurisprudence*, by noting its link to masochistic themes. Such linking is not new. Klimt and Masoch certainly shared an interest in similar subjects. For example, both the writer and the painter, like many other turn-of-the-century intellectuals, were fascinated by the figure of Judith, the female slayer of the Assyrian General Holofernes. Masoch opened his story with a quote from the book of Judith, 'God did punish him and deliver him into a woman's hand', and Klimt painted her image twice, in 1901 and 1909.[111]

Jurisprudence too contains references to masochistic themes. In *Venus in Furs*, the core scene of the story is the one in which Severin finally signs the contract. Immediately afterward, three women come in, each clutching a rope. They tie Severin to a column, his arms behind his back, 'like a man about to be executed', and Wanda proceeds to flog him. The legal act of binding represented by the contract is therefore followed immediately by an act of physical bondage and the fulfilment of Severin's torture fantasy.

Such a scene, it can be argued, is also depicted in *Jurisprudence*. The bottom part of the painting shows a scene of torture with the actual act of torture missing. Instead, what we see is frozen, tableau-like setting which includes a naked man immobilised by a womb-like octopus and three barely-clothed women (Masoch's three African slaves?) who ignore his presence. The scene is characteristic of masochistic imagery, which (according to Deleuze) is based on freezing and suspension, not on action: 'The whip or the sword that never strikes ... the heel that is forever descending

---

[108] Schorske, *Fin de Siecle Vienna*.
[109] DE Curtis and J Resnik, 'Images of Justice' (1997) 96 *Yale Law Journal* 1727 at 1752.
[110] See Likhovski, 'Czernowitz' 622–5.
[111] See Sachar-Masoch, *Venus in Furs* 1; G Fliedl, *Gustav Klimt, 1862–1918: The World in Female Form* (Cologne, Taschen, 2003) 140–41. On the late nineteenth-century fascination with the figure of Judith (and her biblical companion, Salome), see Dijkstra, *Idols of Perversity* 376–401.

on the victim', are expressions 'beyond all movement, of a profound state of waiting'.[112]

If there is indeed a link between *Venus in Furs* and *Jurisprudence*, this means that law is not just found in the upper part of the picture, in the pages of the law books held by the Goddesses. Instead, law is also found at the bottom of the painting, in the form of the octopus-contract holding its willing victim in bondage in an elaborate, ritualistic act. We cannot see the face of this victim clearly, but were we able to see it, would it be too much to speculate that he would have a small, sly smile on his face?

---

[112] *Masochism* 35, 70 and 75.

Part II

Ehrlich's Sociology of Law

4

Ehrlich at the Edge of Empire: Centres and Peripheries in Legal Studies

ROGER COTTERRELL[1]

INTRODUCTION

'I HAD FOUND EHRLICH, and been somewhat crushed in spirit, because he had seen so much.' So wrote the American legal realist Karl Llewellyn about his discovery of Eugen Ehrlich's classic 1913 book on sociology of law.[2] What seems most remarkable now about Ehrlich, nearly a century after he wrote his *magnum opus*, is that it was *as a jurist*, a legal scholar and teacher, that 'he had seen so much'. Ehrlich created his legal sociology as a by-product of juristic inquiries. And it is serious sociology, even if homespun; ambitious social analysis, not the kind of rhetoric of social awareness adopted by many progressive lawyers in the early twentieth century. Ehrlich aimed to save juristic scholarship from itself—from its intellectual narrowness and delusions of self-sufficiency as a science of law—by explaining sociologically the place of that scholarship in society. In a sense, he aimed to promote a new juristic modesty; relating the world of jurists to a larger world of citizens' social experience; arguing, indeed, that the 'centre of gravity' of legal development lies outside the usual work environments of lawyers and state officials.[3] For Ehrlich, more than most pioneers of legal sociology, the question of whether lawyers are to be central or peripheral to social life is of the utmost urgency.

These features of his legal sociology make it especially interesting to study in terms of a dynamics of marginality and centrality in law.

---

[1] I am grateful to Stefan Vogl for his comments on an earlier version of this chapter.
[2] Quoted in NEH Hull, *Roscoe Pound and Karl Llewellyn: Searching for an American Jurisprudence* (Chicago, University of Chicago Press, 1997) 291.
[3] E Ehrlich, *Fundamental Principles of the Sociology of Law*, WL Moll (tr) (New Brunswick, New Jersey, Transaction Publishers reprint, 2002) 390.

His writing is very relevant to any discussion of distinctions between 'internal' (normative) and 'external' (behavioural) viewpoints on law, or assumptions about the existence of a centre and a periphery of legal experience—lawyers usually being assumed to be at the centre. Indeed, Ehrlich raises the whole question of what being a legal insider or outsider means and who has authority to decide such statuses. The issues readily broaden out to more general ones about intellectual and cultural centrality and marginality.

Indeed, it is very tempting (but, this chapter argues, ultimately not sufficient) to try to explain how Ehrlich 'had seen so much' by emphasising his own marginality or 'frontier' situation which gave him a special viewpoint.[4] Certainly, he taught for almost the whole of his career (from 1896 until the disruptions of the First World War closed his university) in a town (Czernowitz) on the remote, eastern-most edge of the vast Austro-Hungarian Empire of which he was a life-long committed subject. Culturally too, he might be seen as located at the periphery of his own (Germanic) cultural universe, living in a region (Bukovina, today part of the Ukraine) populated by many different national and ethnic groups. Furthermore, temporally too, he was surely at a margin, the end of an era, living through the Austro-Hungarian Empire's final years and its dissolution at the close of the World War. In some of his last writings,[5] he argued passionately but fruitlessly, like many other Austrian intellectuals, to save the old Austria as a unified multicultural entity. He wished to preserve a centre that, in fact, would not hold. His life and work related strongly to this centre, and any professional or cultural marginality from it could not have been enough to allow him to achieve what he did.

This chapter attempts, then, to look at Ehrlich's sociology of law not as a product of marginality, but in terms of a *dialectic or interplay of marginality and centrality*, which reflects both Ehrlich's own personal and professional situation and the consistent strategy of his sociology of law. My argument is that this dialectic accounts not only for the most valuable contribution of his sociology of law—its full-frontal challenge to juristic certainties about what legal inquiries encompass and how they are to be pursued—but also for its most serious, most frequently criticised weakness—the vagueness of its concept of law. To develop this argument it will be necessary to consider aspects of Ehrlich's biography and the scholarly reception of his work, as well as the bearing of centre/periphery distinctions on his legal pluralist outlook and his concept of law.

---

[4] Cf A Likhovski, 'Czernowitz, Lincoln, Jerusalem, and the Comparative History of American Jurisprudence' (2003) 4 *Theoretical Inquiries in Law* 621.
[5] See E Ehrlich, E, *Quelques Aspects de la Question Nationale Autrichienne* (Geneva, Édition Atar, 1919).

THE RELATIVITY OF CENTRE/PERIPHERY DISTINCTIONS

As a preliminary, it is important to remember that margins and centres are never absolute locations, but are endlessly re-definable. A situation marginal in some respects, or from a certain point of view, may be central in other ways, or when seen from a different viewpoint. Indeed, a different perspective might show the marginal and the central as reversed. However, legal thought and studies are particularly susceptible to the idea that there really is a fixed centre (and a clearly identifiable, permanent periphery) of law, legal experience, legal studies or legal theory; and that lawyers inevitably occupy the centre of the legal world. A main reason why Ehrlich's work is still important is that it demonstrates the falsity of any reification or hypostatisation of centre/periphery or inside/outside dichotomies in legal studies. Ehrlich's 'living law'—the law that lives in citizens' experience—may not even be law at all from a lawyer's perspective, but merely non-legal social norms. By contrast, 'legal propositions'—the rules that lawyers invoke and to which they most readily attach the status of law—are, for Ehrlich, viewing matters from a sociological perspective, no more than *derivative* law. For him, they are abstract normative generalisations from decisions aimed at resolving conflicts arising in social associations and relationships. Otherwise these legal propositions are rules created by the state that may or may not operate to regulate social relations—their social significance is not to be assumed. Central and peripheral forms of law, as lawyers understand them, appear to be turned on their head in Ehrlich's legal sociology. More accurately, their exact status—how central or peripheral particular kinds of regulation are—is deliberately left theoretically open.

This destabilising of centre/periphery distinctions in law is important for many reasons. Legal sociology is often seen as entirely distinct from juristic legal studies. For some jurists, sociological views about law are 'external' views, outside the scope of juristic debate or scholarship,[6] and some legal sociologists accept this characterisation.[7] Lawyers typically see themselves as at the heart of law and legal experience, treating non-lawyers' legal experience or legal consciousness as, at best, a pale derivative of lawyers' legal understandings, or otherwise as external to any reliable (professional) legal understanding. However, the only reason these views of what is central and marginal can be securely maintained is because of an equally secure sense of what counts as law, and so of what is central and peripheral to it. Ehrlich's work, all the more subversive because it is, itself, the work of a jurist, fundamentally challenges the lawyer's confidence as to what counts and does not count as law. More accurately than any non-lawyer could, Ehrlich aims at the very core of the lawyer's professional sensitivity and security.

---

[6] RM Dworkin, *Law's Empire* (Oxford, Hart reprint, 1998) 13–14.
[7] D Black, *The Behavior of Law* (New York, Academic Press, 1976).

It is this last point—that Ehrlich's sociology is the weapon of a radical jurist—that best illustrates why any claim that his originality reflects professional marginality is unconvincing. His sociology of law gets its power and its enduring interest from the fact that he is a juristic 'insider' no less than a sociological 'outsider' and his book on sociology of law continually moves between these positions, mingling and merging them, playing juristic argument alongside social analysis. The book has many faults: it is poorly structured, gets mired in diversions and distractions, and is repetitive, ambiguous and sometimes seemingly self-contradictory, but it is a virtuoso performance nonetheless. In it Ehrlich not only intertwines juristic and sociological analysis so intimately that attempts to separate them are pointless, but he makes the jurist become a sociological observer of legal processes and legal expectations while he makes the sociologist dig deeply into the intricacies of legal doctrine and juristic thought to see how these directly or indirectly structure and inform social relations and understandings. Ehrlich's whole strategy is to disrupt lawyers' certainties as to what is central and peripheral to law, and what is internal and external to juristic understanding.

Another general point needs to be made about intellectual marginality. In intellectual life, marginality is of interest only if it goes along with a process by which marginal ideas can be seen as integral to a system of thought outside intellectual orthodoxy. It is often said that those on the margins (of mainstream ways of thought, experiences, or cultural reference points) can see more, or even see more objectively.[8] However, that may depend on having recognisable reference points to which they can firmly relate their perspectives. Otherwise marginal thought becomes mere eccentricity. The most productive intellectual marginality may arise when marginal observations can be located in a broader perspective that understands intellectual orthodoxy, but can also *transcend* it, re-interpreting and criticising it from 'outside', from the periphery. This broader perspective might embrace a kind of cosmopolitanism, or an understanding of more than one culture through personal experience, or the accumulated critical and contextual knowledge of a reference group different from that of the intellectually orthodox. Thus, the existence of important reference points for marginal ideas allows them to become (at least potentially) *central* ideas, but in a different intellectual universe—a universe of critique that establishes paradigms of thought in opposition to orthodoxy, and does so by assuming a new parallel orthodoxy of its own.

The development of socio-legal studies in some countries illustrates this process at work. In Britain, for example, for a long time, socio-legal studies were regarded as not really legal research at all, and certainly separate

---

[8] One of the classic sociological sources of this idea is G Simmel, 'The Stranger', DN Levine (tr) in DN Levine (ed), *Georg Simmel on Individuality and Social Forms* (Chicago, University of Chicago Press, 1971) 145.

from orthodox legal research. Orthodoxy in the juristic world relied on ideas of 'black letter law'—officially promulgated legal rules—as almost the sole focus of legal studies. If I may mention my experience (surely paralleled by that of many other socio-legal scholars), much of my early writing on sociology of law in the 1970s was done in conscious opposition to this orthodox legal research paradigm. I rarely attacked the orthodoxy directly or polemically, but I produced work that clearly did not fit it and therefore could have been seen as asserting a place in the law school for scholarly research at the margins. I did not see matters that way, but merely followed my own research inclinations. However, I soon realised the existence of a substantial group of like-minded researchers, and of longstanding intellectual traditions to which 'marginal' socio-legal writings could be related. Within these traditions, and with appropriate reference groups, this marginal research could seem central. Indeed, one could begin to marginalise the orthodoxy!

Now, much later, it is easy to see socio-legal research of many kinds—theoretical, empirical, historical, contextual, policy-oriented and critical—as the centre of contemporary legal scholarship, at least in environments most familiar to me. The old myopic idea of legal scholarship seems so pushed to the margins that the term 'black letter legal research' is often treated as one of disparagement. It seems that few legal scholars now admit to conducting it. Yet everything is a matter of perspective. What is central and what is peripheral in socio-legal research (and, indeed, what this term should be taken to mean) remain controversial, judged differently by different intellectual communities. Furthermore, what counts as valuable legal *theory* is surely judged very differently by socio-legal scholars (in their various constituencies) as compared, for example, with the way it is judged in the heartlands of Oxford legal philosophy. There are few points of contact. Aspects of law and legal study viewed as central or peripheral by one constituency are often given an entirely reversed status by others.

EHRLICH IN EMPIRE AND CULTURE

Any generalisations about Ehrlich's personal and professional situation can only be suggestive. There is insufficient information for firm conclusions. However, the combination of the tantalising, sometimes melancholy evidence available (for much of which we are indebted to Manfred Rehbinder's researches) with the pregnant silences in the historical record makes the multifaceted question of Ehrlich's own marginality or centrality very fascinating. Enough is known, I think, to be able to argue that it is the interplay of his marginal and central positions—intellectually and culturally—that explains most about him; neither marginality nor centrality separately, but both of these, interacting across a range of aspects.

80 *Roger Cotterrell*

Even his obvious geographical marginality suggests interesting ambiguities. Does an empire need a precise centre? Or does empire entail an idea (or ideal?) of rule that can be carried equally into all its regions?[9] Is the heart of empire found in its local manifestations? Surely that depends on how its essence is understood. In the last phase of existence of the Austro-Hungarian Empire, some intellectuals saw the empire as a unity created from cultural diversity, while others saw only diversity given a mere semblance of unity. Optimistic views portrayed the empire as:

> ... a bright colourful garden of nationalities ... Each flower ... was ... praised for its own beauty. But the garden as a whole was imagined as being even more stunning because of the harmonious assortment of its diverse elements.[10]

Austrian banknotes of the time denoted their currency on one side in German and Hungarian and, on the other, in all the other official languages of the Empire.

Ehrlich's writings vigorously defended the empire against charges that it had treated its subject nationalities unfairly.[11] He might well have subscribed to the 'garden theory'. On such a view, the remote Bukovina, the locus of his living law researches, was as integral as Vienna or Budapest to the empire. In his book on sociology of law, he writes about the under-appreciated significance of state law in forming 'the people of a state' (*Staatsvolk*), even a state with different national groups, as a 'unique, unified entity' with a common constitution, capital, army, juristic science, official language, administrative system and economic territory.[12] The idea is of legal-political projection of a meaningful, constitutionally defined unity that does not deny or repress cultural or national diversity. Recent notions of a European constitutional patriotism distinct from nationalism[13] might be seen as reflecting a kind of thinking not unconnected with what Ehrlich had in mind.

Complications multiply when we consider Ehrlich's personal cultural situation. Born into a Jewish family he became a Roman Catholic and wholeheartedly subscribed to an ideal of Jewish assimilation to the dominant Germanic imperial culture.

> I myself belong to a race for which there is no other resolution of the Jewish problem than the complete assimilation of the Jews into the German culture. This

---

[9] Cf P Fitzpatrick, 'The Immanence of *Empire*' in PA Passavant and J Dean (eds), *Empire's New Clothes: Reading Hardt and Negri* (New York, Routledge, 2004) 31.

[10] B Weiler, 'E Pluribus Unum? The Kakanian Intellectual and the Question of Cultural Pluralism', paper delivered at conference on 'The Contours of Legitimacy in Central Europe', European Studies Centre, St Anthony's College, Oxford, United Kingdom, 24–26 May 2002 <http://users.ox.ac.uk/~oaces/conference/papers/Bernd_Weiler.pdf> 3.

[11] See above n 5.

[12] Ehrlich, above n 3, 378.

[13] See, eg J Habermas, 'Why Europe Needs a Constitution' (2001) 11 *New Left Review* (2nd series) 5.

applies not only to Jews living under the Germans but also to Jews here in the East who have their home among the Slavic peoples.

He worried whether anti-Semitism meant that 'this entire plan must now be given up'.[14] He was a member of an often marginalised cultural minority, yet it was one that had a strong presence in his own locality and among the student body of his university. Furthermore, he clearly received recognition for his work. He took his turn as Rector of the University of Czernowitz (in 1906–7)[15] and was well respected for his writings and gifts as a lecturer. However, much is still unknown. He had begun his career as a *Privatdozent* at the University of Vienna in 1894 after publication of his first book, but this was eight years after completion of his doctorate and there seems to be no evidence of what had happened in the interim. Presumably, he was in legal practice. Karl Renner thought that, in later life, the fact that Ehrlich was Jewish had prevented him getting beyond Czernowitz 'despite his research, which would have warranted his appointment at a top-ranking university'.[16]

Bernd Weiler[17] describes culturally marginal intellectuals in the Austro-Hungarian Empire as learning to understand the 'language, values and modes of thinking' of the dominant culture, but often living 'in different cultural milieux, constantly moving across linguistic, ethnic and religious boundaries. Their own marginality combined with a high level of mobility' led them 'to view social life from different perspectives. In their works these intellectuals pointed to the importance of roots and differences. In their practical lives they often felt culturally homeless'. One way to escape the sense of rootlessness, Weiler[18] suggests, was to 'adopt' the supranational identity of the empire, becoming supranational people of the multi-national state. It is certainly not difficult to understand Ehrlich in these terms. In place of (or alongside) cultural marginality is an important idea of *intellectual centrality* within a larger multicultural entity—an entity dependent for its identity on an overarching state structure with its juristic, official law.

---

[14] Ehrlich quoted in M Rehbinder, *Die Begründung der Rechtssoziologie durch Eugen Ehrlich* (2nd edn, Berlin, Duncker & Humblot, 1986) 27. I am grateful to Derek Daniels for assistance with translation from this work.

[15] It seems to have been normal practice (abrogated only during the 1914–18 wartime period) for the office of Rector to be held by each incumbent for a single academic year. R Wagner, 'Fakultäten, Lehrkörper und Rektoren der "Francisco-Josephina"' in R Wagner (ed), *Alma Mater Francisco Josephina: Die deutschsprachige Nationalitäten-Universität in Czernowitz* (Munich, Verlag Hans Meschendörfer, 1975) 130, lists all the Rectors who held office during the period from the university's founding in 1875 until its restructuring as a Romanian institution in 1919.

[16] Quoted in M Rehbinder, 'Neues über Leben und Werk von Eugen Ehrlich' in F Kaulbach and W Krawietz (eds), *Recht und Gesellschaft: Festschrift für Helmut Schelsky zum 65. Geburtstag* (Berlin, Duncker & Humblot, 1978) 405.

[17] Above n 10, 3.

[18] Above n 10, 7.

This alone suggests that Ehrlich's intellectual outlook must not be seen as setting social norms *against* state law (ie periphery challenging juristic and political centre). His project is rather to demand of the state a new, deeper self-awareness to ensure its absolutely necessary survival faced with powerful disintegrating tendencies produced in its periphery.

Everything, indeed, points to the importance of broad, *transnational* points of reference in Ehrlich's life and work. The ultimate intellectual reference point for him was not Czernowitz, the Bukovina, or even perhaps Vienna or Austria-Hungary. He knew an amazing range of languages. His mother tongue was probably Polish, his working language was German, he spoke perfect English and he knew French, Spanish, Italian, Danish, Norwegian, Serbian, Croatian and Hungarian.[19] At the end of his life, at the close of the First World War, he planned to return to Czernowitz to teach in Romanian. 'To get just a mere overview of the subject matter', he explained about his legal sociology, 'I had to learn almost all European languages and undertake much travelling'.[20] A vital key to Ehrlich's scholarly project lies in his commitment to a transnational identity of juristic science: a science with a scope of application as wide as the empire and Germanic legal culture but extending further—as evidenced, for example, by his deep admiration for English law and his frequent advocacy of some of its methods. A science of law 'freed from national limitations' and a 'restoration of international activity in the field of law' promise 'abundant returns', he writes. 'No science has ever grown great in national seclusion.'[21]

This near-global scientific commitment runs alongside a more obvious focus in his work on legal *localism* expressed through his sociological idea of 'living law'—the infinitely varied, effective normative regulation of everyday life. However, the localised study of living law is a necessary correlate of juristic universalism—the corrective needed to prevent juristic science becoming socially out of touch as it is forced to relate to an ever-widening range of social and cultural conditions.

It seems reasonable, then, to see Ehrlich's self-image as that of someone *central* to a new universal legal science as well as a celebrator of many varieties of cultural *marginality* expressed through the local customary practices of living law. As a jurist, he could see himself as a representative of the imperial centre, teaching its law and relating, in all aspects of his juristic formation and primary cultural interests, to its Austro-Germanic dominant culture. As an inhabitant of the empire's '"Far and Wild East", once called "Semi-Asia"'[22] he could observe a cultural periphery in productive ways (even if resisting any thoughts of his own marginality) so as to provide

---

[19] See above n 14, 19 and 23.
[20] Above n 14, 19.
[21] See above n 3, 482.
[22] See above n 10, 1.

resources for reshaping juristic culture from the inside—creating his legal sociology in the process.

RESPONSES TO RADICALISM

I suggested earlier that central and peripheral forms of law, as the lawyer understands them, appear to be turned on their head by Ehrlich's legal sociology. His most important lasting influence might have been a large-scale and permanent disruption of juristic certainties—a genuinely subversive move to shake lawyers' understandings of law to the core. However, his work did not achieve this effect. It suffered the two most common (if opposite) fates of radical ideas: on the one hand, to be co-opted and tamed into forms that allow an appropriation into the mainstream, the centre of orthodoxy; on the other, to be condemned as so bizarre as to be unworthy of consideration, to be irredeemably marginalised.

Co-optation

Roscoe Pound's active promotion of Ehrlich's legal sociology in the United States was not necessarily intended to condemn it to the first of these fates, but it may have helped to do so. David Nelken,[23] and more recently Marc Hertogh,[24] have very properly criticised interpretations of Ehrlich's work that have largely equated his contrast between living law and legal propositions with Pound's influential distinction between 'law in action' and 'law in books'.[25] Ehrlich's concern was not primarily with a contrast between the letter of the law (law in books), on the one hand, and the practice or experience of law (law in action), on the other. It was mainly a concern with the variety of types of law and their interactions, and with the fact that lawyers typically only recognise some of these types (legal propositions, state law and official norms for deciding disputes) and so fail to appreciate the great social significance of other types (the many varieties of living law). Ehrlich's radicalism is to displace state law and juristically developed legal propositions from their pre-eminent position in legal analysis as a whole and to demand the recognition of other kinds of (ultimately more socially fundamental) law that are usually unrecognised by lawyers.

---

[23] D Nelken, 'Law in Action or Living Law? Back to the Beginning in Sociology of Law' (1984) 4 *Legal Studies* 157.
[24] M Hertogh, 'A "European" Conception of Legal Consciousness: Rediscovering Eugen Ehrlich' (2004) 31 *Journal of Law and Society* 457.
[25] Nicholas Timasheff, for example, sees a stress on 'the discrepancies between written law and actuality' as 'the essence of the book of Ehrlich who, I believe, exaggerates it'. See NS Timasheff, *An Introduction to the Sociology of Law* (Westport, Conn., Greenwood Press reprint, 1974) 366.

Ehrlich's work points, therefore, towards a *legal pluralism* (the concept of a plurality of co-existing legal regimes in the same society) that is largely unrecognised by jurists. He asserts that some kind of legal pluralism flourishes even in complex, modern, politically unified societies. Indeed, any society, whatever its nature, will exhibit legal pluralism—it will have a diversity of legal regimes co-existing and sometimes conflicting in the same social space. Some of these legal regimes (indeed, especially those that are socially most fundamental) will not be under the control or supervision of the state or the legal professions.

By contrast, Pound's legal thought lacks almost all of this radicalism. He sees only state law as law: there is no challenge to the idea that the state and lawyers monopolise the whole of law. Pound makes no claim that a different view of the nature and scope of law could be taken in contrast to lawyers' typical views. The contrast between law in books and law in action is a contrast between state law as officially written and state law as experienced in practice. However, the only law considered is the law of the state. For Pound, the central question is: *how* is law experienced? For Ehrlich it is: *what* do people experience as law? Certainly, Ehrlich is also concerned with the effects of state law in action, with 'what is going on in the administration of justice and what the causes thereof may be',[26] but his fundamental claim is that different kinds of law come from different sources.

For Ehrlich, the state makes law, usually in legislative form, but the social associations in which people live their lives also produce law directly as the 'inner order' of those associations. Law is also produced from both social and state sources, in the form of norms by which decisions on disputes are made (*Entscheidungsnormen*). Other law is created juristically as relatively abstract legal propositions, developed from these 'norms for decision' or intended to operate as such norms, or else generalised from state enactments. Finally, Ehrlich[27] analyses the nature of the state itself. He treats it, for most purposes, as one kind of social association and as an organ of society; in this way he tries to complete the link in his theory between state law and the law of social associations in general. If there are many uncertainties and loose ends in the theoretical picture that Ehrlich's legal sociology offers (not least about the role of the state and the legal status of social norms), its vast ambition is not in doubt. However, when it is reinterpreted as a Poundian theory of law in action it is tamed into something unrecognisable: a functional or realist critique of the practical effectiveness of the official law that lawyers professionally serve. If it is true that 'we are

---

[26] E Ehrlich, 'Judicial Freedom of Decision: Its Principles and Objects', E Bruncken (tr) in *Science of Legal Method: Select Essays by Various Authors* (Boston, Boston Book Company, 1917) 47.
[27] See above n 3, ch 7.

all legal realists now',[28] one reason is that this critique of effectiveness has become an accepted part of the legal mainstream in many advanced legal systems. When Ehrlich is treated as a theorist of law in action, co-optation is complete.[29]

Marginalisation

The alternative fate of Ehrlich's sociology of law has frequently been intellectual marginalisation, his ideas being dismissed as too unsound or too lacking in theoretical rigour or sophistication to be taken seriously. 'Who reads Ehrlich now?' an American leader of the law and economics movement once asked me rhetorically in conversation; the implication being: 'Who would want to?' This strategy of denying Ehrlich's work serious consideration on its own terms began early, with Hans Kelsen's critique arguing, inter alia, that sociology of law could not actually deal with law itself; it would be conceptually dependent on, yet unable to contribute to juristic science.[30] The entire legal sociological project could thus not address its purported subject matter 'law'; the conclusion might be simply that it is a non-science, certainly not a science of law.

The historical jurist Paul Vinogradoff, writing in 1920, two years before Ehrlich's death, marvelled that Ehrlich treated ethnological and anthropological issues 'in such a superficial manner' and recommended various texts for him to read. An 'important limitation of our author's range of view and of reasoning', Vinogradoff thought, was that Ehrlich found social phenomena so interesting (even if he studied them in unscholarly fashion) that he neglected juristic logic, thereby throwing out the baby with the bathwater. In any case, sociology 'is yet too indefinite and too incomplete to serve as a scientific basis

---

[28] Cf JH Schlegel, *American Legal Realism and Empirical Social Science* (Chapel Hill, University of North Carolina Press, 1995) 2.

[29] A different kind of (cultural) co-optation is found in Max Rheinstein's striking characterisation of Ehrlich: 'This man, who was born and who spent all his life in the old Austrian Empire, was an American at heart, an individualist and pragmatist, a believer in freedom and the free forces of society. He saw the task of his life in combating government by bureaucracy, which was so characteristic of the old Habsburg monarchy.' See M Rheinstein, *Collected Works, Volume 1: Jurisprudence and Sociology, Comparative Law and Common Law (USA)* (Tübingen, JCB Mohr [Paul Siebeck], 1979) 151. Ehrlich's intellectual prestige was certainly much greater in the United States than in continental Europe: see G Husserl, Review of Ehrlich's *Fundamental Principles of the Sociology of Law* (1938) 5 *University of Chicago Law Review* 330. On one view, although he started no 'school of thought', '[t]he number of [American] jurists who followed him in the sociological or the realist or the relativist approach to legal problems is almost legion': see NO Littlefield, 'Eugen Ehrlich's Fundamental Principles of the Sociology of Law' (1967) 19 *Maine Law Review* 26.

[30] See H Kelsen, *General Theory of Law and State*, A Wedberg (tr) (New York, Russell & Russell reprint, 1961) 162–78.

of law'.[31] In other words, even if grave defects of method could have been corrected, the project would probably still have been a waste of time.

Even some critics who might have been expected to be friendly were not. Nicholas Timasheff, sympathetic to sociology of law, objected to any attempt, such as Ehrlich's, to study social phenomena as 'law' without reference to positive law. He noted that 'Ehrlich's theories are so contestable and so contradictory' that the book in its original German edition had provided no basis for new legal studies.[32] In England, CK Allen[33] noted that 'Ehrlich found the greatest difficulty in setting any boundaries to his subject, and ended up by setting none whatever'. He concluded:

> I mean no disrespect to the labours of a very learned, sincere and original jurist if I call this kind of project Megalomaniac Jurisprudence ... knowledge of everything usually ends in wisdom of nothing.[34]

Behind even measured language in jurists' reviews of Ehrlich, a relentless pincer movement is usually at work. He is often caught between claims that: (i) his social observation is too ambitious or intellectually unsound (sociology often being seen as lacking adequate scientific credentials); and (ii) his juristic analyses are flawed, too generalised, too limited or too unappreciative of the significance of lawyers' doctrinal expertise and reasoning. These kinds of critical strategies have often been used against socio-legal theory since Ehrlich's time. Discomfiting sociological critiques are sometimes brushed off by means of general, unsupported slurs on sociology's intellectual credibility, or suggestions that it lacks legitimacy as an intellectual field.[35] At the same time, attempts to cast doubt on the worth of almost any kind of theoretical inquiry about law are sometimes made through hints that reliable legal knowledge can come only from precise, detailed analysis of rules or judicial decisions and an avoidance of any generalisations beyond those needed to solve specific legal problems.

EHRLICH'S LEGAL PLURALISM

Some of the most severe criticisms of Ehrlich's legal sociology nevertheless have merit. This is a matter to return to in a moment. Equally important,

---

[31] P Vinogradoff, 'The Crisis of Modern Jurisprudence' in *The Collected Papers of Paul Vinogradoff, vol 2: Jurisprudence* (London, Wildy reprint 1964) 222, 223–4.

[32] NS Timasheff, Review of Ehrlich's *Fundamental Principles of the Sociology of Law* (1937) 2 *American Sociological Review* 122. Yet he also saw Ehrlich as 'the outstanding German sociologist of law' and a brilliant critic of historical jurisprudence: see above n 25, 25–7.

[33] CK Allen, *Law in the Making* (7th edn, Oxford, Oxford University Press, 1964) 30.

[34] See above n 33, 32.

[35] See eg the legal philosopher Giorgio Del Vecchio's claim that sociology as a discipline is unnecessary because philosophy and history already cover its field: G Del Vecchio, *Philosophy of Law*, TO Martin (tr) (Washington DC, Catholic University of America Press, 1953) 10–13.

however, is to judge him on his own terms. His enduring contribution lies in his advocacy of a legal pluralist perspective that refuses to be confined by the scope of what lawyers and state officials recognise as law, but which (contrary to some critical perceptions) certainly does take full account of juristic understandings of and contributions to law, and of the state's production of law. Indeed, Ehrlich devotes much of his book on legal sociology to considering the role of lawyers and the state in creating and administering law. Furthermore, as noted above, he insists that state law may make a very important—but insufficiently recognised—contribution to uniting a nationally diverse people constitutionally as a *Staatsvolk* under a unified legal, economic, political and administrative regime. His discussions of the interplay of official (state and juristic) law with the kinds of living law that he sees as growing up spontaneously in the social associations of everyday life are much more subtle and nuanced than is often suggested.

In Ehrlich's view, all social associations of whatever kind—formal or informal, enduring or transient—are organised by social norms that directly reflect the nature of the association and define the position and relations of members in it. Social associations usually also produce norms by means of which conflicts or disputes in the association can be decided. However, such norms for decision cannot always retain the form given by their spontaneous evolution in associational life. They may need greater guarantees of permanence and clarity. Equally, norms are needed to resolve problems *between* social associations. But the practice of making decisions about disputes predates the creation of formal norms for decision. This adjudicative practice, therefore, looks first to the expectations of the associations whose disputes are to be addressed and (later, as courts develop historically) also to the state that guarantees a general judicial authority allowing the imposition of norms. From norms for decision more abstract legal propositions are derived by juristic reflection, and legal propositions are created directly by the state (usually as norms for decision addressed to courts or other tribunals and to state administrative officials).

Thus, Ehrlich's sociology of law presents a complex tapestry of types of regulation and sources of law, with no sharp line between state and society, or between official law and living law. It is clear that his effort to balance these elements in his legal sociology directly reflects a combination of juristic and sociological sensibilities, and an effort to integrate completely these sensibilities in his thinking. From a juristic point of view, law and legal experience exist in many forms, spanning the juristic centre and the social periphery (of normative order beyond lawyers' practice). From a sociological viewpoint, however, law's centre seems initially located in the social associations of life that provide its normative meaning and essential authority, and law's periphery (that is, its derivative or less fundamental forms) is found in state and juristic legal activities.

The real subtlety of Ehrlich's legal pluralism, however, is that because it insists on a vast range of sources of law it seems to suggest, ultimately, that there is no 'objective' means of saying where legal centre and periphery are located. Centre and periphery depend on *standpoint*. In other words, the same complex legal realm might be viewed by lay citizens, state officials, juristic scholars or legal practitioners as, in each case, *their* law, in relation to which they stand in a central place. This dialectic of centre and periphery, which surely derives from Ehrlich's own complex professional and cultural situation, shapes his legal pluralist approach, the most distinctive and original aspect of his legal theory.

It also provides the only possible meaning for his otherwise entirely opaque claim that the centre of gravity of legal development lies in 'society'[36]—which obviously includes lawyers and even, according to Ehrlich, the state as the 'widest', 'most inclusive' of all the social associations.[37] To see law's developmental centre as 'society' is effectively to *decentre* it—to see it as the framework, guarantee, product or expression of innumerable associations or communities, the relative significance of these surely being judged differently from different standpoints, for different purposes, and in terms of different (social, cultural, political, etc) experiences and commitments.

Yet this centre/periphery dialectic also accounts for his theory's most problematic aspect—the ambiguity of what is to count in it as 'law'. Virtually all of the most severe criticisms of Ehrlich's legal sociology focus on this problem, including those referred to earlier as tending towards intellectual marginalisation of his work. They deserve to be taken very seriously, but in a context of appreciating what he tried to do and the difficulties entailed, rather than implying that he would have been better advised to try to do something else.

EHRLICH'S CONCEPT OF LAW

Ehrlich's starting point in explaining the nature of law is the 'inner order' of social associations. A social association is:

> ... a plurality of human beings who, in their relations with one another, recognise certain rules of conduct as binding, and, generally at least, actually regulate their conduct according to them.[38]

---

[36] See above n 3, 390. Cf Husserl (above n 29, 334) criticising Ehrlich's idea of society as 'an abstract construction to which no sociological entity corresponds. His book is entirely wanting in any analysis of such basic social phenomena as a political community, a people, a nation, a community of law, and their interrelation.' Husserl's review is one of the most perceptive early critiques of Ehrlich's legal sociology.
[37] See above n 3, 68, 69.
[38] *Ibid* 39.

Social associations include all kinds of relatively stable patterns or networks of social relations, from contractual relationships, families, religious or political organisations, corporations, social classes and professions to nations and states. The lack of discrimination in Ehrlich's concept of associations does not augur well for it as a basis of rigorous theory. Nevertheless, he sees all social associations as having similar organisational problems, which necessitate rules assigning members their relative positions and roles in the association.[39] A reader familiar with modern social scientific legal pluralism might assume at this point that Ehrlich's view will be that law—in a non-juristic sense—is essentially these associational rules or the most important of them. Although juristic scholars might complain at such a broad redefinition of law that no longer ties it to state or official sources, the germ of a coherent concept of law could emerge from such an approach—the problem would be to ask what degree of formalisation or institutionalisation of social rules would be required before such rules could be recognised theoretically as law.

However, Ehrlich does not take this course. Early in the third chapter of his book on sociology of law, he suddenly stops the reader short with this statement:

> Not all human associations are being regulated by legal norms, but manifestly only those associations are parts of the legal order whose order is based upon legal norms.[40]

The concept of law is ultimately not tied, therefore, to the concept of social association. Some social associations do *not* produce law. Which do? Why these associations and not others? Ehrlich gives no entirely convincing answers to these questions, enabling many of his critics to say that no clear specification of the concept of law, differentiating it from social norms in general, can be found in his work.[41] Thus, Franz Neumann,[42] reviewing Ehrlich's book, complained of its 'entire lack of a genuine legal theory'.

Nevertheless, Ehrlich presents two different strategies for identifying the legal in the social: a sociological strategy, on the one hand, and a psychological one, on the other. The sociological strategy is related to his idea of 'facts of the law' (*Tatsachen des Rechts*). These are foundational social facts that 'the human mind associates' with the organisational rules of social associations.[43] There are, he claims, just four facts of this kind: (i) usage (that is, custom treated as an applicable norm); (ii) relationships of domination and subjection; (iii) the fact of possession (that is, the possibility of actual

---

[39] Ibid 40, 85.
[40] Ibid 40.
[41] See above n 30, 26–8.
[42] FL Neumann, Review of Ehrlich's *Fundamental Principles of the Sociology of Law* (1973) 43 *American Journal of Sociology* 353.
[43] See above n 3, 85.

control over something); and (iv) 'declarations of will'. While usage was an important basis of primitive law (customary law being the central form of this law), it is now, Ehrlich suggests, a merely residual fact of the law. Domination/subjection relationships and possession are legally significant in so far as they relate to matters of general economic importance in society. Law expresses economic conditions in this way. Only two forms of declarations of will—the contract and the testamentary disposition—have been legally fundamental (articles of association linking people in companies or other organisations are basically an expression of usage or agreement).[44]

Ehrlich's view seems to be that all law that arises as the inner ordering of social associations directly reflects these facts—which are clearly a mix of types of social action and types of social relations. The point at which law emerges from social norms cannot be specified precisely. But Ehrlich's view seems to be that law concerns aspects of social organisation that relate to the *Tatsachen des Rechts* and that are considered to be of general (primarily economic) significance in society. As well as law that arises directly in social associations in this way, there is also law in the form of relatively abstract legal propositions enacted by the state or formulated juristically, and law established as norms for decisions by courts and tribunals or various state agencies. So law has a range of sources and forms, but is rooted in the facts of the law, and is regarded (at least by those who formulate or enforce it) as of considerable social importance. Ultimately, the bases of Ehrlich's sociological identification of law seem to be that: (i) law consists of those social norms that regulate matters seen as of general social significance; and (ii) law is rooted in certain specific types of action and relationships that tend historically to assume fundamental economic importance and attract state supervision.

If this seems a weak basis for specifying the distinctiveness of law, Ehrlich's psychological strategy is even weaker.[45] He admits disarmingly that it is very difficult to indicate the precise difference between legal and non-legal norms. But it is 'impossible to deny the existence of this difference' which is 'unmistakable'[46] and revealed in *feelings* about norms. The violation of a law produces a 'feeling of revolt' that is different from and stronger than reactions to breaches of non-legal norms. Law also gives rise to a reaction of *opinio necessitatis*, writes Ehrlich.[47] He does not explain this term, which others have explained as the feeling or instinct of obeying a social necessity.[48]

---

[44] Ibid 104.
[45] Timasheff (above n 25, 140) calls Ehrlich's approach 'a remarkable assemblage of completely vague statements'.
[46] See above n 3, 164.
[47] Ibid 165.
[48] See, eg A Cassese, 'A Follow-Up: Forcible Humanitarian Countermeasures and *Opinio Necessitatis*' (1999) 10 *European Journal of International Law* 797, quoting Georges Scelle.

A theory that avoids defining law in absolute opposition to non-legal norms should certainly not be dismissed out of hand because of that avoidance. On the contrary, to offer a definition sharply dividing law from other social norms would be to subscribe to the kind of rigid centre/periphery dichotomy that Ehrlich's legal sociology properly challenges. Sociology of law does not need a conclusive definition of law of the kind that jurists, for understandable practical reasons, have very often sought. It needs rather a working concept of law to organise empirical research; a concept that avoids dogmatism and so leaves open the possibility of rethinking the scope and character of the research field in various ways to take account of the results of research. Such a provisional 'working concept' also needs to have sufficient coherence and flexibility to allow for productive theoretical inquiries. If sociology of law is to have theoretical integrity as an enterprise of *legal* studies, it needs to be able to identify fields of social experience that can be convincingly characterised as 'legal'—again, at least provisionally. It needs this for the purposes of building coherent socio-legal theory.

What is required is a set of sociological criteria that indicate to what extent it is worth considering social practices as legal practices, and social ideas as legal doctrine, for the purposes of research. However, Ehrlich's characterisation of law's distinctiveness—even if it is treated as merely sketching elements of a working concept of law—is so weak that it gives much ammunition to those seeking to drive his work to the intellectual margins. Why does he get himself into such difficulties? And how might socio-legal theory avoid them?

The cause of the problem for Ehrlich lies in the dialectic of centre and periphery discussed earlier in relation to the juristic and sociological aspects of his work. It is clear that, despite his sociological imagination, he cannot escape his juristic formation, which puts the juristic view of law and legal experience in centre place and arranges other social experience around this as (legally) peripheral. A thoroughgoing modern sociological approach to legal pluralism might well see law as potentially arising in *all* social associations in some form. Perhaps some particular criteria of institutionalisation could then be treated as distinguishing law in these associations from other kinds of social norms.[49] However, Ehrlich does not proceed in this way. He clearly has in mind, as legal problems, the kinds of regulatory problems that jurists and state law address. Thus, when he introduces the idea of facts of the law, virtually all his discussion of these facts relates to juristic doctrine and to problems of regulation familiar to lawyers. It is as though he superimposes, over a (sociological) view of the norms that provide the

---

[49] See, eg R Cotterrell, *Law's Community: Legal Theory in Sociological Perspective* (Oxford, Clarendon Press, 1995) ch 2.

structure of social associations, a quite different (juristic) perception of what is important in lawyers' experience. His discussion of facts of the law represents a very uneasy attempt to reconcile these two perspectives.

The difficulties of Ehrlich's concept of law also clearly show the underdeveloped nature of his social science, which recognises cultural diversity, but does not provide an adequate means of analysing social forces and structures. Thus, when he suggests that laws are social norms that are considered especially important, he does not explain the contexts in which judgments of social importance are made or the conditions that determine whose judgments ultimately count.

It is possible that he envisages a radical pluralism of perspectives in which each group or even each person judges the degree of social importance of a norm that, for that group or that individual, makes the norm 'law'.[50] But this is to read a degree of radicalism into Ehrlich's thinking which is certainly not explicit in his work. One suspects, rather, that he often assumes that the state and the economic and social elites having most direct access to its power will decide what will count practically as law. Ultimately, it seems that he has insufficient interest in sociological inquiry to ask what conditions might render this assumption untenable, or what kind of sociological vision of law might be appropriate where social sources of legal development are so antagonistic to the legal conceptions of the state that a direct confrontation arises as to what should count as 'valid law'. These issues are simply beyond the scope of Ehrlich's sociology of law—perhaps they are just too far from the outlook of a jurist.

Again, if Ehrlich's criterion of law in terms of the perceived social importance of norms is left aside and his alternative 'psychological' criterion is considered, the limits of his social insight are no less apparent. In so far as law is distinguished from other norms by feelings evoked by its breach, there is little recognition in Ehrlich's work that these feelings might vary in patterned ways within and between different social groups, and there is no substantial analysis of possible links between feelings about law and various kinds of social experience.

For all his many remarkable insights, Ehrlich does not ultimately *transcend* a dichotomy between juristic and sociological perspectives. Instead, he juxtaposes these perspectives in his legal sociology. He leaves his sociological insights into the nature of law ultimately undeveloped because, at crucial points, he retreats to juristic assumptions or lacks the incentive or resources to pursue sociological conceptualisations adequately. In this particular respect, the dialectic of centre and periphery is played out in terms of the location from which law is to be conceptualised. Ultimately,

---

[50] He may consider, equally, that the feelings of revolt of each group or each individual in relation to a particular norm is what makes that norm 'law' for the group or the individual.

it seems that Ehrlich understands law in terms of a juristic centre. Beyond that centre, law as a social phenomenon remains vague and undefined in a sociological periphery. Yet, in principle, it should have been possible to shift location: to see law from a sociological centre; in other words, to adopt a significant distancing from (but not a rejection of) the juristic world.

Ehrlich could have achieved this if he had adopted an approach that accepted the kinds of doctrine and practices that lawyers recognise as law, but had treated these juristic kinds of law as special (even perhaps specially important, clear or well-developed) instances within a wider sociological conception of law. There is no reason why a sociological concept of law, taking full account of, but extending well beyond, juristic understandings of the conceptual scope of law, cannot be developed.[51] For example, consistently with his general sociological outlook, Ehrlich could have seen law as one kind of normative regulation of social associations (I should prefer to say, of types and networks of community),[52] distinguished from other kinds of normative regulation by its distinctive *institutionalisation*—that is, by the existence of specific institutions or agencies for creating, interpreting or enforcing normative regulation as doctrine (but not necessarily providing for all three of these activities to occur). This is just one strategy for conceptualising law sociologically. I think it has the merit of creating a working concept that clearly embraces juristic law, but can also extend beyond this to cover many other normative orders based on institutionalised doctrine.[53] However, no doubt there are many other such strategies offering different advantages for socio-legal research.

CONCLUSION

Ehrlich saw 'so much'—and reported it all in his legal sociology—because he could occupy several entirely different standpoints, trying to see as far as he could from each of them. As an Austro-German jurist, he could stand in the centre of a sophisticated legal professional world, which he could envisage as potentially transcending all cultural differences and local social conditions. As a participant observer of imperial provinciality and multiculturalism, however, he could create a different perspective in the social

---

[51] Hans Kelsen's (above n 30, 175) claim to the contrary—ie that any sociological concept of law must be derivative from juristic understandings of law—is surely unwarranted. That legal sociologists may recognise juristic understandings of law (as I think they often should) and even build partly on them in conceptualising law is certainly not an indication that they must derive their working concepts of law from such understandings, or tie these concepts in some way to them.
[52] R Cotterrell, *Law, Culture and Society: Legal Ideas in the Mirror of Social Theory* (Aldershot, Ashgate, 2006).
[53] See above n 49, ch 2.

laboratory that he found on his doorstep in Czernowitz. From that vantage point, the distant imperial centre with its state bureaucracy and official legal order stood at the periphery of a rich if very unstable concentration of local cultures with diverse regulatory expectations and traditions.

Ehrlich may have lacked the sociological insight of some other pioneers of sociology of law—certainly Max Weber or Emile Durkheim. What makes him special and still important is, first, his intricate (if insufficiently developed) conception of legal pluralism and, secondly, the continual unresolved movement of his thought between juristic and wider sociological perspectives. Other pioneer legal sociologists may well have been more systematic in their thinking, better jurists or more profound social analysts, but the dialectic of centre and periphery in Ehrlich's legal consciousness makes his work endlessly fascinating. It presents sociology of law as intimately bound up with juristic perspectives yet also potentially powerfully subversive of them; aiming to respect these perspectives yet also to relativise and decentre them in a broader sociological vision. Perhaps this uneasy, sometimes frustrating combination of approaches still offers legal sociology its best strategies for promoting understanding of (and between) the many varieties of legal experience.

5

Eugen Ehrlich's Linking of Sociology and Jurisprudence and the Reception of his Work in Japan[1]

STEFAN VOGL[2]

THE RECEPTION OF EHRLICH'S SOCIOLOGY OF LAW IN EUROPE, THE UNITED STATES AND JAPAN

EUGEN EHRLICH'S sociological approach to law and his linking of sociology and jurisprudence were controversial among continental European jurists from the beginning. Hans Kelsen accused him of identifying law with society,[3] confusing *Sein* and *Sollen*[4] and applying an unsustainable syncretism of methods.[5] Max Weber denounced his approach as a totally unjustified fight against concepts as such[6] and more recently Niklas Luhmann attributed to his sociology of law an openly hostile attitude towards legislation.[7]

In contrast to the rejection on the European continent, some well-known American jurists highly appreciated Ehrlich's sociology of law. Oliver W Holmes praised his *Fundamental Principles of the Sociology of Law*[8] as 'the best book

---

[1] This chapter is in part a summary version of a doctoral thesis submitted to the University of Frankfurt am Main in 2002 and published in German (*Soziale Gesetzgebungspolitik, Freie Rechtsfindung und soziologische Rechtswissenschaft bei Eugen Ehrlich* (Baden-Baden, Nomos, 2003)).

[2] I thank Roger Cotterrell for his comments on an earlier version of this chapter and Mark Fenwick for discussing the various issues raised over a long period of time.

[3] H Kelsen, 'Eine Grundlegung der Rechtssoziologie' (1915) 39 *Archiv für soziale Gesetzgebung und Statistik* (hereinafter: *ARSS*) 870. (All English translations from literature quoted after the original German title were made by the author.)

[4] H Kelsen, above n 3, 850.

[5] Ibid.

[6] M Weber, *Rechtssoziologie* (2nd edn, Neuwied, Luchterhand, 1967) 209.

[7] N Luhmann, N, *Rechtssoziologie* (2nd edn, Opladen, Westdeutscher Verlag, 1983) 24.

[8] WL Moll (tr), *Fundamental Principles of the Sociology of Law* (Cambridge, Mass., Harvard University Press, 1936). (All titles without author are referring to works of Eugen Ehrlich.)

on legal subjects by any living continental jurist'.[9] Roscoe Pound singled out Ehrlich's Czernowitz 'Seminar for Living Law' as the institution, where 'perhaps the most effective study' in 'sociological jurisprudence' has been done,[10] and Karl N Llewellyn counted Ehrlich among his fellow legal realists.[11] In Japan, Ehrlich's sociology of law became popular in the 1920s, when Suehiro Izutaro,[12] strongly influenced by Ehrlich's concept of 'living law', stopped equating law with the legal concepts received from the West during the Meiji Restoration and started to look for Japanese law in 'practical life', where he hoped to find it 'like fishes in the water'.[13] Today, Ehrlich is regarded as one of the greatest European jurists in Japan and his work is ranked among the classics of jurisprudence.[14]

Ehrlich strongly dismissed the insinuation of confusing *Sein* and *Sollen*[15] during his famous controversy with Kelsen, without being able to convince either Kelsen or his contemporaries.[16] The fact that he 'lost' this debate with Kelsen in the eyes of contemporary jurisprudence[17] confirmed the European scepticism towards his sociological approach ever since.[18] Somewhat ironically, the warmer reception of Ehrlich's sociology of law in the United States and Japan, just building on his 'sociological' or 'realistic' understanding of law as opposed to the traditional dogmatic-normative comprehension, seems to be based on the same misunderstanding that Ehrlich so desperately tried to correct. The rejection as well as the reception of Ehrlich's sociological approach to law have one thing in common: they both expect sociology of law to compete with jurisprudence, or even replace it, on a dogmatic-normative level.

This chapter attempts to elaborate in detail that Ehrlich's sociology of law never intended to *replace* jurisprudence on a dogmatic level, nor to interfere

---

[9] Letter to Pollock, 29 December 1919, in MDW Howe (ed), *Pollock-Holmes letters* 2(Cambridge, Mass., Harvard University Press, 1941) 34.

[10] R Pound, 'The Scope and Purpose of Sociological Jurisprudence' (1912) 25 *Harvard Law Review* 512, fn 94.

[11] KN Llewellyn, 'A Realistic Jurisprudence—the Next Step' in KN Llewellyn, *Jurisprudence. Realism in Theory and Practice* (Chicago and London, The University of Chicago Press, 1962) 29.

[12] Suehiro Izutarô (1888–1951) was a leading law professor at the University of Tokyo and author of influential case books on civil law, law of property and labour law. He founded a 'Seminar for the Study of Civil Cases' in 1921 and did sociological field research on customary law in northern China in the 1940s (R Neumann, 'Berühmte Rechtsgelehrte in Japan' in P Eubel *et al* (eds), *Das japanische Rechtssystem* (Freiburg, Metzner, 1979) 627).

[13] I Suehiro, *Bukkenhô* (Tokyo, Yûhikaku, 1921) 4. (All English translations from literature quoted after the original Japanese title were made by the author.)

[14] R Kawakami, 'Die Möglichkeiten einer Zeitgeschichte anhand von Ehrlichs Biographie und Zustand der Materialienforschung' (1989) 124 *Hôgaku Ronsô* 9.

[15] 'Entgegnung' (1916) 41 *ARSS* 844.

[16] M Rehbinder, *Die Begründung der Rechtssoziologie durch Eugen Ehrlich* (2nd edn, Berlin, Duncker & Humblot, 1986) 119.

[17] M Rehbinder, above n 16, 119 ff.

[18] R Dreier, *Recht—Moral—Ideologie* (Frankfurt/M., Suhrkamp, 1981) 219.

with its genuine evaluative operations.[19] Nevertheless, Ehrlich did link sociology and jurisprudence, however, in a methodologically sensitive way, by distributing different tasks to the two disciplines and striving to profit from their separately gained results in the search for justice. Subsequently, after introducing Ehrlich's concept of law of the *Fundamental Principles* (see second section below), the application of this sociological concept of law in Japanese jurisprudence will be taken up as an example for a methodologically inconsequent linking of sociology and jurisprudence (see third section below). After that, Ehrlich's dogmatic concept of law in *Juristische Logik*[20] and its relation to the sociological concept of law in the *Fundamental Principles* will be analysed (in the fourth section). Based on this analysis, Ehrlich's own way of linking the two disciplines will be explained (in the fifth section) and some conclusions will be drawn (in the sixth section).

CONCEPT OF LAW IN *FUNDAMENTAL PRINCIPLES*

Ehrlich's Claim for a 'Science of Law' without Normative-Practical Relevance

In his *Fundamental Principles*, Ehrlich called for a 'legal science in the proper sense of the term', a 'science of law', which he equated with 'sociology of law'.[21] What did he mean by this 'science of law'?

Already a decade before naming it 'sociology of law' in his *Fundamental Principles*, Ehrlich had started advocating a science of law, which he imagined as a 'free science of law'.[22] Thereby he initially built on Austin's and Holland's analytical jurisprudence, characterising it as a 'general comparative science of law',[23] which 'may break through its national limitations'.[24] However, he later regarded analytical jurisprudence as too narrow an approach for a science of law, because he required his 'free science of law' to deal with legal provisions not only as dogmas, but also as societal forces. Moreover, court decisions, too, were to be analysed not only under

---

[19] Against: J Kraft, 'Vorfragen der Rechtssoziologie' (1930) 45 *Zeitschrift für vergleichende Rechtswissenschaft* 36; and K Larenz, *Methodenlehre der Rechtswissenschaft* (4th edn, Berlin, Heidelberg, New York, Springer, 1979) 73.
[20] *Die juristische Logik* (reprint of the 2nd edn 1925, Aalen, Scientia, 1966).
[21] Above n 8, 25.
[22] E Bruncken (tr), 'Judicial Freedom of Decision: Its Principles and Objects' in Association of American Law Schools (eds), *Science of Legal Method: Selected Essays by Various Authors* (Boston, Boston Book Company, 1917) 76. The German title is *Freie Rechtsfindung und freie Rechtwissenschaft* (Leipzig, Hirschfeld, 1903). Its literal translation would be: 'Free Legal Decision-Making and Free Science of Law'.
[23] See above n 22, 62.
[24] *Ibid* 62.

the dogmatic aspects of 'correct or otherwise',[25] but as a result of various societal forces influencing the judge.[26] For Ehrlich, transcending national borders also meant exploring the 'living content'[27] of the formal abstractions developed by the jurisprudence of various countries, thus requiring an empirical approach. Ultimately, he conceived his 'free science of law' as a 'sociological' science without normative-practical relevance:

> The name sociology of law is an expression of the fact that it is a pure science of law, *excluding any practical application either in jurisprudence or in legal policy* and that this science of law should become a branch of social science and deal with law as a social phenomenon only (emphasis added).[28]

He made it very clear that the normative content of law as such was not a problem for the sociology of law:

> But the question itself how law should be, goes beyond the reach of sociology, because this can neither be described nor proved by scientific methods. What we should do is not a question of how to gain knowledge, but of how to influence one's mind ...[29]

What then was this 'law as a social phenomenon' about which sociology of law was supposed to gain knowledge, but which lacked any apparent utility?

Sociological Definition of Law

Ehrlich defined law as a social phenomenon based on a thorough critique of the practical concept of law in contemporary continental jurisprudence.[30] He realised that according to this practical concept, law was 'exclusively that which is of importance as law in the judicial administration of justice'.[31] That is why law was defined from the point of view of the judge as 'a rule according to which the judge has to decide the legal disputes that are brought before him'.[32] For Ehrlich, this was no scientific concept of law, because it could not grasp the much broader social reality of law, namely 'that which lives and is operative in human society as law'.[33] It only encompassed rules of conduct for 'a small part of the people, ie for the authorities, entrusted with the application of the law, but not ... for the generality of the people'.[34] So he defined law as a 'rule of human conduct' in general, ensuring that in

---

[25] *Ibid* 78.
[26] *Ibid* 78 ff.
[27] Above n 8, 480.
[28] 'Soziologie des Rechts' in M Rehbinder (ed), *Ehrlich, Eugen, Gesetz und lebendes Recht* (Berlin, Duncker & Humblot, 1986) 179.
[29] Above n 28, 180.
[30] Above n 8, ch 1.
[31] *Ibid* 10.
[32] *Ibid*.
[33] *Ibid*.
[34] Above n 8, 11.

his definition 'a rule of conduct was not only a rule according to which men customarily regulate their conduct, but also a rule according to which they ought to do so'.[35] This means that the objects of the sociology of law were indeed norms of law—described, however, as social reality (social facts).

As a consequence of his sociological definition of law, Ehrlich also deviated from the prevailing view in jurisprudence, that law is a compulsory order.[36] If law was no longer only a rule according to which the judge had to decide cases, it was no longer sufficient to distinguish it from other social norms just by a quality of being compulsory. If it was a rule of conduct in general, 'compulsion by threat of penalty as well as of compulsory execution'[37] became a 'secondary matter'.[38] Because people in general 'quite voluntarily' perform the duties in their innumerable legal relations,[39] law ultimately did not depend on compulsion by the state, but similar to any other social norm, on the recognition by the people in everyday life.[40] A distinction between legal and mere social norms could, however, be achieved by social-psychological criteria. Ehrlich suggested the different feelings towards violations of these norms in everyday life as a criterion of distinction,[41] because according to his observation people react with a particular feeling on the violation of a legal norm:

> Peculiar to the legal norm is the reaction for which the jurists of the Continental common law have coined the term *opinio necessitatis*.[42]
>
> The legal norm regulates a matter, which, at least in the opinion of the group within which it has its origin, is of great importance, of basic significance.[43]

This attempt to distinguish between legal and social norms based on social-psychological criteria is not as ridiculous as was presented by its critics,[44] if due consideration is given to the fact that Ehrlich's intention was to distinguish between sociological law in the above explained comprehensive descriptive sense and mere social norms, and not between dogmatic law in its restricted normative sense and mere social norms. It cannot be criticised for being practically useless, because it did not pretend to be of practical use for jurisprudence to distinguish legal norms with binding force for the judge from non-binding social norms.[45] It was not meant

---

[35] *Ibid.*
[36] Above n 8, 20.
[37] *Ibid* 21.
[38] *Ibid.*
[39] *Ibid.*
[40] Above n 8, 167.
[41] *Ibid* 165.
[42] *Ibid.*
[43] Above n 8, 167 ff.
[44] H Kelsen, above n 3, 861: 'Among the many attempts to determine the essence of law this one certainly represents the height of curiosity.'
[45] Against: M Rehbinder, above n 16, 124.

to be a *doctrine of law* serving the judge on a dogmatic level, but to be a *theory about law* for a scientist on a sociological level. So a critique of this theory would have to be targeted at its sociological validity, rather than at its dogmatic utility. The new sociological knowledge that has been gained about feelings and emotions[46] since Ehrlich's time, and the efforts that have been made to operationalise these social-psychological criteria in relation to law,[47] however problematic they might be,[48] do not yet seem to justify a dismissal of Ehrlich's theory as sociologically invalid.

Sociological Typology of Law

Corresponding to his sociological definition, Ehrlich developed a sociological typology of law, which built on an observed difference between law created by the state and law created by society. The latter was not created consciously by a legislator standing above society, but by unconscious social developments penetrating the depths of society.[49] From a sociological point of view, Ehrlich identified two main functions of law, namely to serve as forms of social organisation, ie representing the 'inner order of social associations',[50] and to serve as norms for decisions in courts.[51] According to these criteria, he differentiated law created by society further into the initial form of 'societal law'[52] and the developed form of 'Juristic Law'/'Lawyers' Law'.[53]

Dynamic Input-output Model of Law

In a modern state, law created by the state is made by the legislature, but how does society create law? Ehrlich explained it on the basis of a dynamic input-output model, in which the 'facts of law' are input and 'living law' is the output.

---

[46] Cf J Katz, *How Emotions Work* (Chicago and London, The University of Chicago Press, 1999).

[47] Cf R Schweizer and H Quitt, *Rechtstatsachenermittlung durch Befragen. Bd.I: Die Definitionsphase* (Cologne, O. Schmidt, 1985) 63; and A Podgorecki, W Kaupen, J Van Houtte and B Kutchinsky (eds), *Knowledge and Opinion about Law* (London, Martin Robertson, 1973).

[48] H Rottleuthner, *Einführung in die Rechtssoziologie* (Darmstadt, 1987) 174 ff.

[49] *Beiträge zur Theorie der Rechtsquellen. Erster Teil. Das ius civile, ius publicum, ius privatum* (Berlin, Heymanns, 1902) 237 and 239.

[50] Above n 8, 26 ff.

[51] Above n 28, 91.

[52] Above n 49, 240.

[53] Ehrlich's German term *Juristenrecht* is translated as 'lawyers' law' in *Freedom of Decision* (see above n 22, 54 ff) and as 'juristic law' in the *Fundamental Principles* (see above n 8, 412 ff). Thereafter, the terminology of the *Fundamental Principles* will be used, because it seems to have gained vogue, although the term 'lawyer's law' might be nearer to the original German term.

'Facts of Law' as Input

Ehrlich answered the self-imposed question, 'how factual relations become rights and legal relations',[54] by presenting four social facts as starting points for any organised social group and its corresponding rules:

> A group of human beings becomes an association through organization. Organization is the rule which assigns to each individual his position and his functions. We are chiefly concerned therefore with determining *the facts with which the human mind associates such rules*. ... They are ... the following: usage, domination, possession and declaration of will (emphasis added).[55]

He identified these facts as the 'facts of law' from which also legal norms emerged: 'Legal norms are those norms that flow from the facts of law ...'[56]

This description of the input into law from social facts already highlights the problem of the critique in the tradition of Kelsen, implying that Ehrlich was transposing social facts into legal norms, or deriving legal norms from social facts: it was not the facts of law themselves that Ehrlich regarded as legal norms, but the 'rules', a group of human beings developed from these facts. Hence, it was the evaluation of these facts by 'the human mind' that attached rules to social facts, creating legal norms. So, as far as Ehrlich's legal norms are concerned, there is not a confusion of *Sein* and *Sollen*, but a clear distinction on the sociological level.

Historical evidence convinced Ehrlich that the input into law from the facts of law was confined to societal law and did not affect directly legal propositions in general, because the immediate makers of the legal propositions of 'law created by the state' and of 'juristic law' were jurists,[57] carving out norms of decision from the rules of conduct of societal law in a process of 'universalisation' and 'reduction to unity.'[58]

'Living Law' as Output

Ehrlich's living law was the law that was prevailing in the interaction between the different types of law, and 'which dominates life'[59] as a result:

> Only that which becomes part and parcel of life becomes a living norm; everything else is mere doctrine, norm for decision, dogma, or theory.[60]

---

[54] 'Die Tatsachen des Gewohnheitsrechts' in M Rehbinder (ed), above n 28, 108.
[55] Above n 8, 85.
[56] Ibid 169.
[57] Ibid 175.
[58] Ibid 124.
[59] Ibid 493.
[60] Ibid 41.

Consequently, Ehrlich's living law might consist of any type of law, for example, also of law created by the state, if the latter prevails over societal and juristic law. Even societal law might, however, be dead if its legal norms are successfully suppressed by juristic law or law created by the state. Therefore, Ehrlich's living law can be conceived as the output of an interaction process between the different types of law, which itself is fed by an input from the side of the society by the above-mentioned facts of law. It is a very different concept of law compared with Pound's 'law in action',[61] which in Ehrlich's terminology would only represent 'living law created by the state'. Ehrlich's concept insists on the possibility that social norms might be living law if they are effective in everyday life; and legal norms of statutory law might be dead sociologically if they are ineffective. By relying on effectiveness, Ehrlich again presented a special criterion to characterise one type of sociological law, namely 'living law', which as a sociological criteria is meanwhile frequently operationalised in sociological studies.[62] Unlike Pound, Ehrlich did not use it to narrow down the lawyer's practical concept of law, but to transcend it, thus identifying a new type of sociological law that represented a broader reality of law than the practical concept of law was able to encompass.

Summary: Sociological Concept of Law

In his sociology of law, Ehrlich defined law differently from its dogmatic definition in jurisprudence. Although he partly relied on the traditional 'practical concept of law' ('law created by the state'), law in the sociological sense also encompassed court decisions ('juristic law') that could not be classified as objective law in continental jurisprudence. It even contained norms that from a dogmatic point of view were mere social norms ('societal law'), but from a sociological point of view could be distinguished from them by social-psychological criteria ('feelings towards violations'). The empirical knowledge gained about this law as a social phenomenon, in particular about its effectiveness as 'living law', had no normative-practical implications and was, therefore, explicitly excluded from being applied as such in jurisprudence. It was conceived in the form of empirically derived sociological theories about law and not in the form of legal doctrines. For the sake of scientific analysis, it treated law in general and legal norms in particular as social facts, but did not derive them from social facts.

---

[61] Cf D Nelken, 'Pound and Ehrlich on the Living Law' (1986) Beiheft 9 *Rechtstheorie* 231 ff.
[62] KD Opp, *Soziologie im Recht* (Rheinbeck, Rowohlt, 1973) 190 ff; A Diekmann, *Die Befolgung von Gesetzen. Empirische Untersuchungen zu einer rechtssoziologischen Theorie* (Berlin, Duncker & Humblot, 1980); and E Bardach, *The Implementation Game: What Happens After a Bill Becomes a Law* (Cambridge, Mass., MIT Press, 1977).

EHRLICH'S SOCIOLOGICAL CONCEPT OF LAW IN JAPANESE JURISPRUDENCE

Before contrasting Ehrlich's sociological concept of law with his dogmatic concept, the practical application of his sociological concept in Japanese jurisprudence will be taken up as an example of a methodologically problematic linking of sociology and jurisprudence. I refer to the above-mentioned influential law professor at the University of Tokyo, Suehiro Izutarô (see first section above), whose legal thinking, according to Japanese as well as Western literature, was heavily influenced by Ehrlich's sociology of law.[63] Subsequently, I compare some crucial features of Ehrlich's sociology of law with their application by Suehiro to show how the latter deviated from Ehrlich's account and how this produced problematic results in Japanese jurisprudence.

Sociological Theories about Law as Legal Doctrines

Japanese literature[64] points out that Suehiro received in particular Ehrlich's distinction between 'rules of conduct' and 'norms for decision', Ehrlich's theory of the reception of law and Ehrlich's concept of 'living law'. Whereas Suehiro's biographer Ushiomi Toshitaka presents Suehiro as a Japanese legal scholar,[65] Hirano Yoshitarô refers to him in his biographical article as a sociologist.[66] So as a jurist with a strong affinity to sociology, Suehiro attempted to apply Ehrlich's sociological theories about law directly in jurisprudence.

Laws as Mere 'Norms for Decision' Addressed to the Courts

According to Ushiomi, Suehiro, influenced by Ehrlich, distinguished 'rules of conduct' from 'norms for decision':

> The courts are basing their decisions on 'norms for decision'. Criminal and Civil law consists of norms for decision and *addresses itself only to the Judge*. The

---

[63] Y Hirano, 'Shakaigakusha Suehiro Izutarô' (1951) 23 *Hôritsu Jihô* 745 ff; Z Kitagawa, *Rezeption und Fortbildung des europäischen Zivilrechts in Japan* (Frankfurt und Berlin, Metzner, 1970) 145, fn 13; J Murakami, *Einführung in die Grundlagen des japanischen Rechts* (Darmstadt, Wissenschaftliche Buchgesellschaft, 1974) 77; T Ushiomi, 'Suehiro Izutarô' in T Ushiomi and N Toshitani, *Nihon no hôgakusha* (Tokyo, Nihon hyôronsha, 1975) 335 ff; T Isomura, 'Shimin hôgaku' in T Isomura, *Shakaihôgaku no tenkai to kôzô* (Tokyo, Nihon hyôronsha, 1975) 94 ff and 114; Z Ishimura, 'Rechtssoziologie' in P Eubel *et al* (eds), above n 12, 34; R Kawakami, 'Ehrlich ni okeru hô no rekishishakaigaku no seiritsu' (1982) 111 no 4 *Hôgaku Ronsô* 4; M Rehbinder, above n 16, 23; G Rahn, *Rechtsdenken und Rechtsauffassung in Japan* (München, Beck, 1990) 141, fn 20; and HP Marutschke, *Einführung in das japanische Recht* (Munich, Beck, 1999) 100.
[64] Y Hirano, above n 63, 745; and T Ushiomi, above n 63, 335.
[65] Ushiomi's biographical article '*Suehiro Izutaro*' was published in a compilation with the title: 'Japanese Legal scholars' ('*Nihon no hôgakusha*'), cf above n 63.
[66] Hirano's biographical article was published in the law journal *Hôritsu jihô* under the title 'The Sociologist Suehiro Izutarô' ('*Shakaigakusha Suehiro Izutarô*'), cf above n 63.

'norms for decision' must be distinguished from the 'rules of conduct' that govern everyday life. Otherwise confusion will be the result (emphasis added).[67]

If the criminal and civil law with its norms for decision is addressed only to the judge, the scope of these laws received from the West during the Meiji Restoration is reduced to the courts. It no longer appears as a body of rules governing everyday life, but only as a body of rules instructing the judge how to resolve conflicts. Therefore, it was exclusively the judge who was supposed to be bound by these imported laws.

The distinction between 'rules of conduct' in general and 'norms for decision' in particular can indeed be traced back to the *Fundamental Principles*.[68] However, Ehrlich's distinction was not a legal doctrine allocating different scopes of dogmatic validity to 'rules of conduct' and 'norms for decision'. Ehrlich's distinction was a sociological theory about the difference in the effectiveness of these norms in social reality, explaining the relative normative weakness of 'norms for decision' to govern everyday life. Ehrlich even stressed the basic similarity of these norms from a sociological point of view:

The norm for decision, like all social norms, is primarily a rule of conduct, but only for the courts. It is not, *primarily at least*, a rule for the men who are the doers in life, but for the men, who sit in judgement upon the doers (emphasis added).[69]

A close comparison of the two approaches shows that Suehiro radicalised Ehrlich's sociological theory and simultaneously transformed it into a legal doctrine on a dogmatic level.

Whereas in Ehrlich's theory norms for decision were regarded basically as rules of conduct for everyone (even if not primarily), in Suehiro's doctrine they were attributed binding force only towards the judge. As Ehrlich's distinction was the result of an effort to gain factual knowledge about law, his theory representing this factual knowledge could go no further than stating that although laws were intended to govern everyday life, the normative force of their norms for decision was in reality more or less confined to the judiciary. Therefore, Ehrlich's distinction had no normative implications for law on a dogmatic level. If Ehrlich's distinction was not observed, it could only result in confusion among sociologists, not among jurists, because the judge had to apply law, no matter how it was categorised sociologically. Ultimately, the judge could not even confuse rules of conduct and norms for decision, because they were not dogmatic categories. In shifting Ehrlich's sociological theory to a dogmatic level, Suehiro instrumentalised it as a doctrine, binding exclusively the Japanese judge, while liberating the public

---

[67] T Ushiomi, above n 63, 342.
[68] Above n 8, 10 ff and 121 ff.
[69] *Ibid* 122 ff.

from observing the 'norms for decision' of the received Western law as 'rules of conduct' in everyday life.

Laws as Abstractions without Legal Content

According to Ushiomi, Suehiro gained from Ehrlich the conviction that it was not German law that was received during the Meiji Restoration, but exclusively abstractions and generalisations from Roman law:

> The reception of a German law book by a Japanese law book was only possible, because the German law book doesn't contain the inner order of the German society, but *only* again and again sieved out abstractions and generalizations, which had been transferred from Roman law to German law (emphasis added).[70]

This statement about the object of reception at first glance seems to resemble very closely Ehrlich's reception theory:

> The transformation of a German draft to a Japanese law book was only possible, because this draft didn't *mainly* contain German law, the inner order of the German society, but again and again sieved out abstractions and generalizations, which had been transferred from Roman law. However, for the same reason, that the German draft didn't reflect German law, the Japanese law book doesn't reflect Japanese law, but *mainly* abstractions and generalizations (emphasis added).[71]

It seems to be but a slight difference that in Ehrlich's reception theory it is *mainly* abstractions and generalisations, whereas Suehiro identifies *only* abstractions and generalisations as objects of reception. However, it is again a radicalisation of Ehrlich's theory, which this time not only restricts the scope of the received law from the West, but empties it completely from any substantive German legal content, which in Ehrlich's theory, even if in a reduced form, still existed. This radicalisation of Ehrlich's theory again results in attributing a dogmatic significance to it that was not intended by Ehrlich. Whereas Ehrlich's theory, without stating anything about the dogmatic validity of the received law, does not exclude such validity, Suehiro in denying any substantive legal content implicitly excluded any validity of the received Western law on a dogmatic level.

Dilemma of the Japanese Judge: Bound by Empty Legal Concepts

The dogmatisation of sociological theories about law placed the Japanese judge in a paradoxical situation: on the one hand, he or she was bound exclusively by the norms for decision of the received Western law; on the other hand, this Western law was denied any substantive legal content.

---

[70] T Ushiomi, above n 63, 342.
[71] 'Gesetz und lebendes Recht' in M Rehbinder (ed), above n 28, 236.

106 Stefan Vogl

Consequently, Suehiro had to offer legal content for the judiciary from somewhere else outside the received law.

Sociological Concept of 'Living Law' as Law on a Dogmatic Level

It was Ehrlich's 'living law' that promised to offer the legal content necessary to solve the judge's dilemma. How then did Suehiro activate this sociological concept of law in jurisprudence?

Japanese 'Living Law' as Having Binding Force

Suehiro presented Ehrlich's sociological concept of living law as follows:

> The written law, which jurisprudence recognizes as the only source of law is in contra-distinction with the living law, consisting of the inner order of society. *Its 'living legal norms' are of course binding* in social life and *form in the same way as the legal propositions contained in the law book together with them the legal order* (emphasis added).[72]

Crucially, Ehrlich conceived living law quite differently:

> This then is the living law in contradistinction to that which is being enforced in the courts and other tribunals. The living law is the law, which dominates life itself even *though it has not been posited in legal propositions* (emphasis added).[73]

For Ehrlich, living law was not equipped with binding force on a dogmatic level like legal propositions in general, but nevertheless dominated life factually. Quite the contrary, Suehiro's living law was part of the legal order together with legal propositions. As he attributed to the living law binding force on a dogmatic level in the same way as legal propositions in general were binding, he also dogmatised Ehrlich's sociological concept of 'living law'.

Court Decisions as 'Living Law in the Courtroom'

Suehiro's living law also differed from Ehrlich's living law with regard to the appropriate method of gaining knowledge about it. Suehiro suggested primarily analysing cases decided by the courts:

> *Decisions of the courts* and articles in newspapers and journals are the only appropriate means of recognizing living law. The former is the basis for investigating in how and to which facts law is applied. The latter helps us to know how society is moving (emphasis added).[74]

---

[72] Above n 63, 342.
[73] Above n 8, 493.
[74] Above n 13, 4.

In Ehrlich's opinion, the social order itself had to be examined:

> For the Japanese, it will become an extraordinarily important task, not to content themselves with the cognizance of their law book, but to examine *the social order that constitutes the national background of their law book*: the organization of their family and of the other social groups, the landholding system, the contracts, hereditary succession. This research into living law will become extremely important for all fields of legal life (emphasis added).[75]

Whereas Suehiro regarded court decisions as 'living law in the courtroom',[76] Ehrlich's living law was living in all sectors of society, where it had to be examined by empirical methods of social research. Although Suehiro also referred to society in the form of newspapers and journals, this was only for the sake of understanding how society itself is moving, not for the living law as such. Ehrlich did not deny the possibility of gaining knowledge about living law by analysing court decisions, but he regarded this method as insufficient:

> Only a tiny bit of real life is brought before the courts and other tribunals ... The sociological method therefore demands absolutely that the results which are obtained from the judicial decisions be supplemented by direct observation of life.[77]

Therefore, Ehrlich's scope of research concerning living law, which was as such dogmatically irrelevant, was society as a whole. Suehiro limited his research to the 'living law in the court room', which, however, he regarded as dogmatically relevant.

Solving the Judge's Dilemma

The transformation of Ehrlich's sociological 'living law' to 'living law in the courtroom', with binding force on a dogmatic level, enabled Suehiro to adjust the dilemma of the Japanese judge. He found the substantive legal content that was lacking in the abstract framework of Western law in the judiciary itself, ie in the court decisions, which as 'living law in the courtroom' represented Japanese legal content for him. Consequently, he conceived legal decision-making as a form of law making and openly ascribed to the courts a law-making function, while downgrading the legislator to a provider of an abstract framework: he regarded the courts as 'creators of concrete legal propositions',[78] which filled the 'framework of the law' provided by the legislator with legal content.[79]

---

[75] 'Gesetz und lebendes Recht' in M Rehbinder (ed), above n 28, 236 ff.
[76] The term 'living law in the court room' (in German: *'lebendes Recht im Gerichtssaal'*) is used by Z Ishimura to characterise Suehiro's understanding of 'living law' (Z Ishimura, above n 63, 34 ff).
[77] Above n 8, 495.
[78] I Suehiro, 'Jo' in Minpô Hanrei Kenkyûkai (ed), *Hanrei Minpô I* (Tokyo, Yûhikaku, 1923) 6.
[79] Above n 78, 1 ff.

Suehiro's solution of the judge's dilemma attributed a crucial task to Japanese jurisprudence, namely to continually analyse court decisions in order to gain knowledge of this 'living law in the courtroom'. That is why Suehiro founded a 'Seminar for the Study of Civil Cases' (*Minji Hanrei Kenkyukai*) in 1921: to come to know factually the concrete legal propositions created by the courts.[80] It was not supposed to criticise court decisions from a dogmatic point of view, but to examine them objectively as facts, in order to find out how the judges decide under which constellation of facts.[81] This approach superficially seems to be in accordance with Ehrlich's claim to analyse court decisions as a result of various societal forces influencing the judge.[82] However, whereas Ehrlich attempted to achieve factual background knowledge about juristic law as a 'social phenomenon only', without normative-practical relevance,[83] Suehiro wanted to find practically relevant living law with binding force on a dogmatic level through his factual analysis. To avoid a 'dictatorship of the judges',[84] the judiciary was to be bound by 'reasonable' judgments only.[85] Suehiro thought that this 'reasonableness', ie the justice attained in a decision, could be found by a factual analysis and comparison of different constellations of cases.[86] This demonstrates his conviction that justice could be established scientifically. As will be shown below (in the sixth section), Ehrlich was convinced of the opposite, but nevertheless attributed an important function to sociology of law to achieve justice.

Summary: Dogmatised Sociological Theories Liberating the Judiciary from Statutory Law

By dogmatising Ehrlich's theory concerning 'norms of decision', Suehiro was able to bind the judiciary formally to the received Western law. By dogmatising Ehrlich's reception theory, he deprived the received Western law of any normative content, while upholding it as an abstract framework. The dogmatisation of Ehrlich's concept of 'living law' enabled Suehiro to let Japanese court decisions defined as 'living law in the courtroom' appear as the Japanese content of the received Western law. The problem that Japanese jurisprudence actually regards itself as arguing within a received continental civil law system binding the judiciary to objective law, which

---

[80] Above n 78, 6.
[81] *Ibid.*
[82] Above n 22, 78 ff.
[83] Cf 'Soziologie des Rechts' in M Rehbinder (ed), above n 28, 179.
[84] I Suehiro, *Usô no kôyô* (2nd edn, Tokyo, Nihon hyôronsha, 1981) 33.
[85] *Ibid.* The Japanese term Suehiro uses is *guttaiteki datôsei*, which could also be translated as 'concretely fitting'.
[86] I Suehiro, above n 84, 38.

explicitly does not encompass court decisions as source of law, is circumvented by declaring the received Western law as empty and upgrading the result of a merely factual analysis of court decisions without further evaluation and without taking into account existing legislative law, to a kind of objective law with binding force on a dogmatic level, by virtue of being 'living law'. As a result the judiciary achieved in Suehiro's system the status of a legislator. It must be stressed that Suehiro could achieve this result not by following Ehrlich's sociological theories and his sociological concept of living law as such, but by using them as doctrines in jurisprudence, a usage that was, as we have seen, explicitly excluded by Ehrlich.

Suehiro's approach is not only problematic from a methodological point of view, but also from the point of view of the democratic legitimacy of the judiciary. It allows the judge to follow statutory law formally, while deviating from it substantially, without democratic justification. Indeed, Ehrlich's sociology of law never gave the judge the freedom to deviate from statutory law:

> ... a judge who in the administration of law disregards a statute is guilty of gross violation of duty. Since it is the function of the sociological science of law, like that of every other science, to record facts, not to evaluate them, it cannot possibly as some have believed, tend to establish, at the present stage of human development, a doctrine which might lead the judge to violate his judicial oath.[87]

CONCEPT OF LAW IN *JURISTISCHE LOGIK*

Having highlighted how Ehrlich's sociological concept of law was misunderstood in the Japanese reception of his *Fundamental Principles*, the following sections will shift focus and examine Ehrlich's own account on the proper linking of sociology and jurisprudence. To this end, it becomes necessary to elucidate Ehrlich's dogmatic concept of law as presented in the *Juristische Logik*. This concept was developed through a critique of traditional methods of judicial decision-making and the role of juristic logic.

Ehrlich's Claim for an Alternative Method of Judicial Decision-Making

According to Ehrlich, the traditional subsumption method in jurisprudence, which relies on juristic logic to derive the solution of a case from the law,[88]

---

[87] Above n 8, 389.
[88] Above n 20, V.

was unable to bind the judge to the law.[89] The reason for this failure was the fact that it worked on a purely conceptual basis, without considering whether the interests behind the concepts of a legal proposition really matched the interests involved in a case to be decided. For Ehrlich, the treatment of conflicting interests was the core point of legal decision-making. Juristic logic, however, only made sure that the concretely conflicting interests could still be labelled by the wording of a legal proposition. Therefore, the judge could indeed deviate from the original will of the legislator if he or she found a concept in the legal proposition that could be extended on a linguistic basis to cover a case the legislator did not intend to encompass. Ehrlich characterised this procedure based on 'juristic logic' as a 'construction of legal concepts, not on a legal, but on a linguistic basis'.[90] In search of an alternative method, Ehrlich became one of the founding fathers of the German 'Free Law School'[91] long before he wrote his *Fundamental Principles*.[92] The aim of his alternative method was to bind the judge more effectively to the will of the legislator on the one hand and give him freedom of decision in case of a 'gap' in statutory law on the other hand. It is in this context that Ehrlich developed his dogmatic concept of law.

Dogmatic Definition of Law

From a scientific perspective, Ehrlich had criticised the 'practical concept of law' in continental jurisprudence as too narrow. However, in defining law as a dogmatic phenomenon, he confined its content even further than traditional jurisprudence, namely to the intention of the legislator. The legislator expresses his intentions regularly in 'legal propositions', dealing with various 'legal relations' by using 'legal concepts'. Ehrlich developed his dogmatic concept of law based on an analysis of the dogmatic functions of these three legal instruments used by the legislator.

Legal Propositions and Legal Concepts

Ehrlich regarded legal propositions as decisions of the legislator about a conflict of interests in general terms.[93] A legal proposition indicated which of two conflicting interests was to be regarded as the prevailing one and

---

[89] *Ibid* 299.
[90] *Ibid* 271.
[91] AS Foulkes, 'On the German Free Law School' (1969) LV/3 *Archiv für Rechts- und Sozialphilosophie* 376; and F Wieacker, *Privatrechtsgeschichte der Neuzeit* (2nd edn, Göttingen, Vandenhoek & Ruprecht, 1967), 579. M Rehbinder, above n 16, 87 ff.
[92] Cf *Freie Rechtsfindung und freie Rechtswissenschaft* (Leipzig, Hirschfeld, 1903).
[93] Above n 20, 186.

was therefore to be protected by the courts and authorities.[94] A norm that did not contain such a 'norm for decision' lacked the quality of a legal proposition:

> A legal norm that does not protect an interest against an attack is not a legal proposition, or at least no complete legal proposition.[95]

Therefore, a 'substantive legal proposition containing a norm for decision'[96] had to deal with the following points:

1. the interest worthy of protection,
2. the conditions indicating the circumstances, under which it is worthy of protection,
3. the attack, which is to be averted,
4. the kind and scope of legal protection.[97]

To comprehend the interests to be balanced and decided upon in a legal proposition, Ehrlich acknowledged the necessity of legal concepts.[98] Ideally, they should comprise all of the above-mentioned four components.[99] The concept of 'theft', for example, contained all four of them: the interest (a mobile thing), the conditions of legal protection (a special kind of possession), the attack (dispossession) and the means of legal protection (punishment).[100] As a matter of fact, Ehrlich appreciated legal concepts because they were necessary to comprehend interests worthy of protection. He did not oppose the so-called conceptual jurisprudence because it was orientated towards concepts, but rather because he deemed its concepts as being wrongly constructed:

> The mistake of the so called conceptual jurisprudence is not to deal with concepts, because without concepts there is neither a science, nor a practical application of scientific results. However the construction of its concepts is often misplaced.[101]

Therefore, it can already be stated here that all critics who ascribe to Ehrlich a general aversion to legal concepts[102] or a general incapability to grasp their normative meaning[103] are wrong.

---

[94] Ibid.
[95] Above n 20, 187.
[96] Ibid 188.
[97] Ibid.
[98] Ibid.
[99] Above n 20, 189.
[100] Ibid.
[101] Above n 20, 196 ff.
[102] M Weber, above n 6, 209; EW Patterson, 'Ehrlich, Eugen (1862–1922)' in *Encyclopaedia of the Social Sciences* V (1931) 446; O Behrends, 'Von der Freirechtsbewegung zum konkreten Ordnungs- und Gestaltungsdenken' in R Dreier and W Sellert (eds), *Recht und Justiz im "Dritten Reich"* (Frankfurt/M., Suhrkamp, 1989) 63.
[103] K Larenz, above n 19, 72 ff.

Legal Relations as Interests Protected by Law or Worthy of Protection by Law

Ehrlich defined legal relations as the object of legislative protection, ie the interests grasped by legal concepts, balanced and protected by the legislator against other interests in a legal proposition:

> For the purpose of exploring the nature of juristic logic it is advisable to unite the interest and the conditions of its protection in one concept and thus to contrast the concept of legal relations with the concept of attacks to be averted and the concept of means of protection.[104]

Therefore, a legal relation consisted of two of the above-mentioned four components of a legal proposition, namely of an interest worthy of protection and the conditions of its protection. This means that the concept of legal relation was, on the one hand, narrower than that of a legal proposition, because it only contained the object of balancing and protecting, and not yet the balancing and protecting of interests itself. On the other hand, it was wider because it could also contain mere social interests existing outside of legal propositions:

> A lot of social interests ... remain at least initially, some even permanently, outside of the law laid down in legal propositions.[105]

Nevertheless, they were legal relations for Ehrlich because he rejected to regard 'a legal relation as a relation governed by a law, meaning governed by legal propositions'.[106] Rather it was for him:

> ... a socially recognised relation that consequently *can expect* ... protection by the courts or by the authorities (emphasis added)'.[107]

Therefore, he regarded as a legal relation even a social relation that could only expect protection by the law, ie that was only worthy of protection by law. This means that he actually differentiated between legal relations in a narrow and a broad sense. In a narrow sense, they meant interests already balanced against and protected against concurring interests in a legal proposition. In a broad sense, they also encompassed interests that were only socially recognised and not yet balanced in a legal proposition, thus only worthy of protection by law. In the latter case, they were only potentially protected by law and thus existed without any corresponding legal proposition.

---

[104] Above n 20, 190.
[105] *Ibid* 184.
[106] *Ibid* 191.
[107] *Ibid*.

Interests Worthy of Protection by Law under the Principle of Freedom of Contract and Property

As a relation only worthy of protection by law, a legal relation was not yet law on a dogmatic level, but only an 'interest that struggled for its legal validity in a concrete case.'[108] It had gained the status of a socially recognised relation[109] in 'usages, forms of possession and declarations of will'.[110] Ehrlich marked these usages, forms of possession and declarations of will as the 'basis of legal relations',[111] which means that they represent an interface between the dogmatic concept of law of his *Juristische Logik* and the sociological concept of law, earlier developed in his *Fundamental Principles*. In the *Fundamental Principles*, they were marked as 'facts of law',[112] ie those social facts with which the 'human mind' associates rules,[113] and served as the starting point for his sociological input-output model of law (see second section above). Thus, the legal relations in a broad sense of the *Juristische Logik* appear identical to the 'rules of conduct' of societal law in *Fundamental Principles*, arising from the facts of law.

Based on a comprehensive sociological concept of law as developed in the *Fundamental Principles*, it appears legitimate to reckon with legal relations that are worthy of protection only because they are socially recognised. They were not defined as legal propositions and did not aspire to bind the judiciary. In his *Juristische Logik*, however, Ehrlich wanted to show that 'the methods of legal thinking', too, emerge from society on the one hand and have social effects on society on the other hand[114] as part of a comprehensive 'theory of judicial decision-making'.[115] In doing so, he intended to gain in addition a 'doctrine on knowledge in judicial jurisprudence'.[116] ('*Erkenntnislehre der richterlichen Jurisprudenz*'). Whereas a 'theory of judicial decision-making' would remain on a purely scientific level, Ehrlich's intended 'doctrine on knowledge in judicial jurisprudence' would clearly reach out to a dogmatic level, because this doctrine was supposed to 'teach the judiciary how to apply the law',[117] thus gaining immediate practical relevance. As far as the concept of 'legal relation' in his *Juristische Logik* is concerned, this means that as a 'legal relation in

---

[108] Above n 20, 192.
[109] *Ibid* 191.
[110] *Ibid* 184.
[111] *Ibid* 193.
[112] Above n 8, 83 ff.
[113] *Ibid* 85.
[114] Above n 20, V.
[115] *Ibid* 2.
[116] *Ibid*.
[117] *Ibid*.

a broad sense', ie as a relation legally not yet protected, but only worthy of protection, it was not definable as a legal relation simply because of its social recognition; it would have to prove its legal character specifically from a dogmatic point of view. Therefore, if Ehrlich was to avoid merely transferring his sociological concept of law, namely his societal law as an 'interest worthy of protection by law', on a dogmatic level, which would have meant a problematic conclusion from a socially recognised *Sollen* to a legal *Sollen*,[118] specific dogmatic reasons were necessary to concede a 'legal' character to his 'legal relation in a broad sense' so as to be able to regard these socially recognised interests as also legally worthy of protection on a dogmatic level.

It was the underlying principle of all the continental civil law codes in general, and of the new German *BGB* from 1900 in particular, namely the principle of freedom of contract and property, which provided Ehrlich with the dogmatic justification to qualify socially recognised relations as legal relations. In his *Fundamental Principles*, he explained how societal law fits into the framework of freedom of contract,[119] and in his *Juristische Logik* he marked contractual agreements as one of the possible 'conditions under which legal protection for various interests develops':[120]

> Basically every new agreement, when it appears for the first time, creates a new kind of legal relation, for which a legal proposition cannot yet exist.[121]

By activating the principle of freedom of contract and property as a kind of source of law, Ehrlich only drew the dogmatic consequences from the historic development of Western law 'from status to contract'.[122] As it was acknowledged as a principle of law by the civil law codes, the principle of freedom of contract and property required in his view the recognition of social (societal) interests as legal relations on a dogmatic level, even if no specifically protective legal propositions existed. However, the legal quality of legal relations in a broad sense under the dogmatic conditions set by the principle of freedom of contract and property was limited:

> The existing legal institutions in a society form a legal order, no matter whether they are governed by legal propositions or not. They are dependent on legal propositions, especially from laws, only insofar as they (legal propositions) can determine, how they are to be assessed by the judge, specifically whether the judge has to provide protection to conflicting interests possibly contained in them.[123]

---

[118] Not a conclusion from *Sein* to *Sollen*, as often maintained by his critics.
[119] Above n 8, 401.
[120] Above n 20, 4.
[121] *Ibid* 184 ff.
[122] Cf *Die Rechtsfähigkeit*, reprint of the original edition 1909 (Aalen, Scientia, 1973) 60, where he refers to Henry Sumner Maine's *Ancient Law* (London, 1861).
[123] Above n 20, 219.

Therefore, the function of the principle of freedom of contract and property as a source of law was limited, because legal relations based exclusively on this principle could claim legal protection only in so far as they were not yet balanced against other interests by the legislator in a legal proposition. Only under these circumstances could the judge decide whether to grant legal protection in a concrete case. Neither the interests worthy of protection by law nor the judge's decision, ie from a sociological point of view the 'norm for decision' he created, were ever conceived by Ehrlich as objective law on a dogmatic level. Even the judicial decision to protect a certain interest was only a socially influential 'proposal of a jurist', which had to be confirmed further in the ongoing 'fight of opinions'.[124]

Summary: Dogmatic Concept of Law

Ehrlich's concept of law, as developed in his *Juristische Logik*, did not transfer his whole sociological typology of law automatically onto a dogmatic level. It only allowed the attribution of legal quality on a dogmatic level to 'societal law' as a 'legal relation in a broad sense' under the condition of the dogmatically acknowledged principle of freedom of contract and property. Therefore, it was a legitimate dogmatic concept of law, which provided, however, for an interface to his sociological concept of law.

EHRLICH'S LINKING OF SOCIOLOGY AND JURISPRUDENCE

By upgrading potentially all social relations to legal relations at least worthy of protection by law under the principle of freedom of contract and property, gaps in law became dogmatically relevant because they could contain legal relations. Consequently, gaps could no longer be ignored as a non-legal phenomenon or be filled in by interpreting and applying legal propositions that did not indeed balance and decide on the specific interests conflicting in the gaps. Through this new evaluation of gaps in law on a dogmatic level, judicial decision-making had to change its character not only in case of a gap in law, but also in case of existing legal propositions. Depending on whether an interest was already protected by the legislator in a legal proposition or was only worthy of protection in a gap, legal decision-making had to apply different strategies. It is in this context that Ehrlich linked sociology and jurisprudence, however, neither by transferring his sociological concept of law onto a dogmatic level, nor by having interfere sociology of law with judicial decision-making directly.

---

[124] 'Soziologie und Jurisprudenz' in M Rehbinder (ed), above n 28, 189.

Ehrlich's Alternative Method of Judicial Decision-making

Judicial Decision-making as the Implementation of the Legislator's Balancing of Conflicting Interests

According to Ehrlich, as long as a decision of the legislator to protect a specific interest existed in a legal proposition, the judiciary had to stick to the proposition. This is because the decision of a case by the judiciary had to legitimate itself as a 'judicial balancing of interests subject to the orders of a legal proposition'.[125] On this point, Ehrlich seems to be rather conventional. However, his legal concepts played a different role from that played by legal concepts in the traditional subsumption method. They were not used for subsuming facts, but for comprehending, comparing and protecting interests by the judge.[126] According to Ehrlich's method, like a legislator taking up an interest worthy of protection and including it in a legal proposition, judges had to comprehend conflicting interests—not, however, in order to decide about their protection in a legal proposition, but in order to realise the legislator's balancing of interests in their judgment.

For this purpose, a comparison was necessary. Once the judge had comprehended the conflicting interests in a case, he or she had to compare them, in a second step, with the interests comprehended, balanced and decided on by the legislator in a legal provision[127] in order to make sure 'that the interest that claimed to be protected in the case was not different from the one balanced and decided upon in the legal proposition'.[128] In a third step, after being comprehended, compared and assessed as similar with the interest contained in a legal proposition, the interest involved in a case could be protected by the judge, according to the protection provided for it in the legal proposition.[129] In this process, the concepts gained by the judge in comprehending the interests involved in the case had to be compatible with the concepts used by the legislator to comprehend the interests protected in the legal proposition.[130] Therefore, in every phase Ehrlich's method of judicial decision-making as a realisation of the legislator's decision on conflicting interests required precise legal concepts, because without them a comprehension, comparison or derivation of the protection provided in a legal proposition was not thinkable. This means that characterising the 'judicial freedom of decision' advocated by Ehrlich, as an 'intuitive method of legal decision-making',[131] does not capture

---

[125] Above n 20, 191.
[126] *Ibid* 192.
[127] *Ibid* 191.
[128] *Ibid* 192.
[129] *Ibid.*
[130] *Ibid.*
[131] EW Patterson, above n 102, 446; and O Behrends, above n 102, 50.

his alternative method. Far from being intuitive, it was to guarantee an empirically controllable realisation of the legislator's balancing of interests and rule out arbitrary decisions by the judiciary. That is why he emphasised that his method:

> ... does not mean that the judge is entitled to interpret the legal proposition according to his own interests of expediency: this doctrine which is often advocated nowadays is *absolutely reprehensible*. As long as the judge interprets the legal proposition he has to refer to the interests of expediency of its creator not to his own interests of expediency (emphasis added).[132]

The support of sociology of law became necessary to determine the specific content and range of the legislator's decision on conflicting interests contained in a legal proposition of statutory law and to ensure the empirically controllable realisation of his balancing of interests. This was one of the functions that sociology of law had to fulfil for jurisprudence. Before dealing with it in detail, the other field of judicial decision-making, namely the substitute balancing of interests not yet balanced by the legislator, where the support of sociology of law also became necessary, shall be addressed.

Judicial Decision-making as a Substitute Balancing of Conflicting Interests not yet Balanced by the Legislator

According to Ehrlich, constantly arising new conflicts of interest under the condition of freedom of contract and property actually required an equally constant promulgation of legal propositions,[133] but balancing and deciding all potential conflicts of interest in advance was impossible for a legislator.[134] Of course, a large number of unbalanced and legally unprotected interests that were worthy of protection by law under the principle of freedom of contract and property remained outside of legal propositions. And yet, under the principle of prohibition of denial of justice, the judge had to decide these cases nevertheless, although the decision could not be legitimated as a 'judicial balancing of interests subject to the orders of a legal proposition'.[135] In these cases of a 'gap' in law, the judge could not do otherwise than to decide freely, ie by:

> ... balancing independently the conflicting interests and granting the protection of the courts to the interest he deems as the higher one.[136]

---

[132] 'Die richterliche Rechtsfindung auf Grund des Rechtssatzes. Vier Stücke aus dem in Vorbereitung begriffenen Werke: Theorie der richterlichen Rechtsfindung' in M Rehbinder (ed), *Ehrlich, Eugen, Recht und Leben* (Berlin, Duncker & Humblot, 1967) 226.
[133] Above n 20, 214 ff.
[134] *Ibid* 192.
[135] *Ibid* 191.
[136] 'Die richterliche Rechtsfindung auf Grund des Rechtssatzes' in M Rehbinder (ed), above n 132, 223.

It should be noted that Ehrlich defined gaps in law not depending on the wording of a law, but on whether or not the conflicting interests of a case had already been balanced by the legislator.[137] The key issue was not the range of the meaning of a word, but the range of protection an interest enjoyed in a legal proposition. Therefore, in order to determine the existence and range of a gap, finding out whether and how far the legislator intended to protect an interest against competing interests became crucial. For this purpose, empirical knowledge was needed. It was to be used within the historical rule, which Ehrlich regarded as the only scientific method of interpretation.[138] The task of the historical rule was to find out empirically the decision of the latest historical legislator and not to harmonise a legal proposition with its historical or sociological, factual or normative background:

> What got into the legal proposition from the environment it came from, from the law book it is a part of, from the remaining legal order that surrounds it, is only what was part of the consciousness of the legislator when he created the legal proposition. It is this content of the consciousness of the legislator the interpreter has to clarify, nothing more; if he went further he would not interpret the meaning of the law any more, but give another meaning to it.[139]

By restricting interpretation strictly on a historic-empirically verifiable balancing of interests by the legislator, Ehrlich enlarged the field of unbalanced, or even if balanced, not scientifically verifiable balanced conflicting interests. The possibility of gaps in the law was further enhanced due to the relatively marginal role played by the wording of the law in Ehrlich's approach. The scientifically established will of the legislator was to prevail over the mere words of the law:

> If we find the same word in different places in a law or even in different laws, we are not allowed, like the old jurists, simply to assume, that it always has the same meaning: this would only be justified if the legislator, in every single case really had thought about all the other cases, too.[140]

As a consequence, the range of application of law became considerably limited because the judge had to balance the conflicting interests in a concrete case independently, even if the wording of a law as such covered the conflicting interests, but was not supported by a historic-empirically verifiable balancing of similar conflicting interests. This means that the wording of a law covering a case could no longer exclude the existence of a gap. Hence the traditional juristic subsumption method was no longer applicable.

---

[137] Above n 20, 216.
[138] Above n 20, 137; 'Die richterliche Rechtsfindung auf Grund des Rechtssatzes' in M Rehbinder (ed), above n 132, 222.
[139] Above n 20, 138.
[140] *Ibid* 139.

Instead, Ehrlich offered his new method of balancing interests, also called 'judicial freedom of decision',[141] which—similar to the implementation of the legislator's balancing of interests—was to profit from the support of sociology of law.

The Role of Sociology for Jurisprudence

As in Ehrlich's alternative method of judicial decision-making, rather than knowing the exact linguistic range of concepts, knowing the underlying conflicting interests was important. It is manifest that sociology in general and sociology of law in particular would be central sciences to provide this knowledge. Ehrlich intended to make use of them not only for the sake of the judiciary, but also for the sake of legislation.

Sociology as a Scientific Basis for Legislation

Contrary to a common misunderstanding,[142] Ehrlich's attitude towards legislation was far from hostile. His aim was not to minimise legislation, but to establish a scientific basis for it. Unsatisfied with the naive view that 'all that is necessary in order to abolish an existing evil is to forbid it',[143] he advocated 'an art of legislation resting on a scientific foundation'.[144] This art of legislation was to show 'what can be effected and promoted by the means which the state has at its disposal'.[145] Its scientific foundation was supposed to be sociology.[146]

This does not contradict his definition of sociology of law as a pure science of law[147] if one takes into account that this pure science was supposed to be only the scientific foundation and not yet legal policy itself. He made it sufficiently clear that the theoretical knowledge of sociology gained by empirical methods as such could not yet produce a political or legal doctrine. The theoretical knowledge of sociology still had to be transformed into legislation. The necessity of this transformation process means that although legislation should rely on the factual knowledge of sociology, its knowledge could not be applied automatically as legal policy without evaluating it first. So Ehrlich's own sociological perception of the relation between law created by the state and law created by society as

---

[141] See above n 22.
[142] N Luhmann, above n 7, 24.
[143] Above n 8, 411.
[144] Ibid.
[145] Above n 8, 410.
[146] 'Soziologie des Rechts' in M Rehbinder(ed), above n 28, 194.
[147] Ibid 179.

described in his *Fundamental Principles* could not yet determine the legal policy that was to be applied based on this scientific finding. That is why it is no contradiction that on a sociological level he found out a relative weakness of law created by the state,[148] but nevertheless, far from advocating legislative restraint, called for further legislative efforts to resolve social problems.[149]

Sociology as a Scientific Basis for Judicial Decision-making

As for judicial decision-making, sociology had to fulfil an important function in comprehending the legislator's decision on interests. A scientifically precise comprehension of the legislator's decision on interests was a pre-condition for deciding cases according to the intentions of the legislator. In order to establish the legislator's decision on interests underlying the wording of the law, the judge needed historic-empirically reliable facts. Here, sociology in general and sociology of law in particular assumed the form of a historic-empirical science, focusing exclusively on gaining knowledge about the legislator's decision on interests as a historical fact under certain social circumstances.

In case of a gap, sociology of law was to provide the judge with sufficient empirical knowledge about the conflicting interests worthy of protection by law, including their normative background in society. The purpose of knowing social facts as well as norms, however, was not to realise them in the case of a gap, but to provide the judge with comprehensive factual knowledge, for the free balancing of interests.[150] That is why Ehrlich criticised the frequent misuse of commercial customs in the legal field[151] and attributed the task of opposing 'bad' customs to the legislature as well as to the judiciary, while at the same time stressing that for this purpose 'it is necessary first of all to know the custom'.[152] He demanded from jurisprudence that it withstood the temptation to deal with new conflicts of interest simply by referring to legal propositions or social norms that according to their wording seemed to encompass them, but in reality were not supported by a balancing of the interests in question. Beyond the border of the actual reach of the legislator's balancing of interests, an independent, free

---

[148] Above n 8, 375.
[149] 'Sociale Gesetzgebungspolitik auf dem Gebiet des Deutschen Privatrechts' (1890) 5 *Unsere Zeit* 449 ff; 'Die sociale Frage im Privatrechte' in M Rehbinder (ed), above n 28, 24, 27, 30 and 42; 'Von der Zukunft des Völkerbundes' (1919) 21 *Die Friedens-Warte* 37; 'Die Valutaschwierigkeiten der Schweiz' (1920) 26 *Schweizerische Zeitschrift für Volkswirtschaft und Sozialpolitik* 325; and 'Die "bewährte Lehre und Überlieferung" (Art. 1 ZGB)' (1919/20) 16 *Schweizerische Juristen-Zeitung* 226.
[150] Above n 22, 80.
[151] *Das zwingende und nichtzwingende Recht im Bürgerlichen Gesetzbuch für das Deutsche Reich*, reprint of the original edition 1899 (Aalen, Scientia, 1970) 96 ff.
[152] Above n 22, 80.

balancing of the involved interests by the judicature instead of the missing legislator's balancing became necessary. This free balancing was to be based on justice[153] and not by drawing on social norms. Ehrlich was aware of the fact that the judge who uncritically relied on social norms only favoured certain powerful interests in society.[154]

CONCLUSIONS

Ehrlich's idea of a science-based 'art of legislation'[155] as well as his alternative method of judicial decision-making required a linking of sociology and jurisprudence. Designed to deliver the necessary, scientifically established information about reality for legislation and judicial decision-making, sociology of law implicitly gained an important function for the formation of legal concepts.

Scientific Formation of Legal Concepts by Sociology of Law

As indicated above (see fourth section), Ehrlich did not oppose the so-called conceptual jurisprudence because it was orientated towards concepts, but because he deemed its concepts as being wrongly constructed.[156] In his assessment, jurisprudence failed to fulfil the central task of comprehending social interests because the jurisprudential methods of gaining factual knowledge were pre-scientific and guided by jurisprudential needs. Its concepts were constructed mainly to facilitate the judge's decision-making based on the traditional method of subsuming facts under legal propositions, and tended to miss the interests involved in the facts. Legal concepts reflecting the knowledge gained by sociology of law through modern scientific methods of social research promised to capture not only facts, but also the interests involved. Applying these legal concepts created by sociology of law would prevent jurisprudence from missing the interests. Hence, the scientific formation of legal concepts by sociology of law seemed to Ehrlich more appropriate under the aspect of justice, because the object that was to be treated according to justice, namely the conflicting interests, would not be sacrificed to other purposes.

This change from juristic to scientific formation of concepts, as far as the comprehension of social interests was concerned, implied an institutional

---

[153] Above n 20, 309.
[154] Cf 'Die richterliche Rechtsfindung auf Grund des Rechtssatzes' in M Rehbinder (ed), above n 132, 241 ff.
[155] Above n 8, 411.
[156] Above n 20, 196 ff.

separation of the evaluative tasks of jurisprudence from the fact-comprehending tasks of sociology of law. Sociology of law could, however, build on some rudimentary scientific content of jurisprudence. According to Ehrlich, this rudimentary scientific content was to be split off from jurisprudence in order to become the very starting point of sociology of law, which in turn would enable jurisprudence to concentrate on its genuine evaluative tasks: 'by conceding its sociological-scientific content to sociology of law, it conquers anew its own original field'.[157]

Sociology of Law as a Replacement of Jurisprudence on a Theoretical Level

Although the evaluative task of balancing interests was to remain entirely within the realm of jurisprudence, conceding the formation of legal concepts concerning social reality to sociology of law also meant conceding some indirect preliminary influence on this balancing.

The scientific concepts of sociology of law were to shape perception and comprehension of social interests by the legislator as well as by the judiciary. Through this considerable 'power of definition', sociology of law would determine the factual area of operation of jurisprudence. In its 'anew-conquered' field, jurisprudence could no longer act with its own concepts tailored to its practical needs, but with concepts provided by the sociology of law tailored to comprehend social interests as precise and extensive as possible. Therefore, sociology of law was indeed to replace jurisprudence—on a *theoretical* and not on a *dogmatic* level, however. It was to provide a conceptual framework enabling jurisprudence to deal with reality on a scientifically established factual basis, but not to interfere on a dogmatic level with jurisprudence's evaluative task of balancing interests.

Justice as a Joint Enterprise of Sociology of Law and Jurisprudence

A jurisprudence using concepts created by sociology of law would not necessarily work more smoothly, but nevertheless improve the achievement of justice. It meant creating justice in a 'joint enterprise' of sociology and jurisprudence, which was not only to provide the judiciary with a better factual basis for its decisions, but also to guarantee a judicial decision-making orientated stricter to the will of the legislator.

In this joint enterprise, the scientifically established knowledge and analysis of facts provided by sociology of law functioned as an indispensable

---

[157] 'Soziologie und Jurisprudenz' in M Rehbinder (ed), above n 28, 103.

prerequisite of justice, but not yet as justice itself. As mentioned above (in the third section), this was the tendency in the Japanese approach to regard 'living law' as law on a dogmatic level and to establish its 'reasonableness' by a factual analysis and comparison of different constellations of cases.[158] Ehrlich's understanding of what a 'legal science in the proper sense of the term' can achieve for the sake of justice was more modest:

> Science can be concerned only with those things that are susceptible of scientific demonstration. That a certain thing is just is no more scientifically demonstrable than is the beauty of a Gothic cathedral or of a Beethoven symphony to a person who is insensible to it. ... But although science can teach us nothing concerning the ends, once the end is determined, it can enlighten us to the means to that end. ... Practical juristic science [*Jurisprudenz*] is concerned with the manner in which the ends may be attained that men are endeavouring to attain through law, but it must utilize the results of the sociology of law for this purpose.[159]

Therefore, although Ehrlich neither intended to replace jurisprudence with sociology of law on a dogmatic level nor to establish justice by means of social science, his more modest aim of conceding to sociology of law a say in the making of legal concepts was nevertheless revolutionary for jurisprudence: it meant to compel jurisprudence to deal with social reality as it is and not as a construction subject to jurisprudential needs.

---

[158] I Suehiro, above n 84, 38.
[159] Above n 8, 202. The English term 'practical juristic science' is misleading in this context, because Ehrlich did not regard *Jurisprudenz* as a science at all, but as one of the *praktischen Kunstlehren* (*Grundlegung der Soziologie des Rechts* (3rd edn, Berlin, Duncker & Humblot, 1967) 163), ie part of 'practical technical rules' (above n 8, 202).

Part III

Ehrlich and his Contemporaries

6
Facts and Norms: The Unfinished Debate between Eugen Ehrlich and Hans Kelsen

BART VAN KLINK[1]

THE LAW: DEAD OR ALIVE

Throughout his entire work, Eugen Ehrlich contested what he called the 'vulgar, state-centered conception of law'.[2] In Ehrlich's view, this conception of law could only recognise law produced or sanctioned by the state—'state law' for short—or simply statute law. In this conception of law, the basic legal norms which order society are set by the legislature: the role of the judiciary is limited to applying these norms to individual cases in accordance with the original intent of the legislature. In the (supposedly) rare case when the existing law is unclear or silent, a judge may turn to social norms and give them recognition as customary law which is otherwise non-existent in law. According to this conception, which Ehrlich thought to be especially widespread in the German jurisprudence of his time, law is an instrument in the hands of the state, not of the people. Essentially, it consists of commands to other legal authorities to apply certain prescribed sanctions, in case of non-compliance.

For Ehrlich, the story of the law does not end with the state and its officials, nor does it begin with them. One of the main reasons that it does not end with the state is precisely *because*—according to him—it does not

---

[1] This chapterer is dedicated to the memory of Hildegard Penn, who sadly passed away during its production and was therefore not able to correct the language in her splendid and merciless way. I would like to thank Francesca Dominello and Hans Lindahl for their comments and editorial assistance in the writing of this chapter. I would also like to thank the participants in the Ehrlich workshop, 4–5 May 2006 in Oñati, in particular Salif Nimaga and Stefan Vogl, for their useful comments on an earlier version of the chapter. Final responsibility for the content of this chapter, however, remains with the author.

[2] In the original phrasing: 'die vulgäre staatliche Rechtsauffassung'. Cf E Ehrlich, *Die juristische Logik* (Aalen, Scientia Verlag, 1996, reprint of the second edition from 1925, my translation) 82.

begin there. In *Fundamental Principles of the Sociology of Law*, Ehrlich identified three types or sources of law.[3,4] The first two types of law are still related closely to the state and are, therefore, generally recognised as such, also by adherents of the 'vulgar' conception of law: first, state or public law, set down in statutes; and, secondly, the 'juristic' law developed by judges and legal scholars. Public law in the broad sense consists, on the one hand, of legal norms that constitute the state and its institutions (public law in the narrow sense, including administrative law) and, on the other hand, of legal propositions that contain general provisions (including penal law and procedural law), which aim to protect public law in the narrow sense and 'private' law, ie norms developed in society. On the basis of these general provisions (if available), judges and jurists devise, at a more concrete level, legal norms for decision-making upon which judges rely to resolve conflicts in society.

More important to Ehrlich and also far more controversial was the third source of law that he claimed existed independently of the two aforementioned types of public, state-centered, law: the so-called 'facts of the law'. In his view, the main function of law is to create order in and between associations within society. It does so by providing norms by which people can regulate and coordinate their actions, mostly without the interference of state officials. Moreover, in most cases these order-creating norms are not produced by the state, but flow from the institutions and structures of which the people are a part. Ehrlich referred to these norms as the 'facts of the law'. In other words, facts of the law are social relationships that are also legal relationships. As such, they are a source of social order.[5] Ehrlich calls them facts because their existence can be established by observing actual practices in society. These facts of the law can be classified into four categories: custom or usage; relations of domination and subjection; relations of possession; and declarations of will. According to Ehrlich, the norms contained in these facts of the law have a far greater impact on people's lives, quantitatively as well as qualitatively speaking, than the norms laid down by the state and judicial law. Here is where living law resides, the law made and maintained by the people themselves. By contrast, 'official' law would always run the risk of becoming a mere dead letter by losing touch with the society in which it operates. In a later, if not his very last, publication, Ehrlich compared the attempt to capture the diversity of life in legal propositions to the futile effort to entrap a stream in a pond: 'whatever

---

[3] E Ehrlich, *Fundamental Principles of the Sociology of Law* (New York, Arno Press, 1975, reprint of the 1936 edition), see especially chs V–VIII.

[4] Whenever I think it more useful, I will quote from the German edition: *Grundlegung der Soziologie des Rechts* (Berlin, Duncker & Humblot, 1967, originally published in 1913).

[5] M Rehbinder, *Die Begründung der Rechtssoziologie durch Eugen Ehrlich* (Berlin, Duncker & Humblot, 1967) 32.

comes in, is no longer a living stream, but dead water, and much fails to enter into the pond'.[6]

This blatant attack on the contemporary positivist thought (vulgar or not) prevalent at that time could and would not remain unanswered. It fell to Hans Kelsen, a young and promising legal scholar, to take up the challenge. In 1915, two years after its first edition, Kelsen published a highly critical review of Ehrlich's *Fundamental Principles*.[7] Basically, Kelsen argued that Ehrlich had confused facts and norms in his conception of law—a distinction that would later become the cornerstone of his *Pure Theory of Law*.[8] The main purpose of this chapter is to evaluate the feasibility of Ehrlich's conception of law and its underlying scientific and political objectives in the light of Kelsen's critique thereof. What remains of Ehrlich's work after these 'onslaughts', which were, according to Klaus Lüderssen,[9] not only devastating for Ehrlich personally, but also for the new discipline of the sociology of law in general? To begin, I will identify and discuss the central arguments underlying Kelsen's critique (second section below). As Ehrlich never fully responded to this critique, I will offer three alternate lines of defence: the first based in pragmatism; the second, in natural law theory; and the third, in legal positivism (third section below). Of the three, I will argue that legal positivism provides the strongest framework to sustain Ehrlich's conception of law (fourth section below). Thus, I conclude that Ehrlich's work should not be completely abandoned. Some sacrifices need to be made, but there are aspects of his work that could still be salvaged and developed further.

KELSEN'S CRITIQUE

According to Kelsen, the phenomenon of law can be approached from two different perspectives. On the one hand, the law can be conceived of as a norm, that is, a rule that articulates a specific kind of 'ought': something *ought* or ought not to be done. On the other hand, the law may be taken as a part of social reality, as a fact or regular occurrence. Here, the law takes the form of an 'is' proposition with respect to human behaviour: an action

---

[6] E Ehrlich, 'Die Soziologie des Rechts' (originally published in 1922) in *Gesetz und lebendes Recht. Vermischte kleinere Schriften* (Berlin, Duncker & Humblot, 1986) 243 (my translation).

[7] H Kelsen, 'Eine Grundlegung der Rechtssoziologie' in H Kelsen and E Ehrlich., *Rechtssoziologie und Rechtswissenschaft. Eine Kontroverse (1915/1917)* (Baden-Baden, Nomos Verlagsgesellschaft, 2003).

[8] The first edition of his *Reine Rechtslehre* was published in 1934 and translated in H Kelsen, *Introduction to the Problems of Legal Theory. A Translation of the First Edition of the* Reine Rechtslehre *or Pure Theory of Law* (Oxford, Clarendon Press, 1992).

[9] K Lüderssen, 'Einführung' in H Kelsen and E Ehrlich, *Rechtssoziologie und Rechtswissenschaft*, above n 7, ix. Rottleuthner confirms that this debate was 'to a certain extent' disastrous for the development of the discipline. Cf H Rottleuthner, *Rechtstheorie und Rechtssoziologie* (Freiburg & München, Verlag Karl Alber, 1981) 31.

is or is not done on a regular basis. These two perspectives correspond with two different legal disciplines, respectively, a *normative* science of law that determines deductively which rules are valid, and an *explanatory* sociology of law that establishes inductively a certain regularity for which it tries to find a causal explanation. Thus, the science of law is a normative and deductive science of value, like ethics and logics, whereas the sociology of law, like other branches of sociology, is a science of reality, and conforms more generally to the methodological practices of the natural sciences. It is equally possible and legitimate to study law from both perspectives, but not at the same time. An object cannot be construed as something that is done or happens regularly and that ought to be done or happen simultaneously. Biology, as an explanatory science, may establish a causal link between two factual occurrences (for example, between firing a gun and someone's death), but is not capable of evaluating this link in terms of good/bad or legal/illegal. Conversely, ethics and the science of law, as normative sciences, may dismiss a certain action (for example, killing someone by firing a gun) as evil, if it violates an ethical norm, or illegal, if it violates a legal norm; however, they are unable to explain this action. In Kelsen's view, a combination of both perspectives is 'inadmissible' and would lead to 'methodological syncretism'.[10]

Kelsen criticises Ehrlich for trying to combine what he considers to be incompatible perspectives. Ehrlich seems to waver between an *empirical* conception of law, in which law is a fact, an observable regularity that is subject to the laws of causality, on the one hand, and a *normative* conception of law, in which law is a norm that evades empirical observation and causal explanation, on the other.[11] At the start of his exposé, Ehrlich writes:

> Now it is true that a rule of conduct is not only a rule according to which men customarily regulate their conduct, but also a rule according to which they ought to do so ...[12]

As if stung by a bee, Kelsen reacts: 'Evidently, this sentence is wrong!'[13] According to Kelsen, a rule that contains a causal explanation on the factual level does not give any clue on the normative level about what ought to be done. Of course, there may be norms that prescribe a certain behaviour that has established itself during a long period of time. However, norms like these, in which customary law is embedded, contain prescriptions, not explanations, for specified kinds of behaviour. From the fact that something used to be done, it does not follow logically that this ought to be done. That

---

[10] H Kelsen, H, above n 7, 5.
[11] This corresponds to the internal/external distinction in Hart's theory of law. See HLA Hart, *The Concept of Law* (2nd edn, Oxford, Clarendon Press, 1994) 88–9.
[12] E Ehrlich, above n 3, 11.
[13] H Kelsen, above n 7, 9.

presupposes a (legal, ethical, logical or other) norm, which states that you ought to do what you used to do. Furthermore, vice versa, from 'ought' propositions no 'is' propositions can be deduced. The normative and the factual only coincide in divine power because, for those who believe, He wants the good to be and evil not to be.[14]

When describing the internal order of associations in the course of history, Ehrlich constantly and inconsistently mixes factual observations about law with normative statements about what the law ought to be. If, according to Kelsen, he had stuck to a strictly sociological, empirical and explanatory approach, Ehrlich would have conceptualised the internal order of an association (for example, a family) as a collection of 'is' rules, that is, factual regularities in the behaviour of its members. However, he also made claims about the validity of the rules applied by the members of an association. In that case, the internal order is constituted not by 'is' rules, but by 'ought' rules, which prescribe what counts as legal and illegal behaviour. Ehrlich claimed, for example, that the legal institution of marriage existed in ancient times, although legal propositions formalising marriages were lacking. There were no general legal prescripts promulgated by the state; only contract law applied. In other words, valid marriages could be 'contracted' in the absence of 'official' law. According to Kelsen, this is a normative claim that presupposes a legal point of view. A vow between two persons can only constitute a contract with legal consequences if one at least takes for granted that the legal proposition according to which declarations of will of this kind—not only in one particular case, but in general—ought to be legally binding. 'Otherwise', Kelsen asks rhetorically, 'how can one speak of right and duty?'[15]

Ehrlich, however, denies that legal relationships and legal transactions presuppose the existence of legal propositions. He finds evidence for this claim in history: the concrete establishment of a legal institution has always preceded its abstract regulation: for example, the state was prior to the state's constitution, the family to family law, binding agreements to contract law, and so on. Kelsen dismantles this argument as a 'primitive confusion of temporal and logical relation'.[16] Logically, not temporarily, it must be presupposed that a legal norm precedes a certain state of affairs if these facts require a legal meaning. A fact in itself cannot create a norm. For example, the sheer expression of a last will—such as, 'After my death, my ashes should be spread out over the moon'—does not imply automatically that this will ought to be honoured legally. A legal norm specifies under which conditions a last will is legally valid. Therefore, the norm precedes logically

---

[14] H Kelsen, *Allgemeine Theorie der Normen* (Wien, Manzsche Verlags- und Universitätsbuchhandlung, 1979) 5.
[15] H Kelsen, above n 7, 14.
[16] H Kelsen, above n 7, 16.

the facts to which it applies and which may be prior to it in time. What is at stake here is the epistemological ground of an 'ought' proposition, not the empirical question of causation.[17]

At one point, Ehrlich does distinguish legal propositions from legal norms. The legal proposition is 'the arbitrary universally binding expression of a legal prescript in a statute or a law book', whereas the legal norm is defined as 'the legal command put into practise', applicable in a particular, possibly very small, association. This legal command need not be in writing.[18] As soon as legal propositions have actually been put into practice in an association of people, legal norms will follow from them. However, Ehrlich adds:

> ... in every society there is a much greater number of legal norms than of legal propositions; for there is always much more law that is applicable to individual cases than is applicable to all relations of a similar kind ...[19]

To Kelsen, this does not make any sense at all. Like any rule, legal norms have to be general in character, that is, applicable to more than one case. In the absence of the Aristotelian requirement, 'treat like case alike', rules would be unthinkable. Furthermore, legal norms do not have to be written down (in statutes, or elsewhere) in order to constitute valid law. This holds for ancient law no less than for contemporary law, contrary to what Ehrlich seems to suggest.

Ehrlich's concept of 'facts of the law' suffers from the same methodological confusion. A fact—be it a usage, a relation of domination or possession, or a declaration of will—can never constitute law or a legal relation because this fact, postulated as something that *is*, is in itself value-indifferent. A fact only acquires an objective value if confronted with a norm: it is judged to be good or evil, legal or illegal, beautiful or ugly, and so on. Kelsen argues, however, that usage actually is the only fact of the law. 'Usage' means that a fact is repeated on a regular basis; it is an 'is' rule. Facts, such a declaration of will or a relation of domination, can only become a fact of the law by repetition, that is, by means of a usage. This is only possible under the pre-condition of an 'ought' rule that prescribes that something that used to be done, has to be done. Following this rule, certain facts become legally relevant, that is, facts of the law. In itself, usage is not a fact of the law. Ehrlich's 'facts of the law' are, according to Kelsen, nothing but the possible content or object of legal (or other kinds of social) regulation.

Moreover, Kelsen accuses Ehrlich of failing to explain why the facts he mentions are facts *of the law*. In which respects do the norms that flow from

---

[17] Rottleuthner fully misrepresents Kelsen when he ascribes to Kelsen an *ontological* conception of valdity (see H Rottleuthner, above n 9, 38). For Kelsen, legal validity is not so much a question of ontology, but, as stated above, of epistemology.

[18] E Ehrlich, above n 3, 38. I have corrected the translation when it appears inaccurate or even plainly wrong (eg the German word *zufällig* does not mean 'precise', but 'arbitrary').

[19] *Ibid.*

these facts differ from ethical, moral, religious or other norms? Ehrlich's suggestion that legal norms can be distinguished from other norms by the feelings they evoke,[20] the *opinio necessitatis* that accompanies them, and the importance of their content matter, are not taken seriously by Kelsen. As long as Ehrlich deliberately refrains from referring to the state in defining law, his concept of law would remain boundless and indistinguishable from that of a social norm or a rule in general. As a result, from a sociological perspective, Ehrlich's project 'loses itself'—as Kelsen put it—in an identification of law and society.[21] Consequently, the sociology of law has great problems to establish itself as a separate discipline, independent from a general sociology. Kelsen, by contrast, advocates a clear separation between legal norms and other norms, leading to an identification of law and state. In his view, the state is a 'special form of society' or 'social unity', a 'legal organisation' to which all legal norms can be traced back, whether they are produced by state officials or members of an association.[22] It is the task of the science of law to describe the set of valid legal norms in a certain territory at a certain time, irrespectively of their ethical value and empirical working.

The confusion Ehrlich creates between 'is' and 'ought' could not have been avoided easily, according to Kelsen, and is precisely what makes Ehrlich's project possible and undermines it at the same time. Ehrlich's plea for an official recognition of living law presupposes a leap from the factual—*living law rules!*—to the normative—*let living law rule!* However, what law is, legally speaking, and what it ought to be, ethically speaking, could not, as Kelsen claimed, be established from the viewpoint of legal sociology.

THREE POSSIBLE REPLIES

By way of reply, Ehrlich makes it clear from the outset that he was unwilling to write a counter-criticism. He considers counter-criticisms to be 'inadmissible in general'.[23] Therefore, Ehrlich refrains deliberately from engaging fully in this fundamental debate; he claims only to want to correct some factual errors in Kelsen's representation of his work. However, it is obvious that Ehrlich is quite annoyed by these supposed misrepresentations: 'To accuse someone of confusing an ought rule with a law of nature ... comes close to calling him a fool.'[24] He categorically denies that he had treated the law as if it were a law of nature (physical law), that is, an 'is' rule; instead, he asserted that he always viewed the law as an 'ought' rule. Moreover, he sticks to

---

[20] Below in section 3, this *Gefühlstöne* theory will be discussed in more detail.
[21] H Kelsen, above n 7, 46.
[22] H Kelsen, above n 7, 42–6.
[23] E Ehrlich, 'Entgegnung' in H Kelsen and E Ehrlich, *Rechtssoziologie und Rechtswissenschaft*, above n 7, 57 (my translation).
[24] E Ehrlich, above n 20, 57 (my translation).

his definition of a legal proposition as 'the arbitrary universally binding expression of a legal prescript in a statute or a law book', which could only originate either from the legislature or the judge. Again, he states that this 'official' law does not exhaust the whole of living law, which consists of all legal norms that create order within different associations. He claims not to understand Kelsen's description of a legal proposition as an observational pre-condition for the establishment of legal validity, in German for short: *Betrachtungsvoraussetzung*. As Ehrlich noted, this concept is nowhere to be found in any foreign language dictionary! In his view, a value-indifferent fact does not constitute law or a legal relation, but 'in terms of their evaluation, the perception of law and a legal relation is made from the material that we extract from sensory perceptible reality'.[25] In sum, as Ehrlich sees it, Kelsen has fully misunderstood and misrepresented his work.

In his counter-reply, Kelsen repeats his claim that Ehrlich did not distinguish clearly and consistently between law as an 'is' rule (the factual description of an observed regularity) and law as an 'ought' rule (the postulation of a norm). In Kelsen's view, Ehrlich's methodological syncretism became apparent when Ehrlich argues that he always has subscribed to a normative conception of law and, at the same time, continues to hold on to his conception of legal theory as an explanatory, inductive sociology. You cannot have it both ways, Kelsen argues once again: an empirical science, like other natural sciences, can describe and explain how things are, not how they ought to be. Moreover, he accuses Ehrlich of not understanding that, logically speaking, the general legal norm has to precede any concrete legal relation. The general legal norm enables one to perceive a certain state of affairs from a legal perspective. In this sense, it is an observational pre-condition, or *Betrachtungsvoraussetzung*, for the evaluation of facts in terms of legality/illegality. To Kelsen's dismay, Ehrlich's inability to understand this point only reveals to him that, 'among jurists and legal sociologists, the dictionary of philosophy is a foreign language dictionary'.[26]

The debate, although highly entertaining, is certainly disappointing for its content, and ended up in an unproductive repetition of moves and mutual accusations of misrepresentation and misunderstanding. One cannot escape the impression that Ehrlich has defended himself—energetically but nevertheless—poorly. As a consequence, his plea for an official recognition of the 'living law' lost much of its credibility. How could or should Ehrlich have reacted, if he had been willing to give a more serious reply?

Below, I will sketch three alternative starting points as the bases for a proper defence to Kelsen's criticisms. These possible replies are all, to a greater or lesser extent, derived from Ehrlich's work itself—including *Fundamental*

---

[25] E Ehrlich, above n 20, 63 (my translation).
[26] H Kelsen, 'Replik' in H Kelsen and E Ehrlich, *Rechtssoziologie und* Rechtswissenschaft, above n 7, 72 (my translation).

Principles, The Juristic Logic (*Die Juristische Logik*) and some 'lost' publications—and claim to do as much justice as possible to its overall purposes. Each reply takes its cue from one of the 'strong' positions in legal theory: pragmatism, natural law theory and legal positivism. Since Ehrlich's writings are full of ambiguity, perhaps even plain contradictions,[27] a reconstruction of his work can start from any of these strong positions. Since my purpose is to give a plausible reconstruction of Ehrlich's sociology of law instead of construing a new theory, I will focus on elements of these positions that—in my view—contribute to a better understanding of his work; an understanding that makes it more coherent and defendable against Kelsen's criticisms, regardless of how Ehrlich himself defended it. The first reply denies that the conceptual question about the meaning of law can be settled by scientific means, and resorts, instead, to actual social practises; the second argues that facts and norms are inseparable phenomenologically because social institutions are intrinsically connected to values; and the last explores whether, after the separation of facts and norms, there still can be a meaningful sociology of law (as Kelsen seems to doubt). After having presented these possible replies, together with their main strengths and weaknesses, I will outline in the final section how, in my view, Ehrlich's project can be best presented.

Conceptual Scepticism

In some places in *Fundamental Principles*, Ehrlich appears to be highly sceptical about the scientific possibilities of giving any—let alone a clear and precise—definition of the concept of law. At least, he considered the demarcation between legal norms and non-legal or, more accurately, *extra*-legal[28] norms in general to be very difficult, if not downright impossible. When discussing the origins of judicial norms for decision-making, he wrote:

> Generally speaking, the *extra*-legal norms of morality, ethical custom, and decorum become legal norms so readily that in most cases a differentiation is altogether impossible.[29]

What was a norm of decency or a custom in business one day (for example, 'Deliver your goods within two weeks after payment'), can just swiftly—'so readily'—turn into a legal norm the next day. Because of the permeability of law, *content* does not provide a criterion for distinguishing legal norms

---

[27] In his chapter, Cotterrell speaks kindly of the 'vagueness' of Ehrlich's concept of law that is criticised most frequently.

[28] In the English translation, the German adjective *außerrechtlich* has been translated as 'non-legal'. However, it has to be translated as '*extra*-legal', because these norms do not, in Ehrlich's view, constitute non-legal norms, but rather norms that are not, or not yet, or not in this particular form, part of the 'official', state-centered law. Outside the scope of state law, these norms may still count as 'law' in some other, broader sense.

[29] E Ehrlich, above n 3, 130 (translation slightly adapted, see previous footnote).

from *extra*-legal norms such as these. The only formal, possibly distinctive features Ehrlich thought of were of a rather contingent kind: (i) stability; (ii) determinateness; and (iii) social perception. According to him, legal norms are: (i) more stable, because they can be applied to like cases alike; (ii) more precise, and strictly framed, than *extra*-legal norms; and (iii) they are perceived to be more important and fundamental by society (as is recognised in the legal principle of *opinio necessitatis*). Evidently, these loosely constructed criteria do not, and were probably never meant to, lead to a clean-cut distinction between law and non-law, nor were they intended as a very precise definition of the concept of law.

Ehrlich acknowledges that no easy answers to 'this difficult question' can be expected from the sociology of law:

> The sociological science of law ... will not be able to state the difference between law and morality in a brief, simple formula in the manner of the juristic science that has hitherto been current.[30]

Although the difference between legal and *extra*-legal norms cannot be denied, Ehrlich considers it to be difficult, 'in view of the present state of the science of law',[31] to establish a satisfying demarcation. What is needed is 'a thorough examination of the psychic and social facts',[32] which were not available at the time. The psychic and social facts Ehrlich is referring to in particular are the different kinds, or 'overtones', of feelings (*Gefühlstöne*) that the transgression of the different kinds of norms is supposed to bring about. According to Ehrlich, a violation of law evokes 'the feeling of revolt', a violation of a moral prescript induces 'indignation', indecency is accompanied by 'the feeling of disgust',[33] and so on. In the end, in Ehrlich's view, law is a matter of social perception. The question of what law is and how it is to be separated from other types of norms cannot be answered by social science, nor the science of law, but only by social psychology (which he apparently did not consider to be part of social science as we would today[34]). By carefully observing social perceptions of law, or 'legal consciousness' within society as it is called nowadays,[35] social psychology may in some distant future be able to solve the conceptual issue.

It is clear that, for Ehrlich, it is not possible, given the 'present state of the science of law' at the time, to provide a well-defined conception of law. If there ever was going to be one, it would be the social psychologists' job to find it. However, the few clues that Ehrlich does offer for a social

---

[30] E Ehrlich, above n 3, 167.
[31] *Ibid* 164.
[32] *Ibid*.
[33] E Ehrlich, above n 3, 165.
[34] See also M Rehbinder, above n 5, 39.
[35] M Hertogh, 'A "European" Conception of Legal Consciousness. Rediscovering Eugen Ehrlich' (2004) 31 *Journal of Law and Society* 457.

psychological understanding of law are not very promising. Obviously, emotive reactions aroused by the violation of a legal norm—that is, the 'feeling of revolt'—can never be a serious and solid foundation for law: feelings are in a constant flux and do not, by themselves, involve legal entitlement. People may experience revolt when confronted with their tax assessment; unfortunately for them, it remains a legally binding decision. Conversely, the absence of feelings is also not a very reliable indicator for the existence or non-existence of law: although some cyclists fail to stop at the red light, their behaviour remains a violation of law. Feelings of whatever kind—anger, bitterness, resignation, relief, joy, and so on—are possible by-products of law, never its defining characteristic. As Kelsen observed, '[i]t is an all too cheap pleasure to test Ehrlich's criteria for categorizing social norms'.[36] Other legal scholars, more sympathetic to Ehrlich's work, seem to agree with Kelsen on this point.[37] One may suspect that Ehrlich, by postponing the question of legal validity to an unforeseeable future, and by laying it in the feeble hands of social psychology, appeared to have given up all hope of ever finding a suitable conception of law.

His inability, reluctance and/or unwillingness to address the conceptual issue in a convincing way may stem from a deeply felt scepticism about the possibility of constructing a *scientific* concept of law. For Ehrlich, as well as for Kelsen, the science of law has to be as exact as possible and, like the natural sciences, based on logic and observation.[38] According to Ehrlich, the demarcation between the different kinds of norm was 'undoubtedly somewhat arbitrary'.[39] It is not something that follows from the 'nature of things', but is 'imported into things by man'.[40] Yet, in daily practices the conceptual issue almost never occurs. As Ehrlich acknowledges, it is difficult to draw a line between legal and other norms with scientific accuracy. However, the fact is that this difficulty does not pose practical problems in everyday life.[41] By implication, it may be added, because people know how to distinguish law from non-law, academics should not trouble themselves too much by trying to devise a method for clarifying the distinction. Moreover, there may be an underlying, normative motive for brushing aside the conceptual issue. From a democratic point of view, it should be 'the people' who decide what the law is, and not some elitist group of scholars. After a 'thorough examination of the psychic and social facts', the sociological science of law might

---

[36] H Kelsen, above n 7, 34 (my, somewhat free, translation).
[37] See, for instance, M Rehbinder, above n 5, 105–6; and H Rottleuthner, above n 9, 161–2.
[38] K Lüderssen, above n 9, ix. A crucial difference between Ehrlich and Kelsen is that Kelsen is, in his conception of science and methodology, very much influenced by neo-Kantian thought. See H Dreier, *Rechtslehre, Staatssoziologie und Demokratietheorie bei Hans Kelsen* (Baden-Baden, Nomos-Verlagsgesellschaft, 1968) 56–90.
[39] E Ehrlich, above n 3, 84.
[40] *Ibid.*
[41] *Ibid.*

be able to describe how law originates from these facts; it should, however, refrain from prescribing what has to count as law.

Here we may catch a first glimpse of a serious reply to Kelsen. Factually, it is impossible to differentiate between legal norms and other, non- or *extra*-legal norms with scientific means. In reality, in 'the nature of things', these distinctions do not exist. They are 'imported' by human beings into the social reality they construct together. In this 'man-made reality', distinctions can never be as precise and absolute as science requires. From a pragmatic perspective, it can be argued that language is a tool that should not be measured by its correspondence with 'reality', but by its usefulness for practical matters. Science should take its cue from the fact that people, in the actual practice of daily life, know how to work with the distinctions they have made, however imperfect and transient. At this point, a leap from the factual to the normative takes place, which is typical of pragmatism in general: whatever works in practice should be followed by science. To justify this leap, it is not enough to cite facts that show that the practice at hand actually works and how it works; convincing reasons have to be given as to *why* this practice should be the norm. These normative reasons could, for example, be derived from the value of democracy.

In its present sketchy state, this reply seems to have at least one clear advantage: the 'living law' is saved from the clutches of legal scholars who seek to reduce law to the state or to state law, as Kelsen does. Since it cannot be established scientifically what the law is nor what it ought to be, the sociology of law ought to describe as accurately as possible what is considered to be law in society, at a given time and place. Primarily, law is what people within the social context of their associations perceive as law. However, there are also significant flaws with this line of defence. At a theoretical level, at least three questions arise. First, how is a nominalist/constructivist approach to law reconcilable with the empiricism that Ehrlich also endorsed? Kelsen raises a similar question in his critique.[42] On the one hand, Ehrlich conceived law as a 'matter of an intellectual concept which does not exist in the sphere of tangible reality, but in the minds of men',[43] that is, as a social construction. In his view, '[t]here would be no law if there were no men who bear the concept of law in their consciousness'.[44] On the other hand, Ehrlich argued that:

> ... our concepts are fashioned from the material which we take from tangible reality. They are always based on facts which we have observed.[45]

In this sense, law would not be a mere product of the human mind, but something real, something that can be found in 'tangible reality'. Ehrlich

---

[42] H Kelsen, above n 7, 23–4.
[43] E Ehrlich, above n 3, 84.
[44] *Ibid.*
[45] *Ibid.*

tries to reconcile these positions by stating that perceptions of law are 'facts of the inner life'; although not perceptible, they are still somehow 'observable'.[46] How can law be called a fact if it is buried in the souls of 'men' and not part of the world 'out there'? Kelsen calls this an 'intellectual error':[47] law cannot be both a mental construction and an empirical fact.

This seems to be at odds with the contemporary idea that law can be conceived as 'institutional fact', as described by Neil MacCormick, who builds to this effect on Searle's *Speech Act Theory*. According to MacCormick, legal institutions, such as contracts, rights of ownership, corporations and marriages, may be said to exist, 'by the performance of some act or the occurrence of some event and they continue to existence until the moment of some further act of event'.[48] However, to say these institutions 'exist' in a philosophical sense[49] is to engage in a mental or conceptual operation for the sake of convenience: their 'existence' cannot be read directly from reality, or, as Ehrlich suggests, established by exploring the souls of men. Pre-existing legal norms make it possible to conceptualise certain acts (for example, saying 'yes' at the right moment in the right place) as having legal consequences (for example, to enter into marriage brings forth legal rights and duties). As Kelsen would argue, it is possible to conceive these norms and consequences as 'legal', only if one has already implicitly adopted a normative perspective, that is, the legal point of view. In Kelsen's terms, it would not only be confusing but completely false to call legal institutions facts, which are nothing more than sets of connected legal norms, clustered for practical purposes.

Secondly, the question arises why social practices and usages have to be prioritised over the state or other possible sources of law. As shown above, conceptual scepticism considers actual practices in society to be the only reliable beacon in the conceptualisation of law: science may have a hard time defining law and demarcating it from non-law, but in concrete circumstances people within their associations know what law is and how to get to it. At the same time, Ehrlich had always been well aware that social practices can be very oppressive[50]—for example, in relations of domination like in marriage or slavery—and are not always able to resolve internal conflicts.[51] In these cases, 'official' law (juristic or state law) is an indispensable

---

[46] E Ehrlich, above n 3, 63.

[47] H Kelsen, above n 23, 71 (my translation).

[48] See, for instance, N MacCormick, *An Institutional Theory of Law. New Approaches to Legal Positivism* (Dordrecht, D. Reidel Publishing Company, 1986) 52.

[49] *Ibid* 51.

[50] In his inaugural lecture (1906/1907), Ehrlich already stated: 'In the primal community, the domination is based ... on these two facts: on the defencelessness of the dominated, on his economical and sexual exploitation by the strong ones.' Cf E Ehrlich, 'Die Tatsachen des Gewohnheitsrechts' in *Gesetz und lebendes Recht. Vermischte kleinere Schriften*, M Rehbinder (ed) (Berlin, Duncker & Humblot, 1986) 111 (my translation).

[51] 'But the associations themselves require norms for decision for their own completion and perfection', as Ehrlich writes, see above n 3, 125.

supplement, complementary to living law and capable of overruling it. This supplement should, however, be used very sparingly:

> The legislator ... ought to attempt to mould life according to his own ideas only when this is absolutely necessary; and where he can let life take care of itself, let him refrain from unnecessary interference.[52]

But how does one decide when living law has to rule and when 'official' law is allowed to take over? An answer to this question can only be given from a *normative* perspective, democratic or otherwise—a perspective that an *empirical* sociology of law is neither able nor willing to provide, but must presuppose. In Kelsen's terms, it is an 'observational pre-condition'.

A third question is closely connected to the former: what if the perceptions of law within or between the different associations conflict with each other? In other words, how does one proceed when the beacon of practice is not as reliable as Ehrlich hoped it would be? Precisely because of its scepticism, conceptual scepticism is unable to solve the matter at a conceptual level. If practice is divided on the issue of law—which is more the rule than the exception nowadays—it loses its function as a guiding light. In the absence of a normative, authoritative standard for the assessment of competing perceptions of law, in actual practice power will inevitably trump law: certain norms prevail not so much because a legal authority has issued them, but because some people or groups in society are capable of dominating others. Due to their superiority in terms of physical or intellectual strength, wealth, charisma, and so on, they impose these norms on others. As Ehrlich observed:

> It is a question of social power whether we can consider a norm which is socially valid, but which violates a prohibition issued by the state, a legal norm in the sociological sense.[53]

However, this applies not only to the relation between state and society, but also to the relation between the different associations within society, and between the different members of each association. The 'legal' norms that live in society are the ones that are enforced, not so much by right, on the basis of a legal title, but by might, by the grace of the 'law of the jungle'. Otherwise, there would only be legal validity and no social validity in Ehrlich's sense (or effectiveness in Kelsen's sense). The 'living law' is the 'law' that survives in the social struggle for recognition. In the end, what lives on is not law, but naked power. Alternatively, what boils down to the same thing, both concepts get blurred to the point of indistinction.

---

[52] E Ehrlich, above n 3, 184. Literally, Ehrlich writes that interference by the state is only allowed if life 'cannot function without it' (*wenn es ohne das nicht abgeht*). Cf E Ehrlich, above n 4, 148.

[53] E Ehrlich, above n 3, 170.

Of course, one might argue that, from a certain perspective, law can be seen as a kind of power (in the empirical sense of the ability of imposing one's will on others)—Ehrlich and Kelsen might have agreed on this point— but if it is a kind of power, one still needs to explain what is *distinctively legal* about this kind of power. Because the pragmatist line of defence fails to do so, Ehrlich's sociology of law loses the conceptual ground to differentiate between law and power and between different types of norms, legal or non-legal, official or non-official. As a result, living law becomes an empty slogan without any clear referent. Therefore, it might be worthwhile to explore another line of defence.

Value Essentialism

If we forget about the sceptical and social psychological elements in Ehrlich's work for a moment (not much is lost by that anyway) and return to its sociological basis, we might be able to salvage a more viable position. In every truly sociological study, the primary focus is not on some hidden mental processes, but on the overt interactions between people in the different associations that make up society. In many of his writings, Ehrlich provided ample historical material that showed how facts and norms are inseparable in the institutions created through social interactions. These 'facts of the law', like a marriage, a testament or a contract, not only consist of facts—a woman is married, declares her will or enters into an agreement with another party—but also of normative bindings—specific rights and duties that are attached to each specific institution respectively. For example, in most Western societies a person may only be married to one person at any one time; parties to a contract are expected to fulfil their contractual obligations; and, as a rule, last wills and testaments are binding on a deceased's estate. What may seem to be an oxymoron from a Kelsenian perspective (one can have either facts or norms, not both) is in fact a phenomenological truism: facts are never neutral, but always value-laden. Values are an intrinsic and essential part of the institutions that are created by men and women. Furthermore, these values may be of a 'legal' kind, even though they are, or not yet, recognised by state officials.

According to Ehrlich, the legal propositions that constitute state law are in most cases derived from the judicial norms for decision-making (*Entscheidungsnormen*), which, in turn, are based on the normativity contained in social institutions. In one of his last publications, Ehrlich described the legislative cycle as follows:[54]

> Only state institutions are created by statutes, but the bulk of legal propositions are not brought into being by statutes but by the law of the judge and the jurist,

---

[54] E Ehrlich, above n 6, 247–8 (my translation).

therefore not in advance but afterwards: before judges and jurists can engage with the juridical question in dispute, the institution at hand must exist in life and must have given rise to a dispute.

The claim is not only that certain facts have given rise to law, in the trivial sense that life necessarily precedes law in time; obviously, there must first be a dispute in society before law can enter the scene to end the dispute. Moreover and more importantly, *the facts preceding the law are already infused with law*, which may be, but do not have to be, condensed later, 'afterwards', in 'official' law.[55] The legal proposition, Ehrlich argues, owes 'both its existence and its content' to society.

> It cannot come into being if the social institutions to which it refers do not already exist. And it derives its content from the decisions to which conflicts of interests have given rise that have occurred in society and that, in most cases, have already found their judicial settlement.[56]

Consequently, legal propositions become obsolete as soon as the social institutions that they are supposed to regulate cease to exist. In that case, 'official' law becomes obsolete, that is, sociologically invalid, a mere 'dead letter'.[57] Without the 'breath of life' it has received from society, it is nothing. Here, legal validity and effectiveness collide.

In a crucial, although highly controversial passage, taken from *Fundamental Principles* and discussed in the second section of this chapter, Ehrlich affirmed life's priority over law:

> The state existed before the Constitution; the family is older than the order of the family; possession antedates ownership; there were contracts before there was a law of contracts; and even the testament, where it is of native origin, is much older than the law of last wills and testaments.[58]

For Kelsen, Ehrlich may have simply fallen prey to the *post hoc ergo propter hoc* fallacy (after this, therefore because of this), but there may be more at stake than that. The institutions to which Ehrlich referred are not only prior to law in temporal terms; they are also its existential and empirical pre-condition: 'official' law owes its conception and continued existence to the social arrangements that precede it in time.

More than 20 years before Kelsen launched his *Pure Theory of Law*, Ehrlich accused the '*purely juristic* thinking habits' of his time of 'placing

---

[55] In my reading, Ehrlich's 'facts of the law' do not, or do not only, provide the input or 'germ' for future legal norms, as Stefan Vogl and Salif Nimaga argue in their chapters; rather, they are in some sense *already* legal norms, before being recognised officially. This follows, among other things, from his claim that concepts such as 'state', 'contract' and 'testament' can have legal significance, that is, generate legal rights and duties, without the presupposition of a higher legal norm that renders them legally valid (see further below).
[56] E Ehrlich, above n 5, 250 (my translation).
[57] Ibid.
[58] E Ehrlich, above n 3, 35–6.

the abstract before the concrete'.[59] Obviously, for Ehrlich it has to be the other way round. The concrete—the way in which institutions are shaped in daily life—necessarily precedes, temporarily as well as empirically, the abstract—the way in which these arrangements are condensed into legal propositions. In this process of condensation, law as it has originated in society is transformed: norms become increasingly precise and abstract at the same time, beginning with judicial pronouncements of the law, and ending in legal propositions, possibly but not necessarily incorporated into statutory enactments. However, once abstracted as legal principles, legal propositions always threaten to lose touch with 'real life' and, thereby, to meet their sociological death. The norms that underpin judicial decision-making, however, are more closely connected to reality, because they are created on a case-by-case basis and can be adapted easily, if new circumstances occur.

In his study *Die juristische Logik*, Ehrlich investigates more thoroughly the lawyer's thinking habit which places the abstract before the concrete. One of his main targets is the so-called conceptual jurisprudence, the then-dominant view on how judges apply, or ought to apply, law in individual cases. In this view, as in Kelsen's, a clear and absolute distinction is made between facts and questions of fact, on the one hand, and law and questions of law, on the other. It is the judge's duty to determine the facts in a concrete case and to assess whether these facts meet the pre-given conditions specified in the applicable legal proposition or propositions. Following this view, law application is only a matter of logical subsumption. According to Ehrlich, this is a simplified and false picture of how judges in practice actually find and create law:

> In an extremely simple way, all of the law existing in society is labelled as merely a fact and, thereby, excluded from the law.[60]

In other words, in judicial logic the norms to which people adhere within their associations can only enter the legal calculus on the level of the *minor*, as facts, if they meet the conditions specified in the *maior*. However, these 'social facts' can never occupy the place of the *maior*, that is, they do constitute legal norms on their own right. For instance, the raising of a hand during an auction may considered to be an socially binding acceptance of an offer, but no legal consequences follow necessarily from this gesture. As a consequence of this view, law is presented as a fixed entity, only to be changed by means of legislation, whereas facts appear to be constantly changing.

---

[59] E Ehrlich, above n 3, 36 (my italics).
[60] E Ehrlich, above n 2, 193 (my translation). In E Ehrlich, above n 3, ch XV, a similar criticism is brought to the fore, though in less articulated fashion.

The error of conceptual jurisprudence is not that it works with concepts; science as well as practice cannot do without them. However, in Ehrlich's view, the construction of its concepts is flawed because:

> ... an essential element of every judicial conception is not sufficiently accounted for: the interest that is at stake in the judicial arrangement of the legal relations.[61]

He insisted that the legal institutions, which are present in society, constitute a legal order, whether or not they are embedded in 'official' legal propositions. Conceptual jurisprudence, usually appealing to the unity of law, asks the judge to ignore these legal institutions. Factually, this means that judges must protect interests in society solely on the basis of the legal propositions that are already established. In the actual practice of decision-making, this does not happen, as Ehrlich observed with some relief. In law, principles, fundamental declarations and requirements are being recognised under the influence of natural law, and general clauses, or standards, are promulgated by the legislature. These general prescriptions contain political demands that serve to grant legal recognition to certain interests in society; the weighing of the interests itself is left to the judge. To paraphrase Ehrlich, one may say that they offer judges the soil on which they can freely cultivate their own growth.[62] In this way, living law is offered entry, though by the back door, to the realm of 'official' law.

By challenging the distinction between facts and norms, between questions of fact and questions of law and, by implication, between different types of normativity, Ehrlich moves towards the natural law tradition. However, he is reluctant to acknowledge this explicitly. Sometimes, he mimics the language of natural law by quoting phrases like 'the normative power of the factual'[63] (a phrase taken from Jellinek) and 'from the nature of the thing',[64] but without ever giving up the quotation marks. It is not clear whether, in Ehrlich's view, the standards, fundamental declarations and requirements, which obtain greater recognition by judges under the influence of natural law, constitute law independently of this official recognition. Moreover, Ehrlich establishes a close connection between law and justice, which is, in turn, identified with power: 'Justice is a power wielded over the minds of men by society.'[65] As a 'social force', justice aims at influencing the 'disinterested persons' who are responsible for the creation and

---

[61] E Ehrlich, above n 2, 197 (my translation). The original text contains a couple of venomous wordplays that get lost in translation: 'Aber der Aufbau ihrer Begriffe ist oft fehlerhaft, da darin ein wesentlicher Bestandteil jedes juristischen Begriffs [which means both 'concept' and 'understanding', so I have chosen 'conception' by way of middle term] nicht genügend zu seinem Rechte kommt [literally, is not brought to justice, not recognised in law, sufficiently] ...'

[62] In German it reads as follows: 'Sie [i.e., die allgemeinen Grundsätze, BvK] sind ein freies Feld für den richterlichen Eigenbau.' Cf E Ehrlich, above n 2, 238.

[63] E Ehrlich, above n 2, 86.

[64] E Ehrlich, above n 3, 195 and 357.

[65] E Ehrlich, above n 3, 202.

application of law.⁶⁶ Whether it is powerful enough to do so 'is always a question'.⁶⁷ As a result, law may or may not coincide with justice. In other words, there is a possible and maybe also desirable, but not a necessary or inevitable, connection between law and justice. Even the possibility of this possible connection is a question for Ehrlich:

> *If* there is such a thing as *richtiges Recht* (just law) or to be more exact *richtige Rechtssätze* (just legal propositions), they are those that advance the human race in the direction of its future development.⁶⁸

Ehrlich's reluctance to side wholeheartedly with natural law theory is, of course, fully justified. As a self-acclaimed empirical sociologist, he intends to remain silent on the question of justice. To determine what is just and how the human race should be advanced is:

> ... the function of the founder of a religion, of the preacher, of the prophet, of the preacher of ethics, of the practical jurist, of the judge, of the politician ... Science can be concerned only with those things that are susceptible of scientific demonstration.⁶⁹

In another publication from the same period, Ehrlich states:

> [T]he question itself how the law ought to be is beyond the scope of sociology, because that cannot be described nor demonstrated by means of a scientific method.⁷⁰

Kelsen could not have agreed more. However, in order to sustain his supposedly empirical claim on the inseparability of facts and norms, as well as his overtly normative plea for the official recognition of living law, Ehrlich has to resort to some notion of natural law. In his capacity as a sociologist, he may have argued that he 'only' observed, on a descriptive level, that social interactions create institutions in which facts and norms are inseparable. Whether these norms are good or evil is something that cannot be established scientifically. 'In the forum of science', Ehrlich wrote, the 'trends of justice' existing in society are 'all equally valid'.⁷¹ However, to grant the norms flowing from social institutions a legal title presupposes a transition from the purely descriptive to the normative, from what 'is' (the fact that there are social norms) to what 'ought' to be (the norm that these social norms should be recognised to be legal norms as well). However, by what

---

⁶⁶ *Ibid.*
⁶⁷ *Ibid.*
⁶⁸ E Ehrlich, above n 3, 204 (the first italics are mine; the translation of the German concepts, originally in italics, I have taken from the accompanying footnote on the same page).
⁶⁹ E Ehrlich, above n 3, 202.
⁷⁰ E Ehrlich, 'Soziologie des Rechts' (originally published in 1913/1914) in *Gesetz und lebendes Recht. Vermischte kleinere Schriften* (Berlin, Duncker & Humblot, 1986) 180 (my translation).
⁷¹ E Ehrlich, above n 3, 202.

right are these social norms legal norms? It is not because they are perceived as such in social practices and usages, since perception is an unreliable, and possibly even sometimes an undesirable, guide for the establishment of law, as shown above in the first line of defence. Nor is it because they can be traced back to a higher legal norm which confers authority on the lower level legal norm, as Kelsen suggests, but Ehrlich dismisses offhandedly as '*Kelsenerie*'.[72] Then it must be presumed that every social institution, 'by the nature of the thing', generates values of a legal kind. The law living within society thus owes its legal character to the sheer 'normative power of the factual'. From a sociological point of view, this is bound to remain natural law in quotation marks, 'natural law' that has to manifest itself in the shape of power and has to put its own possibility into question incessantly.

Therefore, the second line of defence, perhaps more plausible at first sight, appears to run into similar, and partly the same, problems as the first line. To begin with, the normative, natural-law-based theory that Ehrlich needed to formulate in order to prove the existence of living law and its empirical priority and moral superiority over 'official' law cannot be construed from his empirical and empiricist sociology of law. It has to be presupposed by way of an observational pre-condition. Subsequently, it may be asked, within the context of such a normative theory, how law can be distinguished from other kinds of norms, especially ethical or moral norms. As Ehrlich neither acknowledged nor entirely denied, there could be possible connections between law and justice. If the relation between the two is construed as a necessary one (law is only law if it is just), as happens in natural law theory, it will be difficult to keep them separate. Inevitably, the question arises of whether the controversy between living law and 'official' law could not better be rephrased in terms of the moral, ethical or political quality, or acceptability, of the law created by state officials. In other words, is there still a need for the concept of 'living law'?

Finally, a contrary but equally devastating objection can be raised from a sociological perspective. Whereas in ethics justice may be construed as an undivided and universally applicable concept, in sociology it has to appear as a pluralist notion. In society, there are—as Ehrlich puts it—many different 'trends of justice' that compete for social and legal recognition. Law cannot do justice to all those trends that are framed as interests: some interests are recognised in law, while others are not. Sociologically speaking, living law is just one of these trends of justice striving for recognition, a trend, however, that distinguishes itself from other trends by being powerful enough to assert itself at the expense of the others. That is precisely why it

---

[72] E Ehrlich, above n 20, 64. The word '*Kelsenerie*' is difficult to translate, but can be described as Kelsen's fabrications or fabulations, not to be taken very seriously.

can be called 'living': it has proven to be the dominant conception of justice at the cost of weaker conceptions. In this light, justice can indeed be seen as 'a power wielded over the minds of men by society'. If that is true, Ehrlich's controversy is not so much about different conceptions of law, but about the power to rule: which rules, legal or not, remain in the social struggle for survival?

Either way, normatively or empirically, living law threatens to lose its right to exist: normatively, because it becomes indistinguishable from justice; empirically, because it coincides with power.

A Positivist Sociology of Law

In one last effort to evaluate the feasibility of Ehrlich's project, I turn now to the question of what actually would happen if facts and norms were separated as rigorously as Kelsen suggests. Despite Ehrlich's rejection of *Kelsenerie*, Kelsen's theory of law may offer some valuable clues for developing a sociology of law on a positivist basis.[73] In fact, there are, despite the obvious differences, some fundamental similarities between the two positions that justify this exploration: like Kelsen, Ehrlich acknowledges the distinction between 'is' and 'ought'—as he himself declared in anger, to suppose otherwise would come close to considering him 'a fool'.[74] Moreover, he rejects a normative sociology of law and, instead, advocates an empirical sociology that takes a neutral stance towards the different 'trends of justice' in society. Also, at times he shows a keen awareness that what, from a normative perspective, is called law or justice, is empirically speaking nothing more than the exercise of power: from an empirical perspective, norms may be perceived as either sustaining or challenging existing relationships of domination in society. Kelsen criticises Ehrlich, not because Ehrlich fails to make these distinctions, but because he does not make them consistently. Therefore, the question is: what aspects of Ehrlich's project can be saved and what must be sacrificed, if its empirical, descriptive and explanatory, motives are stressed and its normative claims are downplayed?[75]

---

[73] There are, of course, other ways of constructing a positivist sociology of law. See recently, eg Brian Z Tamanaha, *A General Jurisprudence of Law and Society* (Oxford, Oxford University Press, 2001). In the following, I will focus on Kelsen, partly on the contingent ground that the debate at hand is between Ehrlich and Kelsen, and partly on the principal ground that Kelsen offers one of the most radical and consistent kinds of legal positivism thinkable. My claim is that if a reconstruction of Ehrlich's theory meets Kelsen's critique in a convincing way, it surely can stand the test of other positivist approaches as well.

[74] E Ehrlich, above n 20, 57.

[75] In opposition to what seems to be the general opinion (see, for instance, M Rehbinder, above n 5, 98–104; H Rottleuthner, above n 9, 31–41; and K Lüderssen, above n 8, xviii–xxi), Vogl argued during the Ehrlich workshop that Ehrlich's sociology of law, in its present state, already fully complies with Kelsen's demands. Vogl's reconstruction of the work of Ehrlich can be found in his chapter in this book and, more substantially, in his monograph *Soziale*

Beginning with the sacrifices that are required, the first step would be to reject Ehrlich's inclination to regard every regularity in social practices that serves a fundamental end as 'law'. Social perception offers only shaky ground for the delineation of law *and* it makes law indistinguishable from power, which may not be a problem for a general sociology, but definitively is such for a sociology *of law*, and even more so for a *normative* sociology of law that aims at rehabilitating living law. According to Kelsen's positivist conception of law, a norm is a legal norm if and only if it can be traced back to a higher legal norm that authorises the creation of the legal norm on a lower level. Ultimately, as he would argue later in his *Pure Theory of Law*, the validity of all legal norms depends on the implicit acceptance of the basic norm, or *Grundnorm*, of a legal system.[76] The basic norm states that the norms of a state's first constitution constitute law and, by implication, the norms following from the first constitution also constitute law. Whereas Ehrlich is unable to differentiate between law and power, Kelsen does so, but only under the assumption that a person is willing to adopt the legal perspective. Someone who does not recognise the basic norm perceives the enforcement of norms as nothing but the exercise of naked power. Thus, for Kelsen, law is a matter of perception, too; but, in his case, not as a social fact, but rather as a transcendental presupposition: in order to identify norms as legal, a person has to assume that the 'existence' of a prior higher legal norm that validates all other legal norms that follow from it.

The second necessary step to take if this *legal* perspective is accepted would be to reverse Ehrlich's prioritisation of life over law or, in his own terms, of the 'living law' over 'official' law: from the positivist perspective, legal norms, irrespective of how and by whom they are created, owe their validity to the state, not society. In Kelsen's view, the state is a 'special form of society' or a 'legal organisation' to which, ultimately, all legal norms can be traced back (see second section above). By implication, no principal distinction can be made in the creation of law between 'ordinary' people and state officials: everyone who is authorised to issue legal norms is, by definition, part of the state.[77] That does not exclude the possibility that most, or the most fundamental, norms are produced by the people within associations and not by higher state officials, such as the judge or the legislature. Moreover, norms that have their origins in society may very well, as Ehrlich claims, constitute the empirical precondition for law to exist, in the

---

Gesetzgebungspolitik, freie Rechtsfinding und soziologische Rechtswissenschaft bei Eugen Ehrlich (Baden-Baden, Nomos Verlagsgesellschaft, 2003). However, as I will show below, some fundamental adaptations in Ehrlich have to be made first before he and Kelsen can be made compatible.

[76] See above nn 8 and 13.

[77] Kelsen would later elaborate this point in *General Theory of Law and State* (translated by Anders Wedberg, New York, Russell & Russell, 1973) in particular at 181–206.

sense that a legal norm possibly owes both its content and its acceptability to other, non-legal norms. However, a norm can only be called a legal norm if there is a higher legal norm available that authorises the creation of this norm. For example, a contract between two parties is valid only if it is entered into on the basis that there is a higher legal norm that recognises the contracting parties' rights to enter into a contract. The validity of this higher legal norm has to be recognised prior to the determination of the contract rules on a lower level. And even then, the contract will only be binding on the parties involved if it conforms to the legal norms regulating contractual relationships. In this sense, the abstract necessarily precedes the concrete—again, not in time, but logically.

The third and final step, closely related to the former, is to reject Ehrlich's identification between legal validity and effectiveness. According to Ehrlich, 'official' law would live under the permanent threat of becoming obsolete, a 'mere dead letter'. Because of its abstract character, it tends to lose touch with the concrete circumstances on which it has to be applied. The 'living law', on the contrary, is supposed to be the 'real' law because it consists of the norms that people in society actually obey. If law has to live to *be* law, legal validity equals effectiveness. In his *Pure Theory of Law*, Kelsen shows that both concepts, although connected at some point, should fundamentally be distinguished from each other.[78] The validity of the legal system as a whole would depend on the fact that it is by and large effective, that is, that its norms are in general applied and obeyed. In a by-and-large effective legal system, a particular legal norm does not owe its validity to its effectiveness, but to its derivation from a higher legal norm and, ultimately, from the basic norm. Legal norms are valid, not *because* they are effective, but *as long as* they are largely effective. A particular legal norm that seems to be dead from a sociological point of view can be reanimated at any time by a legal authority, if it has not been withdrawn officially.[79]

Necessarily, there is a discrepancy between law and reality, between what is and what ought to be, albeit within reasonable limits. At an upper limit, law cannot afford to be fully out of step with reality because then it would cease to exist. On the other hand, at a lower limit, law cannot coincide with reality, because that would make its existence superfluous:

> Indeed, there must exist the possibility of a discrepancy between the normative system and what actually takes place within its scope, for without such a possibility a normative system is meaningless.[80]

---

[78] H Kelsen, above n 8, 58–62.

[79] Against Rottleuthner, I do not see how the sociology of law may contribute to the establishment of the validity of legal norms (in the technical-legal sense, see H Rottleuthner, above n 9, 62). That remains an exclusive matter for the science of law. Only competent legal authorities can decide when, according to some standard, a legal norm is not effective and therefore—ie for reasons of *desuetudo*—has to be abolished.

[80] H Kelsen, above n 8, 58–9.

A complete correspondence between 'is' and 'ought', as much as a complete discrepancy, means the death of law. It may be a joyous death, which can be welcomed with the well-known words of the Portuguese poet Pessoa: '[I]f I die now, I will die happy / Because everything is real and everything is right'[81]—but still, it is death.

After abandoning these three convictions, cherished so dearly by Ehrlich and his kindred spirits, a sociology of law may still be able to contribute to legal inquiry as an *empirical* phenomenon. However, this inquiry would have to accept that it is incapable of defining its own object—the law—because that presupposes a *normative*, in particular a legal, point of view. It would first have to adopt a normative definition of law from a position beyond its conceptual horizon in order to then investigate law from an empirical perspective. In this regard, two traditional and important fields of sociological research remain to be explored: the origin and the effectiveness of law.[82] To begin with, a sociological perspective on law may shed light on how legal norms have come into being. From an empirical perspective, though, it must be remembered that they are nothing but social psychological facts. What are the sources of these facts conceived as valid legal norms? How did they manage to penetrate the realm of law? What is the role that courts play in channelling social norms into the law? Which conflicts of power lie hidden behind the creation of legal norms? For these kinds of question, Ehrlich's pioneering work into the normative institutions existing within the different associations is very useful. From a legal perspective, these institutions do not contain 'facts of the law', as Ehrlich called them, but social norms that may or may not be turned into legal norms, and are dependent on the surrounding forces to assert them and be accepted as law. Subsequently, it might be interesting to know whether legal norms, once they are created, are adhered to by society. Is law effective, in general and in particular instances? What do citizens know about the content of the law and the access to law? How can the apparent lack of effectiveness of law be explained sociologically? Given these sociological conditions, how can the efficacy of legal norms be improved? Here, Ehrlich's work provides some general clues: legal norms should be of practical use for the institutions to which they apply and they should accord, as much as possible, with the normativity already contained in these institutions.

---

[81] In the poem 'When Spring Comes' from the series *Detached Poems*, Pessoa writes literally 'I will die satisfied' ('contente'), also translated as 'peaceful'. However, 'happy' is more in the spirit of the poem. A couple of lines earlier he stated: 'I feel an enormous joy.' See, eg <http://www.electricguild.com/Pessoa/Caeiro/Pds/pds19.html> accessed 23 July 2008.

[82] In general, I subscribe to the eight themes of inquiry that H Rottleuthner (above n 9, 68–77) attributes to an empirical sociology of law, among which are access to law, knowledge and opinion about law and evaluation studies.

Facts and Norms: Eugen Ehrlich and Hans Kelsen   151

Kelsen tried to curb even this last attempt to save Ehrlich's sociology of law. At the end of his critique, Kelsen queries whether a sociology of law along these positivist lines is really of interest to social science:[83]

> Because it is the normative conception of law that demarcates its problems, its demarcations have to appear as arbitrary from the viewpoint of the science of which it [i.e., the sociology of law] has to be an offshoot, i.e., *sociology*. Whether the norms, whose effects determine social behaviour, are legal norms or norms of decency or moral norms, does not really matter from a sociological perspective. From a purely sociological standpoint, there is no *essential* difference between these norms, that is, *between the psychological facts, the perceptions, which constitute the content of these norms*.

In my view, Kelsen pushes his point too far here. He may be right that there is, from a 'purely' sociological point of view, no essential difference between legal and other norms. For one thing, sociology as an empirical science is not qualified to construe a typology of norms. Its job is to describe regularities in social behaviour that necessarily appear as facts, psychological or otherwise. However, as soon as sociology seeks to find explanations for these regularities in social behaviour, it does matter whether or not the norms at hand are supported by the state. The violation of legal norms may be followed by pre-given sanctions such as fines and imprisonment, whereas other (religious, moral, customary) norms are enforced predominantly by public opinion.[84] If that would not make a difference, an essential difference indeed, one may wonder why there is an *empirical* need for the state anyway. Moreover, if not essential, it is still scientifically worthwhile, as long as there is a state, to find out how and why it sometimes succeeds and, at other times, fails to influence people's actions.[85]

For his part, Ehrlich would have no reason to be very happy with this solution either. From a legal point of view, the 'living law' has to be identified with valid legal norms. Norms that are not valid, that is, norms that do not follow from higher legal norms, are not law in this sense. This means that law cannot be thought of independently of the state. Obviously, many legal norms are produced by non-governmental actors in contracts, collective labour agreements, testaments, and so on, but to be law it must be possible to trace them back to the legal norms that are produced by state officials and, ultimately, to the basic norm.[86] All legal norms are part of the unitary legal system that Kelsen equated with the state. Many norms

---

[83] H Kelsen, above n 7, 53–4 (my translation, original italics).

[84] Here I have adopted the rough distinction Mill made between coercion exerted by law and by public opinion. Cf John Stuart Mill, *On Liberty* (Harmondsworth, Penguin, 1985 (1859)) 64 ff.

[85] On this point I fully agree with Rottleuthner—see above n 9, 39.

[86] If this is possible, the non-governmental actors become state officials themselves. As argued above, from the viewpoint of law creation the later Kelsen drew no fundamental distinction between state and society.

that govern people's daily life, even when perceived as being fundamental or morally just, do not belong to this system. In this sense, Ehrlich was absolutely right in saying that the law is not able to contain the 'diversity of life'. As quoted in the first section above: 'whatever comes in, is no longer a living stream, but dead water, and much fails to enter into the pond'. Therefore, what may seem to live from a sociological perspective can, from a legal perspective, appear to be non-existent or dead. Conversely, what appears to be sociologically dead may very well be alive and kicking, legally speaking. So, after all these explorations, the question remains: what is left of living law?

RESURRECTING LIVING LAW

As shown above, the three possible replies to Kelsen's critique—following a pragmatist, a natural-law-based and a positivist line of defence respectively—all seem to end up in the death of living law: it becomes indistinguishable either from power (both in the first and second reply) or from justice (in the second reply), or it is incorporated in the 'official', state-centred law (in the third reply) from which Ehrlich had originally tried to separate it. In my opinion, the final, positivist reply is preferable to the first two replies, even from Ehrlich's point of view, because it offers at least some chance that living law survives, albeit in the *Fremdkörper* (foreign body) of the state's law. In merging with justice, living law may meet a happy death (recall Pessoa's vision of everything that is real, is right), whereas its equation with power may be a more cruel way to die (it is the 'law of the jungle' that survives in the end). In both cases, the days of the law seem to be numbered, since any clear criteria for its identification are lacking. Only the positivist reply is able to explain what is distinguishingly legal about living law and, thereby, how it can differentiate itself both from other types of norms and from power. Moreover, it does not fall prey to methodological syncretism like the other two positions that confuse systematically empirical and normative claims. What ought to be cannot be inferred from how things are, either in an established practice or in some idealised description of reality (ie the supposed 'nature of things'), but is a matter of subjective evaluation for which no objective scientific criteria can be given.[87]

Consequently, the best way to resurrect living law is to present it not so much as an *alternative*, but as a possibly valuable *addition* to law created by the state. Basically, there are two ways in which living law can penetrate

---

[87] See H Kelsen, 'What is Justice?' in *What is Justice? Justice, Law, and Politics in the Mirror of Science. Collected Essays by Hans Kelsen* (Berkeley, University of California Press, 1971).

'official'[88] law: first, the norms contained in living law may, under the conditions specified in the last part of the third section above, acquire a legal title—as a valid contract, collective agreement, testament, and so on. Alternatively, secondly, these norms may be a source of inspiration to higher state officials who create law, in particular, to the judge and the legislature. In this latter process of transformation, part of the 'liveliness' of living law gets inevitably lost, that is, its flexibility or adaptability to new circumstances or changes in public opinion. As soon as social norms are turned into legal norms—in particular, the norms that Ehrlich called 'legal propositions'—their meaning is fixed and cannot be changed that easily. That is the price that has to be paid for legal certainty. What is gained, however, is that, in their transformation to legal norms, the scope of the social norms is widened: they are not only applicable to the cases that originally gave rise to their creation, but also to other, similar cases.

If living law is indeed a mere addition to the state's law and becomes indistinguishable from it as soon as it is added to the state's law, it may be asked whether there is a *scientific* need for the concept of living law. Strictly speaking, there is not. From a normative perspective, law is either valid or invalid, as determined by legal science. From an empirical perspective, law is either effective or ineffective, as determined by social science. Depending on the perspective, 'living law' is synonymous either with valid law or effective law. Therefore, in scientific terms, the concept has no added value. Its main function lies in the *rhetorical-political* sphere, where it may elicit powerful pleas for the recognition of norms that have originated in society, independently of the state. This actually happened in Japan and Indonesia, as Stefan Vogl and Franz and Keebet von Benda-Beckmann respectively show in their chapters. However, such a normative programme transcends Ehrlich's project of a self-acclaimed empirical sociology of law, and brings it into the domain of ethics, religion and politics that it seeks to avoid (see the second part of the third section above). Empirically, it cannot be proven that the norms produced in the different associations of society have to be prioritised over the state's law, even though they may—as Ehrlich himself acknowledged—be oppressive. By implication, Kelsen's reverse prioritisation of the state over society cannot be founded empirically either; therefore, it should not be misconstrued as the moral or political claim that state-produced law is in general 'better', that is, more just or useful, than other social norms living in society. Kelsen's *Pure Theory of Law* only aims at establishing the validity of law, not its legitimacy, that is, its compatibility with moral, religious, economical or other normative standards.

---

[88] The quotation marks are needed because, from a Kelsenian perspective, the whole of the law is 'official' in the sense that it is, at least in Western legal systems, unthinkable without the concept of the state (see also the last part of section 3).

Although the notion of living law has predominantly a rhetorical-political function, the ideas that are, rightfully or wrongfully, connected to it may be still of value to science. In my view, the scientific significance of Ehrlich's project can be summarised in four observations: (i) the driving force behind the creation and development of law has to be located in society, not in the higher ranks of the state—most legal norms are either created by non-governmental actors or inspired by norms created by non-governmental actors; (ii) the validity of law does not equal its effectiveness—the norms people actually obey are not necessarily those endorsed and enforced by the state; (iii) the effectiveness of the state's law depends to a large extent to other social norms existing in society; and, therefore, (iv) the state's possibilities to change existing patterns of behaviour and thinking are necessarily limited.

Supposing that Kelsen would accept the empirical evidence provided by Ehrlich, Kelsen would have no difficulty in endorsing these observations. He calls the first observation a 'truism' (*Binsenwahrheit*).[89] Moreover, it does not touch his *Pure Theory of Law* at all, because it 'only' concerns the origin of law, not its status *as* law. The same counts for the next three observations that relate to the effectiveness of law, and in particular to the conditions of its effectiveness. By focusing on law as a normative phenomenon, Kelsen immunises himself against empirical data. Reality hits the self-enclosed world of law only at one point, namely when the legal system as a whole does not function. In that exceptional case, the validity of law is affected by its effectiveness. One important lesson than can be learned from Ehrlich is that the state, if nothing else in view of its own survival, should pay close attention to factual developments in society beyond the centre of power. In this respect, I subscribe to Cotterrell's view in this volume, when he characterises Ehrlich's project in the following terms:

> ... Ehrlich's intellectual outlook must not be seen as setting social norms *against* the state law (ie, periphery challenging juristic and political centre). His project is rather to demand of the state a new, deeper self-awareness to ensure its absolutely necessary survival faced with powerful disintegrating tendencies produced in its periphery.

However, I cannot see that this so-called centre-periphery dialectic inevitably leads to the kind of legal pluralism Cotterell has in mind. In the final analysis, as Kelsen points out, legal norms have to fit the existing legal system. Therefore, the room for plurality—that is, the possibility of integrating social norms into the existing legal order—is, by necessity, limited.

If one, by way of conclusion, combines these two perspectives and tries to link together the truths that they produce in their own right, one would arrive at the following legislative aporia: law is necessarily *a part of* society, as Ehrlich argues, as well as *apart from* society, as Kelsen claims. While it

---

[89] H Kelsen, above n 7, 54 (my translation).

cannot but extract its norms from society, law necessarily deviates from these social norms. This inevitable gap between law and society, which simultaneously acts as a bridge, prevents that law is ever identical with justice and power *and* that it is fully separable from both. By necessity, law will entertain some relationship with justice (or social perceptions of what is right) and power (conceived as a social force or might that makes right), but it cannot coincide with them completely because then it would vanish. The law lives as long as facts and norms exist that, although do not overthrow it, conflict with it *in realis* or, at least, *in potentialis*.

7

Pounding on Ehrlich. Again?

SALIF NIMAGA

'"Law in books" refers solely to rules and norms. It is only in this way that it can be distinguished from the "law in action". But 'norms for decision', which are said to be its equivalent, include in Ehrlich's usage not only norms and rules but also the actual patterns of decision by legislative and judicial bodies. Conversely, "living law" does not correspond to what Pound meant by the "law in action" because it refers essentially to obligatory norms rather than action. Indeed, from the point of view of the members of a group, "living law" represents their "law in books" as compared to what actually happens in practice when the norms are breached, avoided or transformed. Ehrlich's concept of "norms for decision" therefore encompasses most of what Pound was getting at in his discussions of "law in books" and "law in action". But Ehrlich's notion of "living law" has no parallel in Pound's distinction. Its nearest relative is the idea of informal norms within formal organisations.'[1]

INTRODUCTION

ROSCOE POUND'S CONCEPTS of 'law in the books' and 'law in action' were often linked to Eugen Ehrlich's 'norms for decision' and 'living law'.[2] It is tempting to assume that this is due to the

---

[1] D Nelken, 'Law in Action or Living Law? Back to the Beginning in Sociology of Law' (1984) 4 *Legal Studies* 165. I am deeply indebted to David Nelken's enlightening clarifications on similarities and oppositions in the writings of Eugen Ehrlich and Roscoe Pound and if it were not for this paragraph, on which I will comment in detail in my concluding remarks, these reflections—comprising an addition rather than a critique—would not have been written.

[2] See, eg WJ Chambliss and R Seidman, *Law, Order and Power* (2nd edn, Reading, Addison Wesley Publishing Company, 1982) 69, who equate 'living law' and 'law in action' and oppose it to 'formal law' and 'law in the books'. The concepts are used with similar meaning in JW Harris, *Law and Legal Science. An Inquiry into the Concepts of Legal Rule and Legal System* (Oxford, Clarendon Press, 1979) 27; and JF O'Day, 'Ehrlich's Living Law Revisited. Further Vindication for a Prophet Without Honour' (1966) 18 *Case Western Law*

fact that the 1936 English translation of Ehrlich's groundbreaking work *Fundamental Principles of the Sociology of Law*[3] came with an introduction by Pound.[4] However, neither this introduction nor the book reviews that accompanied this publication[5] provide much support for this assumption.[6] It may be true that '[t]erms do take on meanings beyond their origins' and that therefore the term '"law in action", as it has developed in the law and society tradition, includes both Pound's and Ehrlich's ideas'.[7] However, these new meanings should prevent us from linking them to the prominent exposition in the works of both Pound and Ehrlich, in which these terms have an irreconcilable content, as Nelken has rightly pointed out.[8] Here, I would like to go a step further and include Ehrlich's concept of 'legal propositions'. I will argue that a reconstruction of his conceptual framework based on legal norms, norms for decision and legal propositions does more justice to the complexities of his work and facilitates a comparison to the terminology used by Roscoe Pound in his famous 1910 article 'Law in Books and Law in Action'—if one wants to undertake such an endeavour.

Review especially at 214 and 216. Even M Rehbinder, 'Einleitung' in M Rehbinder (ed), *Eugen Ehrlich, Recht und Leben. Gesammelte Schriften zur Rechtstatsachenforschung und zur Freirechtslehre* (Berlin, Duncker & Humblot, 1967) 8 uses the terms 'living law' and 'law in action' synonymously. J Stone, *Social Dimensions of Law and Justice* (London, Stevens & Sons Ltd, 1966) § 21, especially at 67 mentions Ehrlich alongside Pound in a discussion of 'law in books' and 'law in action', but overall his book draws on many of Ehrlich's insights and is a valuable resource.

[3] E Ehrlich, *Fundamental Principles of the Sociology of Law* (Cambridge, Harvard University Press, 1936). The German original, *Grundlegung der Soziologie des Rechts*, was published in 1913. Usually, I will refer to the English edition, quotes to the German original refer to the 4th edition (Berlin, Duncker & Humblot, 1989).

[4] R Pound, 'Introduction' in Ehrlich, above n 3, xiv.

[5] See the book reviews by M Ginsberg (1937) 1 *The Modern Law Review* 169; F Neumann (1937) 43 *The American Journal of Sociology* 351; NS Timasheff (1937) 2 *American Sociological Review* 120; G Husserl (1938) 5 *The University of Chicago Law Review* 330; AM Kidd (1938) 38 *Columbia Law Review* 383; and M Rheinstein, 'Sociology of Law. Apropos Moll's Translation of Eugen Ehrlich's Grundlegung der Soziologie des Rechts' (1938) 48 *International Journal of Ethics* 232. Only SP Simpson (1937) 51 *Harvard Law Review* 191–2 states: 'It [Ehrlich's 'living law'] resembles in one aspect Pound's "law in action", as distinguished from the "law in the books" which consists of legal propositions; but it is a broader term, since law in action means the law in the books in action, while Ehrlich's "living law" may never have been in the books at all—indeed, the contrary may be in the books.' This formulation reappears in O'Day, above n 2, 214.

The American reviews that discussed the original German publication of Ehrlich's work, namely GC Butte, (1915) 9 *The American Journal of International Law* 569; and P Vinogradoff, 'The Crisis of Modern Jurisprudence' (1920) 29 *Yale Law Journal* 312, do not include such a comparison, either.

[6] The introduction to the 2002 edition of the *Fundamental Principles* by Ziegert points to the difference between Ehrlich's and Pound's concepts (K Ziegert, 'Introduction to the Transaction Edition' in E Ehrlich, *Fundamental Principles of the Sociology of Law* (Transaction Publishers, New Brunswick, 2002) xxxix).

[7] S Macaulay, 'The New versus the Old Legal Realism. Things Ain't what They Used to Be' (2005) *Wisconsin Law Review* 387.

[8] Nelken, above n 1.

EUGEN EHRLICH

Legal Norms

For Ehrlich, the distinction between legal norms and legal propositions is crucial.[9] A 'legal norm' (*Rechtsnorm*) is 'the legal command, reduced to practice, as it obtains in a definite association, perhaps of very small size, even without formulation in words'.[10] Legal norms are rules of conduct that provide for the inner order of the social association;[11] they are the 'primary normative order' and are supplemented by a 'secondary normative order' which is established not to shape, but to perpetuate and to protect it.[12] Ehrlich thus proposes a concept of law that does not depend on the existence of the state and its agencies.[13] He further claims that legal norms can be distinguished from other social norms by the 'overtones of feelings' they release—in the case of law the *opinio necessitatis* accompanied by a 'feeling of revolt that follows a violation of law'.[14] The merits of this approach, namely that such a wide concept of law allows for the analysis of pre-state societies and associations at the sub- or super-state level and its problems, mainly the lack of conceptual rigidity and practical usefulness, have ever since divided the scholarly world.[15]

Norms for Decision

Of a different nature are the 'norms for decision' (*Entscheidungsnormen*). Primarily, they are addressed to and/or found by the judges:

> The norm for decision, like all social norms, is primarily a rule of conduct, but only for the courts. It is not, primarily at least, a rule for the men who are the

---

[9] See Ehrlich's remark in his exchange with Hans Kelsen: 'Da ich in meinem Buche ziemlich oft wissenschaftliches Neuland betreten habe, so mußte ich dafür zum Teile eine eigne wissenschaftliche Terminologie schaffen. Dazu gehört die Unterscheidung zwischen Rechtssatz und Rechtsnorm' (see E Ehrlich, 'Entgegnung' in H Kelsen and E Ehrlich, *Rechtssoziologie und Rechtswissenschaft. Eine Kontroverse (1915/1917)* (Baden-Baden, Nomos, 2003) 59 (originally published in (1916) 41 *Archiv für Sozialwissenschaft und Sozialpolitik* 844)). My translation reads: As in my book I have quite often stepped on scholarly uncharted territory, I had to create in part my own scientific terminology. This includes the distinction between legal proposition and legal norm.

[10] See Ehrlich (1936), above n 3, 38. The first part of the German original is different: '*der ins Handeln umgesetzte* Rechtsbefehl, wie er in einem bestimmten, vielleicht ganz kleinen Verbande herrscht, auch ohne jede wörtliche Fassung' (Ehrlich (1989), above n 3, 44; emphasis added) refers to a *legal command transformed into action*. This crucial inaccuracy in the translation was first pointed out by Husserl, above n 5, 334.

[11] Ehrlich (1936), above n 3, 40.

[12] *Ibid* 55.

[13] See *ibid* 160: 'The view that law is created by the state therefore will not bear the test of historical analysis. And we may therefore say that it has been refuted; for if it be essential to the concept of law that it be created by the state, how could it have been in existence without the state throughout long epochs of history?'

[14] *Ibid* 165.

[15] For a good summary, see BZ Tamanaha, *Realistic Socio-Legal Theory. Pragmatism and a Social Theory of Law* (Oxford, Clarendon Press, 1997) ch 4.

doers in life, but for the men who sit in judgment upon the doers. In so far as the norm for decision is a legal norm, it appears to be a legal norm of a special kind, different from the legal norms that contain general rules of conduct.[16]

Several things are important in this regard. First, we have to understand that Ehrlich uses very wide concepts of 'courts' and 'judges'. In principle, these terms do not require a state connection, even though in the course of history, the state has gained control over most of the courts of other social associations.[17] Secondly, norms for decision are to be based on 'the inner order of the associations as it existed at the beginning of the quarrel', that is, 'the facts of the law', which are usage, relations of domination and possession, and contracts.[18] These facts of the law are a reflection of the peaceful order of the association and do not contain solutions for the conflict in question. However, the knowledge and analysis of this peaceful order provide guiding material for the judge in his or her creation of a norm for decision. In this sense, norms for decision are mainly juristic law because they are found by a professional group dealing with conflict resolution. Thirdly, we have to keep in mind the normative character of norms for decision, which Ehrlich, provoked by Kelsen's critique,[19] felt the need to clarify at a later point:

> Ich erkläre, daß ich in meinem ganzen Buche das Recht immer nur als Sollregel und nie als Naturgesetz, als 'Seinsregel' behandelt habe, und daß sich darin kein Wort findet, das die Kelsensche Behauptung rechtfertigen würde.[20]

Obviously, Ehrlich was eager to keep apart the categories of norms and facts, which only seemingly collapse in the case of norms for decision. A specific norm for decision contains only information about the decision of a singular case. Actual patterns of judicial decisions cannot be analytically extracted from norms for decision. This information can only be gathered if one systematically studies how cases are decided by judges. This data collection yields two sets of information, which are not to be confused: one regarding patterns of decisions, the other concerning 'norms for decision',

---

[16] Ehrlich (1936), above n 3, 122–3.
[17] Ibid 121.
[18] Ibid 123 ff. On the concept of 'facts of the law', see ibid 83–120; and M Rehbinder, *Die Begründung der Rechtssoziologie durch Eugen Ehrlich* (Berlin, Duncker & Humblot, 1967) 29–34. It seems that one should stress the first part of this opaque notion. In relation to the law-generating effect of the most fundamental fact of the law, namely usage, Ehrlich (1936), above n 3, 85, states that it is built on the principle of 'The custom of the past shall be the norm for the future'. The first part of the sentence refers to usage and merely rests on the observation of a regularity of behaviour, whereas the turn towards the emergence of a legal norm in the second half of the sentence ('... shall') requires a psychological turn towards the normative, which is either consensual or imposed.
[19] H Kelsen, 'Eine Grundlegung der Soziologie des Rechts' in H Kelsen and E Ehrlich, *Rechtssoziologie und Rechtswissenschaft*, above n 9, 1.
[20] Ehrlich, above n 9, 58. My translation reads: 'I declare that in my whole book I have always treated the law as an Ought-rule and never as a rule of nature or "Is-rule" and that it does not contain one word that would justify Kelsen's allegation.'

that is, 'the general proposition on which the decision is based',[21] which are advanced as their normative basis.

Legal Propositions

A 'legal proposition' (*Rechtssatz*) is in Ehrlich's terms 'the precise, universally binding formulation of the legal precept in a book of statutes or in a law book'.[22] Every norm for decision already contains the grain of a legal proposition, based on the tendency that the former serves as a precedent from which, through further abstraction and final expression, the latter can be created; a process Ehrlich refers to as the 'law of the stability of norms'.[23] In the light of this law of the stability of norms and due to formulations such as 'the norm for decision *in the form of* the legal proposition' (emphasis added),[24] one might conclude that the distinction between norms for decision and legal propositions is superfluous, as the former term embraces the latter. To do so, however, means not only to ignore Ehrlich's choice to differentiate between the two,[25] but also to miss the subtle points that come with this distinction. As we will see, the overlap between legal propositions and norms for decision is only in part, as there are legal propositions that are not norms for decision and vice versa.

State Law

> State law is created by the state, not indeed as to its form, but as to its content; it is law that came into being solely through the state, and that could not exist without the state.[26]

State law refers to: (i) the inner order of the state, the *Staatsrecht* or the public law in the narrow sense;[27] (ii) norms for decision; and (iii) administrative norms.[28] The fact that Ehrlich chose as the basis for the distinction

---

[21] Ehrlich (1936), above n 3, 132.
[22] Ibid 38; cf Ehrlich (1989), above n 3, 44. Again, we find a problem in the translation: the German '*zufällig*' is better rendered as 'arbitrary' than as 'precise'.
[23] Ehrlich (1936), above n 3, 132.
[24] *Ibid* 136.
[25] Compare *ibid* chs VIII and IX, which are dedicated to the creation and structure of legal propositions!
[26] *Ibid* 137.
[27] *Ibid* 143.
[28] *Ibid* 367. The term administrative norms is a direct translation of *Verwaltungsnormen*, the term used by Ehrlich later (see 'The Sociology of Law' (1922) 36 *Harvard Law Review* 132) and is more embracing than '*Eingriffsnormen*, ie norms directing state agencies to proceed' used in *Fundamental Principles*. See Rehbinder, above n 18, 52 for a description of how this change towards the very end of Ehrlich's career relates to his evaluation concerning the effectiveness of state law.

of state law a substantive and not a formal criterion forced him to introduce some qualifications. Whereas the first and the third category are always state law, norms for decision are only state law insofar they are 'designed to subserve the purposes of the state' and 'have arisen independently of juristic law':[29]

> The borderline between state law and juristic law is not easily determinable. In the first place juristic law consists of the norms for decision which the jurist has created by universalisation. State law consists of commands directed by the state to its tribunals. The jurists cannot issue commands, they can only find law. The state does not find law, it can only command.[30]

Furthermore, state law appears mainly in the form of legal propositions, within the civil law context primarily in the form of statutes.[31]

The turn towards state law includes for Ehrlich also a change of perspective. Whereas the movement from the facts of the law over legal norms and norms for decision to legal propositions is an evolutionary description that is bottom-up, the perspective of state law is top-down with imperatives issued by the state to its administrative or judicial agencies in an attempt to directly (administrative norms) or indirectly (norms for decision) shape social relations.[32] In this regard, he assumed that the 'effect of state norms for decision is usually very much over-estimated'[33] and that '[d]irect action by the state is much more effective than a norm for decision'.[34]

Synthesis

> The norm for decision, like all social norms, is primarily a rule of conduct, but only for the courts.[35]

> Every legal proposition which is to serve as the basis for judicial decisions is itself a norm for decision, formulated in words, and published in an authoritative manner, asserting claim to universal validity, but without reference to the case that may have occasioned it.[36]

Due to remarks such as these, which introduce partial overlaps, it is difficult to arrange Ehrlich's key concepts systematically and almost impossible to

---

[29] Ehrlich (1936), above n 3, 367.
[30] Ibid 188.
[31] Ibid 368.
[32] See ibid 192: 'New facts of the law therefore can be established not only, as in past centuries, by the application of force, or, as is usual in our days, by the silent, unobserved sway of social forces ... but also, at least indirectly, by means of legal propositions.'
[33] Ibid 368.
[34] Ibid 371.
[35] Ibid 122.
[36] Ibid 171.

draw neat boundaries; something the concepts might have in common with the phenomena they try to grasp. I will show, however, that most of the confusion can be avoided if we understand that there are basically two sets of threefold distinctions operative in his argument, namely that between legal norms—norms for decision—legal propositions on the one hand and legal norms—norms for decision—administrative norms on the other.

The first set of distinctions can serve as a synopsis of Ehrlich's view on legal evolution, mainly in terms of *formal* characteristics of legal rules. In regard to these formal qualities, law emerges from the facts of the law[37] in the form of legal norms that have an intuitive quality and can exist 'even without the formulation in words'. In formal terms, law reaches its highpoint of abstraction in legal propositions, which are considered to be 'the precise, universally binding formulation of the legal precept in a book of statutes or in a law book'.[38] Norms for decision occupy a middle ground and point to the varying degrees of abstraction in between these two extremes.[39]

Crucial is Ehrlich's emphasis on legal norms, the fact that they provide for a coexistence that is essentially conflict-free and especially his choice to qualify these norms as legal, even though they are developed within associations (potentially) existing and operating at great distance from the centre of state authority. In an attempt to explain this development in Ehrlich's theoretical outlook, one can attribute it to a large extent, loosely spoken, to the Bukovina factor.[40]

The tension created by the ambivalent relation of the concepts of 'norms for decision' and 'legal propositions' is one reason to hold on to this distinction. Another is the determination of the original contribution to the law-creating process by judges:

> This concrete norm for decision, which the judge has deduced from the facts, is introduced between the legal proposition which contains the general norm for decision and the ascertainment of the facts by the judge. Whether the judge, therefore arrives at his decision independently of a legal proposition or on the basis of a legal proposition he must find a norm for decision.[41]

---

[37] The facts of the law are themselves not included in this distinction of *normative* phenomena, see above n 18.
[38] All quotes from Ehrlich (1936), above n 3, 38.
[39] See *ibid* 172: 'This norm for decision, indeed, is not as yet a legal proposition. It lacks the formulation in words, the claim to universal validity, the authoritative publication, but it is a part of the valid law, for if this were not true the judge would have no authority to decide the litigation according to it.'
For a more complex account of Ehrlich's views on legal evolution, compare KA Ziegert, 'The Sociology behind Eugen Ehrlich's Sociology of Law' (1979) 7 *International Journal of the Sociology of Law* 225.
[40] Cf A Likhovski, 'Czernowitz, Lincoln, Jerusalem, and the Comparative History of American Jurisprudence' (2003) 4 *Theoretical Inquiries in Law* 621.
[41] Ehrlich (1936), above n 3, 173.

Ehrlich's emphasis on norms for decision can be seen as the scholarly counterpart to his activity in the Free Law Movement, heightening the professional self-esteem that had suffered from the great German and Austrian codifications of the second half of the nineteenth century, which allegedly produced a hermetic system of legal propositions.[42]

This does not render the concept of 'legal propositions' superfluous. Their characteristic is a high degree of abstraction that makes them particularly suitable for organisational purposes in large political entities. In Ehrlich's account, the full differentiation of legal rules, therefore, tends to coincide in historical perspective with the appearance of the state. Therefore, he tends to treat state law as legal propositions and vice versa.

In reviewing the main actors in the process of norm production, we can broadly equate legal norms with social law as generated by the associations, norms for decisions with juristic law and legal propositions with state law. This aspect needs modification, however, as Ehrlich points out that a juristic norm for decision—the majority of norms for decision—if promulgated by the state merely becomes a 'norm for decision *in the form of* [a] legal proposition' (emphasis added).[43]

This last qualification will become clearer when we examine the second set of distinctions, which focuses on *functional* aspects of these rules. In functional terms, legal norms constitute the backbone of the inner order of all legal associations: of the social associations in general where the centre of the law development occurs; it can refer to the order of a court or a system of courts, even though this aspect is not addressed explicitly by Ehrlich; and finally as the *Staatsrecht* or the public law in the narrow sense,[44] pointing to the legal order of the state as a particularly important association, utilised by society as an organ 'to impose its order upon the associations belonging to it'.[45]

Secondly, norms for decision in this account primarily aim at dispute resolution. They become necessary in cases of conflict for which the inner order of an association—based on the legal norms resulting from the facts of the law—does not provide solutions. It has already been mentioned that Ehrlich distinguishes norms for decision according to their (juristic or state) origin.

Lastly, administrative norms, the norms directing state agencies to proceed, are tied to the development of administrative agencies and are in Ehrlich's account primarily found at the level of the state.

---

[42] For historical and theoretical background, see R Ogorek, *Richterkönig oder Subsumtionsautomat? Zur Justiztheorie im 19. Jahrhundert* (Frankfurt aM, Vittorio Klostermann, 1986).
[43] Ehrlich (1936), above n 3, 136. See also *ibid* 171, quoted in the text accompanying n 36.
[44] *Ibid* 143.
[45] *Ibid* 154.

Pounding on Ehrlich. Again? 165

In summary, each level of law, therefore, serves a different function:[46] Legal norms provide the foundation for a peaceful life within an association, as they order human relations. Norms for decision are found or created by judges in their efforts to contain conflicts and thus serve primarily the function of dispute resolution. Legal propositions comprise both of the former, but in addition can perform the task of social engineering based on an instrumental understanding of state law, mainly by guiding the administrative bodies in their proactive intervention into social relations. It seems that Ehrlich saw law's potential to successfully fulfil these tasks as decreasing in the movement from legal norms to legal propositions. This distinction is overlooked by those who claim that law according to Ehrlich reinstitutionalised custom and ought to do so.[47] To him, this reference to the singularity of law would not make sense, as he spent his time pointing to the existence of a plurality of legal orders that differ in their origins, their functions, their forms and contents. Table 1 can serve as a visualisation of the preceding analysis:

Table 1—Two Sets of Norms According to Ehrlich

Formal	*Functional*		
	Legal norms	*Norms for decision*	*Administrative norms*
Legal propositions (state law)	Precision, universality/ *Inner order*	Precision, universality/ *Dispute resolution*	Precision, universality/ *Social engineering*
Norms for decision (juristic law)	Not mentioned[48]	Medium abstraction/ *Dispute resolution*	
Legal norms (social law)	Reduced to practice, even w/o formulation/ *Inner order*		

Living Law

One may be startled by my omission of what appears to be Eugen Ehrlich's major contribution to the sociology of law, that is, the term 'living law'.

---

[46] See also S Vogl, *Soziale Gesetzgebungspolitik, Freie Rechtsfindung und Soziologische Rechtswissenschaft bei Eugen Ehrlich* (Baden-Baden, Nomos, 2003) 358.
[47] Cf Chambliss and Seidman, above n 2, 68.
[48] Even though this aspect is not addressed explicitly by Ehrlich, the inner order of a court or a system of courts might fit into the functional differentiation without problems. It is in the vertical movement from legal norms to norms for decision and legal propositions where the inner order of the courts does not really fit in. This problem occurs because Ehrlich does not use different terminology in order to refer to substantive or formal characteristics of these norms.

In earlier writings, it is widely used and it gave the name to his seminar at the University of Czernowitz created in 1909. In *Fundamental Principles*, it certainly informs the core of the argumentation, yet it does not play an important conceptual role. Only towards the very end, in the chapter about 'The Methods of the Sociology of Law', Ehrlich gives us his definition:

> This is then the *living* law in contradistinction to that which is being enforced in the courts and other tribunals. The living law is the law which dominates life itself even though it has not been posited in legal propositions.[49]

From the terminology that is applied here, one can assume that the living law is identical with the total number of legal norms in the formal sense,[50] which are not contained in legal propositions. Whether the last restriction is really elementary to Ehrlich's understanding of the living law can be questioned because at another instance he speaks about how a legal proposition can act back on the order of the social associations and by dominating it can turn into a legal norm.[51] It can be argued that in the definition of 'living law' given above, Ehrlich excluded legal norms that were turned into legal propositions only in order to direct more attention to the enormous number of legal norms that are not legal propositions at the same time.[52]

ROSCOE POUND

With all its defects, often pointed out, Ehrlich's *Grundlegung der Soziologie des Rechts* is one of the outstanding books of this generation. He had only the beginnings of a technique of ascertaining customs of popular action and getting at the relations of these customs to the law in the books and the judicial and administrative processes in action. But he set us to studying such things and the technique

---

[49] Ehrlich (1936), above n 3, 493. See the equivalent expression in 'Die Erforschung des Lebenden Rechts' in Rehbinder (ed), above n 2, 19, stressing the evolutionary aspect by stating 'though it has not *yet* been posited in legal propositions' (my translation, emphasis added).

[50] Cf Ehrlich (1936), above n 3, 40: 'In all legal associations the legal norm constitutes the backbone of the inner order; it is the strongest support of their organization.'

[51] See *ibid* 192–3: 'A legal proposition which dictates to the courts and the administrative tribunals the course of action which they are to follow contains what amounts to a legal norm for the courts and administrative tribunals as soon as these bodies actually carry it out; it becomes a rule of conduct only when the social relations are actually being ordered thereby.' See also *ibid* 41: 'Rules of law that have remained mere norms for decision, that become effective only in the very rare cases of legal controversy, do not take part in the ordering of the associations. This may be said, a fortiori, of those legal propositions, in reality quite numerous, that do not affect life at all ... Only that which becomes part and parcel of life becomes a living norm; everything else is mere doctrine, norm for decision, dogma, or theory.'

[52] In a short paragraph concerning Talmudic law, Ehrlich mentions three possible relations between the living law and legal propositions: (i) a legal proposition that through its actual acceptance has turned into living law; (ii) living law that results from a misunderstanding of the legal proposition; and (iii) living law that developed autonomously from legal propositions. See 'Das Lebende Recht der Völker der Bukowina' in Rehbinder (ed), n 2 above, 45.

has been developed. ... His idea of the inner order of groups and associations and relations as the basis of the legal order, giving us the living law, should be compared with what the economic determinist sees as imposition of the will of the socially dominant class. His idea of the reaction of 'living law' upon generalizations and formulas, and of precepts and formulas which no longer reflect the inner order of significant associations and relations, should be compared with the view of the skeptical realists who can see nothing but individual behavior tendencies of individual judges. He made a significant beginning of a sociological comparative law (or shall I say a comparative sociological jurisprudence?) which is palpably developing at present.[53]

This slightly longer passage from an article by Roscoe Pound on jurisprudence can serve as a summary of the author's appreciation for the work of Eugen Ehrlich.[54] Pound had taken notice of the original German publication of *Grundlegung der Soziologie des Rechts*.[55] He was an important actor in the preparation of Ehrlich's visit to the United States in 1914, which had to be cancelled due to the outbreak of the First World War and which could not be realised later.[56] It is tempting to relate his interest in Ehrlich in the 1930s, which led to the translation and publication of *Grundlegung der Soziologie des Rechts* in 1936, to the debate between Karl Llewellyn and Roscoe Pound concerning the Legal Realism movement, but information on this matter is scarce.[57] It is safe to assume, however, that while Ehrlich was not one of the main influences on Pound's work, he had

---

[53] R Pound, 'Fifty Years of Jurisprudence' [Part III] (1938) 51 *Harvard Law Review* 805–6. The reference at the beginning concerning the law in the books and the judicial and administrative processes in action shows that Ehrlich's living law was in Pound's view a third and distinct category.

[54] For the relationship between Pound and Ehrlich, see Nelken, above n 1; Likhovsky, above n 40; and M Hertogh, 'A "European" Conception of Legal Consciousness. Rediscovering Eugen Ehrlich' (2004) 31 *Journal of Law and Society* 457.

[55] See, eg Pound's letter to John Chipman Gray, 3 February 1915, RPP, 156-11, quoted in NEH Hull, *Roscoe Pound and Karl Llewellyn. Searching for an American Jurisprudence* (Chicago, The University of Chicago Press, 1997) 110: 'If you have not seen it, Professor Ehrlich's *Grundlagen der Soziologie des Rechts* would be well worth looking at. I think it is the best thing that has been written recently.'

[56] Cf R Pound, 'An Appreciation of Eugen Ehrlich' (1922) 36 *Harvard Law Review* 129. Ehrlich was supposed to lecture at the Lowell Institute in Boston and to address the Association of American Law Schools. The latter presentation was replaced by William Page's 'Professor Ehrlich's Czernowitz Seminar of Living Law', see the reprint in Jerome Hall (ed), *Readings in Jurisprudence* (Indianapolis, Bobbs-Merrill, 1938) 825.

[57] This debate culminated in their famous exchange in the Columbia and Harvard Law Reviews: KN Llewellyn, 'A Realistic Jurisprudence. The Next Step' (1930) 30 *Columbia Law Review* 431; R Pound, 'The Call for a Realist Jurisprudence' (1931) 44 *Harvard Law Review* 697; and KN Llewellyn, 'Some Realism about Realism. Responding to Dean Pound' (1931) 44 *Harvard Law Review* 1222. While including Ehrlich in a list of forerunners to Legal Realism because of his attempt 'to go beyond theorizing, to move, along such lines as these, into the gathering and interpretation of facts about legal behavior', Llewellyn (1930) at 454 consciously omitted Pound from this list. From this point of view, the introduction of Ehrlich's major work to the American (scholarly) public might have appeared advantageous to Pound at the time.

sympathy with and admiration for his *oeuvre*, which remained unaffected throughout the years.

The mixture of longevity and productivity makes it virtually impossible to do justice to the writings of Roscoe Pound in their entirety.[58] The aspects presented here were chosen for their connection to the elements of Ehrlich's work already discussed and are based on Pound's article 'Law in Books and Law in Action',[59] published slightly earlier than the German original of *Fundamental Principles*.

Introducing the difference between 'law in the books' and 'law in action', Pound considers the first to consist of 'the rules that purport to govern the relations of man and man', whereas the latter is understood as the rules 'that in fact govern' these relations.[60] This is as much of a conceptual clarification we receive from Pound and he does not return to this distinction in later writings. Although the underlying thought is vital to his conception of sociological jurisprudence, it can legitimately be claimed that these are not its conceptual building blocks. This dichotomy can also be seen as an example for how concepts can take on a life of their own, independently from the weight their creators accorded to them. The scarcity of the definition labelling a (by now!) common-sense insight might have contributed to this success. Uncritical usage of these terms, however, will inevitably brush over some problematic aspects. Without wanting to indulge into 'Pound-pounding'[61] here, I want to focus on three of those aspects that were chosen because they are standard problems of legal theory and sociology and bear resemblance to some of the issues with which Eugen Ehrlich was concerned. Turning first to the term 'law in action', which appears to be the more problematic of the two, opens up the possibility to discuss the distinction between norms and facts and the distinction between legal and non-legal norms. The term 'law in the books' seems to be self-evident to such a degree that the issue of the indeterminacy of law does not readily suggest itself. It is, however, quite pertinent to the analysis of this concept.

For a documentation of the Llewellyn-Pound debate and the origins of Legal Realism, see NEH Hull, 'Some Realism about the Llewellyn-Pound Exchange over Realism. The Newly Uncovered Private Correspondence, 1927–1931' (1987) *Wisconsin Law Review* 921; and Hull, above n 55.

[58] For a detailed review of life and work, see D Wigdor, *Roscoe Pound. Philosopher of Law* (Westport, Greenwood Press, 1974); EB McLean, *Law and Civilization. The Legal Thought of Roscoe Pound* (Lanham, University Press of America, 1992); and the bibliography by FC Setaro, *A Bibliography of the Writings of Roscoe Pound* (Cambridge, Harvard University Press, 1942).

[59] R Pound, 'Law in Books and Law in Action' (1910) 44 *American Law Review* 12.

[60] Ibid 15.

[61] See S Presser, 'Revising the Conservative Tradition. Towards a New American Legal History' (1977) 52 *New York University Law Review* 712, who stated that it 'has been a favorite indoor sport for legal historiographers for almost forty years'.

Norms and Facts

The distinction between law in the books and law in action is one between two sets of rules. So, only looking at law in action for the moment, how is it possible to determine the content of rules if in fact we only have the observable social interaction of individuals?

Based on Pound's concept of law, a restriction enters into this description, as for him not any interaction of individuals will suffice; rather, only the acts of judicial and executive personnel can put the law in action, so to speak. This element of official application of law is necessary, and thus in crucial opposition to Ehrlich whose definition of law does not require any involvement of state agencies. Yet, the official element alone is not sufficient for Pound, either:

> [L]aw is not what is done officially but the measuring of what ought to be done officially and how it ought to be done.[62]

Similar to Ehrlich, Pound also strives to keep up the line between the normative and the factual. However, the difference between a rule *for* behaviour and a regularity *of* behaviour makes it all the more difficult to understand his concept of 'law in action'. It seems to require a regularity in the application of norms: consequently, isolated instances of norm application that do not conform to the law in the books must be regarded as misinterpretations or misapplications and, therefore, they do not form the basis for law in action. The mere fact that a certain behaviour by state officials occurs regularly cannot suffice to create *law* in action, either. A reference to the claim of the normative power of the factual, first made by the German theorist Jellinek and then taken up by Ehrlich,[63] might suggest otherwise. However, this statement should only be read as a commentary on the *evolutionary* aspect of the *ought* out of the *is* and not as casting doubt on the *analytical* difference between the two. Therefore, we must assume further that Pound conceives law in action as a set of rules that can be discerned from a pattern of comparable application of legal rules by judicial or executive agencies—rules that might or might not match those prescribed by the law in the books. Unfortunately, Pound fails to provide the criteria for the determination when these behavioural patterns are actually rule-governed, which is of particular importance in the case where the behaviour does not comply with the formulated provisions in the books. There is not even an allusion to a methodology of how to derive the norms from the observable

---

[62] R Pound, 'The American Idea of Government' (1944) 30 *American Bar Association Journal* 501. In this vein, see also the mocking remark in the introductory quote from Pound regarding the 'view of the skeptical realists who can see nothing but individual behavior tendencies of individual judges'.

[63] Ehrlich (1936), above n 3, 86.

behaviour.[64] What remains, in the end, is the striking parallel to the two aspects contained in Ehrlich's norms for decision, one referring to the pattern of judicial decisions, the other to their normative content.

Legal and Non-legal Norms

The second issue—the distinction between legal and non-legal norms—is less troubling for Pound than it is for Ehrlich. The latter's distinction between different classes of norms according to the 'overtones of feelings' (*Gefühlstöne*) they release[65] has attracted much criticism, and even mockery, due to the lack of conceptual rigidity and practical usefulness. Pound's 'imperative theory of law coupled with a Realist stress on effective prediction of legal outcomes' may be little satisfactory, as the effectivity criterion is not applied rigorously.[66] Still, Pound does not allow for the existence of law production at the general level of society, and as a result avoids many of the problems encountered by Ehrlich. The examples provided in the article, for instance, the rise of wills in ancient Rome,[67] highlight that not social practices by themselves but only their recognition by state agencies charged with the task of social control become legally relevant.[68] Precision is facilitated by a restriction of the actors involved in norm-creating processes: the general population cannot but create mere social, that is non-legal, norms, whereas the state's coercive apparatus creates and applies legal norms. From this perspective, Pound's distinction between legal and non-legal norms is more satisfactory than Ehrlich's proposal.

The Indeterminacy of Law

Up until now, the term 'law in the books' has been used as a readily understandable standard against which to measure the activities of state agencies. However, as the debate concerning the indeterminacy of legal rules suggests, this should be far from obvious. Wittgenstein's remark that 'no course of action could be determined by a rule, because every course of action can be made out to accord with the rule'[69] points towards an

---

[64] Illustrative in this regard is the questionnaire Ehrlich developed to document the 'living law of the people in the Bukovina', which aims at collecting information both about the practice of the people as well as their conceptions of legality that accompany it: see Ehrlich, above n 52, 49–60.

[65] Ehrlich (1936), above n 3, 165.

[66] Nelken, above n 1, 160.

[67] Pound, above n 59, 13.

[68] It is interesting to see Ehrlich's discussion of the topic: he sees the same practice regarding the rise of wills in ancient Rome as legal norms without the necessity of their recognition in norms for decision or even legal propositions; cf Ehrlich (1936), above n 3, 193–4.

[69] L Wittgenstein, *Philosophical Investigations* (3rd edn, New York, MacMillan, 1958) 81.

extreme rule scepticism that one needs to take into account. This seems to be even more the case if we leave the level of particular legal rules and turn to their interplay within a normative system whose qualities as being complete and free of contradictions have long been disputed and notably by Ehrlich and the Free Law Movement.[70] Building on Bloor's action-based theory of meaning, Tamanaha concludes that only a given practice, for example, that of judging, can eventually determine the meaning of norms, as they are otherwise inevitably open to change.[71] However, if it is true that norms acquire their (definite) meaning only through an act of interpretation by those who apply them, then the distinction between the categories of law in the books and law in action collapses. If we do not accept the notion that out of the multitude of possible interpretations of a rule only one is right—and there seems to be no ground of impartiality from which to make such a claim—then this incertitude inevitably extends to the legal realm. Thus, we can no longer assume of one standard derived from the law in the books against which we can measure the law in action; rather, we have to accept that content and meaning of every rule are continually actualised and these actualisations relentlessly compete for acceptance.

> A process of judicial lawmaking has always gone on and still goes on in all systems of law, no matter how completely in their juristic theory they limit the function of adjudication to the purely mechanical.[72]

Given this stress on the importance of the judiciary for legal renewal, especially in opposition to legislation and juridical tradition, we find a starting point in Pound's thought, which already casts doubt on the clear opposition between law in the books and law in action. Therefore, it is even more surprising that Pound did not expand on this. The reason for this might be that Pound was already steeped in anti-formalism that was to become one of the major tenets of the movement of American Legal Realism and thus he might have considered references to this anti-formalistic critique

---

[70] See E Ehrlich, 'Über Lücken im Recht' in Rehbinder (ed), above n 2, 80. The Free Law Movement and its influence on American Legal Realism is described by JE Herget and S Wallace, 'The German Free Law Movement as the Source of American Legal Realism' (1987) 73 *Virginia Law Review* 399. They show that covert reception of Ehrlich's work, among that of other members of the Free Law Movement, was widespread. This reception, however, was not centred on *Fundamental Principles*, but rather on *Freie Rechtsfindung und Freie Rechtswissenschaft* (Leipzig, Hirschfeld, 1903), which appeared in the translation of E Bruncken and LB Register in *Science of Legal Method* (Boston, Boston Book Co, 1917) 47.

A famous argument in favour of the determinacy thesis, in the sense of the existence of one right decision for every case, can be found in R Dworkin, *Taking Rights Seriously* (Cambridge, Harvard University Press, 1978) ch 4; for the corresponding critique, see M Cohen (ed), *Ronald Dworkin and Contemporary Jurisprudence* (Totowa, Rowman and Allanheld, 1984).

[71] Tamanaha, above n 15, 165.

[72] R Pound, *The Spirit of the Common Law* (Boston, Marshall Jones, 1921) 172.

superfluous.[73] The problems that I have pointed out in reviewing the relationship between law in the books and law in action would have taken away much from the impact of Pound's article, whose aim was mainly to convince. Given the influence on the scholarly field exerted by his call for a sociological jurisprudence, the reader may decide for him- or herself whether this goal was attained.

It has become apparent in the course of my argument that I have also detected a three-layered division at the base of Pound's thought, namely of: those who make law; those who apply or enforce law; and those that are mere users, addressees or objects of the law. These groups can be approximated to the legislature, the judiciary and administration, and finally the general population. The distinction between the first and the second level is blurry as on the one hand Pound highlights the innovative, law-creating role that the judiciary and the executive can play, most notably with his emphasis on judge-made law. On the other hand, Pound relies on the productive antagonism that arises between the two. He stresses, for example, that the judiciary is best equipped to further the goal of protecting and furthering civilisation, as it is bound by the received precepts, techniques and ideals developed by legislation and inherited legal method, which open a margin of discretion within professionally legitimated boundaries.[74] Pound's call 'not be afraid of legislation' and to 'welcome new principles, introduced by legislation, which express the spirit of the time'[75] is based on his model of legal development and his distinction between phases of legal stability and flexibility. In the current phase of the 'socialisation of law', which finds its theoretical equivalent in 'sociological jurisprudence', he deemed the legislator to be in an important position to employ influences from the social sciences in order to promote a new and more concrete version of individual equality that adjusts 'burdens with reference to ability to bear them'.[76] In summary, it is this ambivalence which prevents a sharp division, but it is also important for the description of the gap that comes to exist when the law in action does not accord to the law in the books.

The fact that Pound and Ehrlich were kindred spirits in this regard can best be revealed if one accepts my reconstruction of the threefold distinction between legal propositions, norms for decision and legal norms, as the mere dichotomy of living law and norms for decision allows for no space to locate this gap. As mentioned above, Ehrlich's argument also contains this ambivalence, with only a blurry line dividing legal propositions and

---

[73] In regard to the anti-formalistic traits of American Legal Realism, see the recent summary by H Dagan, 'The Realist Conception of Law' (2007) 57 *University of Toronto Law Journal* 611–22.
[74] See McLean, above n 58, 281 ff.
[75] Pound, above n 59, 35.
[76] R Pound, *Jurisprudence*, vol 1 (St Paul, West Publishing, 1959) 431.

norms for decision. However, this productive tension allowed for stressing the original contribution of judges to the law-creating process. For Ehrlich, working in a civil law context, this was of even greater importance. From his perspective the position of the common law judge served as an ideal for him, with England providing a particularly laudable example.

The two authors, however, part intellectual companionship in reference to the third level. Consider Ehrlich's one-sentence summary of his book:

> At the present as well as at any other time, the center of gravity of *legal* development lies not in legislation, nor in juristic science, nor in judicial decision, but in society itself (emphasis added).[77]

This is, of course, diametrically opposed to Pound's view that allows for no law creation outside the activity of state agencies. It seems that this difference makes any comparison between the two very difficult. The closest match that we can find in Pound's article concerning the observable phenomenon of social order that is attributed by Ehrlich to the existence of 'legal norms' is that of 'extra-legal notions of conformity to the views of the community'.[78]

CONCLUSION

After this conceptual rearrangement stressing rather a threefold than a twofold distinction in both the works of Ehrlich and Pound, let me return to the initial quote by Nelken, which can serve as a foil to demonstrate where this change of perspective yields different results. First of all, the way in which he describes the relationship between law in the books and law in action contains in a nutshell the first and the third problem that I have highlighted in the discussion devoted to Pound, which led to the result that one needs

---

[77] Ehrlich (1936), above n 3, xv.
[78] Pound, above n 59, 19. Stone, above n 2, 45–7 points to seven possible gaps to be researched, namely: '(1) between what courts say and what they do; (2) between the words of statutes and what courts do under them; (3) between instructions to juries and what juries do; (4) between the formulae for executive action and what executive officials actually do; (5) between rules formulated for conduct on a matter by statute or judicial decision or juristic writing, and the conduct of citizens which actually occurs; (6) between the object assumed or expressed by legislature or court in formulating a rule, and the actual consequences which flow from observance of it; (7) between "facts" as found by judges and juries on the issues raised in adversary procedures, which in the light of the applicable rule determine the results, and the "true facts" which do not emerge.' In a footnote, he attributes the fifth constellation to Ehrlich and phrases it as the gap between 'legal propositions and rules for official decision' and 'living law'. According to the understanding of Ehrlich that I presented, one should be more precise and see the gap between rules formulated for conduct on a matter by statute or judicial decision or juristic writing and *the rules that govern* the conduct of citizens which actually occurs. However, Stone is essentially right and more importantly it becomes clear that this gap is beyond Pound's concern, as the second set of rules cannot make up *law* in action. It seems that Pound was mainly interested in the gaps number (2) and (4) of Stone's list.

by all means to maintain the normative quality of the law in action. In this sense, law in action contains, however, additional information, that is, a pattern of behaviour by law applying state agencies, a trait it has in common with the here-proposed narrower meaning of 'norms for decision'.

Secondly, there is agreement in the evaluation that living law cannot correspond to what Pound meant by law in action, simply because the former lacks state recognition which is vital to Pound's definition of law. However, the first explanation provided by Nelken is not convincing on both accounts. As law in action necessarily refers to a set of rules in order to avoid the collapse of the separate categories of norms and facts, *both* living law and law in action reveal an obligatory character inherent in their normative nature. The second part, the alleged lack of action in Ehrlich's concept of 'living law', is irritating, but might be attributed to the imprecise translation, which speaks of the 'legal command, reduced to practice', whereas 'the legal command transformed into action' is closer to the original.[79]

Proposing that the living law is the law in the books for the members of a social association is confusing in that Ehrlich claims that the legal norm can and usually does exist without any formulation in words.[80] Furthermore, it is problematic in the sense that Ehrlich describes the living law as the base for the peaceful order of the social life within an association, whereas the law in the books in Pound's understanding is rather the latest form of normative attempts of social control and intervention by the state. The functions performed by these two sets of norms in the view of their authors are not easily reconcilable. In this sense, Ehrlich's bottom-up proposition of the normative development from legal norms over norms for decision to legal propositions conflicts with Pound's top-down approach of social engineering by legal means.

For Ehrlich, the normal condition of any social association is by definition one of order and peace. Legal norms or the living law reflect this condition and therefore adequately show what *actually* happens. This shift of emphasis is his attempt to correct the lawyers' distorted vision of a world consisting primarily of conflict and norm violations.[81] Therefore, legal norms do not provide an answer for what happens in the case of norm violation, although lawyers should try to derive their norms for decision from the order provided by the living law. However, if the distinction between 'law in the books' and 'law in action' has any significance at all,

---

[79] Ehrlich (1936), above n 3, 38; cf Ehrlich (1989), above n 3, 44.
[80] Ehrlich (1936), above n 3, 38.
[81] According to Gurvitch, this comes for the price of an impoverished description of the law of associations, which might at times be more abstract in formal terms and also inclusive of autonomous bodies of conflict resolution. See G Gurvitch, *Sociology of Law* (New York, Philosophical Library, 1942) 155.

then it is certainly not from the first category that we learn what norm transgression entails, but only from the second, since it is only the law in action which provides the additional information of that which 'actually happens in practice'. It appears that Nelken's remark in this context rather refers to Ehrlich's distinction between the primary and the secondary normative order, the one proscribing the norms which when followed lead to the peaceful coexistence within an association, the second providing norms to stabilise it in the case of conflict.

To end my reflections, I repeat the point that it appears damaging to the reconstruction of Ehrlich's theoretical as well as political endeavours to assume that his 'norms for decision' comprise both Pound's 'law in action' and 'law in the books'. It leads to the collapse of the gap between Pound's two categories, whose preservation is even more important for Ehrlich. Pound eventually wants to close the gap by making the 'law in the books such that the law in action can conform to it'.[82] Within Ehrlich's framework with his stress on the need for the judge to find appropriate norms for decision for every case as well as the different functions assigned to legal norms, norms for decision and legal propositions, this is not a meaningful suggestion. Making norms for decision and legal propositions that are more sensitive to the order provided by the living law does not mean that these categories lose their distinguishing features.

That leaves us with Nelken's last statement and with this I can totally agree. Legal norms in Ehrlich's sense are inconceivable for Pound and they are exactly what make Ehrlich's approach so unique. And this should have put more problems to Pound than it seems to have had. Ehrlich's 'legal norms' are the foundation for an image of society that is infinitely more polycentric in regards to law. It is this contribution to the sociology of law that makes Eugen Ehrlich's writings so valuable as a starting point for both theoretical as well as empirical research[83] and it is Nelken's intent and achievement to restore this. An achievement that is by no means diminished by the criticism advanced here, as the main thrust of his argument remains untouched by it.

In his debate with Hans Kelsen, Ehrlich warned against the attempt to read his book with a different terminology in mind.[84] Remembering this warning, I would hesitantly propose, with all the restrictions presented earlier, that there are affinities between Eugen Ehrlich's 'legal propositions'—'norms for decisions'—'legal norms' and Roscoe Pound's concepts of 'law in the books'—'law in action'—'extra-legal notions of conformity to the views of the community'.

---

[82] Pound, above n 59, 36.
[83] The most recent effort in this vein is Hertogh's proposition of a European conception of legal consciousness, see n 54.
[84] Ehrlich, above n 9, 61.

8

The Social Life of Living Law in Indonesia

FRANZ AND KEEBET VON BENDA-BECKMANN

INTRODUCTION

WHEN WE WENT to Indonesia the first time in 1973 to discuss our research plans on disputing and property and inheritance with members of the local university in Padang, West Sumatra, the concept of adat law, the customary, traditional law of the ethnic population groups in the Indonesian archipelago, was no longer valued. It was strongly associated with the old pre-colonial adat law. When we explained that we did not want to study this old adat law, but to find out what nowadays could be called law, what kind of law was used in village decision-making and in court judgements, they brightened up: 'Ah, you want to research living law; yes, that is a good and necessary activity.' There was some general understanding of what living law was. It was not old but contemporary law, not law on paper but actually valid and practiced, and it was more than just adat law. At this very general level, we had understood each other, yet we felt that we only had used magic formulas because neither of us could say with great clarity what should be understood under the concepts of living law and adat law.[1]

In this very first beginning of our research, we did not know yet that the concept of 'living law' (Indonesian: *hukum hidup* or *hukum yang hidup*) had had an interesting career in Indonesia. That such a concept had a career at all must be astonishing for everyone familiar with the writings of Ehrlich and his elaboration of living law. While Ehrlich[2] had developed his concept in contrast to conventional legal doctrines and theories, in Indonesia, living

---

[1] F and K Von Benda-Beckmann, *Om de Taak van den Onderzoeker. Herdenking van de 100ste Geboortedag van Cornelis van Vollenhoven* (Leiden, 1975) 75.

[2] E Ehrlich, 'Die Erforschung des lebenden Rechts' (1911) 35 *Schmollers Jahrbuch für Gesetzgebung, Verwaltung und Volkswirtschaft im Deutschen Reich* 47; E Ehrlich, *Grundlegung der Soziologie des Rechts* (4th edn, Berlin, Duncker & Humblot, [1989], 1913); and E Ehrlich, *Fundamental Principles of the Sociology of Law* (New Brunswick and London, Transaction Publishers, 2002).

law was incorporated into legislative texts and court judgments, in which it became the decisive ground and justification for establishing court jurisdiction and substantive inheritance law. This raises the question of how the concept of living law found its way to Indonesia, and whether Ehrlich's writings have anything to do with it (for Ehrlich's ideas *did* find their way to academic and political discourses in other countries).[3] As Nelken, Ziegert and others have pointed out, Ehrlich's writings and his notion of living law in particular had also considerable influence on later sociological and anthropological approaches to law.[4]

In our contribution, we show that in the case of the Dutch East Indies and later Indonesia, the living law (German: *lebendes Recht*) which made such an amazing career in Indonesia was not the one that Ehrlich had found, but the living law discovered and labelled '*levend recht*' by the Dutch scholar Cornelis van Vollenhoven (1874–1933), who started using it in 1907.[5] Nothing points to the two authors being familiar with each other's work. Yet their understanding of law, and of living law, was rather similar. Similar also were legal conditions which led them to talk in terms of living law as the 'really relevant law for people' and as the subject to which a social (and legal) science of law, but also law application, ought to direct interest. In Ehrlich's case, these conditions were formed by the complex plural legal conditions in the Austro-Hungarian Empire; in Van Vollenhoven's case, it was the even greater complexity of law in the colony of the Dutch East Indies. Van Vollenhoven, it seems to us, was probably the most congenial of Ehrlich's contemporaries, despite the fact that his academic and political project differed from Ehrlich's and his other contemporaries.

We shall first briefly sketch Van Vollenhoven's use of the term *levend recht*, living law. We shall then trace its way to the Dutch East Indies and the significance it obtained in Indonesian law. Finally, we will examine Ehrlich

---

[3] Podgorecki mentions that the concept of living law, transmitted to Japan through the writings of Ehrlich, was sought as a political instrument by the Japanese communists who intended, in the 1930s, to intercept power through parliamentary, not revolutionary, means (A Podgorecki, 'Unrecognized Father of Sociology of Law: Leon Petrazycki. Reflections Based on Jan Gorecki's Sociology and Jurisprudence of Leon Petrazycki' (1981) 15 *Law and Society Review* 183 at 191, fn 10). On the social life of the term in Japanese jurisprudence, see Vogl in this volume. On the notion of 'living customary law' in South African jurisprudence, see T Bennett, 'The Contribution of Legal Theory and Judicial Practice to the Future Development of Customary Law' in G Glover (ed), *Essays in honour of AJ Kerr* (Durban, LexisNexis Butterworths, 2006).

[4] See M Rehbinder, *Die Begründung der Rechtssoziologie durch Eugen Ehrlich* (Berlin, Duncker & Humblot, 1967); M Rehbinder, *Einführung in die Rechtssoziologie* (Frankfurt am Main, Athenäum Verlag, 1971); D Nelken, Law in Action or Living Law? Back to the Beginning in Sociology of Law' (1984) 4 *Legal Studies* 157–74; J Griffiths, 'What is Legal Pluralism?' (1986) 24 *Journal of Legal Pluralism* 23; G Teubner, 'Global Bukowina: Legal Pluralism in the World Society' in G Teubner (ed), *Global Law without a State* (Aldershot, Ashgate, 1997); KA Ziegert, 'Introduction to the Transaction Edition' in E Ehrlich, n 2 above; and R Banakar, *Merging Law and Sociology: Beyond the Dichotomies in Sociolegal Research* (Glienicke and Madison, Galda and Wilch, 2003).

[5] Ehrlich founded an Institute for living law in 1910, see Ziegert, above n 4, xxiv.

and Van Vollenhoven and some of their other contemporaries and compare how Ehrlich's understanding of living law relates to Van Vollenhoven's.

VAN VOLLENHOVEN AND LIVING LAW (*LEVEND RECHT*)

Van Vollenhoven earned his fame as founder and master of what became known as the Adat Law School.[6] He was a professor in international law, but devoted most of his academic work to the variety of mainly unwritten legal orders of ethnic groups in the Indonesian archipelago.[7] These laws were summarily called adat laws, and Van Vollenhoven's spent much time synthesising and systematising the patchwork literature written so far by European travellers, early anthropologists, lawyers, administrators and judges.[8] The first and second decade of the twentieth century was primarily devoted to the 'discovery' of adat law rather than its application in the courts. Van Vollenhoven's division of adat laws into adat law circles (*adatrechtskringen*) and a full-scale presentation of all aspects of their legal systems set the agenda and provided the categories through which research on adat was to be undertaken. His pupils later wrote comprehensive accounts of individual adat systems and more specialised accounts of certain fields of law.[9] Great amounts of ethnographic detail were collected and published

---

[6] The development of Dutch anthropology of law until the early 1980s has been described and analysed in great detail by J Griffiths, 'Recent Anthropology of Law in the Netherlands and Its Historical Background' in K von Benda-Beckmann and F Strijbosch (eds), *Anthropology of Law in the Netherlands* (Dordrecht and Berlin, Foris Publications and Walter de Gruyter, 1986). For other accounts, see F Strijbosch, *Juristen en de Studie van Volksrecht in Nederlands-Indië en Anglofoon Afrika* (Nijmegen, Instituut voor Volksrecht, 1980); F Strijbosch, 'De Rechtsantropologie in Nederland en België' in J Griffiths (ed), *De Sociale Werking van Recht: Een Kennismaking met de Rechtssociologie en Rechtsantropologie* (Nijmegen, Ars Aequi, 1996); F von Benda-Beckmann, 'Rechtsantropologie in Nederland' (1981) 28 *Themanummer Sociologische Gids* (Meppel, Boom) 297; JF Holleman, *Van Vollenhoven on Indonesian Adat Law* (The Hague, Martinus Nijhoff, 1981); K von Benda-Beckmann and F Strijbosch, 'Introduction' in K von Benda-Beckmann and F Strijbosch (eds), *Anthropology of Law in The Netherlands* (Dordrecht and Cinnaminson, Foris Publications, 1986); P Burns, 'The Myth of Adat' (1989) 28 *Journal of Legal Pluralism* 1; P Burns, *The Leiden Legacy: Concepts of Law in Indonesia* (Leiden, KITLV Press, 2004); K von Benda-Beckmann et al, *Living Law in the Low Countries* (Special issue of the Dutch and Belgian Law & Society Journal Recht der Werkelijkheid) (The Hague, Vuga, 1991); and F and K von Benda-Beckmann, 'Anthropolgy of Law and the Study of Folk Law in the Netherlands after 1950' in H Vermeulen and J Kommers (eds), *Tales from Academia: History of Anthropology in the Netherlands*, Pt 2 (Saarbrücken, Verlag für Entwicklungspolitik Saarbrücken GmbH, 2002).

[7] For more information on Van Vollenhoven, see JF Holleman, *Von Vollenhoven on Indonesian Adat Law* (The Hague, Martinus Nijhoff, 1981); and DS Lev, 'Book Review: Van Vollenhoven on Indonesian Adat Law' (1984) 22 *Journal of Legal Pluralism* 147.

[8] One has to bear in mind that what in 1817 became the colony of the Dutch East Indies had been established in various parts of the archipelago around 1600, while other regions (Bali, Aceh) were only incorporated at the turn of the nineteenth century.

[9] See, eg FD Holleman, *Het Adat-grondenrecht van Ambon en de Oeliasers* (Delft, Molukken Instituut, 1923); FD Holleman, *Het Adatrecht van de Afdeeling Toeloengagoeng (Gewest Kediri); Een Onvoltooide Studie* (Buitenzorg, Archipel Drukkerij & Boekhandel, 1927); VE Korn, *Het Adatrecht van Bali* ('s Gravenhage, Naeff, 1932); VE Korn, *De Dorpsrepubliek*

between 1910 and 1955 in the *Adatrechtbundels*, and this information was again systematised in the *Pandecten van het Adatrecht* between 1914 and 1936. In terms of quantity and quality, the information gathered and processed during the first three decades of the twentieth century was unique.

Van Vollenhoven's main work on adat law was published in three volumes between 1906 and 1933. The concept of 'living law' was frequently used, mostly in a rather matter-of-fact way. The earliest source we could trace was in 1907, when he wrote the chapter on 'the study of adat law', later to become chapter IV of volume I.[10] Van Vollenhoven also refers to living law in his book on *Misconceptions of Adat Law*, where he speaks of 'living folk law'[11] and at several places in his book on *The Discovery of Adat Law*,[12] where living law is contrasted to 'described law'.[13] He contrasted his understanding of adat law with the more classical understandings of customary law, as it had developed in Roman law and later in European legal thought,[14] and compared his ideas to and distinguished them from earlier 'theories' of customary law of Suarez, Savigny, Puchta, Kelsen and many more. These theories, he said, seem to be dialectically deduced, logically derived, from a set of own premises never based on the observation of reality. He rejected in particular the notion that adat customary law had to be old, based on *inveterate consuetudo*, and emphasised its dynamic nature and changes.

Adat law for Van Vollenhoven was law in its own right, irrespective of the existence of a state or a state's coercive power. Adat law was adat with legal consequences. It was dynamic, having its own ideas about change.[15] It mainly emerged and was maintained in *rechtsgemeenschappen*, 'jural communities' in Holleman's translation.[16] Van Vollenhoven never defined the concept strictly, but its meaning is clear from the consistency of his usage. It refers to the larger or smaller constituent corporate units of an organised indigenous society, which, in Van Vollenhoven's conception, derive their distinct, legal autonomy in domestic affairs from the fact that each

---

Tnganan Pagringsingan (Santpoort, Mees, 1933); R Soepomo, *Het Adatprivaatrecht van West-Java* (Batavia, Departement van Justitie, 1933); and JC Vergouwen, *Het Rechtsleven der Toba-Bataks* ('s Gravenhage, Martinus Nijhoff, 1933). However, there was also life outside the adat law school, for instance, Willinck's monumental work on the legal life of the Minangkabau, rarely quoted and praised, because he was not part of the adat law 'school': GD Willinck, *Het Rechtsleven bij de Minangkabausche Maleiers* (Leiden, Brill, 1909).

[10] This was written in his critique of German ethnological jurisprudence, where he criticised the not distinguishing data from living and scriptural law (in, eg Muslim or Hindu law, Van Vollenhoven, below n 18 (1918), 74 and 65–91; and Holleman, above n 6, 31).

[11] Van Vollenhoven, *Miskenningen van het Adatrecht* (Leiden, Brill, 1909) 50 and 51.

[12] *De Ontdekking van het Adatrecht* (Leiden, Brill, 1928).

[13] *Ibid* 109; see also 97, 131 and 160.

[14] Van Vollenhoven, below n 18 (1931), II: 397. Also, Dutch authors had said that custom could only become legal if the judge recognises it as such.

[15] Van Vollenhoven, below n 18 (1918), 66.

[16] JF Holleman (ed), *Van Vollenhoven on Indonesian Adat Law* (The Hague, Martinus Nijhoff, 1981) 43.

has: (i) its discrete representative authority; and (ii) its discrete communal property, especially land, over which it exercises control.[17] Already in his inaugural lecture of 1901,[18] Van Vollenhoven stated that in order to unravel the exceeding complexity of legal forms and processes in Indonesia, one should focus primarily on these communities as the fundamental sources and places of law, and on the 'common product law' only in the second place.[19] In volume II,[20] Van Vollenhoven elaborately discussed the mechanisms through which adat law is maintained and changed. In his view, the processes of law application through judges in court procedures is one important, but possibly the least significant, way. Much more important are 'voluntary observance' and the processes of 'supported observance', later called 'preventive law care'.[21] These were processes in which representatives of the community, by virtue of their participation, validated important social transactions, confirming that the transactions did not violate other people's rights and were in accordance with the principles of adat law.

In the Dutch adat law literature, Islamic law was not a possible candidate for 'living law'. It was regarded as mainly 'external' law, outside the realm of the common people and their living law. However, the position of Islamic law was hotly disputed around the turn of the nineteenth century. There were and are two major positions regarding the role of religious law. Van den Berg and others took a rather extreme position when they held that:

> ... it is generally accepted that the family and inheritance law of the population of Java and Madura who have accepted the Islamic faith is governed by Mohammedan law (*sarat*).[22]

The adat law scholars reacted sharply against such a legalistic interpretation.[23] In the view of most adat law specialists, in order for Islamic legal elements to become folk law, it had to become part of adat law. This applies also to Van Vollenhoven, be it that he paid more attention to Islamic law than later scholars of adat law.[24] Even in his work there is a tendency to

---

[17] *Ibid*: for Indonesia, Van Vollenhoven identified four general types of jural community: genealogical groupings; territorial and genealogical groupings; territorial groupings without genealogical communities; and voluntary corporate associations.

[18] C Vollenhoven, *Het Adatrecht van Nederlands-Indië*, 3 vols (Leiden, Brill, 1918, 1931, 1933) III: 3 ff.

[19] Holleman, above n 16, 19.

[20] Vollenhoven, above n 18 (1931).

[21] JF Holleman, 'Trouble Cases and Trouble-less Cases in the Study of Customary Law and Legal Reform' (1973) 7 *Law & Society Review* 585.

[22] LWC Van den Berg, 'De Afwijkingen van het Mohammedaansche Familie en Erfrecht op Jave en Madoera' (1892) 41 *Bijdragen tot de Taal-en Volkenkunde van Nederlands-Indië* 454.

[23] Starting his account of Central and East Java, Van Vollenhoven writes: 'Much too often one still is inclined ... to look for [Javanese inheritance law] ... primarily in Moslem regulation' (Van Vollenhoven, above n 18, 589).

[24] This is shown in his elaborate summary and analysis of materials on religious law in the Dutch East Indies (Van Vollenhoven, above n 18 (1931), ch III). Significantly, chapter III is entitled 'Religious parts of adat law'.

treat the reality of Islamic law mainly in terms of its deviations from the *fiqh* and of its incorporation into adat law, or its 'penetration of little pieces of Muslim law into the adat law'.[25] The idea that folk law could consist of 'folk' legal ideas stemming from different sources, among them religion, and that there could be an Islamic folk law that differed from scriptural Islamic law, was as foreign to his approach as it was to others. In our view, the most prominent reason for equating folk law with adat law and excluding the possibility of religious law as folk law is that researchers were too strongly preoccupied with proving that adat law was law, and with the recognition of that adat law in the context of state structures.[26] Adat law, in order to be legitimately supported, had to be folk law, in the sense of an indigenous law, which, although dynamic, had a long historic continuity into which Islamic law, and later colonial law, had intruded. In this line of thinking, religious legal elements were only seriously taken into account as far as they were adat-ised and thereby transformed into indigenous law. Underlying this type of argument lay a deep distrust of Islam and a more or less a priori disregard of the fact that in some areas Islam had been part of people's social and religious life for several centuries before the European colonisers came. The fact that Islamic scriptural law was also a legal system and was maintained as such for centuries and that, as a system, it was clearly distinct from adat, or from state law for that matter, probably added to this view.

THE TRAVEL OF LIVING LAW TO THE DUTCH EAST INDIES

The notions of living law and living adat law, which were to become part of the state legal system after Indonesia's independence, thus had been important concepts in the adat law scholarship in the Netherlands and its colony. The metaphors were common in the circle of the pupils of Van Vollenhoven, many of whom were Indonesians. Furthermore, these notions moved with them to Indonesia, especially after the establishment in 1924 of the Law College (*Rechtshogeschool*) in Batavia, the capital of the colony (now Jakarta).[27] Here, the first generations of Indonesian lawyers were trained having to follow intensive courses in adat law and ethnology.[28] Many of these students, some of whom wrote PhD dissertations based on research on adat law, were to play a prominent role in high positions during

---

[25] Van Vollenhoven, above n 18 (1931), 163.
[26] F and K von Benda-Beckmann, 'Islamic Law as Folk Law' in H Slaats (ed), *Liber Amicorum Mohammad Koesnoe* (Surabaya, Airlangga University Press, 1993).
[27] This is a nice example of how concepts 'travel'; see W Twining, 'Have concepts, Will Travel: Jurisprudence in a Global Context' (2005) 1 *International Journal of Law in Global Context* 5.
[28] See GS Resink, 'Rechtshogeschool, Jongereneed, Stuw en Gestuwden' (1974) 130 *BKI* 428.

and after independence. Indonesia's first Minister of Justice, Supomo, had studied in Leiden and had completed his PhD under Van Vollenhoven in 1927.[29] In the 1920s, adat law played an important role in finding an all-Indonesian identity. In addition, post-war writings on adat law, and on law, took over the language of adat law, adat law as living law and living law. When Wignjodipuro[30] reviewed the definitions and circumscriptions of adat law of Supomo, Sukanto, Bellefroid, Djojodigoeno, Van Vollenhoven, ter Haar and Hazairin, these always came down to the idea that adat law was (mostly) unwritten and dynamic. Adat law is a law that lives, because it mirrors the true legal feelings of the population. Therefore, adat law is in a continuous process of emergence and growth, as life itself.[31] Living law, to some extent as living adat law, but sometimes used in a wider sense, remained an important concept for lawyers and anthropologists until the 1970s.[32]

Living Law Becomes Lawyers' Law: Living Law (*hukum yang hidup*) in Indonesian Legislation, Court Decisions and Academic Writing

Independent Indonesia carried over the burden or richness of a plural legal system, in which the various adat laws, Islamic law (as the most important of the religious laws) and state laws co-existed, the latter mainly being colonial laws. These legal orders all had their own institutional basis for law application, adat courts, religious courts and state courts. Although adat and religious courts had been influenced or even constituted by the colonial administration, they were clearly regarded as an alternative to the state system. Islamic law and political Islam had been systematically suppressed under colonial rule and now claimed a more prominent position in the legal

---

[29] Strijbosch, above n 6, 93.

[30] S Wignojodipuro, *Pengantar dan azas-azas hukum adat* (Bandung, Penerbit Alumni, 1973) 2.

[31] *Ibid* 29. Ihromi, a well-known anthropologist and lawyer, also identifies adat law with the law that lives in society: *Adat perkawinan Toraja Sa' dan tempatnya dalam hukum positip masa kini* (Yogyakarta, Gadjah Mada University Press, 1981) 157, fn 1. She mentions that the understanding of adat law after 1945 was different from the pre-war understanding (p 171). This was directed against the notion that adat law was (purely) local law within its adat law circles. According to Ihromi, adat law was not a priori bound to one locality (p 173). Koesnoe saw the emphasis on adat law as one of the reasons for a unified Indonesia by the young pre-revolutionary elite, expressed in the 'Oath of the Young Generation' (*Sumpah Pemuda*): MH Koesnoe, *Penelitian Hukum Adat di Bali dan Lombok 1971–1973: Laporan Pokok* (Surabaya, Universitas Airlangga, 1975); and MH Koesnoe, *Opstellen over Hedendaagse Adat, Adatrecht en Rechtsontwikkeling van Indonesië* (Nijmegen, Instituut voor Volksrecht, Nijmegen University, 1977). See also Ihromi (1981) 174; and Resink, above n 28, 428.

[32] At the Seminar on Adat Law in 1975, Satjipto Rahardjo, an Indonesian sociologist of law, gave a paper on 'The Understanding of adat Law, Living Law in Society, and National Law' (Ihromi, above n 32, 179). Imam Sudiyat, one of the grand old adat law professors, gave a paper in 1974 on 'Legal Innovation and Living Law: Adat Law as Element in the Development of National Law' (Koesnoe, above n 32, 175).

and political system of the new republic. Any new legal development had to find some balance in this triangle of state-Islam-adat. In the sphere of substantive private law, in many regions of Indonesia the main tensions were between adat and Islam, and here the most hotly disputed issue being which law was valid for inheritance problems. In this context, living law was used to flexibly navigate between the demands of adat, Islam, the existing state law and the demands for a new, Indonesian national law. These developments occurred during the period in which the parliamentary constitution of 1950 was replaced with a strong executive constitution, and the 'rule of law' mindedness gave way to the 'law of revolution'.[33] As Lev notes, 'living law' was used during the revolution to allow the judges to avoid the rigidities of colonial concepts of adat law.[34] The concept of 'the living law of society' appeared for the first time in a draft bill in 1948 to justify a continuing role for adat authorities outside the new civil courts.[35] The living law formula was then used in Emergency Law 1 of 1951, which had:

> ... abolished or anticipated the abolition of adat courts everywhere in Indonesia, except religious justice where according to the living law such justice forms an independent part of adat justice.

The first systematic post-independence regulation of the competence of religious courts in Indonesia, Government Regulation No 45 of 1957, stated that Islamic courts would be competent in the issues mentioned (including inheritance) to the extent 'that according to the living law these issues are to be resolved according to the law of Islam'.[36] This formulation was a compromise between the Departments of Religion and of Justice. According to Lev, lawyers sympathetic to Islam had hoped that this formula would offer an opening for Islam against traditional adat. The regulation seemed to be a major victory for Indonesian Muslims, because it provided a basis for religious courts and the enforcement of Islamic law all over Indonesia.[37] As it turned out, the formula was mainly used the other way around, for the living law which came to be interpreted by judges in the civil law court system, including the Supreme Court of Indonesia, and their interpretation of living law was mainly adat law. As Lev said:

> ... one has to read 'living law' as being equal to adat law plus, in reality, the discretionary judgment of civil law judges about what social rules remain in effect.[38]

---

[33] DS Lev, 'The Lady and the Banyan Tree: Civil-law Change in Indonesia' (1965) 14 *The American Journal of Comparative Law* 289.

[34] DS Lev, *Islamic Courts in Indonesia* (Berkely, University of California Press, 1972) 79 and fn 21.

[35] J Bowen, *Islam, Law and Equality in Indonesia* (Cambridge, Cambridge University Press, 2003) 53.

[36] Lev, above n 35, 116; and F von Benda-Beckmann, *Property in Social Continuity: Continuity and Change in the Maintenance of Property Relations through Time in Minangkabau, West Sumatra* (The Hague, Martinus Nijhoff, 1979) 126.

[37] Lev, above n 35, 89.

[38] Above n 35, 116.

In the relation between adat as applied in civil courts and Islam as applied in Islamic courts, the living law formula was thus used in the defence and continued protection of adat. One important instance making this clear was a decision by the Supreme Court in a case that had originated from Makassar, which stated:

> ... the Supreme Court regards it as clear that in all of Indonesia with respect to inheritance it is essentially the adat law which applies, which in areas in which Islamic law is strong contains more or fewer elements of Islamic law.[39]

In terms of substantive law, on the other hand, the notion of living law was used to change elements in adat law that were deemed to be old fashioned and unjust. The yardstick for 'appropriateness' and 'justice' was not derived from Islamic law, but from the spirit of modernity and equality. In the 1950s and 1960s, the Supreme Court took on the task of reconstructing local adat laws to fit post-revolutionary national sensibilities.[40] Its President, Wirjono Prodjodikoro, wanted to establish a widow's inheritance right to her husband's property in these societies.[41] Most of the Supreme Court judges at that time were Javanese and during this early period the attempts of change concerned the position of widows on Java only. The court was far more reluctant to intervene in the adat systems of the so-called Outer Islands (outside Java and Madura). In 1959, Wirjono signalled an increasing trend to support the rights of women nationally. In January 1959, the Supreme Court ruled that:

> ... according to the knowledge of the Supreme Court itself ... Batak adat law at the present time provides that both widows and children inherit community property.[42]

This development was, for some time at least, a matter of contention amongst Supreme Court judges. Wirjono Prodjodikoro recurred to formulas such as that adat law had to be evaluated according to 'society's sense of justice'. This was also fed by the egalitarianism of the revolution, pressure of women's organisations, world opinion and by his own

---

[39] Lev, above n 35, 68.

[40] IJ Simbolon, 'Peasant Women and Access to Land: Customary Land, State Law and Gender-based Ideology: The Case of the Toba-Batak North Sumatra' (PhD Thesis, Wageningen University, 1998); and J Bowen, *Islam, Law and Equality in Indonesia* (Cambridge, Cambridge University Press, 2003) 53. In his research on Supreme Court inheritance decisions, Lev analysed the legal interventions of the Supreme Court on adat law in the 1950s, especially in cases where the question of whether widows or daughters could inherit in adat laws with patrilineal and bilateral systems was at stake: DS Lev, 'The Supreme Court and Adat Inheritance Law in Indonesia' (1962) 11 *The American Journal of Comparative Law* 205. See also Bowen (2003) 55; F von Benda-Beckmann, above n 37, 340, quoting the judgment from R Subekti and J Tamara, *Kumpulan Putusan Mahkamah Agung mengenai Hukum Adat* (Jakarta, Gunung Agung, 1965) 198; and HH Hadikusuma, *Hukum Adat dalam Yurisprudensi: Hukum Kekeluargaan, Perkawinan, Pewarisan* (Bandung, PT Citra Aditya Bakti, 1993).

[41] Lev, above n 41, 215.

[42] *Ibid* 221.

evaluation.[43] There also was an increasing ease with which judges justified their interventions. In the mid-1950s, the Supreme Court had still rejected too easily declarations of change in adat law, stating that 'to determine a change in adat law it is necessary to show clear evidence, based on real events on conditions'. Later on, judges tended to be more laconic in their statements 'that there had been change in the respective adat law'.[44]

The Supreme Court decision No 179 K/Sip/1961 recognised that women (daughters) and men (sons) had equal inheritance rights. In its considerations, the Supreme Court stated that:

> ... Batak adat does not recognise women's inheritance rights, but ... that on the basis of general feelings of humanity and justice and of absolute equal rights between men and women, it should be considered the living law throughout Indonesia that daughters and sons are equally entitled to the parental inheritance.[45]

This was the beginning of the end in a development where the Indonesian Supreme Court, and especially its President Wirjono, had introduced gender equality in intestate inheritance rights for widows and daughters into adat law systems that did not recognise such rights: bilateral inheritance was declared to be 'living law throughout Indonesia'.[46] In Indonesia, the concept of living law did not remain limited to adat. It could be used to reinterpret adat as living law, but living law could also be put against adat and state law. It could even be applied to Islamic law in order to soften demands of a full validation of the *Sharia* as official law. In the debates surrounding the 1989 Law on the Jurisdiction of Religious Courts, a drafting committee of Supreme Court justices and people from the Ministry of Religious Affairs interviewed 166 religious authorities (*ulama*) on the 'living *fiqh*', a concept that extended the Supreme Court's living adat law idea into the realm of the *fiqh*.[47]

---

[43] Ibid 217.

[44] The major change in Minangkabau inheritance law by Supreme Court decision 39K/sip/1968 contained the not further substantiated statement 'that according to the present stage of development in Minangkabau' (F von Benda-Beckmann, above n 37, 340).

[45] Case Reg No 179K/Sip./1971; Lev, above n 35; H Slaats and K Portier, 'Legal Plurality and the Transformation of Normative Concepts in the Process of Litigation in Karo Batak Society' in K von Benda-Beckmann and F Strijbosch (eds), *Anthropology of Law in the Netherlands* (Dordrecht and Berlin, Foris and Walter de Gruyter, 1986) 233; Simbolon, above n 41, 104; and Bowen, above n 41.

[46] R Subekti and J Tamara, *Kumpulan Putusan Mahkamah Agung mengenai Hukum Adat* (Jakarta, Gunung Agung, 1965) 85; see also MA Jaspan, 'In Quest of New Law: The Perplexity of Legal Syncretism in Indonesia' (1965) VII *Comparative Studies in Society and History* 262; and Bowen, above n 41, 53.

[47] Bowen, above n 41, 190. The result of these consultations was made into a 'compilation' of Islamic law. The compilation was introduced as an *Instruksi Presiden* no 1-1991. About the compilation of Islamic law, it was said that 'in its essence the Compilation is the living law [in English] that has been voluntarily applied for centuries ...' (Bowen, above n 41, 192).

LIVING LAW AS DEAD LAW

The ideas about living law expressed in the judgments and political legal rhetoric had, however, lost firm connection with the ground, the 'inner order of social associations'. It was not a living law that was widely shared or appreciated by the majority of the population, or at least, there was little interest in such law. Some people, including judges in the lower courts, felt that the Supreme Court had gone too far in deviating from the adat law, so far indeed that the court was disregarding social realities in certain areas and had gone 'beyond the people's true sense of justice'.[48] One Supreme Court judge went even so far as to say that the new inheritance case law was not based on any written source or immediate observation, but was judge-made law.[49] Commenting on the Karo Batak inheritance case mentioned above, a book on Karo Batak adat law published in 1979 stated that the court's decision was unfortunate and, had it been followed, it would have caused extensive social disruption.[50] Ihromi, a Batak feminist and professor in law and anthropology, and very sympathetic to the cause of gender equality, in 1981 characterised the 1961 judgment as 'rather brave and not really based on empirical regularities'.[51]

Therefore, living law here functioned as a legitimisation of a kind of *Freie Rechtslehre*, allowing and justifying the adaptation of law in decisions to changed circumstances and demands. In post-revolutionary Indonesia, this was a *Freie Rechtslehre* by the legal elite and judges of the highest court, while it was largely opposed 'below' by the majority of the population and lower court judges. Living law in Indonesia had thus become contrary to what Ehrlich meant by the term and what Van Vollenhoven understood as *levend recht*. However, the new Indonesian lawyers were less influenced by Van Vollenhoven than by Ter Haar, Van Vollenhoven's disciple who became professor at the Law College in Batavia. While Van Vollenhoven had always distinguished folk law and living law from lawyers' law, Ter Haar made the adat law science into a branch of positive law. His 'decision theory' (*beslissingenleer*) pointed at decisions as the place where adat law was to be found by the judge.[52] With the increasing knowledge of adat law principles

---

[48] Lev, above n 41, 222.
[49] Ibid 224.
[50] Bowen, above n 41, 54.
[51] Ihromi, above n 32, 174. Sitorus did research in the 1990s. Old adat experts insisted on the adat rule that daughters could not inherit, while young adat leaders said that daughters could inherit. In practice, variation, but cases in which daughters received some portion were found. There were also cases where it was said that daughters had no rights, but still received part of the inheritance: MTF Sitorus, 'Hak Waris Janda dan Anak Perempuan Batak Toba' in Masinambow (ed), *Hukum dan Kemanjemukan Budaya* (Jakarta, Yayasan Obor, 2000). See also S Irianto, *Perempuan di antara bebagai strategi pilihan hukum* (Jakarta, Yayasan Obor Indonesia, 2003).
[52] In 1939, Ter Haar characterised the judge finding and applying adat law as the poetic troubadour (*dichter troubadour*) of adat law: see F and K von Benda-Beckmann, above n 1, 20. See also F Strijbosch, above n 6 (1980), 73. For an early critique, see FD Holleman,

and a pressing need to make them suitable for court and administrative decision-making, the character of adat law studies changed. Van Vollenhoven had never tried to give an authoritative definition of adat law, and he had cautioned against making sharp distinctions between law, custom and morals.[53] Ter Haar's version of adat law studies, in contrast, was specifically directed at finding the unwritten law in order to help colonial judges and to develop adat law studies as a positive legal science (*positieve rechtswetenschap*), different only from other legal science by the unwritten nature of its object, which had to be extracted out of social reality.[54] This required a clear distinction between adat and adat law. Ter Haar's approach has been influential on post-independence Indonesian adat law scholars such as Djojodigoeno, Supomo and Koesnoe. Descriptions of adat law made by later Indonesian adat law scholars, although not meant as prescriptive legal codes, were clearly and primarily meant to help guide court decision-making.[55] Ter Haar's teachings resulted in a kind of case law doctrine for adat law, based on the assumption that it was possible in principle to apply to new cases the law as defined in earlier decisions. Influenced by American legal realist ideas (Grey), he developed his decision theory (*beslissingenleer*): adat law was to be found in decisions taken in and outside disputes. Pragmatic reasoning had taken over from the attempt to come to a descriptive account that was as close as possible to the conceptual logic of adat systems and their ideas about proper decision-making.

After the 1970s, living law gradually disappeared from the main legal discussions. It shared the demise of adat law studies in the Indonesian law faculties and the loss of social significance of adat in many regions of Indonesia. However, after the autocratic regime of Suharto had fallen in 1998, adat law was revitalised, especially in the field of land law where adat law was mobilised against state law.[56] And with this new rise of adat law, notions of living law also reappeared. Furthermore, this living law is no longer a construction of progressive judges as in the post-revolutionary period, but goes back to 'the law of the people', to living law in the earlier sense. This is nicely illustrated in a cartoon series published by an Indonesian Human Rights organisation, HuMa. After having traced the history of European thought on folk or people's law (Kant, Austin, von Jhering,

'Mr. B. ter Haar Bzn's Rede, Het Adatrecht van Nederlands-Indië in Wetenschap, Practijk en Onderwijs, Besproken door Holleman' (1938) 147 *Indisch Tijdschrift voor het Recht* 428.

[53] Van Vollenhoven, above n 18 (1933), 3; Koesnoe, above n 32; and Holleman, above n 6, 23. F von Benda-Beckmann spoke of 'law *in* adat', above n 37, 117.

[54] B Ter Haar, *Het Adatrecht van Nederlands-Indië in Wetenschap, Practijk en Onderwijs* (Batavia, 1937).

[55] Strijbosch, above n 6.

[56] See F and K von Benda-Beckmann, 'How Communal is Communal and Whose Communal is it? Lessons from Minangkabau' in F von Benda-Beckman, K von Benda-Beckmann and MG Wiber (eds), *Changing Properties of Property* (Oxford, Berghahn, 2006).

The Social Life of Living Law in Indonesia 189

[Comic panels with the following text:]

Panel 1 (R. Soepomo): Adat law is a law that lives, because it manifests the true legal feelings of the people in line with its own character. Adat law is continuously emerging and growing like life itself.

Panel 2: If this is so, it is already clear: there is law made by the government called legislation

Panel 3: There is also a law that is born and grows together with society, which is called people's law or adat law.

Panel 4: The plantations think that they have a right to expropriate and abuse our land on the basis of legislation.

Panel 5: Conversely, our objection to this exploitation and abuse is based on people's law or adat law.

Binder, Marx, von Savigny), the cartoon moves to quoting Supomo, adat law scholar and Minister of Justice:

> Adat law is a kind of law that lives, because it expresses the true legal feelings of society ... adat law is in a constant process of emergence and growth as life itself.[57]

COMMON ROOTS? PARALLEL DEVELOPMENTS?

There are many similarities and some differences in Ehrlich's and Van Vollenhoven's thinking about law, and not surprisingly, they have been criticised for similar 'faults':

a) Both defined law as conceptually independent from creation, recognition or sanction by the state. As Ziegert points out, for Ehrlich such

---

[57] HuMa, 'Hukum Adat, Hukum Kami' (2002) Nos 1 and 2, *Seri Komik Adat dan Masyarakat* (Jakarta, HuMa) 31. It is interesting to compare these developments with the role which the notion of 'living customary' or 'indigenous law' has received in South African legal scholarship and in judgments of the Constitution Courts (see *Alexkor Ltd and another versus The Richtersveld Community and others* 2004 (5) SA 460 (CC), and *Bhe versus Magistrate, Khayelitsha and others (Commission for Gender Equality as Amicus Curiae)* 2005 (1) SA 580, 2005 (1) BCLR 1 (CC). Living customary law is distinguished from codified (and obsolete) customary law, and judges and academics grapple with the problem of how to find or establish living customary law. See also AJGM Sanders, 'How Customary is African Customary Law?' (1987) 20 *CILSA*; and Bennett, above n 3.

kind of definition was neither reasonable nor scientific.[58] It was the same for Van Vollenhoven.[59] Such concept of law has been criticised, and as the many discussions of the concept of 'legal pluralism' show, it remains contested.[60] A similar reproach has been made to Van Vollenhoven.[61] Van Vollenhoven, however, did talk about more than just norms, rules or values. While acknowledging that the category of 'adat' encompassed customs, morality and law and that a sharp distinction between these adat elements was difficult if not impossible, and for him neither desirable nor necessary, he spoke of adat law as such adats (uncodified rules and principles) which had sanctions or legal consequences. In the fields of marriage, inheritance, economic transactions and political office, the rules, principles and procedures were pretty clear. Moreover, many adats had their own internal subdivisions into several kinds of adat and distinguished legal from other principles.[62]

b) Neither author confined living law to one type of law (societal law or folk or adat law).[63] Both saw communities as the main source and social environment in which law emerged and was maintained. Van Vollenhoven's notion of *rechtsgemeenschappen*, legal communities, is rather similar to Ehrlich's *'innere Ordnung der gesellschaftlichen Verbände'*.[64]

---

[58] Above n 4, xli.

[59] In fact, legal realist thought has seriously restricted the conceptual and methodological approaches of Anglo-American anthropology of law, by confining the locale for finding law to decisions taken in trouble cases. Dutch adat law realism, for instance Ter Haar's decision theory, was always wider than the trouble-biased American realism and included decisions in 'trouble-less cases' (Holleman, above n 21). Ehrlich's ideas also provide a better perspective than a focus on 'law in action' of the legal realists, because the idea of living law is less isolated from sociological theory (Nelken, above n 4, 169).

[60] See F and K von Benda-Beckman, above n 6; and F and K von Benda-Beckmann, above n 57. Nelken, above n 4, 163 and 173, for instance, takes up the criticism that Ehrlich did not make a distinction between the norms of the living law and other norms and lists a number of questions following from this. For a discussion of this reproach, see Ziegert, above n 4, xli.

[61] See among others Burns, above n 6.

[62] See Koesnoe, above n 32; and F von Benda-Beckmann, above n 37.

[63] Rehbinder emphasises that living law may not be identified with societal law. It is a societal law at a higher level, namely influenced through the reactions to lawyers' law and state law. Only at that level law is a factually lived order, the legal norm a norm of social action (Rehbinder, above n 4, 32).

[64] Van Vollenhoven sympathised with Struycken's opinion that there is a more realistic wind blowing through legal science which has blown away the ultra-legalistic ideas of the nineteenth century. 'Struycken could have added' (so Van Vollenhoven, above n 18, II: 400) 'that not only the belief in exclusive legislative law had been blown away; also the belief in exclusively judge-made law was broken by what reality shows us'. Struycken wrote (correctly) that inasmuch as social life contributes independently to the life and maintenance of law, this rarely occurs in the form of legal rules, but nearly always in the form of concrete legal relations, contracts and practices. There is also an echo of Ehrlich's emphasis on legal documents here, from the content of which the living law must be won.

c) An important difference, at least at first glance, is that Van Vollenhoven dealt with unwritten law, while Ehrlich thought in terms of written sources such as contracts, testaments and so on. Yet we can look behind these differences and see similarities again, namely in the kind of social processes that both authors regarded as the main sources of living law: processes of validating the inner order of associations and/or important social, economic and political transactions, such as pledge agreements, testaments and marriage arrangements—all instances considered to be preventive law care or supported law observance by the Dutch adat law scholars.

d) Ehrlich and Van Vollenhoven had much in common, even though their commonality often concerns what they disliked and criticised. Ziegert mentions that concepts such as *Volksrecht* and possibly also living law 'were in the air'.[65] So perhaps we should not make too much of the words themselves, which both authors used. Even if not acquainted with each other's work, they were acquainted with the writings of Savigny, Beseler and Puchta.[66] However, both Ehrlich and Van Vollenhoven distanced themselves from the teachings of von Savigny and Puchta about customary and folk law. Ehrlich criticised them for not thinking in terms of a parallel development of different kinds of law, but for seeing *Volksrecht* in a historical, rather evolutionary sequence, with no eye for the fact that also in contemporary times *Volksrecht* could emerge directly from society.[67] For a sociological science of law, he argued, 'the concept of customary law of conventional jurisprudence is useless'.[68] Van Vollenhoven also contrasted his understanding with the more classical understanding of customary law, as it developed in Roman law and later in European legal thought, and distinguished his ideas sharply from von Savigny and Puchta.[69]

e) The political and legal conditions, which led them to talk about living law as the 'really relevant law for people' and to declare living law the subject to which a social (and legal) science of law ought to direct its interest, were also similar. Both scholars developed their ideas in the context of a (colonial) empire (the Austro-Hungarian Empire for Ehrlich and the Dutch East Indies for Van Vollenhoven), characterised

---

[65] Above n 4, xxviii and xlvii.
[66] Burns (above n 6) links Van Vollenhoven's work to the German historical school, to Savigny and Puchta.
[67] Ehrlich, above n 2, 393 ff.
[68] *Ibid* 396.
[69] Dutch authors like Fromberg had said that custom could only become legal if the judge recognises it as such, a point that van Vollenhoven did not share (Van Vollenhoven, above n 18, II: 398).

by the co-existence of multi-ethnic population groups and a variety of status and ethnicity-based political organisations within the encompassing state. Under these conditions, the existence of non-state and legal-science-based forms of normative ordering and social significance of these orders could hardly be overlooked. Scholars interested in the law that really governed people's lives, therefore, would notice and reflect upon these forms, theoretically and with respect to legal practice. Yet there were also important differences in the kind of empire they were dealing with, which also influenced the audience they chose for their writings. While both Ehrlich and Van Vollenhoven challenged conventional wisdom, their approaches were different, and these differences concerned the law they were dealing with. The region in which Ehrlich was working in was an integral part of the Austrian Empire, subject to laws that in principle were the same for all. There was no distinct colonial civil service as in the Dutch colonies overseas and no partial recognition of 'native law and custom' within the legal system, and a judiciary which had to apply this. Ehrlich thus had to address his colleagues in the law schools and civil service. His ethnographic findings had to be interpreted in a general theory of law. He wanted to develop a real 'science' of law in the living law and all elements it comprised became the subject of a unified approach, now called sociological.[70]

Van Vollenhoven pursued a different project altogether. He worked on the legal conditions in an overseas colony separated in space from the mother state.[71] The colonial administration had a top layer of Dutch civil servants who supervised 'native authorities', who were incorporated either as self-governmental or as directly governed units. Even in the directly governed regions, however, a range of administrative and dispute management tasks had been left, or given, to native authorities. For the Indonesian indigenous population, the colonial government had recognised adat civil law (*adat privaatrecht*) as the applicable law. Moreover, it had created a dual court system of local institutions of adjudication and colonial courts based on Dutch law. Van Vollenhoven's writings to a large extent were a critique of colonial legal policies. In particular, he defended the validity of the local populations' living laws and the economic rights based in these laws against Dutch colonial legal interpretations, which did not interpret these rights as rights and thus allowed expropriation of the huge resource areas termed wastelands (*woeste gronden*).[72]

---

[70] '*Soweit wir eine wirkliche, theoretische Wissenschaft vom Rechte haben, ist sie historisch oder ethnologisch*' (Ehrlich, above n 2, 400).
[71] Strijbosch, above n 6, 25.
[72] Van Vollenhoven, *De Indonesiër en zijn Grond* (Leiden, Brill, 1919).

The Social Life of Living Law in Indonesia 193

> Van Vollenhoven is a professor of the law faculty of Leiden University in the Netherlands. He had quite some followers.

> I oppose the Agrarian Law of 1870 and all regulations that do not respect the living law which lives in the society of the indigenous populations.

> It is clear that creating state land in the Dutch East Indies is an unjust action towards the indigenous population.

> Indigenous — what does this mean?

> YAA, adat communities such as us.

HuMa 2002   SERI KOMIK HUKUM DAN MASYARAKAT 21

In the early twentieth century, the Dutch Government announced plans to create a uniform private law for the Dutch East Indies, which was to facilitate economic growth. Van Vollenhoven argued that it was impossible to simply impose a foreign, written law on millions of indigenous people.

It would require the cooperation of the local population. Moreover, he argued that these plans showed a lack of respect for adat and expressed a misplaced sense of superiority.[73] The political fight lasted 25 years until the return to a policy of dualism and has left a deep imprint on his academic work. His plea was not for a pristine adat: he pleaded for integration and a development of a 'good' judicial and administrative system. For this, a well-founded knowledge of adat, based on research, collection of adat case law and a good training of adat judges, was of fundamental importance.

In his work, Van Vollenhoven mixed two scientific genres. He was a social anthropologist when describing and analysing adat law, trying to understand its inner logic, and discussing contradictions as found on the work floor. However, when it came to the relationship between adat and state law, or when discussing case law, he switched and argued as a lawyer, and he took position on the basis of normative evaluations, participating in legal political arguments as any other lawyer.[74] But his audience remained, in contrast to Ehrlich, a colonial audience: academics, lawyers, politicians and civil servants working in the colonial context. It remained a debate outside the mainstream of legal scholarship.

Ehrlich, Van Vollenhoven and Other Contemporaries

Ehrlich's work has been placed alongside that of another author, Petrazycki (1867–1931), who developed notions of 'intuitive law', a law beyond the law of the state, courts and lawyers.[75] In fact, as Podgorecki points out, Petrazycki's first publication in German in 1907 antedates Ehrlich's article on living law and his *Fundamental Principles*.[76] According to Podgorecki, Petrazycki's work was 'more precise and adequate'.[77] However, as Banakar points out, there are important epistemological differences between the two.[78] As in the case of Van Vollenhoven, there is no evidence that the two knew of each other's work, but in contrast to Van Vollenhoven, Ehrlich and Petrazycki both shared the ambition to develop a social science of law,

---

[73] Strijbosch, above n 6, 31.
[74] *Ibid* 59–64.
[75] Banakar, above n 4, 206; and Podgorecki, above n 3. See also A Podgorecke, 'Intuitive Law versus Folk Law' (1982) 3 *Zeitschrift für Rechtssoziologie* 75.
[76] Ehrlich, above n 2, first published in 1913. See L Petrazycki, *Law and Morality* (Cambridge, Mass., Harvard University Press, 1955). Podgorecki quibbles about the term 'folk law', which he sees mainly adequately used in relation to societies (often wrongly) called primitive. He would rather call them and their law also as intuitive law in Petrazycki's sense. See also Gorecki (above n 3).
[77] Above n 3, 76. See his four types of law (Banakar, above n 4, 208).
[78] Above n 4, 211 and 212. Podgorecki (above n 3, 191, fn 10) mentions that Licki had claimed that Ehrlich took the idea for living law from Petrazycki's intuitive law. Ehrlich was quite sensitive to reproaches of borrowing; apparently one had accused him of taking over insights developed by the Kroation scholar (Ehrlich (1989) 392).

sociology of law. The notion of living law was also frequently compared to Pound's and other American legal realists' conceptions of law in action. Nelken convincingly demonstrates the differences between Ehrlich's categories of law and Pound's distinction between law in the books and law in action, the latter being oriented at law made by legislators or courts. Ehrlich's living law does not correspond to law in action.[79] Nelken concludes: 'Both were convinced that judges needed to be relieved of the belief that their role was a narrow one.' Pound insisted that judges should adapt the law to changing circumstances, Ehrlich polemicised for 'free law finding', by which he meant the attempt to base judicial decisions on the appropriate criteria which emerged from a situation under consideration rather than from legal propositions. However, while Pound was concerned with the unmet social needs which were made evident by these social circumstances, Ehrlich was more concerned with the existing normative orders which it would be perilous to disregard.[80] Ziegert, deploring the absolute methodological void in legal science, also shows the differences between Ehrlich and the legal realists, and argues convincingly that living law is a far more radical sociological concept than the notion of the legal realists.[81]

Van Vollenhoven was more sophisticated than Ehrlich (or Petrazycki) in methodological respect, even if he reserved his considerations to the living law or adat law and not to the totality of the plural legal order. Although he frequently expressed his disdain for 'theorising', Van Vollenhoven went much further in identifying the social mechanisms through which people were socialised with law, learnt (about) law during ceremonies and public hearings and used law to give validity and legal certainty to important social, economic and political transactions. Van Vollenhoven called these processes 'supported law observance'. In the spirit of conceiving 'law as process', Van Vollenhoven was far ahead of his time and other thinkers. Besides, his ideas about research techniques, observation and interviews are further developed than in Ehrlich's writings.[82]

CONCLUSIONS

Van Vollenhoven, writing about living law in Indonesia, seems to be the most congenial of Ehrlich's contemporaries. However, when looking at the project for which the concept was designed, the conscious development of a social science of law in general, others like Petrazycki may have been closer. Van Vollenhoven's project was to understand the wide range of

---

[79] Above n 4, 165.
[80] Above n 4, 169.
[81] Above n 4, xxxiv and xlvii.
[82] See also Strijbosch, above n 6, 58 ff and 80 ff.

very different adat laws. His frame of reference consisted of his critical stance to the historical school, general anthropology and the (German) Ethnological Jurisprudence of Post and Kohler, and to authors who took up their ideas when researching Indonesian adats, such as Wilken.[83] The law cartoons published since 2002 by HuMa (an Indonesian Human Rights Organisation) make a different historical link. Here the understanding of adat and folk law before and after Indonesia's independence is embedded in a historical review of legal thinkers who did or did not conceive of and sympathise with law beyond state production, recognition and dogmatic scholarly elaboration. In a remarkable historical reconstruction, the makers of the comic parade and comment upon Kant, Austin, Von Jhering, Binder, Marx, von Savigny and then Supomo, the foremost adat law scholar and later Minister of Justice in independent Indonesia, following the trajectory of periods in which the existence of living law was denied and was acknowledged. As the comic (see p 189) shows, living law is emerging in a new incarnation:

> Adat law is a law that lives, because it expresses the true legal feelings of society … adat law is in a constant process of emergence and growth as life itself.[84]

This brings us to the preliminary end of the social life of living law in Indonesia. This latest use of the concept again goes back to the beginning, when Van Vollenhoven's use of living law was mobilised against the exploitation of people's resources on the basis of state law.

In 1984, David Nelken asked 'Is there life in Ehrlich's concept living law?'—a question he answered to the positive. Ehrlich's arguments, he wrote, have been an essential starting point for those writers, often anthropologists, concerned to emphasise the 'legal pluralism' of Western societies.[85] Similarly, Banakar stresses that many theories run parallel with and are more or less stimulated by Ehrlich's insights into law and organisations.[86] This is often acknowledged, for instance by Rehbinder,[87] Griffiths,[88] Teubner[89] and Ziegert,[90] to name just a few. Ziegert in particu-

---

[83] Weber (1864–1920) and Durkheim thus probably were irrelevant, and neither their evolutionistic assumptions nor their typologies would have been much help in dealing with the varieties of local ethnic laws and the different extents of religious legal influences in Indonesia. The manuscript of Weber's sociology of law was of 1913 (E Baumgarten '*Einleitung*' in M Weber (ed), *Soziologie Universalgeschichtliche Analysen-Politik* (Stuttgart, Kroener, 1973) xxxiii).
[84] Supomo as quoted by HuMa, above n 58, 30.
[85] Nelken refers to John Griffiths' (1981) paper on legal pluralism, later to be published as J Griffiths, 'What is Legal Pluralism' (1986) 24 *Journal of Legal Pluralism* 1–55, and to Moore's (1973) notion of the semi-autonomous social field (Nelken, above n 4, 169 and 171). S Moore, 'Law and Social Change: The Semi-autonomous Social Field as an Appropriate Subject of Study' (1973) 7 *Law and Society Review* 719.
[86] Banakar, above n 4, 216 and 217.
[87] Above n 4.

lar follows Ehrlich's ideas and critiques of Ehrlich's (mis)interpretations in the Anglo-American anthropology of law of Hoebel and Pospíšil.[91]

Our contribution, I think, has shown a rather different life of the concept. One was its continued existence as descriptive, analytical concept to capture a particular set of social phenomena as 'law', phenomena outside the conventional definitions of law in legal science and much sociology (of law) as well. We have shown how this idea travelled to Indonesia, where it was used in the writings of sociological, anthropological and legal scholars. However, its life in Indonesia took a turn. In one respect, this was a turn from an analytical instrument towards a legal (folk) concept incorporated into the official legal and judicial machinery of the state, and to some extent as a weapon to invalidate 'the real' living law, for instance, Batak inheritance law as practised by the majority of the Batak population. Living law had become lawyers' law, leading a rather marginal life in legal texts and some court judgments. However, under the current adat law revival, the concept is used once more in its older meaning. As far as its usefulness and continued inspiration for social science approaches to law is concerned, it lives on, and not just in the list of references. Furthermore, its basic ideas—that there is much law outside of and independent from its recognition by the state and dominant legal theory, that much of this law is found in the organisation of social formations, that the respective orders do not exist in isolation but are interdependent—are shared by many scholars and have been elaborated in different ways. Those like ourselves, familiar with Ehrlich and the writings of the Dutch adat law scholars,[92] have had the luxury of being able to build on both Van Vollenhoven and Ehrlich, using Van Vollenhoven's ideas developed for unwritten law emerging outside the state law for looking, in Ehrlich's sense, at all law.

---

[88] Above n 4, 1.
[89] Above n 4.
[90] *Ibid.*
[91] Above n 4, xl.
[92] See, for instance, F von Benda-Beckmann, above n 37, 38.

Part IV

Ehrlich and Contemporary Socio-legal Studies

9
Naturalism and Agency in the Living Law

JEREMY WEBBER[1]

INTRODUCTION

THERE IS A common tendency in some branches of the sociology of law—especially in the literature of legal pluralism—to see social norms as being deeply rooted in patterns of human interaction. There is some variation in how this relationship is described, but many approaches speak of norms emerging from social interaction in a manner that suggests that: (i) any prolonged human interaction tends to generate norms; and (ii) this occurs spontaneously rather than through deliberate human action. Indeed, the temporal ordering I have suggested here—interaction occurring first, with norms then being generated from that relationship—may understate the connection posed by some theorists. Some treat norms as being virtually coeval with any peaceable human relationship.[2] On this view, any ordered interaction implies the simultaneous existence of norms in the same way that the physical constitution of an organism presupposes its skeleton. There is a strong implication of necessity, then, in such visions of normative orders. A normative order is considered to be a natural dimension of any human interaction, generated through the day-to-day business of human life, perhaps even definitional of the existence of society.

The tendency to present norms as emerging naturally out of human interaction also typically presents a society's normative order as non-contentious. A normative order consists of those rules that the members of society recognise and obey. The norms are not the result of argument and

---

[1] My thanks to Marcia Barry, Christina Godlewska and Crystal Reeves for their able research assistance, and to Kate Gower, Crystal Reeves and the participants in the workshop on 'Living Law: Rediscovering Eugen Ehrlich', International Institute for the Sociology of Law, Oñati (especially Franz and Keebet von Benda Beckman) for their trenchant comments on earlier drafts of this chapter.

[2] For example, R Sacco, 'Mute Law' (1995) 43 *American Journal of Comparative Law* 455.

imposition; they are inscribed in members' conduct. Implicitly, then, these approaches align with theories of social organisation based on consent. The parties may not have deliberately chosen the norms by which they are governed, but they have internalised those norms, living them. The socially grounded law is portrayed as a unified and harmonious body of norms, highly adapted to a particular social milieu and exempt from disagreement and contention. It is not so much that disagreement is denied, but that it has no point of entry into the theory. The law is given directly by social interaction, not by processes of human debate and decision-making. Processes that maintain the normative order are conceived as mechanisms for the enforcement of pre-existing rules, not as devices by which the content of those rules is itself determined. Not only does this distort the nature and role of those processes (as I discuss below), it also opens up a deep gulf between social law and the state's law. The former is natural, consensual, communal and conflict-free; the latter is artificial, coercive, peremptory and conflict-ridden.

In this chapter, I want to defend a view that all law—non-state law as well as state law—is inherently non-consensual, that it is always to some extent peremptory and imposed, establishing a collective position against a backdrop of deep-seated normative disagreement. All legal orders, of whatever kind, have to have mechanisms for fashioning these collective positions out of the welter of disagreement. This does not undermine the key insights of the theorists of the social law, but it does warn us against the tendency to treat the social law as natural, as emerging harmoniously from practice. Instead, it insists on the existence of contestation and dissent and focuses attention on the means by which contestation is settled. In so doing, it emphasises the sources of dynamism and change in the law and provides a foundation for the more nuanced comparison of, and examination of the interaction between, state and non-state legal orders.

I will explore these questions specifically in relation to Eugen Ehrlich's *Fundamental Principles of the Sociology of Law*,[3] examining the extent to which he falls prey to the naturalising fallacy. As will become clear, I believe that he falls into this danger in crucial parts of his argument—although in drawing attention to those failings, I do not mean to deny the great force of his accomplishment in emphasising that law is intimately entangled in social interaction more generally. On the contrary, I accept his foundational insistence that we focus our attention on how law is lived in day-to-day interaction and that we examine the close structural relationship between state law and other forms of social normativity. My argument is that we understand

---

[3] E Ehrlich, *Fundamental Principles of the Sociology of Law*, Walter L Moll (tr) (New York, Arno Press, 1975 [1936]) (hereinafter: simply 'Ehrlich'). I am grateful to Alex Ziegert for my first substantial introduction to Ehrlich: KA Ziegert, 'A Note on Eugen Ehrlich and the Production of Legal Knowledge' (1998) 20 *Sydney Law Review* 108.

those dimensions best when we take normative disagreement seriously. Indeed, the very essence of law—and of normative orders generally—involves the fashioning of an emphatically social outcome in the face of disagreement.

Precisely because I share Ehrlich's concern with the relationship between state law and other forms of normativity, I will generally avoid the term 'law' when presenting my own views, referring to 'norms' or 'normative order' instead. For many legal theorists, especially those influenced by legal positivism, 'law' is necessarily and indissolubly tied to the state. The application of the term to norms produced by other mechanisms therefore prompts an immediate and dogmatic objection. I want to sidestep that stumbling-block. I do not deny that the involvement of state institutions makes a difference to our analysis of the legitimacy, salience and means of operation of norms. (Although it is often too simple to say that the difference flows merely from the fact that the norms are 'state norms': it is generally necessary to examine what kind of institution has produced them by what means—legislature? civil service? courts? specialised administrative agency? Their scope of application, means of enforcement and even legitimacy will vary depending on the precise way in which the state is implicated. Moreover, if there is considerable mobility between non-state and state norms—if, for example, state institutions draw their standards in part from the activities of trade associations or from largely self-regulating professions, or depend upon non-state means for their enforcement—the very task of establishing the line between state and non-state norms can be challenging). However, even granted that it is important to distinguish between state-sanctioned and non-state-sanctioned norms for some purposes we still need to preserve a space for comparing different modes of social regulation and examining the interconnections between them, as Ehrlich does to such illuminating effect. That objective is sometimes best achieved by treating state and non-state norms as species of a single genus. That is what I do in this chapter. Indeed, my primary purpose is to establish that non-state norms share a fundamental characteristic with state norms: they all confront the fundamental problem of how to establish a common standard in the face of pervasive normative disagreement.

But is this just a straw man? Surely any scholar of law—jurist, sociologist or anthropologist—will acknowledge that in any real society opinions about norms vary and that any system of social regulation must possess ways to settle these disputes. The anthropological literature—on which legal pluralists rely—is replete with descriptions of authority, disputation and dispute resolution in non-state orders.

This is true, but nevertheless the temptation to naturalise non-state orders, portraying them as actuated by a unified set of beliefs, is a real one, well worth recognising and guarding against. Such a tendency is common, for example, in anthropological accounts that seek to describe the internal rationality of normative orders, especially accounts that try to establish the distinctness and integrity of those orders in comparison to other ways of organising social life. Often, the author wants to defend a subaltern order against a dominant one, and this increases the temptation to minimise internal disagreement and emphasise cohesion. This can be true of hermeneutic approaches, which seek to explain social norms in terms of a comprehensive and internally consistent world view. Clifford Geertz's work, stimulating though it is, is vulnerable to this criticism. He acknowledges complexity especially in the existence of legal *mixité* (in one striking passage he notes the many legal traditions present within Ethiopia and argues for an 'abnormal' or 'non-standard' discourse to deal with it).[4] However, it is difficult to see how this fits with his primary emphasis on the internal rationality of normative world views. One suspects that, for Geertz, legal *mixité* primarily serves as a source of disorder and destabilisation in relation to world views conceived in much more consistent and unified form. For Geertz, disputing mechanisms are primarily means to re-affirm, elaborate and defend the internal rationality of the order. They tend to take the latter as given, not as something that has to be made and remade through the agency of social actors, as this chapter will insist.

Indeed, we can fall prey to the temptation to minimise conflict and naturalise social orders whenever we try to describe those orders primarily in terms of their substantive content. This is, of course, a common approach in ethnography, where one sets out to describe the beliefs and concepts of a particular culture. It is also very common—indeed standard—in the general run of doctrinal literature in law, which seeks to present a rationalised, systematised, coherent and comprehensive understanding of an area of the law.[5] There is good reason to attempt accounts of content: broad differences certainly are apparent when one compares different normative orders; differential content determines much of the texture of day-to-day life in those societies; and in its broad lines, that content may have stability and resilience through time. However, we should never lose sight of the fact

---

[4] C Geertz, 'Local Knowledge: Fact and Law in Comparative Perspective' in *Local Knowledge: Further Essays in Interpretive Anthropology* (New York, Basic Books, 1983) 167 at 221.

[5] This invocation of both ethnographic description and juristic literature in this paragraph obscures an important difference between them. They both involve simplified, one might even say idealised, portraits of the normative order, and it is in this respect that they are cited together in this paragraph. However, the juristic accounts do so precisely in order to bring more consistency to the legal order. Part of jurists' role is consciously to define an order that only imperfectly exists; they actively promote the goal of consistency and justice in the law. In terms I have coined elsewhere, their role is exhortative rather than merely descriptive: J Webber, 'Legal Pluralism and Human Agency' (2006) 44 *Osgoode Hall Law Journal* 167 at 192. Ethnographers, on the other hand, are more clearly in the descriptive camp. They necessarily simplify in order to communicate—the desire to defend a subaltern order can lead them to simplify still further, in order to portray that order as more consistent and unified than in fact it is—but they nevertheless seek to describe rather than refashion.

that those portraits are simplified, tidied-up versions of the contexts they purport to describe. To adopt a phrase commonly used by lawyers, they represent the 'best view' of the law, in which the writer seeks to establish more coherence and consistency than exists in the phenomena themselves. In contrast, any real legal order is characterised by the co-existence of variant interpretations, variant conceptions of justice, variant theories of the whole. Any order must have mechanisms to address those contending positions and make authoritative determinations, at least provisionally. When those mechanisms are taken seriously, the specific content becomes less significant. Descriptions of content appear more like snapshots in time, instructive in themselves, but immediately subject to mutation and change. To fully understand a normative order, one has to understand the processes of change: what drives it; how it works with the past; how it is regulated; and how provisional outcomes are determined and applied.[6]

There is, in short, a temptation in the practical or empirical literature to treat normative orders as more consistent than in fact they are, and to minimise the role of human agency in fashioning and refashioning that content. The temptation is also manifested in the theoretical literature. It is not uncommon to see consciously made orders contrasted to orders that emerge out of practice, with the latter treated as though they are the product of something other than conscious decisional processes. To take one recent example, Simon Roberts adopts the adjective 'acephalous' to describe non-state orders. He does so to distinguish orders based on centralised political control from orders that do not involve imposition by a governing class; he wants to confine 'law' to the former (although he does acknowledge that the latter are normative orders). However, surely 'acephalous' connotes more than the mere dispersion of decision-making. It obscures human agency altogether in the establishment of order, suggesting that there is no directing intelligence or combination of intelligences, or if there is, such an intelligence works purely by consensual negotiation.[7] In doing so, the gulf between highly centralised state-structured orders and non-state orders is exaggerated.

---

[6] In some ways, the argument in this chapter runs parallel to debates that have occurred in anthropology over how history and process should be incorporated into ethnography, instead of presenting a unified and fundamentally static vision of cultures. See, eg G Marcus and M Fischer, *Anthropology as Cultural Critique: An Experimental Moment in the Human Sciences* (Chicago, University of Chicago Press, 1986) 77; and S Moore, 'Explaining the Present: Theoretical Dilemmas in Processual Ethnography' (1987) 14 *American Ethnologist* 727.

[7] S Roberts, 'After Government? On Representing Law Without the State' (2005) 68 *Modern Law Review* 1. Compare Lon Fuller's cogent criticisms of approaches to customary law that see them as located in simple habit: L Fuller, 'Human Interaction and the Law' (1969) 14 *American Journal of Jurisprudence* 1 at 3–5. Perhaps the strongest claims of spontaneous ordering are not in the localist or culturalist mode of this and others, but of a more universalist cast, marked by a strong commitment to market ordering. The prime example is the work of Friedrich Hayek: FA Hayek, *Law, Legislation and Liberty: A New Statement of the Liberal Principles of Justice and Political Economy* (London, Rouledge & Kegan Paul, 1973–79).

I suspect that one reason for this tendency is a desire to affirm the integrity of non-state orders against the state, because the state is seen as distant, unresponsive, repressive and (with respect to subaltern orders) colonialist. There are strong affinities between this literature and classical anarchism, as writers seek to affirm means of social organisation that are taken to be consensual, untainted by authority and imposition. I share the need to take non-state orders seriously. I acknowledge that state orders can do great violence to non-state mechanisms of social ordering. However, we cannot achieve an adequate understanding by portraying non-state orders as more unified and conflict-free than they are and by obscuring the mechanisms of decision within those orders.

Ehrlich's theory strays into this naturalising fallacy, especially (as I will argue) in his fundamental distinction between 'rules of decision' and 'rules of conduct'. And although a full assessment lies beyond the scope of this chapter, one wonders whether Ehrlich was tempted by the attractions of anarchism. The period is right, and Ehrlich shares Proudhon's and Kropotkin's hostility to the state running roughshod over more local orders, an idealisation of local orders as more consensual and responsive than the imposed order of the state, and Proudhon's particular concern with the role of localised associations and voluntary acts (especially various contractual forms) in creating normative communities.[8] One would not want to conclude too much. Characteristically, Ehrlich hedges his bets; there are passages, for example, where Ehrlich appears to accept the inevitability of state institutions. But the parallels are thought-provoking.

Ehrlich's work is subtle and rich, carrying great insight. It is not my purpose to pigeon-hole much less to dismiss him. This chapter is premised on the value of engaging with Ehrlich's approach, an engagement from which I have learned much. Moreover, as other contributors to this volume make clear, Ehrlich's work is exploratory and (perhaps for that very reason) not always systematic. Often, Ehrlich appears to have been on the track of the insights for which I will be arguing, but those insights were inadequately integrated into his theory. My fundamental argument is that, when engaging with Ehrlich's work, we get a better sense of the nature and dynamics of law and of the presence of agency within its formulation if we take the true extent of social disagreement seriously.

INTERPRETATION AND THE LIVING LAW

Let me begin the primary argument of this chapter with a story. In the 1990s, I was a member of a research group concerned with developing a

---

[8] For an excellent discussion of these themes, see G Woodcock, *Anarchism: A History of Libertarian Ideas and Movements* (Harmondsworth, Penguin, 1962) especially 20, 22, 106–9, 123–5, 130 and 187 ff.

conceptual framework for the sociology of law, working especially with the notion of 'the emergence of norms'.[9] Most of the members of the group approached the issues in the spirit of legal ethnographers, locating norms within a thick description of the circumstances in which the norms were formed. However, one of our colleagues took a distinctly different approach. He too was concerned with the emergence of norms, but he conceived of that emergence entirely in terms derived from the work of Friedrich Hayek, as the spontaneous ordering of the market.[10] His interpretations did not fit at all well with those of the rest of us. We were attempting to provide rich cultural accounts of the emergence of the norms, highly attentive to the peculiarities of each context; he provided what seemed to us to be stripped-down and functionalist accounts, accounts which filtered all human action through the self-regarding rationalism of economic man. There were times when we wondered whether our colleague and we were engaged in the same type of intellectual endeavour.

There was indeed—and still is—a deep gulf between Hayek's vision of human interaction and those I find persuasive. However, I now think that there was more in common in the approaches taken by our Hayekian colleague and by the rest of us than I had initially realised. Every attempt to derive legal rules from the lived interaction of the members of a particular society is necessarily interpretive, necessarily simplifying, seising upon particular dimensions as especially significant. We make decisions as to which are the best among rival interpretations. We impose greater order upon the material than the practices alone generate. The Hayekian approach was particularly far-reaching in its abstraction, universalising in its assumptions about human behaviour, and thorough-going in its individualism, as it proceeded to reduce human interaction to the self-interested deployment of one's property. However, as an attempt at theorisation it was not profoundly different in spirit from our more culturalist approaches. Our approaches too took a complex and ambivalent experience and simplified it, producing a unified portrait of a normative order said to have emerged from interaction.

In doing so, we tended to occlude variant interpretations, disagreement and the mechanisms by which that disagreement was settled in the various contexts in which we worked. We tended to reduce contending interpretations to a single vision of the normative order. We might have avoided such a highly simplified account. Instead of attempting to state the emergent law of a particular context as though it were a set of determinate rules engrained in human action, we might have set out to describe the legal culture of that context. We might have explored the diversity of normative arguments that had become entwined with the practices, identified the salient

---

[9] The papers resulting from the group's research were published in the collection: J-G Belley (ed), *Le droit soluble: Contributions québécoises à l'étude de l'internormativité* (Paris, Librairie générale de droit et de jurisprudence, 1996).

[10] Hayek, above n 7.

fault-lines within the society, described the relative strength of the various interpretations of the normative order, determined the relationship to practice that gave those interpretations their strength, and suggested how the social milieu's normative debates tended to be settled.[11] We would then have portrayed a more contentious milieu, albeit one that took distinctive shape and structure from its practices, traditions and historical interaction.

Now, I think there is a reason why we were induced to push beyond this picture of a diverse and somewhat untidy normative field to an account of what we took to be the milieu's unified and coherent system of right. Those responsible for maintaining, interpreting and applying a normative order do aspire to such unity and coherence; they do attempt to fashion a consistent normative order for the social field with which they are concerned. Our mistake lay in thinking that this was accomplished fact, and in purporting to describe the intended normative order as though it were already ingrained in interaction. We failed to realise that any normative order always involves the continual creation and re-creation of that order in the face of disagreement. We short-circuited that process, treating the order as though it were already achieved when it was very much under construction, indeed perennially so. Moreover, when describing the nature of that order, we would often pick what appeared to us to be the best interpretation of the order's norms, in a manner that seriously confused our role as observers with the role of those participants charged with providing authoritative interpretations of that normative order.[12]

Normative orders are, in a sense, always open, always subject to further interpretation, refinement, elaboration and extension. This is true even of the social law—in Ehrlich's terms, the 'living law'. The normative meaning of practices is always subject to ambiguity and disagreement. The practices may well furnish grounds for evaluating rival interpretations, providing a basis for arguing why one provides a better understanding of the practices' normative significance than another. In that sense, norms can be fashioned and then evaluated in relation to practice. That is the great truth in theories of social law, providing the foundation for our intuition that practices and norms evolve together and allowing us to argue intelligibly about the principles that might best order our societies. However, given the complexity of practices in any actual social field, and given the variety of considerations that are used to shape and interpret them, the practices themselves are never so univocal that they simply generate norms. At most they support

---

[11] See D Nelken, 'Using the Concept of Legal Culture' (2004) 29 *Australian Journal of Legal Philosophy* 1; and J Webber, 'Culture, Legal Culture, and Legal Reasoning: A Comment on Nelken' (2004) 29 *Australian Journal of Legal Philosophy* 27. To be fair, I may be overstating the defects of our research group's work for rhetorical effect. The resulting collection, above, n 9, is very fine indeed.

[12] See the discussion of the descriptive versus the exhortative mode in Webber, above n 5.

a range of normative considerations, which then have to be narrowed and adjudicated (in the broad sense of adjudication described below) to determine a single rule for society.

Every normative order aspires to have such single rules, at least to govern some matters. If people want to live in an ordered society, in which at least some matters are resolved by means other than brute force, there have to be ways of coming to a resolution despite the persistence of normative disagreement. Those mechanisms may well rely upon—indeed they should rely upon—knowledge of social practices so that the resolution fits well with the pattern of normative traditions present within the society, and so that the ultimate resolution complements those practices (or, if the intention is to change the practices, so that one knows accurately what one is changing). However, that knowledge will only rarely result in a single unambiguous conclusion. Generally, there will be a range of conflicting interpretations which then have to be adjudicated. That adjudication can occur through a wide variety of means: legislation; adjudication by a judge or panel of judges; agreement; or normative assertion, compromise and acquiescence. One can even, in some circumstances, agree to disagree. One can recognise continuing spheres of normative autonomy. However, in all of these cases, mechanisms exist for determining what the societal resolution to the divergence of interpretation will be. This resolution will always be artificial, in the sense that it will always establish a single or at least greatly simplified outcome in the face of disagreement. It will always be, in this sense, peremptory. Moreover, the underlying disagreement will generally continue. It may resurface and prevail in some future controversy.

In fact, it is not too much to say that this last, decisional stage of settling norms is fundamental to our idea of law as an emphatically social order, which governs us regardless of our individual agreement or disagreement. Law necessarily imposes a socially determined rule against a more complex and ambiguous background of normative assertion and counter-assertion.

An example may help to clarify what I mean. To establish that the argument applies in the case of non-state norms, I have chosen a clear case of a socially generated rather than governmentally decreed norm. In Vancouver, British Columbia, it is generally accepted that when a traffic light turns amber, not one but two cars that have been waiting to turn left across a line of oncoming traffic are permitted to make their turns, once the line of oncoming traffic has come to a stop. This seems such an invariant practice as to amount to a rule of customary law. Drivers accustomed to Vancouver almost universally understand this rule: those turning left feel justifiably aggrieved when oncoming drivers come through the intersection on a late amber, encroaching on the left-turners' time to turn; drivers waiting to turn left behind the first two cars are annoyed if one of the first two cars doesn't turn, thereby delaying the rest of the line; and drivers on the cross street will patiently wait for the left-turners to complete their turns before they enter the intersection.

Now, one can see how such a rule would come to exist. It is clearly structured by particular aspects of the situation. All have experienced the frustration of waiting to turn left when faced with a continuous line of cars coming in the other direction. All drivers can understand that left-turners must be given an opportunity to turn or a long line of cars will develop at busy intersections, all trying to turn left. The changing of the lights appears to be the best moment to allow them this opportunity. Moreover, if the oncoming traffic stops promptly when the light turns amber, there is often enough time for two cars to turn before cars on the cross street can get started. Finally, at many large and busy intersections, if on a green light the left-turners advance to make their turns, there will be two cars in the intersection.

However, it is also clear that the solution adopted in Vancouver is not a foregone conclusion. (In fact, in my city, Victoria, there appears to be no such custom, even though we are just across the Strait of Georgia from Vancouver, in the same province, with many drivers who would have driven extensively in Vancouver.) A strict rule against a car entering an intersection to turn left before the route was clear might have been enforced. The practical challenge of turning left could have been solved by greater reliance, by the city, on advance-arrows and left-turn lanes. The Vancouver solution would appear to depend upon the wider existence of norms of courteous behaviour; it may be breaking down as traffic volumes increase and drivers become more aggressive, running through intersections on late amber lights or surging ahead when their light turns green.

How, then, did the customary rule come to be established? As with many social rules, it is impossible to know, but I suspect it happened something like this: faced with heavy traffic and several cars waiting to turn left, drivers of the second left-turning car began to take the opportunity to follow through with their turn after the light turned amber. Other drivers, recognising the value of more than one car clearing the intersection, acquiesced, and did not press into the intersection when their light turned green. Moreover, when they too were in a left-turning situation, they began to adopt the practice. The police, realising the benefit to the flow of traffic, tolerated the practice. The custom became generalised. Note two things about this: first, there is a time before the establishment of the norm when its existence has to be settled. Here, it is settled by assertion and acquiescence, followed by its reproduction in other contexts. Secondly, note that it is not mechanically produced by the practice. A process of reasoning and justification enters in. The acquiescence flows from the parties' recognition that the practice carries a number of benefits. There is an element of implicit deliberation. This reinforces a point made by Lon Fuller: customary law is not merely the sedimentation of habit; it is always a reasoned solution.[13] In the case of this simple norm, where all drivers from time to time find themselves in the

---

[13] Fuller, above n 7.

same predicament, all understand the considerations in issue, and the range of potential solutions is limited, assertion and acquiescence is sufficient to settle the norm. In more complex situations, a more elaborate mechanism would generally be required: in the case of non-state norms, determination by an elder or other authority figure, compromise among the members of a family, recommendation by a trade association, debate leading to a majority opinion backed by the threat of ostracism and denunciation, and so on.

There are, then, two dimensions to all law that is grounded in social practices: (i) an interpretive dimension, in which participants propose and deliberate about rules, justifying their solutions on the basis of the exigencies of the situation, the lessons of experience, and broader attitudes already established within society; and (ii) a decisional dimension, in which a collective resolution is established from among the proposed interpretations. The former involves arguments of justification on the basis of practice and tradition, and forms the foundation for the legal pragmatist's or legal anthropologist's assumption that norms are derived from practice and culture. However, practice and culture do not speak with a single voice, and there therefore have to be mechanisms for settling upon a specific outcome. That gives rise to the second dimension, which forms the foundation for legal theories that emphasise jurisdiction, authority and command. It furnishes the kernel of truth in positivistic accounts of law.

Virtually all normative orders involve both dimensions, blended in different proportions sometimes in different institutions. Even structures that seem to depend overwhelmingly upon jurisdiction and command, such as legislatures, undoubtedly rely on interpretive methods in their deliberations. In addition, the success of legislative norms depends on their appropriateness to social life and not simply on their coercive enforcement (as Ehrlich argued at many places in *Fundamental Principles*)—although different institutions may perform such interpretive roles better or worse depending on their particular make-up, and a complex society may well adjust institutional role to institutional form. Institutions may also be subject to criticism on the basis of the scope of experience to which they refer when crafting their rules. They may look exclusively to the practices of a dominant cultural group, for example, neglecting those of a powerless minority. This may be one reason for adjusting the jurisdiction of institutions to conform to deep and pervasive cultural divisions (as in the case of indigenous self-government). However, all law, both state and non-state, is articulated against a backdrop of experience, with mechanisms for bringing normative debate to a close. All law is both interpretive and, to a degree, peremptory.

NATURALISM AND AGENCY IN EHRLICH'S SOCIOLOGY OF LAW

How are these dual dimensions of law reflected in Ehrlich's sociology of law? Although Ehrlich acknowledges their presence in what he calls juristic law (statements of law that result from the synthesising and systematising efforts of scholars), he tends not to treat other forms of law as embodying both dimensions. He treats the 'living law' (the rules of conduct which he sees as being embodied in social life) as though it were simply latent in social practices. The decisional dimension is virtually absent in his account of living law and even the interpretive dimension gets short shrift: the only interpretive role that he directly acknowledges is that of the legal scientist, who observes the legal order and attempts to describe its character as a matter of fact. He pays very little attention to *how* the norms of the living law are established and their definitions maintained. As for elements of state law other than juristic law, Ehrlich is still less clear. His stress upon the alienation of state law from the rules of conduct within a society—his emphasis upon the top-down quality of state law—tends to suggest that it has a decisional but not an interpretive dimension, although he does acknowledge the possibility of statutes being grounded in practice when discussing the arguments of the Historical School of Jurisprudence.

However, this brief summary of Ehrlich's position obscures as much as it reveals. It is worth discussing these matters in detail.

To begin, I should emphasise that there is a great deal of value in Ehrlich's magisterial work even if one accepts the view I take of social ordering. This is true of his emphasis on the primacy of customary law—of law grounded in practice or, as I would prefer to say, justified in relation to practice. His arguments for the primordial quality of that law and for the insufficiency of state law—his attempts, in other words, to remove state law from the centre of legal theory—are very well taken.[14] He also makes many telling criticisms of the view that state enforcement is fundamental to law, insisting that social sanctions are primary even in the enforcement of the norms found within state law.[15] Furthermore, he makes an exceptionally strong case that we need to take seriously how legal forms are habitually employed, not merely the rules that regulate their creation, if we are to understand their social roles.[16] His discussion of the use of distinctive contractual forms to structure economic relations, and of the close connection between particular productive systems and specific clusters of contractual interrelationships, is very revealing.[17] In his account, law is more particularistic, more fully adapted to particular economic circumstances, than is suggested in thinned-down doctrinal approaches to law. In that respect, his comments about the attempts to universalise norms through adoption, refinement and extension by the state, and the perils of that process, are

---

[14] See, eg Ehrlich, above n 3, 162, 488 and 497–8. See also Fuller, above n 7. This decentring is a theme of many of the contributions to the present volume.
[15] Ehrlich, above n 3, 20–23 and especially 64 ff.
[16] *Ibid* 43.
[17] *Ibid* especially 44.

especially thought-provoking.[18] Finally, his emphasis on the importance of associations, relationships and institutions to our understanding of law is immensely valuable.

However, all of those accounts would be strengthened and given added subtlety if the mechanisms by which the living law comes to be determined were more fully discussed. Ehrlich recognises that state law is incomplete, requiring continual development through conscious decision, but he generally fails to recognise that the same is true of non-state law. He tends to treat the living law—non-state law—as a coherent and comprehensive body of rules, engrained in determinate form within human associations, recognised but not created through conscious decision-making. Here are some examples of how he describes it:

> The legal norm is the legal command, reduced to practice, as it obtains in a definite association ... even without any formulation in words.[19]

> ...we may consider it established that, within the scope of the concept of the association, the law is an organisation, that is to say, a rule which assigns to each and every member of the association his position in the community ... and his duties ...[20]

> A social association is a plurality of human beings who, in their relations with one another, recognise certain rules of conduct as binding, and, generally at least, actually regulate their conduct according to them.[21]

When discussing the social law, he greatly minimises the role of any decision-makers in establishing and interpreting these rules, treating the law as though it were simply observed in practice. He mentions that decision-makers have a role in developing norms that transcend those of the 'cells' of a particular society or respond to new developments in society, and does refer cursorily to dispute settlement procedures in 'primitive' social orders,[22] but generally he treats the living law as consensual and non-contentious. Indeed, that assumption seems to be built into the very foundation of his distinction between rules of conduct and rules for decision, with the former being the province of the living law. He goes so far as to suggest that rules of conduct are rules that obtain only when the association is at peace. If contention arises, the rules of conduct run out and must be supplemented from some other source.[23]

This emphasis on the unity, coherence and determinacy of the living law is complemented by Ehrlich's adoption of the historical school of

---

[18] *Ibid* 137.
[19] *Ibid* 38.
[20] *Ibid* 24.
[21] *Ibid* 39.
[22] *Ibid* 118, 120 and 140–41.
[23] *Ibid* 123–4.

jurisprudence's position that law reflects a specific people's character—that if custom is to create law, 'it must be an expression of the general legal conviction of the people'.[24] The living law is harmonious and closely associated with the collective beliefs of a particular human community and, perhaps at a broader level of generality, with the nation. All members of the community hold to the rules as a matter of their collective identity.

Now, it is absolutely correct to emphasise (as the above quotations do) that law is about ordering relations in a particular context. However, it is a mistake, I believe, to treat that order as though it were organically inscribed in the community, so that all members simply live by its demands. It is better to think about law as driven by an aspiration towards order, by a will to live in an ordered community, but where that order has to be made and remade. The agent that makes this order need not be the state. Ehrlich is absolutely right in drawing our attention to the plurality of contexts in which rules are created and maintained. There may be a very strong ethic that those norms should be sought through reflection on the society's own practices, so that one attempts, to the extent possible, to resolve new challenges in a manner that maintains consistency with past interactions. This is especially so in the case of societies which have a strong sense of commonality, of solidarity, combined with a will to maintain that solidarity into the future. However, even there, it is best to think of such societies as proceeding on the basis of a presumption of order—a sense that one has to postulate the existence of a common rule to regulate the society's interactions in an ordered fashion—rather than simply embodying a set of unambiguous and determinate rules. In any disputed case (and disputed cases are frequent in any actual society), one will have to deliberate over what the common rule is and (what often amounts to the same thing) what it entails in these specific circumstances. And that deliberation is almost always concluded by some means of ultimate determination.

Now, in that process of deliberation, fidelity to the practices of the society may well serve as the principal ground for argument. Detailed appeal to those practices may dominate discussion. Extended deliberation, citing past practice, may produce something approaching consensus, but the acceptability of the final outcome does not depend upon all participants agreeing that the final resolution gets the practice right. Individuals have good reason to acquiesce in the outcome even if they disagree with it, simply because they value living in community with others or can see no possibility of doing otherwise.[25] It is in this manner that we should understand Ehrlich's

---

[24] Ibid 444 and generally throughout ch 19.
[25] I explore some aspects of this challenge in J Webber, 'Rapports de force, rapports de justice: la genèse d'une communauté normative entre colonisateurs et colonisés' in Belley, above n 9, 113, published in English as J Webber, 'Relations of Force and Relations of Justice: the Emergence of Normative Community between Colonists and Aboriginal Peoples' (1995) 33:4 Osgoode Hall Law Journal 623.

insistence on the 'autonomous' as well as 'heteronomous' nature of all 'rules of conduct'—his argument that such law is imposed from within, not merely from without.[26] It is not imposed from within because everyone agrees with it; it is acknowledged and followed because people realise that if the community is to continue, there have to be ways of bringing social controversy to an end and, in a community in which people do not always agree, those outcomes cannot simply be the ones that each member would pick. Indeed, Ehrlich recognises that the autonomous nature of the law cannot imply that:

> ... the norm must be recognised by each individual. The norms operate through the social force which recognition by a social association imparts to them, not through recognition by the individual members of the association.[27]

In important ways, then, the commitment to live in community precedes and determines one's commitment to that community's normative order. One realises the necessity of living in community with people with whom one disagrees, and that prompts one to accept the order that enables that to occur. One's primary attachment is very much to the idea of order, not necessarily to the rules embodied within it. One is willing to accept a range of ordering principles as long as some reasonable and peaceable structure is maintained. Indeed, this may go a very long way towards explaining the force of arguments based on past practice and tradition: those arguments, drawing their content directly from reflection upon our past lives together, stay closest to our commitment to community for community's sake. We rely upon our experience of living together because, in the last analysis, the very fact of being able to live together is what is most important to us.

Ehrlich sometimes suggests that the rules are primary. He says, for example:

> Every human relation within the association, whether transient or permanent, is sustained exclusively by the rules of conduct. If the rules cease to be operative, the community disintegrates; the weaker they become, the less firmly knit the organisation becomes.[28]

This comment is unexceptionable, however, if one realises that underlying these rules and accounting for their hold on individuals is those individuals' foundational need for community. At a variety of points, Ehrlich emphasises precisely this dynamic. He speaks of people clinging to their group, noting with respect the force of social norms:

> He therefore who is in need of the support of the circle to which he belongs—and who is not?—does wisely if he conforms, at least in a general way, to its norms.

---

[26] Ehrlich, above n 3, 166–8.
[27] *Ibid* 167.
[28] *Ibid* 40.

> He who refuses to conform to them must face the fact that his conduct will loosen the bonds of solidarity within his own circle.

At another point he suggests that even a well-advised 'moral anarchist' will conform to the rules of his community:

> ... if for no other reason, because he does not wish to lose the advantages which he gains by doing so, because he wishes to avoid the disadvantages incident to rebellion.

Furthermore, he says that a normative order:

> ... may be a poor one, may perhaps afford undue advantages to its leaders, may impose heavy burdens upon the others, but it is always better than no order at all.[29]

All of this opens up the possibility that one can have a perfectly viable association, one that seeks to draw upon its own history as its principal source for its normative order, while still harbouring considerable disagreement and debate over the very content and interpretation of that normative order. That is the usual situation of human communities; at the very least, it is a more persuasive conception than one that sees those communities as naturally unified around a wholly determinate set of rules. All communities then must have processes for settling upon particular resolutions to particular questions. Both dimensions are present: the interpretive and the decisional.

This, however, has fatal consequences for Ehrlich's key distinction between rules of conduct and rules of decision. This distinction dominates *Fundamental Principles*. Early in the volume, Ehrlich says:

> The first and most important function of the sociological science of law ... is to separate those portions of the law that regulate, order, and determine society from the mere norms for decision, and to demonstrate their organising power.[30]

The distinction largely underlies Ehrlich's separation of the living law from the vast bulk of state law. He uses it at the foundation of his notion of 'legal proposition'. He suggests that rules of decision are much more limited than rules of conduct, for the former are directed only at official decision-makers, while the latter are observed in life. Indeed, he suggests that rules of decision tend to be alienated from their societies, confined to officialdom, invariably appearing 'as the result of an inspiration of higher power and wisdom'.[31] Ehrlich does not intend this as flattery. He argues that a true science of law must focus on the law that people actually live by, not the norms that are used merely to resolve controversies.

---

[29] *Ibid* 62–3, 167 and 61–2. See also 27–8 and 214–15.
[30] *Ibid* 41.
[31] *Ibid* 122.

There may well be merit in Ehrlich's suggestion that state law can become alienated from society, and there is certainly much to be said for the view that a traditional, sources-based, dogmatic approach to law can miss much that is significant to legal relations. However, it is not helpful to think of these matters in terms of a contrast between rules of conduct and rules of decision.

As we saw above, Ehrlich portrays rules of conduct as engrained in human behaviour. He suggests that norms of decision, however, go beyond what is present in behaviour precisely because they have to provide solutions where the rules of conduct have failed:

> ... for a relation as to which there is a dispute is something different from the same relation at peace. That which before had been adaptable and flexible has become rigid, immovable; vague outlines have become clear and sharply drawn, and often a meaning must be read into the words that the parties had never been clearly conscious of.[32]

He suggests that the process of deliberate decision is alien to the rules of conduct. In his view, any such decision would have to draw on rules that are independent of the association's internal order:

> ... in every case when a quarrel or controversy arises, the associations have usually got out of their established order into a state of disorder. It would be foolish thereafter to try to make the norms of the association the basis of a decision, for the latter have lost their ordering power in the association.[33]

However, if the practices are not univocal—if they always need to be interpreted and in that interpretation people differ, with people then having to find ways of resolving their differences for the purposes of sustaining a social order—processes of decision are entirely interwoven with the living law. These mechanisms need not be alien to the association's internal order, deriving their content entirely from the outside. They may well involve the kind of intensive deliberation on past practice that I sketched above and they may be performed by parties that are by no means alienated from society, such as respected elders or, in a commercial context, trade associations publishing advisory opinions or arbitrators named from among the participants themselves. Nor need they result in rigid conclusions: resolutions can take the form of compromises; they can involve processes of restoration and rededication to the relationship; they can be expressly limited to the particular case, without propounding an abstract rule. Again, Ehrlich's position stumbles over an excessive emphasis on agreement as the foundation for the living law, leading him to neglect interpretive and decisional processes that are inherent in all examples of the living law.[34]

---

[32] *Ibid* 123–4.
[33] *Ibid* 125–6.
[34] See, eg the heavy emphasis on consent in the living law in Ehrlich, above n 3, 126–7 and 140–41.

To put the same point another way, Ehrlich is right to see social norms as never being definitively stated and as existing in close relationship to the pattern of practices that lie beyond the expression of the rule. That, after all, is the great insight in Wittgenstein's theory of what it means to follow a rule.[35] However, those rules do have to be made articulate, especially when a choice between varying interpretations is necessary, and especially when they are to be used to resolve a particular dispute—in the very circumstances, in other words, in which a rule is necessary. And that is accomplished through probing the practices, considering their implications, reviewing past normative commitments and deciding how the norms should now be developed (and indeed Ehrlich describes this process of interpolation, although he suggests that the practices provide unique answers, without any need for the further determination I have been emphasising).[36] The expression of the social rule is not, then, antithetical to its nature. Ehrlich is right that the formulation of the rule does not precede its application, so that the rule's application is simply the logical consequence of the previously articulated rule.[37] There is always room for further consideration of practice and further development of the rule's normative content in consequence, a development prompted by the very act of applying the rule to new circumstances. However, the formulation and reformulation of norms through the making of decisions is part and parcel of how one works with all law, non-state as well as state. Llewellyn and Hoebel's focus on decision-making as the key arena in which to understand Cheyenne law was not just common-law casuistic bias, but the recognition of a fundamental and inevitable dimension of all legal orders.[38]

It is worth enquiring into the nature of these decisional mechanisms in non-state orders. Any recognition of a normative order involves not just the recognition of a set of rules, as Ehrlich seems to suggest, but also a structure of authority which settles, interprets and applies those rules. Those structures of authority require our attention. Questions about their adequacy should not be hidden behind the fiction that non-state orders are natural and non-contentious.

It is also possible for state institutions to settle societal norms in a manner that is attentive to the normative implications of human interaction. Indeed, once one recognises that non-state orders too require decisional mechanisms, the contrast between the orders becomes much less sharp.

---

[35] L Wittgenstein, *Philosophical Investigations*, GEM Anscombe (tr) (2nd edn, Oxford, Blackwell, 1958).

[36] Ehrlich, above n 3, 172. See also 460–61, where he talks of scientific labour in law being productive, 'but its productivity consists in discovering the content of existing law, not in creating new law'.

[37] Ehrlich, above n 3, 171.

[38] KN Llewellyn and E Adamson Hoebel, *The Cheyenne Way: Conflict and Case Law in Primitive Jurisprudence* (Norman, University of Oklahoma Press, 1941).

Gerald Postema's theory of the common law is a persuasive portrait of just how normative reasoning can be driven forward by intense engagement with past human interaction.[39] There is a substantial body of scholarship in administrative law which suggests that specialised tribunals too can develop regulatory regimes in a manner responsive to their particular domains.[40] The alienation between state institutions and the living law postulated by Ehrlich is possible, but by no means necessary. In fact, Ehrlich notes that the role of state law has grown in conjunction with the intensification of solidarity within national societies; he acknowledges that juristic law (state law developed by judges) has grown by hermeneutic extension, often working from the rules developed in the inner order of associations; and, as already mentioned, he appears to accept the suggestion of the historical school of jurisprudence that statutes too can be grounded in practice.[41]

There is, in the end, a great deal in common between non-state and state legal orders in their manner of functioning. One wonders whether Ehrlich's fundamental concern is best understood not on the basis that one legal order is engrained in conduct and the other imposed as a rule of decision, but rather flows from his regret at the generalisation of norms beyond the rich cohesion of a local community. He is concerned with the application of rules on a state-wide basis, so that they are imposed beyond the contexts that originally produced them, overriding local norms.[42] He emphasises that the abstraction and universalisation of norms separates them from their communities, and he markedly prefers particular and localised norms (although he acknowledges that some universal norms have taken hold among 'the whole human race' and have now become, in his terms, rules of conduct for them).[43] Some of his criticisms of state law can be read as attacks on professionalisation and the potential for alienation that that involves. Indeed, this seems to be the key point underlying his contrast between customary and juristic law in the work of the historical school.[44] However, if this is so, we are not dealing with two fundamentally different kinds of law—rules of conduct and rules of decision—but with a unified phenomenon which can be pursued with greater or lesser sensitivity

---

[39] GJ Postema, 'Classical Common Law Jurisprudence (Part I)' (2002) 2 *Oxford University Commonwealth Law Journal* 155; and GJ Postema, 'Classical Common Law Jurisprudence (Part II)' (2003) 3 *Oxford University Commonwealth Law Journal* 1.

[40] P Nonet and P Selznick, *Law and Society in Transition: Toward Responsive Law* (New York, Octagon Books, 1978); HW Arthurs, 'Understanding Labour Law: The Debate over "Industrial Pluralism"' (1985) 38 *Current Legal Problems* 83; HW Arthurs, '*Without the Law*': *Administrative Justice and Legal Pluralism in Nineteenth-Century England* (Toronto, University of Toronto Press, 1985); I Ayres and J Braithwaite, *Responsive Regulation: Transcending the Deregulation Debate* (New York, Oxford University Press, 1992).

[41] Ehrlich, above n 3, 155–6, 175–80, 289, 444, 446 and 449–51.
[42] Ibid 124–5.
[43] Ibid 81.
[44] Ibid 452 and 456.

to place, with greater or lesser responsiveness to experience and tradition, with greater or lesser respect for norms of equality, individuality and participation, with greater or lesser openness to moral learning, revision and change, and within spheres of jurisdiction that are more or less attuned to patterns of experience and culture. It is along these vectors that the comparison of state and non-state orders should proceed.

CONCLUSION

Thus, we obtain a better sense of the nature and dynamics of law and the presence of agency within its formulation if we take normative disagreement seriously. How would this change our pursuit of Ehrlich's project?

To begin, we would pay careful attention to the decisional dimension that exists in all normative orders, state and non-state. We would enquire into the nature of decision-making processes, their partiality and the elements of imposition that all normative orders embody. We would attend to dissent: where dissent is located, how it is manifested, whether and how it influences outcomes, how social norms are settled. When we stepped from the task of understanding normative orders to the question of how and why they should be accommodated—when we moved, that is, from science to policy—we would not base our decisions on an easy equation of norms and communities so that issues of contestation and control were rendered invisible. On the contrary, we would be alert to the mechanisms by which norms are made and would gauge our responses to those mechanisms' claims to authority. I would like to think that this might produce a stance of constructive engagement among members of different orders, where one would presume that norms had a measure of adaptation to context (precisely because the norms had been developed within that context), but where that presumption operated in relative terms and did not foreclose an assessment of social agency. We would pay careful attention to who claims to speak for whom, whose voice is predominant and the justification for that predominance. And we would always be careful to turn similar scrutiny back on ourselves.

At the same time, we would subject the interpretive dimension of normative orders to more detailed examination. Orders are not simply a projection of social practices. Those practices have to be perceived, formulated, their implications explored and their ostensible lessons re-translated into action. An act of interpretation is always interposed. The practices do provide the foundation for the range of interpretations. This recognition furnishes the basis for arguments that suggest that at a broad level of generality, the normative order is constrained by, perhaps even determined by, social conditions. However, note that this conditioning of norms operates only at a level of generality; the detailed determination of norms and their application still involves the kind of agency identified here. Furthermore, one would also want to be careful in employing the language of constraint or determination even at a general level. Norms can be relative to practices and shaped by them without being absolutely constrained by them. Practices can be susceptible to such a variety of interpretations that there is room for quite different conclusions. Norms themselves help to structure practices; there can therefore be change in the conditioning environment over time in part as a result of past normative decisions. Once again, our attention should be drawn to questions of agency. And in that agency we see the relevance of culture—of the resources and linguistic frameworks within which phenomena are expressed and understood—to all law. Law is never simply a functional adaptation to context. The pragmatic and the cultural are always conjoined.

Finally, note that these comments apply equally to state and non-state normative orders. Indeed, there is a deep and abiding structural similarity among all norms. All are framed in relation to practices; all are premised on interpretations of practices (in which culture inevitably plays a role); all require means for resolving interpretative disagreements in order to establish today's norm (at least provisionally). The paradigmatic feature of the law has often been thought to be coercion; the principal agency of coercion is the state; hence the equation of state and law. This chapter suggests that the emphasis on physical compulsion is itself misconceived. Legal institutions' fundamental role—their quintessentially legal function—is to specify norms, to render them determinate. They may also apply coercive pressure, but that is supplementary, not indispensable. Indeed, if there is anything that the sociology of law, including Ehrlich, has taught us, it is that direct coercive enforcement of the law is rarely necessary to secure even a high degree of social compliance. Specification of the law—making clear what the social norm is in the face of normative disagreement—is often fully sufficient to achieve conformity, given individuals' commitment to living in society—a commitment that itself underlies informal, indirect inducements to comply.

10

World Society, Nation State and Living Law in the Twenty-first Century

KLAUS A ZIEGERT

EHRLICH AND THE GROUNDING OF A SOCIOLOGICAL THEORY OF LAW

THERE ARE FEW texts in the socio-legal literature, compiled over the past 100 years or so, which stand out as a true 'companion' text and one which can be recommended as such comprehensively and without hesitation to students and scholars of sociology of law. Ehrlich's 'Grundlegung'[1] certainly is one of them and perhaps the only one. Whenever one consults this book, dealing with a contemporary issue of sociology of law in research or for a lecture, one is struck by the longevity

---

[1] It is also rare that all guiding ideas and theoretical concepts of an author are systematically presented in just one book. However, E Ehrlich, *Grundlegung der Soziologie des Rechts* (Wien/Leipzig, 1913) appears to be such a book. In the following, most of the references will be to the more or less contemporary translation of Walter Moll (E Ehrlich, *Fundamental Principles of the Sociology of Law* (Cambridge, Mass., Harvard University Press, 1936, reprinted and with a new introduction, Transaction Publishers, New Brunswick, 2002). While overall Moll's translation works remarkably well, it has difficulties in dealing with Ehrlich's inimitable and for that matter 'untranslatable' sarcastic style in the German original. These difficulties start with the title: the English 'Fundamental Principles' does not carry the same gravity but also pretension as the German 'Grundlegung' does—a very deliberately chosen provocation of the German-speaking academic establishment, but also a very accurate description of Ehrlich's pedagogical project. That the book remained the only major publication of Ehrlich's sociological theory of law is due to the difficult circumstances of Ehrlich's work in the last years of his life and happened by default. Ehrlich worked apparently on a trilogy of his sociological theory of law, dealing with the principles, legal reasoning and judicial decision-making in turn. Of these, he published the *Grundlegung (fundamental principles)* 1913 and *Die juristische Logik (Legal Reasoning)* 1917/1918. The latter was apparently a rushed version, first published in a law journal (1917) and then as a separate edition (Tübingen, 1918) and, as far as I am aware, has not been translated into English. *Die richterliche Rechtsfindung auf Grund des Rechtssatzes (judicial decision-making)* appeared only fragmented in the form of four chapters in *Jherings Jahrbücher* (1917).

of the arguments that Ehrlich drew from his observations of law as it happens and his acutely felt sense that law was only a part of the historical and social (evolutionary) process of humankind's coping with everyday life, moving along only on the basis of a sustainable order—or not at all. An impatient reader today may quickly abandon the text and its often long-winded excursions into legal history, nineteenth-century philosophical anthropology and political theory, perhaps disappointed while in search for a ready-made answer to his or her research question. However, there are reasons for the timelessness of this text and its solid position as one of the enduring canons of sociology of law over time. The following chapter is an attempt to present them in more detail, with a special focus on the question as to the fitness of Ehrlich's sociology of law for twenty-first-century global society. We will find that being guided by Eugen Ehrlich on a round trip through society's law can be highly illuminating and time well spent. At the very least, it is never boring.

The more often one returns to Ehrlich's momentous work, the more one is surprised to see that modern sociological theory of law is only vaguely and then highly selectively informed about what Ehrlich actually observed and wrote. It seems that the concurrent socio-legal discussion is treating Ehrlich's work as part of the history of ideas, but cannot show that it has come much further in providing fitting constructs for understanding the operation of law when compared with Ehrlich's timeless contextual concepts. Of course, he does not—could not—come up with contemporary buzzwords like legal pluralism, legal culture, communication, semi-autonomous fields, legal systems and so on. However, he would have—in his judicious empirical way—adopted some of the underlying concepts as fitting and rejected others as not, while he could rest assured that the respectively assessed 'legal facts' were already—and are still—accounted for in his sociological theory of law. Consequently, the main reason why Ehrlich wanted to lay the ground for a theory of law sociologically was his vision of a universal theory of law.[2] This was not meant to 'take over' from or substitute for the doctrinal (normative) theory of law (allgemeine Rechtslehre), but to complement and refine it with a scientific (empirical theory) of law. He arrived at this view by his growing and, after decades of research, deeply held conviction that the unity of law was constituted by society and not by law however theoretically conceptualised—least of all as a doctrine of state law circulated by the contemporary legal academics as a legitimation for imperialist nation states. In this radical call for a general

---

[2] See E Ehrlich, *Fundamental Principles*, above n 1, 25. Moll translates Ehrlich's definition 'die Soziologie des Rechts ist die wissenschaftliche Lehre vom Recht' (sociology of law is the *scientific theory*/doctrine of law) as 'theoretical science of law' and so distracts from Ehrlich's major argument as to why lawyers needed to learn and know sociology.

sociological theory of law, we can find the connection to a modern general theory of world society and its law.[3]

Inevitably, such a design of a theory of law had to provoke stern resistance of the legal academic establishment and, by that authority, all lawyers with their contemporary exclusive focus on state law, including such eminent scholars as the lawyer-sociologist Max Weber.[4] However, even today when we look into contemporary theoretical approaches, their concept of law and especially the relationship of law and state or norm and sanction, we find, except for some notable exceptions, evasive answers, such as differences between 'hard' and 'soft' law, diffuse references to legal cultures or 'legal pluralism'—none of which define the operation of society's law as clearly, definitely and comprehensively as Ehrlich worked out with his formula of the 'living law'. More or less they too are wedded to the idea that law is a state affair or even a 'national' arrangement. Contrary, then, to the criticisms that Ehrlich's neglect and occasional derision of state omnipotence in his sociological theory of law were a serious flaw in his theory disqualifying it from twenty-first-century consumption, we must assume that his relentless dissection of the infatuation of legal theorists with state power or more or less democratic 'people power' in order to explain law is one of the fundaments on which the robustness of Ehrlich's sociological theory of law rests.

Accordingly, this chapter will revisit the controversy of statist legal theory versus a sociological theory of law and state with the benefit of the hindsight of 100 years of further development of law and state since Ehrlich made his famous analysis and in view of a world which perhaps has not changed all that much since then and certainly not as much as many would like to make us believe. With that focus on twenty-first-century world society in mind, we will re-examine Ehrlich's constructs of society and law (see second section below) and what they hold, especially, in defining the role and function of the state for ordering world society (see third section below). Here we will compare Ehrlich's findings with the writing of his near contemporary *Herbert Spencer* (1820–1903), who appears to have been an important source for Ehrlich, especially in respect to a social science which is informed by evolution theory.[5]

---

[3] See N Luhmann, *Die Gesellschaft der Gesellschaft* ('World Society as a Social System') (Frankfurt, Suhrkamp, 1997, no English translation available) as the sum of modern systems theory of society, including law. We use this theoretical approach as our vantage point from which we interpret Ehrlich's lasting contribution in this chapter.

[4] See M Weber, *Wirtschaft und Gesellschaft* ('Economy and Society') (Tübingen, Mohr & Siebeck, 1922) 511. Significantly, however, Weber does not comment on Ehrlich's sociology at all, but criticises Ehrlich's call to lawyers to be aware of social norms.

[5] A collection of the most critical essays of Herbert Spencer was published in 1884 (Herbert Spencer, *The Man versus the State* (London, 1884, reprinted Liberty Fund, Indianapolis, 1982)), but Ehrlich's references to Spencer leave in the dark what he had read or, for that matter, received through contemporary sociological adaptations of Spencer by both Ferdinand

In the light of such an exploration of both the contribution of Spencer's evolutionary systems theory and Ehrlich's appreciation of it, a question is in order as to whether Spencer has been dismissed too lightly as a 'social-Darwinist' or has been forgotten too readily as a serious, early critic foretelling the many adverse and often paradox effects of the 'progress of human civilisation' in the name of the rule of law. Nevertheless, we will find that between the engineer—and savage critic of law and lawyers—Spencer, and the lawyer Ehrlich, both working from the same empirical sociological foundations and often coming to the same conclusions, Ehrlich's understanding of society's law, with his more accurate observations of the mixed blessing of state power, connects better to the world society and its living law in the twenty-first century (see fourth section below).

EHRLICH ON SOCIETY AND THE 'INNER ORDER OF ASSOCIATIONS'

Applying the 'test of time', Ehrlich's construct of society stands out as a truly original theoretical innovation, pre-empting in many respects much later developments in sociological theory, but going unnoticed by general sociology until today. The fortunate rejuvenation of the discussion of Ehrlich's work in the past three decades[6] has set out in sufficient detail the many aspects of Ehrlich's sociological approach to law, so there is no need for a reiteration of the many aspects of Ehrlich's account here. Instead, we want to concentrate on what makes Ehrlich's findings so remarkable and what is worth heeding in contemporary sociology of law.

As an expert of Roman law and comparative legal history and keen to put his research findings on a purely empirical (scientific) foundation, Ehrlich captured the essence of evolution theory as it relates to the human species. He designed his theoretical construct of society as a structural network of relations that individuals entertain together and with each other. Individuals can do their 'own thing', but what they can do meaningfully and productively, and above all reliably, they can only do in association with their associations. This construct clearly distinguishes society as a support structure for individuals as

---

Tönnies (1855–1936) in his *Gemeinschaft und Gesellschaft* (1887) and above all Emile Durkheim (1858–1917) in *De la division du travail social* (1893). However, Ehrlich seems to have consulted Spencer's work directly and not through the contemporary sociologists to whom there is no reference in Ehrlich's works.

[6] See the exemplary and today most systematic cataloguing of Ehrlich's output and the literature dealing with Ehrlich's work in all its aspects in S Vogl, *Soziale Gesetzgebungpolitik, freie Rechtsfindung und soziologische Rechtswissenschaft bei Eugen Ehrlich* ('Ehrlich on social security law policies, free finding of law and sociological jurisprudence') (Baden-Baden, Nomos, 2003). His research is mostly directed at the life and work of Ehrlich in order to extract a profile of Ehrlich's political values and engagement in social policy issues and less on a discussion of Ehrlich's sociological theory of law.

different from both individuals and a mere aggregate of individual wills and actions. In setting this empirical construct in sharp contrast against the legal doctrinal concepts of a nation or, preferably, nation-state society on the one side and psychologically generalised individuals on the other, Ehrlich could leave it to concrete empirical observation which specific 'society' he had in mind. He could apply the construct of association widely across the historical and comparative spectrum of all cultural forms of social life, maintaining consistently and deliberately the singular (society) for indicating the unity of the plurality of associations which give form to society:

> Society is the sum total of the human associations that have mutual relations with one another ... extending far beyond the bounds of the individual state and nation ... [that] constitute a society to the extent that acting and reacting upon another is all that is perceptible among them.[7]

Evidently, this construct is not just a simple generalisation of an 'ethnographic' account of a 'global Bukowina' akin to the region at the provincial periphery of the Austro-Hungarian Empire, where Ehrlich worked and lived,[8] but a functional-structural concept of society with the concept of differentiation in the form of modernisation built in:

> [In society] a man becomes a member of associations of the most diverse kinds; his life becomes richer, more varied, more complex. And in consequence, the once powerful genetic associations languish, and in part, fall into decay. Only the house community of the nearest blood relatives, who dwell under the same roof ... has been able to maintain itself in full vigour down to our day.[9]

Ehrlich did not need to 'psychologisise' or double-guess what 'makes', motivates or drives individuals to do what they are doing, including 'organising' themselves. He was satisfied that the unity of society is bounded exclusively by the—universally observable—'actions and reactions' of individuals upon each other in the (normative) forms of their associations.

Structural form, then, is the key for understanding what Ehrlich meant with his concept of 'association'. This concept identifies the relational social norms or rules of conduct as the formative element of associations and what constitutes their 'inner order'. Social order emerges as a relational and structural result of generalised, practised observation of others, that is, having respect for the actions and reactions of the other members of the association. This order cannot be singularly 'hijacked' or commandeered by any one individual. It develops over time, and becomes entrenched so deeply that the original, practical reasons for those 'actions and reactions' get lost in the cultural, intergenerational transmission. What there is to

---

[7] See E Ehrlich, *Fundamental Principles*, above n 1, 26.
[8] See on the biographical data of Ehrlich's life and work most comprehensively, S Vogl, above n 6, 73–139.
[9] See E Ehrlich, *Fundamental Principles*, above n 1, 27–8.

be 'vigorously' kept and preserved by the associations are the forms of relational conduct, that is, social norms. Giving form to the social relations in associations, norms are self-evidently successful, and so self-perpetuating and self-rewarding. They are not a special apparatus for enforcement or implementation. Violations of the norms are infrequent, compared to the overwhelming frequency with which they are observed. However, reactions to violations are highly demonstrative and—as part of that—often violent. Social norms are attributed with a high degree of certainty (of expectation) and the inner order of associations is predominantly communicative, peaceful, stable and predictable. This is the 'way' of the association,[10] or in another word, its law.

Ehrlich stressed his observation of the self-regulation of associations by their inner order so forcefully because he considered it to be, everywhere and at all times, the only factual and sustainable social order. He arrived at this observation by applying sociological methodology far from conjuring up an idyllic picture of past or provincial village life, and used it to draw attention to the fact that this universal primary order and its functionality were overlooked in legal theory and doctrine which made their statements without scientific foundation. Therefore, he rightly claimed that also in modern society it is the inner order of associations, and nothing else, which provides society with the effectiveness of its existing norms.[11]

The finding of the use of norms in sustaining the relations of the association allowed Ehrlich to define norms sociologically. Norms according to Ehrlich's concept of society are not a description of an ideal state of affairs (the sphere of 'ought'), but the observable expectations of the members of an association as to how things were (always) done. In this empirically measurable way, the effectiveness of norms correlates with the stability, or certainty, of a socially acceptable and accepted practice. Social norms are maintained by society because the members of the association factually achieve what they set out to do. The successful performance is the only inducement (but also reward) for keeping to norms and for doing what norms 'want'. There is, therefore, basically no need for further measures of enforcement. Consequently, threats and terror (deterrent), for instance in the form of sanctions and especially punishment, have very little and often an aversive effect.[12] Rather, sanctions are an expression of power and power relations, not an expression of law.

---

[10] See, for instance, this approach in legal anthropology at KM Llewellyn and EA Hoebel, *The Cheyenne Way: Conflict and Case Law in Primitive Jurisprudence* (Norman, University of Oklahoma Press, 1941).

[11] See the assessment of especially this point in the context of twenty-first-century world society in the fourth section below.

[12] In this point and generally, Ehrlich acknowledges the great benefit that he derived from consulting the work of a fellow transcarpathian legal scholar, Karl Georg Wurzel (1875–1931),

As Ehrlich observes, the order which emerges as the relational structure of the associations, and in particular of the 'genetic associations',[13] is self-reproducing. Law comes to this order as an accessory after the fact and is not a source for this order. Nor can legal norms displace social norms. As far as legal norms have an ordering effect, they can only achieve this if they are based on social norms:

> A study of the beginnings of human society discloses the fact that the force of the legal norms which at the time is as yet undifferentiated from the norm of religion, or morals, or ethical custom, is based exclusively on the influence exerted upon every individual by the members of the narrower association of which he is a member.[14]

Law, then, in the sense that lawyers think of it, is pursuing a different objective from actually ordering society. It fulfils a different and special function in the course of the differentiation of society. This is the function of making decisions about norms. It is a misconception to believe that the mere legal decision or legal proposition has a social effect—other than being declared law—or that a legal proposition is a statement about the actual effect of law on the reflexive structure of associations and respective members.[15] Rather, distinguishing legal norms creatively from social norms, lawyers produce a different set of norms which assist them to make decisions about (social) norms. Legal history shows that lawyers' law becomes increasingly preoccupied with legal propositions which serve the sole purpose of reproducing norms for decision-making or decisional norms (*Entscheidungsnormen*).

---

who introduced the concept of projection as a scientific definition of norms in his research of normative decision-making and legal reasoning (see E Ehrlich, above n 1, 402: 'perhaps the best book that has appeared on the Continental juristic method of the present time'). Wurzel is today forgotten, but was a respected scholar in Viennese academic circles at the time. As far as I know, he published only one work (*Das juristische Denken* ('Legal Reasoning') (1904, 1924 and reprinted 1991 as Vol 92 of H. Winkler (ed), *Forschungen aus Staat und Recht* (Vienna-New York, Springer)). This work was also published in the United States as *Methods of Juridical Thinking*, in ch X of *The Science of Legal Method* (1917), and favourably quoted by J Frank, *Law and the Modern Mind* (New York, 1930) and L Fuller, 'Legal Fictions' in *Illinois Law Review* XXV 1930–31. Both Ehrlich and Wurzel contend that the consequences of the ignorance of lawyers in particular in relation to the social function of norms compound in the overuse of sanctions in legislation and state law; see below, third section.

[13] Ehrlich uses here the biologicistic language of the day; contemporary anthropology used a more descriptive distinction of primary versus secondary groups, where primary groups are associations into which individuals are born through their organic (genetical/biological) and cultural (social) births and secondary groups are associations into which members select themselves more or less by their own volition.

[14] See Ehrlich, above n 1, 73.

[15] Adam Podgórecki expressed this crucial finding of Ehrlich very well when he suggested that lawyers and then legislators and politicians operated a 'light-switch model of law', which supposed that law worked just by being deemed to be law; see KA Ziegert, 'Adam Podgórecki's Sociology of Law: The Invisible Factors of the Functioning of Law Made Visible' in: (1978) 12 *Law & Society Review* 151.

The sociological observation of the historical differentiation of lawyers' law from the social norms of the associations leads Ehrlich to coin the term of the 'living law'.

The pressure of the unceasing differentiation as all forms of association cope with the practicalities of everyday life forces about a proliferation of legal decisions and the further differentiation of decision-making norms. This is primarily a reflection of the rapid differentiation of lawyer's law and not necessarily a reflection of the deficiency or even disintegrating inner order of the association. However, also the lawyers' law and legal decision-making must have regard for the operation of the social order and express that creatively in the legal propositions. It is in this sense of understanding and reinforcing the reflexive structure of society that lawyers' law is not divorced from living law, but, on the contrary, an important and constructive component of living law.

Evidently, then, Ehrlich directed his efforts of reforming legal education and scientific legal thought at positioning sociology of law in its proper domain, that is, educating lawyers how to observe society and, understanding it, make effective, that is, fitting, legal decisions. There is no pluralist understanding of law operating on different levels or in different 'social fields' in Ehrlich's work, only a new, enlightened view of what constitutes the unity of law:

> Just as we find the ordered community, wherever we follow its traces, so we also find the law everywhere, ordering and upholding every human association.[16]

There is, then, a unity of law, but it is not the unity of legal propositions. 'Legal propositions only form a unity in the context of society in which they have an effect',[17] that is a combination of the lawyer's creation of legal propositions and the social order which is contained in the legal relations of the associations. In other words, Ehrlich discovers a dual mode of the operation of law, in which each mode is dependent on the other, but each mode operates seemingly independently of the other. Ehrlich claims that lawyers are trained to be blind to this factual operation of law and to tacitly assume that they capture the social order in 'a giant net of legal propositions' in which they rule supreme. As a result, they believe that they can 'domesticate' any troublesome reality simply by pronouncing (normatively) legal propositions.[18] In the event, they create a decision-making system which allows legal decision-makers to treat society as an object of law. In turn, however, the decision-making mode of law supports (selectively!) the social order by maintaining an internally consistent practice of legal decision-making in respect to that order which is confined to the lawyers'

---

[16] See Ehrlich, above n 1, 25.
[17] See Ehrlich, *Grundlegung*, above n 1, 146.
[18] *Ibid* 135.

law. The social 'inner' order of associations regulates itself and respects the lawyers' law—or not—where it is practical.

In the final count, the concept of living law allows Ehrlich to draw attention to the lack of scientific methodology in legal decision-making and its adverse effects:

> To attempt to imprison the law of a time or of a people within the sections of a code is about as reasonable as to attempt to confine a stream within a pond ... Legal propositions are not intended to present a complete picture of the state of the law.[19]

Scientific methodology can assist in breaking the stranglehold of normative legal reasoning and address a more complex reality of law:

> The living law is the law which dominates life itself even though it has not been posited in legal propositions. The source of our knowledge of this law is, first, the modern legal document, secondly, direct observation of life commerce, of customs and usages and of all associations, not only those that the law has recognised but also of those that the law has overlooked and passed by, indeed even of those that it has disapproved.[20]

EHRLICH ON STATE AND LAW

Ehrlich's functional analysis of society's law explains law as the 'always coming into being'. This society-centred view of law rests on a wide array of scientific arguments directed at the normative constructs of legal theory and legal doctrine in Ehrlich's time. This construct holds that law is created by the state and it is the coercive force of the state which maintains the legal and social order. Ehrlich attacks this legal concept of state. In his observations, neither force nor the monopolised power of state is a decisive factor in the dynamics of living law and a sustainable peaceful social order. Rather, the fact that the state administration has a massive force at its disposal is a reason for suspicion that the role of the state in law is that of an interested party. Accordingly, the state is only one, even if particularly authorised and powerful, association among the many overlapping associations in which individuals are or can become members. They all co-evolve, co-exist and cooperate with the association 'state'.

Ehrlich was not alone in this outspoken, and for his time certainly radical, finding. In Herbert Spencer, he found an important source for his sociological

---

[19] See Ehrlich, *Fundamental Principles*, above n 1, 488.
[20] See Ehrlich, above n 1, 493.

theory of law and state.[21] There, Ehrlich found support for his critical assessment of the role of the state in society and for his sociological construct of the evolving normative order of society. He also shares his empiricist scientific approach based on evolution theory with Spencer. However, he apparently ignores the strongly Victorian individualist and liberalist overtones of Spencer's social philosophy, which made Spencer such popular reading in late-nineteenth-century England and especially the twentieth-century United States and which made it easy to overlook the finer points in Spencer's critical analysis of his contemporary and any imperialist society.[22]

Herbert Spencer was educated privately by his father and grandfather, and later argued vehemently against the introduction of general public education through legislation. He went to technical college and trained as a mathematical statistician and civil engineer. As such, he was involved in major infrastructure projects as a renowned expert, building mainly bridges and railroads, but led a lonely life, living mainly in hotels and taking up political and subsequently sociological writing as an outsider to the political and academic establishment. He had no disciples and did not leave a school of likeminded scholars.[23]

The key for the attraction of Spencer's work for Ehrlich was Spencer's commitment to a scientific methodology for assessing social organisation, which Spencer flaunted incessantly and often overly schoolmasterly. Evidently, he was highly skilled to handle statistical data and he employed statistics adeptly to support his observations and findings, and especially in polemic arguments. Ehrlich also sees in empirical research the strongest argument in his no-less-polemical debate with the legal academic establishment. He used his work in the 'Seminar of Living Law' at the University of Czernowitz to great effect and publicity. There, Ehrlich taught his law students how to collect empirical data on the social practices and usages of the 'tribes' populating Bukovina. Based on these observations, Ehrlich cannot agree with Spencer—who can only refer to secondary statistical data—on the strong individualist ideology of the latter. Spencer was keen to demonstrate that 'improvement in character' of both the welfare of a society and the 'justice of its arrangements ... resulted from carrying on peaceful industry under the restraints imposed by an orderly social life";[24] Ehrlich was not concerned with 'improvement in character' and

---

[21] See Ehrlich, above n 1, 150, 392, 400 and 401. Unfortunately, Ehrlich—who probably only follows the practice of legal writers in his time—does not reference his sources in the works of Spencer in any detail; see also above n 4.

[22] So, for instance, his clearly ironic use of the concept of the 'survival of the fittest' in criticising the 'civilisation' of militarist-imperialist England: see also below and n 28.

[23] See on the life and work of Herbert Spencer comprehensively M Kunczik, 'Herbert Spencer (1820–1903)' in D Kaesler (ed), *Klassiker der Soziologie* ('Classical sociologists') (3rd edn, Munich, CH Beck, 2002) 74–93.

[24] See H Spencer, above n 5, 69.

held that only a sober description of living law mattered. While Spencer can go on:

> The defective natures of citizens will show themselves in the bad acting of whatever social structure they are arranged into ... there is no political alchemy by which you can get golden conduct out of leaden instincts,[25]

Ehrlich observes factually: 'One who is engaged in the practical affairs of everyday life is anxious to deal peaceably with people'.[26] Interestingly, both use 'peaceful' as the objective of the respective order that they have in mind. Notwithstanding these differences, Spencer provided Ehrlich with useful observations and illustrations for a sociological rather than legal view on the relationship of state and law. Spencer saw the evil of aggressive state coercion as part and parcel of this form of social organisation throughout the evolutionary history of humankind: 'It is unquestionably true that Government is begotten of aggression and by aggression'[27] and 'the aggressiveness of the ruling power inside a society increases with its aggressiveness outside the society'.[28]

> Thus by survival of the fittest, the militant type of society becomes characterised by profound confidence in the governing power, joined with a loyalty causing submission in all matters ... while these ruling classes are subject to a moral discipline consisting of six-sevenths pagan example [feats in battle] and one seventh Christian precept there is no likelihood that there will arise such international relations as may make a decline in governmental power practicable, and a corresponding modification of political theory acceptable. While among ourselves the administration of colonial affairs is such that native tribes, who retaliate on Englishmen by whom they have been injured, are punished, not on their own savage principle of life for life, but on the improved civilised principle of wholesale massacre in return for single murder, there is little chance that a political doctrine consistent with unagressive conduct will gain currency ... it is impossible to unite the blessings of equity at home with the commissions of inequity abroad.[29]

What, then, is the 'proper sphere' of government? For Spencer it is:

> ... [S]imply to defend the natural rights of man—to protect person and property—to prevent aggressions of the powerful on the weak, in a word to administer justice. This is the natural, the original office of government. It was not intended to do less, it ought not to be allowed to do more.[30]

Ehrlich shares Spencer's position on state power. He also deplores ignorant and inept legislation and state regulation. However, his construct of society—in

---

[25] See *ibid*.
[26] See Ehrlich, above n 1, 497.
[27] *Ibid* 71.
[28] *Ibid* 72.
[29] *Ibid* 172–3.
[30] See *ibid* 187 and again, almost verbatim, Ehrlich after him, see below n 36.

contrast to Spencer's individualist concept—allows Ehrlich to attribute a legal realist role to the state. According to him, the factual power of the state is limited by living law, and also as far as legislation is concerned regulatory effects are limited: historically, 'great changes were always taking place in law that were not brought about by legislation', even 'at a time when the state had already gained control over legislation'.[31]

> Three elements therefore must, under all circumstances, be excluded from the concept of law as a compulsory order maintained by the state—a concept to which the traditional jurisprudence has clung tenaciously in substance, though not always in form. It is not an essential element of the concept of law that it be created by the state, nor that it constitute the basis for the decisions of courts or other tribunals, nor that it be the basis of a legal compulsion consequent upon such a decision.[32]

Ehrlich also addresses the issue of the 'proper sphere of government', almost in Spencer's terms:

> On the whole the effect of the coercive order of the state is limited to the protection of one's person, of one's possession, and of claims against those who are outside the pale of society. Whatsoever else the state may do in order to maintain the law is of less significance, and one might reasonable maintain that society would not go to pieces even if the state should exercise no coercion whatsoever.[33]

LIVING LAW IN THE TWENTY-FIRST CENTURY

Today, the benefit of hindsight allows us to see the observations and warnings of Ehrlich and Spencer in a harsher empirical light. We can see that the world has not necessarily become a 'better place', but living law has prevailed. This raises the potential for a sustainable global human order of material wealth, well-being, peaceful coping with everyday life and an effective law. Ehrlich's sociological construct of society is as valid today as it was when he presented it to the unimpressed public in 1913. Far from being a simplistic description of pre-industrial society, Ehrlich's construct of a general sociological theory brings social analysis to a point that is crucial for understanding human society. This point is that there is no limit to the overload of norms that humans can entertain individually and collectively, but there is a limit to the social order that they can sustain with whatever social relations they make normatively safely expectable. Ehrlich's radical distinction between the world in which people live, the social norms of

---

[31] See Ehrlich, above n 1, 391.
[32] See Ehrlich, *Fundamental Principles*, above n 1, 24.
[33] See Ehrlich, above n 1, 71.

everyday life and the world of normative propositions, the political ones in the form of ideologies and the legal ones in the form of legal propositions, is a lasting contribution to sociological thought and a warning against aggressive interference with any forms of social and political order. We are well advised to heed Ehrlich's warnings. The society that modern sociologists are so excited about and preoccupied with plays out largely in the world of normative propositions; the world of 'living' social norms is far more glacial and changing only little by little through an 'inner order' that dictates which norms can be sustained in everyday practice and which norms can be safely ignored.

The society, then, that Ehrlich had in view is society in general, that is, the socially organised world society—then and now. It is also this global human society derived by evolution which drives the differentiation of its functional subsystems worldwide—there is no patent or, to use Spencer's words: 'alchemy'—for how family, economics, politics or law should develop. However one can say, in the light of Ehrlich's findings, that these functional systems are a performance of society which radiates, under given local circumstances differently, from the local practice of associations and their norms to the different specialised and formally extended forms of association and their normative propositions. In other words, not only lawyers, but also and especially sociologists of law, should pay more, and at least equal, attention to primary social structures than to secondary structures where most of the normative noise of modern society is generated, but very little of their 'inner order'.

The case in hand is living law. It is not bounded by local practices or local legal propositions and, yet, emerges as a unity which comprises not only the legal propositions or lawyers' law, but also the 'social order of existing legal relations'.[34] Ehrlich can include seamlessly international law in that unity and also cast a prophetic glimpse at the emerging world law of human rights.[35] This living law of the world society is reminiscent of Kant's design[36] of a cosmopolitan civil society of non-governmental 'associations' supported by law (international legal decision-making), together with the power play of states held in check by treaties. This civil society

---

[34] See Ehrlich, *Grundlegung*, above n 1, 146.

[35] '[At least among the select thinkers of the world] there exists a conception of a morality which embraces all human beings, of law not confined within any boundaries. Although it is at present time nothing more than a dream of the noblest and best which promises a better future, it has been realised in the living law to the extent of securing, in the seats of the highest civilisation, life, liberty, and property to every human being' (see Ehrlich, *Fundamental Principles*, above n 1, 82 (translation by KAZ)).

[36] See *Immanuel Kant* and his construct of a peaceful order in which 'eternal peace' is achieved by keeping the 'military-industrial-financial complex' sustaining and being sustained by aggressive state power in check with international law, that is, a cosmopolitan legal order of world citizens (see I Kant, *Zum ewigen Frieden* ('On eternal peace') (Königsberg, 1775)).

does not have nor needs to have a corresponding 'world government', but is anchored in and promoted by non-aggressive and humanitarian states, which respect—with the rule of law, or in Ehrlich's words 'administration of justice' in place—domestically and globally the 'proper sphere of government'.

This kind of world society is no longer a mere dream 'of the noblest and best', but the ever more clearly emerging living law of (world) society in the twenty-first century—civil society, international legal decision-making and non-aggressive states are fact today. However:

> This [global legal order] is not a developed order but a developing one, which has always to be regained again and again by dissolving the controversial interests entertained in the social relations into legal ordering in due course.[37]

---

[37] See Ehrlich, *Grundlegung*, above n 1, 146.

11

Ehrlich's Legacies: Back to the Future in the Sociology of Law?

DAVID NELKEN

Social research on law has been characterised by a repeated discovery of the other hemisphere of the legal world. This rediscovery is often associated with Ehrlich.[1]

INTRODUCTION

WHAT IS MEANT by 're-considering' Ehrlich—and why should we want to? In this chapter, I shall be discussing this question in relation to the influence Ehrlich's work has had on later writers—what can be called Ehrlich's legacy—or, as we shall see, legacies.[2] I shall first contrast two reasons for studying classical writers. I will then go on to provide examples of the ways in which Ehrlich's writings have been used by later scholars in the light of changing conditions and perspectives. In order to show how his work has served as a point of reference to deal with problems in the sociology of law, I describe how Ehrlich continues to inspire research into the evolving phenomena of the 'living law'. Then, as an illustration of the way in which scholars try to update his ideas so as to make them relevant as theory advances, I discuss the way he is currently being re-read and re-written in the light of Luhmann's social theory of law.

---

[1] M Galanter, 'Justice in many rooms: Courts, private ordering and indigenous law' (1981) 19 *Journal of Legal Pluralism* 1 at 20.
[2] This will necessarily be a selective overview of the influence of some of Ehrlich's key ideas about law in society, and will not touch, for example, on the influence or implications of his arguments about free law-finding. Even so, following up their influence will take us across a range of interdisciplinary approaches to law, including comparative law, international law, conflicts of law, legal philosophy, law and economics, and social theory. For a brief previous effort to show Ehrlich's influence in different disciplines see KA Ziegert, 'A Note on Eugen Ehrlich and the Production of Legal Knowledge' (1998) *Sydney Law Review* 4–17.

I conclude by suggesting that the process of interpreting the message of a 'founding father' is never ending. Without pretending that we can find in Ehrlich's work ready-made answers to our current challenges, I do hope to show why the questions he asked are still of contemporary relevance.

WHY STUDY A CLASSICAL AUTHOR? CONTEXTUALISATION, DE-CONTEXTUALISATION AND RE-CONTEXTUALISATION

Why should we still be interested in Ehrlich's controversial philosophical, historical, psychological or sociological propositions? There are many reasons to be concerned with the work of great writers of the past, but for our purposes it is helpful to contrast the aim of seeking to get *a writer's ideas right* with that of trying to decide whether the ideas themselves *were right*. These certainly seem like relatively distinct exercises. Put most sharply, the first of these approaches could be said to aim at adding to the footnotes on Ehrlich, while the second focuses on the way in which Ehrlich figures as a footnote in the work of later writers.

The importance of context varies for the two enquiries. For the first approach it is of the essence to understand Ehrlich in his time and place. We might, for example, try to explain how a scholar of Roman law could have come to make this sort of breakthrough to sociological fieldwork, or examine the similarities and differences between his idea of living law and the ideas about 'social law' in the work of earlier writers such as Savigny or Tonnies. In the second type of enquiry, however, our interest is more about what has been made of a scholar's ideas—and on what can still be made of them. So the point would be more the need to get Ehrlich 'out of context' in the sense of describing how his work has been (or can be) made to transcend his setting in Bukovina at the beginning of the twentieth century.[3] If, in the one case, we would engage in careful exegesis in order to grasp what Ehrlich *meant*, in the other we would be more concerned with showing what Ehrlich *means* for us today.

In practice, however, although there are important differences in emphasis, these enquiries cannot entirely be kept apart. Even if our research is focused on the way in which Ehrlich's work influenced later authors, we will still need to engage in some exegesis of what he actually said. It would be question-begging to speak of *Ehrlich's* influence unless we can be sure that the ideas used by others are those *actually* espoused by Ehrlich. In fact, writers who try to get Ehrlich right are frequently motivated by the desire to show that the way in which other commentators have got him wrong is

---

[3] This is over-simplifying. It could be argued—it has been argued—that it was the marginality of Ehrlich's context—'on the periphery' of the Austro-Habsburg empire—that enabled him to see 'more' than his contemporaries.

not merely a matter of mere antiquarian interest. Thus, in an earlier paper, I devoted considerable attention to distinguishing Ehrlich's ideas from the ways in which they had been re-presented by Roscoe Pound.[4] However, at the same time, I also argued that the reason why this mattered was that Pound's summary obscured the way in which Ehrlich's contribution could still be of value for us. Clearing up the misconceptions about what Ehrlich was supposed to have argued was therefore a prerequisite to going on to reveal the relevance of what he actually said for current debates. As I shall seek to show later, a return to the text not only—typically—accompanies the claim to have uncovered the 'true' or 'real' historical Ehrlich, it can also serve as a take-off point when searching for new meaning in older texts.

Our interest in relating Ehrlich to his context will also depend on our conception of how the sociology of law progresses. On one (scientistic?) view of sociology of law as a 'science', our prime task is to subject Ehrlich's de-contextualised hypotheses to empirical testing. To contextualise him involves making an imaginative leap back before not only the birth of the discipline of sociology of law, but also before there were studies of 'law and psychology' or 'law and economics'. Ehrlich's contribution would then have to be considered as of mainly historical interest on a par with other writings in the sciences of his period. If the sociology of law can 'progress' scientifically, or rather, just because it can progress, we should not expect the founder of the discipline to do more than set out directions to follow. We can learn from Ehrlich only by leaving him behind.

However, most writers (including major textbook writers such as Treves or Cotterrell) see the sociology of law as less assimilable to this idea of scientific progress.[5] They would encourage us to return to Ehrlich, as to other founding fathers, such as Durkheim, Weber or Marx, less because of the empirical validity of their specific claims and more because of the continuing relevance of the fundamental issues they dealt with and the way in which they dealt with them. On this view, Ehrlich's arguments, as also the criticisms made of them at the time, may be as relevant today as they were then. The earliest reviewers of his work wondered about the relationship between legal sociology and legal history,[6] but the issue of disciplinary boundaries is as problematic now as it was then. Critics complained about Ehrlich using the term 'law' in talking of living law—most notably in Kelsen's controversial attack on what he saw as Ehrlich's failure to defend the rights of citizens as declared by state law.[7] Furthermore, there are still

---

[4] D Nelken, 'Law in Action or Living Law? Back to the Beginning in Sociology of Law' (1984) 4 *Legal Studies* 157.
[5] See, eg L Friedman, 'The Law and Society Movement' (1986) *Stanford Law Review* 763–80.
[6] P Vinogradoff, 'The Crisis of Modern Jurisprudence' (1920) 29 *Yale Law Journal* 312–20.
[7] See ch 6 of this volume.

heated debates about the normative implications, if any, of claiming that societies are characterised by regimes of legal pluralism.[8]

Even where Ehrlich gets things 'wrong', this can be instructive. Many of the early comments, both on the original German edition and on the later American translation, echo those still being made today. Max Rheinstein, a hard though not unsympathetic critic, applauded Ehrlich for opening jurists' eyes to the relations that actually exist between family members, the way in which wealth is actually transferred from the dead to the living, and how people actually buy and sell. However, he also accused him of peddling half truths. He considered it a (politically motivated!) mistake to describe custom as law; social behaviour patterns do not always coincide with what people really believe are the right values. It was important to see that law does make space for other normative systems, which it may then incorporate. However, it was wrong to treat this as the general rule. Ehrlich's arguments applied mainly, Rheinstein claimed, to what can be called 'stop gap law', the rules people make for themselves in private transactions. In terms of legal practice, he argued, it was misleading to reduce legal science to sociology. In addition, whilst legal sociology can be of assistance to judges, questions of justice involve matters of political prudence which do not and often should not be resolved by appealing to popular sentiment.[9]

The philosopher and jurist Morris Cohen, for his part, thought Ehrlich was overreacting against the historical school.[10] He too criticised Ehrlich for confusing law with custom. The practice of tipping waiters, he pointed out, is custom not law, and there is nothing to be gained by calling it law. By contrast, the arcane details of wills are law—and not custom. Businesses may make their own agreements irrespective of the law, but they always act (in his prescient words) in its shadow. The state may not dictate everyday life, but its importance should never be underestimated. It would otherwise be difficult to understand why such hard battles are fought over who should control the government.[11]

The fact that many of the issues raised by his work still do not seem to have found agreed solutions shows how far Ehrlich's ideas do transcend their original context. Nonetheless, it is important to see that any 'return' to Ehrlich also involves a process of re-contextualisation. Later writers give *new* meaning to older authors as they 'appropriate' classical texts so as to make them speak to and for present purposes. Furthermore, it is this use which makes them classics in the same way that 'traditions' enable 'the past

---

[8] See, eg later in this chapter, the arguments Michaels deployed against Teubner and others.
[9] M Rheinstein, 'Sociology of law, Apropos Moll's translation of Eugen Ehrlich's Grundlegung der soziologie des Rechts' (1938) 48 *Journal of Ethics* 232–9.
[10] MR Cohen, 'Recent philosophical-legal literature in French, German, and Italian' (1912–14) 26 *International Journal of Ethics* 528–46 at 535–7.
[11] MR Cohen, 'On Absolutisms in Legal Thought' (1936) 84 *University of Pennsylvania Law Review* 681–715 at 684.

to live in the present'.[12] Even if we were to set out only to repeat exactly what Ehrlich is thought to have said, introducing his ideas can have different 'meaning' depending on the changing context in which he is quoted. They would, for example, likely have a different impact at a time when there is concern about too much state intervention or 'juridification', as compared to a period of extensive privatisation. However, most returns to classical authors in any case, to a greater or lesser extent, also involve explicit attempts at (re)interpretations. Since any interpretation of what a past writer has written is contestable, other commentators will often allege that the new interpretation represents a departure from the correct meaning—and it is through such debates that traditions develop and earlier scholars' arguments are given new life.

A given response to Ehrlich often tells us as much if not more about the interpreter than it does about what is being interpreted. Rheinstein, for example, thought Ehrlich's arguments were vitiated by their political sub-text. The desire to legitimate only the kind of law that was popularly accepted—what he described as the 'postulate of complete and homogenous democracy'—was being disguised as science. For him:

> Ehrlich's basic proposition that the norms of law are nothing but the actual customs and habits of the people does not withstand the scrutiny of methodological analysis. It is the statement not of a scientific truth but of a political postulate. Nevertheless, Ehrlich's work occupies a high rank in legal sociology.[13]

By contrast, Maoist writers in China (first introduced to Ehrlich's sociology of law by Pound) wrote of 'the reactionary essence of Ehrlich's sociology of law'.[14] In addition, as we shall see, Ehrlich's ideas have been pressed into service both within a framework of Pound's common-law cultural presuppositions and projects, and in terms of Luhmann's continental and civil law assumptions.

This raises the question of what yardstick to use in order to decide whether the work of an earlier writer has been interpreted (or misinterpreted) to such an extent as not to deserve to count as an example of his or her influence. It would have been possible, as in my earlier discussion of Pound on Ehrlich, to write this chapter in the form of a protest at the way in which Ehrlich continues to be 'appropriated' by later scholars in ways that often pay scant attention to what he really said. As we shall have cause to note, there is indeed more than a little special pleading in the more recent accounts of Ehrlich offered by leading authors such as Alex Ziegert (again) or Gunther Teubner. However, my main purpose in this revisiting of Ehrlich

---

[12] M Krygier, 'Law as Tradition' (1986) 5 *Law and Philosophy* 237–62.
[13] Rheinstein, above n 9, 238–9.
[14] JW Dong, 'Sociology of law in China: Overview and trends' (1989) 23 *Law and Society Review* 5 at 903–14 at 904.

is *not* to try, yet again, to 'save' Ehrlich from his interpreters by offering a better reading of his text. If we are concerned with the usefulness of Ehrlich's contribution to the discipline, we need also to ask questions about which interpretations have more heuristic value. However, once we do this, to insist that we are only interested in setting the record 'straight' about what Ehrlich actually said smacks not only of pedantry, but ingenuity.

If the meaning of an author is inevitably subject to different interpretations, the search for the most useful interpretation will often tread a fine line between misinterpretation and creative reinterpretation. Questions about interpretation can arise not only where scholars claim to be explaining what Ehrlich really meant, but also where they argue that he got things wrong. And they of course also apply to our efforts to 'correctly' interpret Ehrlich's interpreters. So we need always to ask how any given interpretation *becomes* authoritative. This does not mean that any interpretation of Ehrlich is as good as any other. There must be some limits to how far we are entitled to rewrite past thinkers in the light of current concerns. However, it does suggest that the heuristic value of an interpretation may change from one context of time and place to another.

I may have been justified in trying to prise Ehrlich away from the embrace of Pound's socio-legal engineering if, at the time I wrote, such an interpretation of his work was as serving as a block on the development of sociology of law. However, that still leaves open the question of whether Pound may have made 'good' use of Ehrlich in his own time. Under current conditions, it is arguable that attempts to re-read Ehrlich in the light of a major sociological theorist of the range and sophistication of Niklas Luhmann should not be rejected *tout court*, even if, again, these interpretations do require some straining of Ehrlich's prose. In other words, we also need to ask if reading Ehrlich's work in the light of autopoietic theory of law as a communicative sub-system of society may be helpful in advancing the discipline.

When dealing with Teubner's recent reinterpretation of Ehrlich's ideas in his influential paper about Global Bukowina,[15] it would be inappropriate, for my purpose of understanding Ehrlich's legacies, to concentrate only on the question of whether Teubner captures what Ehrlich meant at the time he wrote. We also need to see why his paper also represents a highly creative effort to apply Ehrlich's ideas to new challenges in the light of new ways of theorising social change. Moreover, as we shall see when discussing his arguments in detail, the question of how we should respond to Teubner's presentation of Ehrlich's work becomes even more complicated because he *admits* that he is also changing the ideas that he has borrowed from him. As this, and the other examples I shall be presenting, will illustrate, efforts at

---

[15] G Teubner, 'Global Bukowina: Legal Pluralism in the world society' in G Teubner (ed), *Global Law Without a State* (Dartmouth, Aldershot, 1997) 3–28.

re-contextualisation produce an unstable compromise between the aims of contextualisation and de-contextualisation—between getting Ehrlich right and claiming that he is right.[16]

THREE ASPECTS OF LIVING LAW

The canonical definition of what is meant by 'living law' is usually taken to be Ehrlich's statement that:

> The living law is the law which dominates life itself even though it has not been posited in legal propositions. The source of our knowledge of this law is, first, the modern legal document; secondly, direct observation of life, of commerce, of customs and usages and of all associations, not only those that the law has recognised but also of those that it has overlooked and passed by, indeed even of those that it has disapproved.[17]

However, this definition has some remarkable features. In the first place it is in large part mainly an indication of method. It tells us where to look (and how to look) for something, but the existence of that something is predicated on unspecified theoretical grounds. It is also difficult to see what his examples have in common other than the fact that they may all be illustrations of normative phenomena that elite lawyers in Vienna may not know about—or even want to know about. In any case, as is usual in the development of academic disciplines, what is presented by Ehrlich as one theoretical category is seen by later writers as grouping together a number of not necessarily homogenous phenomena. Following up the later reception of Ehrlich's work in the relevant secondary literature, we will find that we have to deal with different legacies rather than assume that scholars have all taken the same message from what he wrote.

In his description of living law, Ehrlich puts together the creation or employment of law by lawyers (and others), the rules and usages of associations that are 'recognised' by or will develop into (state) law, as well as, most remarkably, the shared practices of associations that are disapproved of by the state and have no aspiration to be included in the sway of its law. Some later scholars who follow him have mainly shown interest in what else law does—the actual practice of legal officials, administrators as well as all those who use or are affected by the law. Others have focused more on what else does law, even to the extent of detecting the existence of rival legal systems. Finally, yet others are searching for the sources of normative order, what

---

[16] My 1984 paper on Ehrlich was no exception. In the final footnote, I proposed drawing on Ehrlich to construct a more 'ecological' approach to law reform (something which Gunther Teubner later asked me to elaborate on).

[17] E Ehrlich, *Fundamental Principles of the Sociology of Law*, WL Moll (tr), with introduction by Roscoe Pound (New York, Russell and Russell, 1936/62) 493.

Durkheim called 'the pre-contractual basis of contract'.[18] For the purposes of illustration, it may be helpful to distinguish developments in the study of law beyond the law (law other than that contained in statutes and judgments), law without the state (especially the co-existence of plural legal regimes) and order without law (the implicit norms that make order possible).

There is certainly some overlap between the phenomena that are studied under each of these rubrics, and this goes beyond the common denominator that we cannot afford to restrict ourselves to the study of legal codes and court decisions if we want to understand 'law in society'. However, there are also important differences in the issues that each of them raise. We may wonder how far Ehrlich was justified in combining into one category examples such as youngsters giving over the pay for their work to their parents, and businessmen not insisting on being paid by their debtors. But the situation becomes even more complex when we seek to include as examples of living law an even greater variety of phenomena, including the avoidance of legal relations by automobile dealers, the alternative sanctioning mechanisms used by diamond merchants and the typical practices of queuing for the cinema.

The Law Beyond the Law

The first part of Ehrlich's definition reminds us, as he would put it, that law 'cannot imprisoned in a code'. We need to go 'beyond' the law books so as to take into account both the role of society in generating state law and judicial sentences and the way in which it shapes laws and decisions as they seek to influence social life. Ehrlich's exemplar, the 'modern legal document', might not at first sight seem to be the most obvious starting point for grasping this aspect of living law. However, those who engage in the sociology of substantive areas of law certainly can learn a great deal from focusing on legal documents. Many of the books in the path-breaking 'law in context' series (published in the United Kingdom from the 1960s onwards) did exactly this, gathering information about the contracts used by consulting engineers, or the standard-form contracts of hire purchase or dry cleaners, so as to reveal a world of law at variance with that presupposed by the more traditional textbooks. Giving attention to documents is also crucial to understanding the construction of transnational legal agreements and regulatory modes by legal professionals.

It is impossible to trace the full influence of Ehrlich's insights here—these are now woven into the warp and woof of sociology of law. Ehrlich's claim that 'the centre of gravity of legal development lies not in legislation, nor in juristic science, nor in judicial decision, but in society itself' could well

---

[18] E Durkheim, *The Division of Labour in Society* (New York, Free Press, 1964).

be taken as the leitmotiv of the contributions to the field by Lawrence Friedman, one of the most distinguished contemporary social historians of law. More generally, the argument that there is more to law than what can be found in statutes and court decisions is constitutive of any interdisciplinary approach to law. All of the most famous studies over the last 50 years (mainly, it has to be said, coming from the United States), such as those by Macaulay 'on the non-reliance on contracts'[19] or Galanter 'on why "the haves' come out ahead"[20] mainly concern the way in which non-legal factors shape the use of law.

However, the idea that there is 'law beyond the law' has not always been taken in the same direction. Many have followed Pound and the Legal Realists in studying the 'Law in action' so as to explore the practical implementation of laws or of judicial and administrative decisions.[21] But others have sought rather to understand the 'legal consciousness' of those who use or are affected by the law, showing how ideas of legality and what it represents circulate and shape such consciousness at least as much as they are its product.[22] Marc Hertogh has recently sought to integrate Pound's common law and Ehrlich's more continental approach in order to investigate the interaction between law in action and legal consciousness. His case study of the use of discretion by housing officials shows how they mediate between the legal principle of formal equality enshrined in the *Rechtsstaat* and a wider popular legal consciousness which values responsiveness and material equality.[23]

At the same time, the claim that law has more to do with its given local context than with the wider process of rule production in the legislature and courts has never been uncontroversial. As Rheinstein pointed out in an early appraisal of Ehrlich's work,[24] this is likely to vary by types of law. Later empirical research showed that forms of law, such as that to do with labour relations, did not necessarily correspond to particular forms of social organisation in ways that would be expected.[25] There have also been some attempts to break out of the whole paradigm of trying to fit 'law' to

---

[19] S Macaulay, 'Non-contractual relations in Business' (1963) 28 *American Sociological Review* 55.

[20] M Galanter, 'Why the "Haves" Come Out Ahead: Speculations on the Limits of Legal Change' (1974) *Law and Society Review* 9 at 95–160.

[21] The alleged equation between 'law in action' and 'living law' is examined critically in Nelken, above n 4.

[22] S Silbey and P Ewick, *The Common Place of Law* (Chicago, University of Chicago Press, 1998); and S Silbey, 'After Legal Consciousness' (2005) 5 *Annual Review of Law and Social Science* 323–68.

[23] M Hertogh, 'A "European" Conception of Legal Consciousness: Rediscovering Eugen Ehrlich' (2004) 31 *Journal of Law and Society* 457–81.

[24] M Rheinstein, above n 9.

[25] S Henry, *Private Justice: Toward Integrated Theorizing in the Sociology of Law* (London, Routledge and Kegan Paul, 1983); D Nelken, 'Beyond the Study of "Law and Society"' (1986) *American Bar Foundation Research Journal* 11.2 at 323–38; and G Iskowits, 'Social Theory and Law: The Significance of Stuart Henry' (1988) 22 *Law & Society Review* 949–62.

'society'.[26] Most radically, Luhmann, first in his systems theory approach, and even more in his autopoietic social theory, insisted that law could only relate to its own communicative constructions of its environment rather than actually have direct connections with it.

Legal historians and comparative lawyers have often stressed that law can be out of step with society, or be linked to foreign sources rather than being embedded in the society in which it is found.[27] The obvious response is that the law that 'really' matters will always be that which is actually operating and therefore being shaped locally. However, this risks being tautological. On the other hand, for others, including both critical legal scholars and some post-modern social theorists, law is even more tightly bound up with society than Ehrlich thought. It is state law, official law, which shapes society's deepest conceptions quite as much as the reverse. Some speak here of law's 'constitutive' role. In a recent discussion of intellectual property law, for example, Rosemary Coombe and Jonathan Cohen argue that:

> ... a critical cultural legal studies reveals that law is fully imbricated in shaping lifeworld activities, bestowing propriety powers, creating markets, establishing forms of cultural authority, constraining speech, and policing the public/private distinction (that protects corporate authors from social accountability).[28]

As they go on to say:

> Law is a palpable presence when people create their own alternative standards and sanctions governing the use of corporate properties in the moral economies that emerge in law's shadows.

Intellectual property law does not function in a rule-like fashion as a regime of rights and obligations, but also acts as 'a generative condition and prohibitive boundary for practices of political expression, public-sphere formation, and counter-public articulations of political aspiration'.[29]

For Ehrlich, the key to the unfolding of law was to be looked for in the role of associations. Amongst the many important developments of this idea may be noted Karl Renner's demonstration—this time as seen from Vienna, rather than from the periphery—that codified property law could easily become no more than a dead husk in respect of the actual developments in

---

[26] D Nelken, above n 25; and D Nelken, 'Changing Paradigms in the Sociology of Law' in G Teubner (ed), *Autopoietic Law: A New Approach to Law and Society* (Berlin, De Gruyter, 1987) 191–217; D Nelken, *Beyond the Study of Law in Context* (Aldershot, Ashgate, forthcoming).

[27] D Nelken, 'Comparativists and Transferability' in P Legrand and R Munday (eds), *Comparative Legal Studies: Traditions and Transitions* (Cambridge, Cambridge University Press, 2003) 437–66.

[28] R Coombe with J Cohen, 'The law and late modern culture: Reflections on "between facts and norms" from the perspective of critical legal studies' (1999) 76 *Denver University Law Review* 1029 at 1031.

[29] *Ibid* 1043.

the actual organisation of capitalist firms or large rented tenements.[30] From the 1950s onwards, the work of Lon Fuller at Harvard and Philip Selznick at Berkeley examined the roots of (and the need for) 'legality' within the structure of organisational life.[31] The most recent studies by Lauren Edelman and her collaborators, also based in Berkeley, using the approach of institutional sociology to focus on the role of organisations, confirm Ehrlich's ideas about the role of associations in creating the living law. On the other hand, they also show that official norms and those of the organisations themselves are (now) far more intertwined and interdependent than Ehrlich envisaged when first contrasting living law and 'norms for decision'.

In one recent paper, which deals with organisationally constructed symbols of compliance following the 1964 Civil Rights Act,[32] Edelman *et al* coin the term 'legal endogeneity'. This refers, they say, to 'a subtle and powerful process through which institutionalized organizational practices and structures influence judicial conceptions of legality and compliance'. They argue that:

> ... organizational structures such as grievance procedures, anti-harassment policies, evaluation procedures, and formal hiring procedures become symbolic indicia of compliance with civil rights law...as they become increasingly institutionalized, judges begin to use their presence or absence in evaluating whether or not an organization discriminated. Ultimately, these structures become so closely associated with rationality and fairness that judges become less likely to scrutinize whether they in fact operate in a manner that promotes non-discriminatory treatment.

As Rheinstein suggested, however, we should be careful before generalising too much from intellectual property law or anti-discrimination law. As Edelman *et al* themselves note, law-making that sets forth broad and often ambiguous principles gives organisations particularly wide latitude to construct the meaning of compliance.

Law Without the State

The second approach to living law that we can trace back to Ehrlich is one less focused on how official law is shaped or reshaped, and more interested in uncovering the existence of legal regimes that do not have or appear to

---

[30] K Renner, *The Institutions of Private Law and their Social Function* (London, Routledge and Kegan Paul, 1949).
[31] L Fuller and K Winston, *The Principles of Social Order* (Oxford, Hart, 2001); and P Selznick, *Law, Society and Industrial Justice* (New York, Russel Sage, 1968).
[32] LB Edelman, LH Krieger, SR Eliason, C Albiston and VA Mellema, 'When Organizations Rule: Judicial Deference to Institutionalized Employment Structures', 21 June 2006, 1st Annual Conference on Empirical Legal Studies Paper <http://ssrn.com/abstract=910940> accessed 24 July 2008.

need the backing of the state. The key problem here is how to take into account the fact that there can (also) be non-state law and sub-state private legal regimes. As Teubner puts it, for this literature, 'law or not law is the question'.[33] Although Gurvitch has stronger claims than Ehrlich to having developed a rich (even over rich) sociological theory of plural legal orders,[34] discussions about legal pluralism often refer to Ehrlich's writings and current debates continue to make explicit reference to his ideas. Unfortunately, however, many writers still tend to reduce Ehrlich's contribution to the importance he allegedly attributed to preserving ethnic and cultural pluralism. However, the varied examples of living law he offered, which included businessmen not insisting on claiming their debts, give the lie to such reductivism.

Ehrlich famously argued that the state does not have a monopoly over the law. He would also have agreed with Llewellyn (who in fact was an admirer of his work) when the latter argued later that 'law jobs' do not have to be done by state institutions. Although Ehrlich focused mainly on the jurisgenerative propensities of communities and associations, his writing has also rightly been taken as inspiration for those have gone on to argue, more broadly, that more or less autonomous 'social fields' can create their own set of norms and sanctioning mechanisms.[35] The focus of more recent writing, however, is on the way in which globalisation is increasingly 'uncoupling' law from the state. Transnational enterprises and transnational forms of communication and regulation have thus emerged as an important new source of legal pluralism.

Two key examples of such new forms of legal pluralism which have provided the occasion for rediscovering Ehrlich's ideas about living law are *lex mercatoria*, as discussed for example in Teubner's collection *Global Law without a State*,[36] and the governance of the internet, as in Rowland's discussion of 'Law in Cyberspace'.[37] For these authors, as for many other commentators, the question of whether these regimes can be described as law is strongly linked to the issue of whether they *should* be so recognised (as if 'calling' them law will help make them so). And the answer is not necessarily the same for each of these examples. Whilst the first has to do more with norm-making by or for businessmen as an attempt to create

---

[33] G Teubner, 'Foreword: Legal Regimes of Global Non-state actors' in G Teubner (ed), *Global Law without a State* (Dartmouth, Aldershot, 1997) xiii.
[34] G Gurvitch, *Sociology of Law* (London, Routledge Kegan Paul, 1947).
[35] SF Moore, 'The Autonomous Social Field as an Appropriate Subject of Study' (1973) 7 *Law & Society Review* 719–46; and L Bernstein, 'Opting Out of the Legal System: Extralegal Contractual Relations in the Diamond Industry' (1992) 21 *Journal of Legal Studies* 115.
[36] Teubner, n 15 above.
[37] D Rowland, 'Cyberspace—A Contemporary Utopia?' (1998) 3 *The Journal of Information, Law and Technology* <http://www2.warwick.ac.uk/fac/soc/law/elj/jilt/1998_3/rowland> (last accessed 11 Aug 2008).

interstitial order for their interests, the other has to do with an allegedly virtual space open to all.

In a valuable article in which he examines both phenomena from the point of view of an expert on conflicts of law, Ralf Michaels compares them in relation to the different criteria that can be used for defining law.[38] He accepts that both *lex mercatoria* and the internet can promote social ordering and social control. However, he claims that whilst the new law merchant also aims at dispute resolution, this is less clear with the internet. Moving to the structural criterion, law merchant imposes binding obligations on tradesmen, while the internet, he rightly suggests, 'controls rather through its technology, its architecture'.[39] Law merchant is referred to by some (although not all) participants as law; this again, is less true for the internet. Certainly, merchants consider themselves to be some kind of 'community'; the same may be true of users of the internet. He concludes that while the new law merchant has a good claim to qualify as 'law' under most named criteria, proponents of an autonomous internet law have a more difficult case to make.

Nonetheless, Michaels insists that, from a juristic perspective, neither of these regimes, nor any other legal system that can be shown to be only semi-autonomous, can be rightly described as law. The crucial point for him is that they all require the state to 'recognise' their legal validity. The state has three ways to cope with other normative orders: incorporation, delegation and deference. Through incorporation, which applies, for example, to *lex mercatoria*, rules count as law only in so far as they become part of the law of the state. This, he argues:

> ... is perfectly compatible with Ehrlich's insight that the production of law mainly happens on the periphery, within society. Yet the insight loses its revolutionary potential. The state is able to domesticate this potentially subversive development through the incorporation of the norms that are created. It recognizes non-state communities as generators of norms, but it denies these norms the status of autonomous law. Instead, by incorporating these norms into state law, the state reiterates its own monopoly on the production of legal norms.[40]

Michaels also refers to Ehrlich's arguments when discussing the strategy of deference. '(T)he state', he explains:

> ... may leave it to commercial practices and professional standards to develop the appropriate standard of care, the typical expectations necessary for interpreting contracts, etc.[41] This is the approach most frequently seen as an answer to Ehrlich's 'living law'. Again, living law is not ignored by the law of the state, but

---

[38] R Michaels, 'The Re-Statement of Non-State Law: The State, Choice of Law, and the Challenge from Global Legal Pluralism' (2005) *Duke Law school working papers series paper 21.*
[39] Ibid 18.
[40] Ibid 28.
[41] Ibid 24.

neither is it recognized as law. The state and its law do not conceptualize their relation to such spaces of private ordering as a relation to foreign laws, to be handled by rules of conflict of laws. Rather, the state refrains from interfering, or, put differently, it defers to the private interactions of individuals. The whole public/private distinction, as we know well by know, takes place within the framework of the state's law. Private ordering enters the substantive law of the state at the time of enforcement as fact—as customs, general expectations, etc, that must be taken into account in the application of the state's laws, but that do not constitute such norms in themselves.

Finally, Michaels tells us:

> A third operation, somewhat similar to deference, treats such orders as legal orders separate from the state's own law, but still denies them full autonomy. This process can be called delegation. Instead of regulating on its own, the state defers to the self-regulation by interested groups. Examples of delegation abound. Autonomous labour agreements between unions and employers have the force of law; codes of conduct of regulated or unregulated industries substitute possible regulation by the state, etc. Indeed, this idea of the contract was one basis for the idea of the new law merchant ('contrat sans loi'). In the very moment in which they are attached and subordinated to the state and its law ... Non-state law turns into sub-state law.[42]

Michaels is very wary of crediting 'communities and fields with the power to create law'. However, he admits that his juristic perspective, one 'intrinsic to operations of the legal system itself', is not the only way to look at the question. '[L]egal pluralism, legal sociology and legal anthropology', he explains, 'may well have different definitions of law, because they are interested in different aspects of law'.[43] Furthermore, for their part, even those sociologists and anthropologists most committed to the idea of legal pluralism will concede that the state does usually seek to deny the legitimacy of rival regimes. Michaels is quite willing to admit that, from a sociological or anthropological perspective, it may (or may not) make sense to refer to all normative orders in communities as 'law'.

In fact, like legal scholars, social theorists are be found on both sides of the divide regarding whether we should describe rival or sub-state legal regimes as law. Legal scholars such as Berman (with whom Michaels polemicises) argue that communities have the power of 'jurispersuasion'.[44] Anthropologists have been amongst those most convinced that state law is far too narrow a perspective for many of the societies they study.[45] In a

---

[42] Ibid.
[43] Ibid 30.
[44] PS Berman, 'From International Law to Law and Globalization' (2005) 43 *Columbia Journal of Transnational Law* 485.
[45] For a strong statement, see F Von Benda-Beckmann, 'Comment on Merry' (1988) 22 *Law & Society Review* 897–902.

provocative recent essay, Melissaris even extends the notion of communities to aggregates such as queues, arguing that:

> Only when the legal commitment of clubbers who queue patiently at a bouncer's orders is treated as seriously as the legal commitment of communities with religious or other moral bonds will the pluralistic study of the law be able to move away from the essentially positivistic external study of groups to the study of legal discourses.[46]

However, on the other hand, many would say this was a *reductu ad absurdum*.[47] Social theorists such as Brian Tamanaha argue that what is crucial is the way in which people use the term 'law'—which usually privileges state law.[48] It has even been argued that extending the label 'law' to non-state regimes means imposing a state-like definition of law. For Simon Roberts:

> Law, long so garrulous about itself, is now, in its contemporary enlargement, graciously embracing others in its discourse, seeking to tell those others what they are.[49]

However, whether or not social scientists are entitled to use the term 'law' as they wish, a more important question concerns how far Ehrlich's notion of living law helps or hinders our understanding of these emergent phenomena. Take, for example, law-making by cyber communities. In a relatively early paper on this topic, which explicitly takes its inspiration from Ehrlich, Rowland makes an effort to tease out the living law of such communities. She argues that:

> ... [the] impact of new communications technology on both social relationships and law-making processes is still in its infancy ... [t]here are myriad political processes at work in all societies but the decentralized nature of the Internet makes it particularly difficult to understand either the manner in which power can be exercised, by whom and within what limits.

For her, we need to face the fact that cyber communities 'challenge state-based models of lawmaking as well as many of our preconceptions of the attributes of society and community'.[50]

Rowland expresses concern about 'imposing on the organization and use of the Internet a social construct which is entirely inappropriate both in idea and substance'. 'Thus far', she argues:

> ... legal rules external to Cyberspace have not been conspicuously successful at regulating the global computer network ... [and] ... may only succeed in regulating

---

[46] E Melassaris, 'The More the Merrier? A new take on Legal Pluralism' (2004) 13 *Social and Legal Studies* 57–79 at 75.

[47] However, see the views of Reisman discussed in the next section.

[48] BZ Tamanaha, 'The Folly of the "Social Scientific" Concept of Legal Pluralism' (1993) 20 *Journal of Law & Society* 192; and BZ Tamanaha, 'A Non-Essentialist Version of Legal Pluralism' (2000) 27 *Journal of Law and Society* 296.

[49] S Roberts, 'Against Legal Pluralism' (1998) 42 *Journal of Legal Pluralism* 95.

[50] Rowland, n 37 above, 7.

Cyberspace when the social conditions pertaining in cyber communities are acknowledged and understood.

One can imagine Ehrlich sharing such cautions. At the same, however, she suggests, law may be forming itself 'from below'. Legal rules, she tells us:

> ... may already be emerging from amidst the chaos of Cyberspace ... in some respects the cyber community, at this juncture, could be regarded as a 'pre-legal' world and the change to a legal world will inevitably involve the creation of rules dealing with change, adjudication and recognition of rights. Most communities will regulate themselves, in practice, by a combination of formal or 'book law' ('top-down' rule formation) and also by acknowledgement of the customary rules which have evolved to supplement this source of law and to cater for what 'actually happens' ('bottom-up' regulation). Examples are the rites of passage, initiation or induction for newcomers to that community which either enable them to integrate more easily, or, conversely, create a barrier to entry to the society which must be successfully negotiated.[51]

For Rowland, progress towards a self-regulating internet law is at best uneven. Although certain customs in cyber communities:

> ... appear to be in the process of being elevated to the status of customary rules ... many rules remain purely customary, having no enforceable sanction attached to their non-adherence, indeed it is doubtful whether a universally enforceable sanction can be applied in Cyberspace.

Rowland concedes that we do not have to:

> ... measure the success of custom as a regulatory mechanism purely by the availability of express sanctions. Successful customs may be obeyed, not so much because of the threat of sanctions, but for fear of standing out from the crowd. Such rules may be adhered to not out of personal conviction, but, rather, as an indication that such conduct is conventionally accepted and so participants are happy to accept it as a standard of assessment. People may also accept rules not necessarily because of any issue of morality but possible out of fear, self-interest, coercion or habit.

Nonetheless:

> ... what is not apparent in cyber communities is such an assurance of acceptable behaviour, at least as judged by the prevailing standards and mores of the physical world. In comparison, the range of norms and values in cyber communities seems to cover a much wider and more diverse range. What may be absent in the virtual world is the necessary degree of uniformity and unanimity defining a custom which has the capacity to metamorphose into a legal rule and become both binding and obligatory.[52]

---

[51] *Ibid.*
[52] *Ibid.*

The literature on internet law has grown exponentially since Rowland posted her reflections (although it does not, as far as I am aware, make much reference to Ehrlich). The question of what norms are appropriate for cyberspace (and providing them with a history or legitimacy) has changed as the internet itself has developed from an idealised utopia of caring and sharing—with its folkloristic evolution of norms of good manners—to an ever-expanding site for commercial activities as well as the exploitation of the less attractive aspects of human sociability. It is less and less possible to think of users mainly in terms of online communities—and some of the communities that do exist in this space use the internet to disseminate hate propaganda aimed at others.[53] However, net users continue to surprise. Pressed into service by the market, they can sometimes rise up against property rights as where users collectively reveal trade secrets. Seemingly feeble in the face of the armed might of the state, the diffusion of video photographs provides the evidence to protest at the conduct of military operatives and secret police from that in US military installations to police stations in Egypt.

The internet is not a world apart. It belongs to and helps further those economic developments by which consumers (those who can afford to consume) come more and more to play the role of producers. The real and virtual worlds intersect as shown through the application of copyright law or privacy protections. The problems it throws up mirror many of the crimes and civil wrongs found in the real world. What goes on in the virtual world of 'second life' is all too reminiscent of what happens in ordinary life. The internet provides occasions for blogging feuds, cyber bullying, defamatory Google bombing, misuse of 'spiders' or cookies, and the all-too-evident spread of spamming. Enforcement of norms is complicated by the use of anonymity and the difficulty of knowing when users can be assumed to be informed of norm changes. On the other hand, sanctions from which there is no appeal, for example, where users are banishing users from given sites, may be considered too severe to be left to private parties.

In so far as the internet does maintain a sort of autonomy, there is scope for more investigation into how far group exercises in rule making and rule application are constructing a distinctive form of living law. The collective encyclopaedia Wikipedia, for example, does use law-like procedures for rule making and fact finding as ways of deciding whether an article's content is sufficiently evidenced, whether links to other entries are justified, what counts as an insult, and so on. However, there is a need here too for protection from the guardians. In March 2007, for example, there were reports about a fake professor known as Essjay whose 'authority' to arbitrate disputes and remove site vandalism about articles on religion turned

---

[53] A Roversi, *Hate on the Net* (Aldershot, Ashgate Press, 2008).

out to be based on false credentials: he was obliged to resign from his role because, as the co-founder explained, the encyclopaedia relies on 'trust and tolerance'.

Order Without Law

The third literature that can be connected to Ehrlich's ideas about living law is one less interested in how associations impose their norms and more in how patterned behaviour gives rise to the working orders of associations. Order, rather than law, is the focus here, as seen in such titles as Robert Ellickson's celebrated *Order without law—How neighbours settle disputes*,[54] or Eric Posner's *A theory of norms*.[55] The same is true even of Michael Reisman's *Law in Brief encounters*—despite having law in its title.[56] This line of enquiry can be distinguished from the previous literatures considered so far in so far as it refuses legal centralism not by contrasting the centre and the periphery or by hypothesising the existence of rival legal regimes, but by questioning the centrality of law as compared to norms. Writers seek to explain the origin and content of norms, in particular they develop theories of norms in the context of cooperation, collective solutions and welfare maximisation. Even if not all writers on these topics take their cue from Ehrlich, at least some of this work can also be traced back to him. Especially relevant is his advice to move from studying conflict to understanding order, to distinguish situations 'at war' from those 'at peace', and to think about expectations as much as sanctions—or of expectations as sanctions. His controversial attempt to distinguish legal from other types of norms also shows him addressing these issues.

There is by now an enormous multi-disciplinary library—ranging across evolutionary biology, psychology, philosophy, law, economics—and sociology—which deals with the source and efficacy of norms. Sociology of law alone will not be able to master this subject. However, once Ehrlich's ideas about living law are seen to embrace a wide range of normative phenomena, this leads to a richer set of questions than merely whether the norms of semi-autonomous associations count as law. We are led to investigate the relationship between law and norms. How and when do norms turn into law (as in the case of the internet or *lex mercatoria*)? How does law become normative? When do norms mandate not following or using law? How far do norms depend on associational life? How big or amorphous must such associations be? What about the fact that we are simultaneously members of very many associations? As this suggests, research on order without law tends to be

---

[54] R Ellickson, *Order without law: How Neighbours settle disputes* (Cambridge, Harvard University Press, 1991).
[55] E Posner, *Law and Social Norms* (Cambridge, Harvard University Press, 2000).
[56] WM Reisman, *Law in Brief Encounters* (New Haven, Yale University Press, 1999).

more radical than merely looking for 'the law beyond the law'. Take, for example, Macaulay's famous findings about the extent to which businessmen did not conduct their exchanges on the basis of contract law, relying instead on the shared norm of 'keeping one's promises' and 'standing behind your product', which provide the underpinnings of normal business behaviour.[57] Those interested in norms would then want to go further and ask about the social origins of such norms and they way in which they are reproduced.

Whatever plausible links can be drawn between this sort of work and Ehrlich's writings, in practice it can often be difficult to assess his actual influence. This can be well illustrated by considering the reference made by Ellickson to Ehrlich in his book, *Order without law*. Ellickson's claim is that 'impersonal norms are among the most magnificent of cultural achievements'.[58] To understand them better, he sets out to synthesise insights from the sociology of law and economics and law. He criticises sociologists of law for treating the content of norms as exogenous and being too satisfied with thick descriptions rather than cumulative testable theory. He argues that we must learn what norms are, not just how they are transmitted. Law and economics writers, on the other hand, he sees as too obsessed with the relationship of norms to wealth maximisation and the problems of how groups can overcome the problem of 'free riders'. Ellickson's goal is to produce a 'general theory of social control', one that could predict, on the basis of independent variables describing society, the content of the society's rules. These would in turn need to be distinguished as substantive, remedial, procedural and controller-selecting.

In this book, however, he settles for the more modest aim of illustrating the logic of one social sub- system, that of 'informal social control'. To develop his predictions, Ellickson draws on his own empirical study of rancher's communities as well as historical research into dispute resolution in whaling communities. To explain the rationality of cooperation in the absence of law, he describes the details of dispute processing, the events that trigger sanctions, and how relevant information is gathered. What is of interest for us is that it is not until page 150 that he actually makes any reference to Ehrlich. At this point, he tells us blithely that 'Ehrlich believed that law is relatively unimportant and that social forces tend to produce the same norms in all human society'.[59] Ellickson then goes on to explain that Ehrlich (like Durkheim) is to be seen as a functionalist who saw the sanctioning of norms as the way in which social groups maintained their solidarity. And he complains that functionalist arguments are circular because they do not say for which groups the function is being performed and assume that organisms have an objectively determinable state of health.

---

[57] Macaulay, above n 19.
[58] Ellickson, above n 54, 184.
[59] *Ibid* 150, fn 62.

Ellickson is not obliged to provide us with a rounded analysis of Ehrlich work. However, it is still surprising to find such a superficial reading coming from such an eminent scholar. Did Ehrlich really believe that 'law is unimportant'? Ellickson just assumes that whatever Ehrlich is talking about it is not law, because he (along with many others) insists that state law is likely to be inefficacious unless backed up by other norms. However, it could as well be argued that by introducing the concept of 'living law', Ehrlich exaggerates the importance of law by finding it everywhere. Certainly, this is the interpretation favoured by those legal pluralists who take Ehrlich as a warrant for characterising rival normative schemes as law, to all effects. As far as the charge of functionalism is concerned, Ehrlich may indeed be interested in showing us how associations use law-like norms to solve problems of functioning and reproduction, but he also offers examples of behaviour, as for example where businessmen do not insist on collecting their debts, which go beyond this role. More fundamentally, his book also contains discussions of how norms reflect changing interests, which is the judges' task to reconcile in the direction of progressive social change.

Ellickson's synthesis of economics and law and sociology of law leans towards a rational actor perspective. Most of the many other recent studies of norms tend to be even more influenced by the individualistic bias of economics of law and game theory. A recent study by Eric Posner, for example, also links norms to the question concerning the rationality of cooperation.[60] Posner sees norms as rules that distinguish desirable from undesirable behaviour and give third parties authority to punish. He is particularly interested in showing how norms play a role in allowing actors to avoid dilemmas of non-cooperation by signalling their willingness to be reliable collaborators rather than act as free riders. He offers some valuable insights into how and when the following of norms can help participants distinguish genuine from false signals. He also discusses how law tries to harness the strength of norms and when legal regulation should or should not be used instead of relying on norms.

However, for all its plausibility, the claim that order relies more on shared norms than on official legal processes has also been criticised. In so far as Ellickson's arguments are based on empirical research, they are open to counter-examples based on other case studies. Some research has shown that resort may be made to official law even in what would appear to be ideal conditions for maintaining order without law. Eric Feldman, an expert on Japanese law, has recently offered a fascinating and finely grained account of the workings of what he calls the tuna court in the Tokyo fish market.[61] Here, post-auction disputes between dealers and buyers, mainly regarding

---

[60] Posner, above n 55.
[61] E Feldman, 'The Tuna Court: Law and norms in the world's premier fish market' (2006) 94 *California Law Review*: 2.

hidden defects in the fish, are routinely and expeditiously resolved by judges in ways that reinforce rather than substitute for the cooperation between the participants. Feldman claims that his case study goes against what Bernstein, Ellickson and others would predict, given that these participants form a community of continually interacting players who could be expected to create their own informal normative order. In Ehrlich's language, we see here an illustration of the way in which 'norms for decision' can also guarantee peaceful co-existence. What is more, this preference for court-like procedures is found in a culture which many (though not Feldman himself) see as one normally geared to the avoidance of law.

Ellickson's work and, in general, the arguments of the so-called 'new norms jurisprudence', have also been subjected to more fundamental theoretical objections. As we have already noted in discussing 'the law beyond the law', it is also (increasingly) difficult to draw the line between sources of order within and outside a given setting. Even if it is not official law that produces order, there is likely to be some symbiosis between its projected order and the actual order shaped by and within the association or organisation. It can be a mistake to credit the idea that norms produce order independent of models in the larger environing framework. Mitchell, for example, has recently complained that:

> ... there is little attention paid to the way in which group norms or private law systems relate to or are influenced by either legal, moral or customary norms that permeate the society as a whole ... norms—whether the norms of the Elks Club, the New York Diamond Merchants Exchange, various religious groups, or the automobile insurance industry, are at some level inseparable from the web of norms that influences the behaviour of each of the members of these groups.[62]

Mitchell proposes that we speak not of 'order without law', but 'order within law'.[63] As he says:

> The private law systems noted by Ellickson and Bernstein are grounded on the notion of legal obligation and legal order that pervades our society. Or, to put the claim more modestly, the legal systems which these private law systems mimic have been so pervasive in our society for so long that it seems unlikely that the new norms theorists can separate out the influence of the legal order upon the creation of private law norms.[64]

Mitchell's point is that official law serves as a model even when its details are unknown or misunderstood. 'The problem with Ellickson's work', he says:

> ... is not the valuable field study but rather the conclusions he draws. Ellickson found what he took to be a startling conclusion. When neighbours had border

---

[62] LE Mitchell, 'Understanding Norms' (1999) 49 *University of Toronto Law Review* 177–258 at 255.
[63] *Ibid* 237.
[64] *Ibid*.

disputes or arguments over fences or over trespassing livestock; they didn't sue each other—they negotiated out their difficulties in a way that—given the repetitive nature of the issues—became regularized. This he viewed as the spontaneous generation of order and the irrelevance of law, supported by the fact that, when surveyed, most of his interviewees either didn't know the governing law or got it wrong.

Ellickson's ranchers might not have known the law. They might have thought they knew the law but gotten its principles wrong. They might have made up their own rules to avoid litigation. But there is one thing that I am certain that they did know; there was law, that law governed the kinds of disputes in which they engaged, and that law was available to them should they choose to use it (as sometimes they did). In other words, Ellickson's ranchers were resolving their disputes on the broad background of an understanding of legal obligation that is immanent in our society and derives from the notion of a society governed by a system of laws—when one person causes damage to another's person or property, there are circumstances under which the law (if invoked by lawsuit) will hold that party to account. The idea of legal order already existed in Shasta County—what Ellickson found that was different were the principles that were applied.[65]

The fact that the literature about norms is so vast also means that it is riven by almost as many disagreements as is the case for arguments about the nature of law. Differences in definitions, regarding, for example, how far norms should be seen more as instruments or as cultural constraints on action, tend to reproduce major divisions in sociological approaches to society. Others reflect the choice between privileging a more macro or micro focus on social life. Some efforts to locate the source of normative order go beyond the level of Ehrlich's focus on associations or the interactions of people involved in repeated relationships. Michael Reisman, a leading professor of international law, claims to have discovered what he calls the micro-law of relatively fleeting relationships. In a series of well-observed descriptions, Reisman shows that people handle the problems of everyday life as if they were small-scale analogies of the larger problems of legal order.[66] He explains how norms enable people to have a sense of what is and is not appropriate in situations such as those of looking at others, in talking with equals or with the boss, in making queues and holding places for others in line. Decisions about such matters cannot be and are not arbitrary or else such valuable institutions as the queue would break down.[67]

Although he entitles his book *Law in brief encounters*, what Reisman actually sets out to describe is (only) a form of de facto 'living law'. He cannot mean that the rules generated in these situations are already (official)

[65] Ibid 236.
[66] However, it has been objected that the individuals Reisman discusses tend to be middle-class people with middle-class responses.
[67] Reisman, above n 56, 59.

law because he goes on to ask when law should recognise or interfere in these micro-legal orders. In general, he is favour of keeping state bureaucracy out of such matters. However, (because of his background as an international lawyer?) he also suggests that there are some standards that micro-law must pass and 'that the practices of all groups must be appraised in terms of the international code of human rights' so that 'practices inconsistent with the international standard be adjusted'.[68] As this suggests, though Reisman does not seek to anchor his insights in older writers, there are certainly many parallels with Ehrlich's concerns. It is interesting too to find that Reisman insists that the norms he discusses are kept alive not so much by the sanctioning of breaches (albeit that this can and does take place), but by the decision of the norm-abider to reaffirm the existence of the norm despite the breach.

If authors such as Reisman emphasise the parallels between legal order and micro-order in society, others, such as Jutras, think it important to ask 'does the normative structure of everyday life mirror the architecture of official law?'[69] They urge us to look for differences as well as similarities. It may be instructive, for example, that the everyday 'feels' non-legal, whilst the law appears self-contained. Tamanaha, too, considers it is an error to confuse legal and social order.[70] It is important, he argues, to see that law is not necessarily a source of social order and social order is not necessarily law-like.[71] This leads him to be ambivalent about Ehrlich's claims concerning normative order.

> In an important sense, Ehrlich's observations raised a sharp critique of the mirror thesis and the social order function of law ... In another important sense, however, Ehrlich's work is the ultimate extension of the mirror thesis and the social order function of law. In effect his argument is that if positive law does not mirror social norms and does not in fact maintain social order, it has lost its superior entitlement to the claim of being the law, and the label must be given back, or at least shared with the 'living law', the actually lived social norms that do satisfy these criteria.[72]

Tamanaha argues that:

> The traditionally assumed relationship gets things precisely upside down. It is state law that is dependent on these other sources of social order if it is to have a chance of exerting an influence.[73]

---

[68] *Ibid* 158.
[69] D Jutras, 'The legal dimensions of everyday life' (2001) 16 *Canada Journal of Law and Society* 45–65.
[70] BZ Tamanaha, *A General Jurisprudence of Law and Society* (Oxford, Oxford University Press, 2001).
[71] I am relying on the thorough re-analysis in W Twining, 'A Post-Westphalian Conception of Law' (2003) 37 *Law and Society Review* 199–258.
[72] Tamanaha, above n 70, 31.
[73] *Ibid* 224.

But, of course, this exactly takes us back to what it is that Ehrlich was trying to tell us!

RE-WRITING EHRLICH: FROM 'LAW IN ACTION' TO LEGAL AUTOPOIESIS

We have dealt so far with authors who use Ehrlich's work as a precedent or inspiration without necessarily going into detail about what he actually wrote. In this section, I want to discuss more elaborate appropriations of Ehrlich, and show how they shape efforts to 'go back to the beginning' or 'back to the future' in the sociology of law. For a long time, there was a tendency (especially, but not only, in English-language discussions) to assimilate Ehrlich's arguments to Anglo-American ways of talking about 'law in society'. This certainly facilitated drawing on him in dealing with socio-legal problems as they are posed in common law jurisdictions. This is most clearly seen in Pound's original introduction to the first translation of Ehrlich's *Grundlegung*.[74] However, what we are now witnessing is in some respects an opposite trend, one which treats Ehrlich's work as belonging to the world view of Continental legal systems and adopts him as a forerunner of one of the most advanced schools of continental sociology of law, that associated with Niklas Luhmann. Curiously, this re-presentation is again expounded in the introduction, this time to the new English translation of Ehrlich's magnum opus.[75] In this novel framing of Ehrlich's ideas, we are told that Ehrlich represents an approach for which Luhmann's sociology of law can be seen 'the continuation'[76] if not the sociological culmination. All of this even though Luhmann himself does not even refer to Ehrlich!

When I last wrote about Ehrlich, more than 20 years ago, my main goal was to set out the differences between his ideas and those of Pound. Ziegert (one of the few to appreciate the continuing relevance of this then half-forgotten pioneer) argued then that Pound's distinctions between 'law in books' and 'law in action' 'could only be' that put forward by Ehrlich.[77] In my article, I claimed that, on the contrary, the ideas were different. In fact, even Pound himself, in a retrospective towards the end of his career, admitted that he had (as he put it) 'developed' living law into the somewhat

---

[74] R Pound, 'Introduction to Ehrlich, E.' in *Fundamental Principles of the Sociology of Law*, WL Moll (tr) (New York, Russell and Russell, 1936/62). Pound's use of Ehrlich was endorsed by Alex Ziegert in his 'The Sociology behind Eugen Ehrlich's Sociology of Law' (1979) 7 *International Journal of the Sociology of Law* 225.

[75] KA Ziegert, 'Introduction' in E Ehrlich, *The Fundamental Principles of Sociology of Law* (New Brunswick, Transaction Publishers, 2001) 19–44.

[76] *Ibid* xxxi.

[77] Zeigert, above n 74.

different concept of 'law in action'.[78] Whilst acknowledging that there was some overlap between the concepts of 'law in action' and 'living law', I set out to show that Ehrlich's original idea of living law should be considered a more promising and richer starting point for an approach more open to mainstream sociological concerns and less geared to the problem of legal effectiveness.

I was convinced then of the overriding importance of correcting Pound's misinterpretations: getting Ehrlich 'right' was the only way that his valuable insights could be recovered. I would still argue that Pound's use of Ehrlich limits the potential contribution of the idea of living law. However, whilst it is good that more scholars (including Ziegert) have come to agree that it is important to recognise the differences between these two authors, I would now add that simply claiming that Pound got Ehrlich 'wrong' oversimplifies the issue of how classical authors are made relevant to contemporary problems. To a great extent, it is impossible to read a past author except through current lenses.[79] What Pound took from Ehrlich can be seen as having special relevance for his own time—and may be an interpretation that could still be salient in other times and places. Equally, alternative 'readings' have to 'prove' their superiority, now and in the future.

Ziegert in his new introduction aims both to present a faithful picture of Ehrlich and also to show that he is a forerunner of Luhmannian thinking. This leads to interesting, if sometimes surprising, reformulations. We are told that Ehrlich is the founder of the 'genuine social level apart from the individual'. For Ehrlich, like Luhmann, in thinking about law, 'expectations not sanctions matter'. What Ehrlich was trying to say in speaking of living law was that:

> ... the norm structure in inner order of associations is what individuals need as a reference point to construct themselves as 'behaving individuals' and to expect from others what they can reasonably expect from themselves ... this reflexive domain is the domain of law and has nothing to do with the state governance [sic] or sovereignty.[80]

Likewise, the account of Ehrlich's policy sympathies, although put in unfamiliar language, is not implausible. He is said to be against the self-aggrandisement of lawyers and state functionaries, but to believe that 'society' will keep these in check. Ehrlich, we are told, shows law's 'blind spot' which results from the fact that law is 'a trade', and lawyers refer back only to legal practice and so don't see what else is happening. In a few

---

[78] Pound, above n 74. In his introduction to Ehrlich's book, he had already complained that 'Europeans had a phobia of the state'. However, he was living in the new deal United States of the 1930s, not as a citizen of strong—and soon to be totalitarian—European states.
[79] HG Gadamer, *Truth and Method* (New York, The Seabury Press, 1975).
[80] Ziegert, above n 75, xii.

cases though, Ziegert's interpretations seem particularly forced ones. For Ehrlich, we are told:

> ... [the] evolution of legal decision-making through legal practice conditions the social order for further evolution and specialises the court-based decision-making system as the effective hub of the living law.

However, whilst it is fair to say that Ehrlich did admire the common law and the (somewhat idealised) way he assumed it operated, describing what courts do as 'the hub of the living law' seems a strange way of re-presenting a book that (pace Luhmann) sought to describe how living law was actually rooted in the everyday life of associations.

Arguably, Ziegert's reformulations of Ehrlich also do a disservice to Luhmann by blurring the way in which his approach to socio-legal theorising has involved a 'paradigm' shift from 'open system' to 'closed system' theorising about law in society.[81] On this point, Ziegert explains that 'Ehrlich does not deny the need for, or the fact of, legal specialisation (differentiation)'.[82] However, 'non denial' is hardly the equivalent of the theoretical breakthrough which Luhmann builds on the back of his radical differentiation of legal and other communicative systems. Ziegert goes on to say that, for Ehrlich:

> What makes legal propositions legal is not a higher normativity but the specialised differentiated performance of a subject of social operations responding to pressures of uncertainty.[83]

Here, too, it would seem more correct to say that, unlike Luhmann, Ehrlich mixes discussions of law and morals at the level of social pressures, but seeks to distinguish them in terms of the psychology of the individuals deciding whether to recognise their legitimacy.

The same applies when Ziegert tells us that, 'like Luhmann, Ehrlich is a scientific observer of law in its social context'.[84] Again, it would seem better to recognise that 'context' has more of a technical meaning for Luhmann, at least as explained by Teubner, his leading interpreter in legal sociology. Law *makes* its own context—and there are a series of contexts depending on what subsystem we start from. Likewise, when Ziegert affirms that, for Ehrlich, '[l]aw can never control the factual order itself', we need to avoid confusing two senses of 'control'. Ehrlich thinks that only a better informed form of legal decision making could—and should—do justice to the facts of the living law (this was his legacy to the American Legal Realists). However, for Luhmann, order comes from, or is imposed on the 'noise', of the outside world, and law's role includes maintaining normative expectations by 'not

---

[81] Nelken, above n 26.
[82] Zigert, above n 75, xxxiii.
[83] Zigert, *ibid*, xxiii.
[84] *Ibid* xv.

Ehrlich's Legacies: Back to the Future in the Sociology of Law? 263

learning' from the antinomian facts of social life. If Ehrlich's message is that we must stop buying into jurists' way of seeing the world, for Luhmann 'scientists' must make a 'second-order' assessment of law's way of observing the world—or as Teubner puts it, of 'how the law thinks'.[85]

Although we should appreciate the effort to make Ehrlich speak to present concerns, we need also, I think, be cautious about assimilating him to conventional wisdom rather than using him to gain a perspective on it. Whereas Ziegert once told us that Ehrlich's work could provide a valuable resource for improving efforts at social engineering,[86] he now tells us that Ehrlich, like Luhmann, is sceptical about such efforts and that time has shown the sense of this scepticism.[87] However, the current period is different from the early 1980s. An obsession with the limits of 'legal effectiveness' can easily become a theoretical dead-end in a period where everyone assumes an instrumentalist role for law and exaggerates its ability to produce social change. However, matters may be different at a time where there is too much cynicism about law's ability to deliver social progress. The same applies to the closely related research obsession with the so-called 'gap' between law's promise and achievement.[88] What is a tired approach within pragmatic, technically oriented, Anglo-American legal cultures may be much more heuristically useful in places, such as some continental European jurisdictions, where the 'gap' between legal promise and implementation is typically so wide that it is just taken for granted.[89] In such societies, filtering Ehrlich's message through Luhmann's formulas may be less innovative than it might otherwise seem.

However, all depends on what is done with these ideas. In this respect, it is interesting to contrast Ziegert's re-presentation of Ehrlich with Gunther Teubner's argument about 'Global Bukowina'.[90] Teubner, like Ziegert, is engaged in a rewriting of Ehrlich in Luhmannian terminology. However, whereas, for Ziegert, Ehrlich's ideas were right when they were first put forward and (when properly reformulated) are still valuable now, Teubner, more surprisingly, argues that Ehrlich was actually wrong in his own time and only really comes into his own now at a time of globalisation. In addition, whereas both Ziegert and Teubner treat Ehrlich as a forerunner of the Luhmannian doxa, Teubner is explicit about the need also to change and 'update' Ehrlich's arguments.

These differences are linked to the topics which these authors use Ehrlich to address. Ziegert is concerned with his relevance to law in the nation

---

[85] G Teubner, 'How the Law Thinks' (1989) 23 *Law and Society Review* 727–57.
[86] Ziegert, above n 74.
[87] Ziegert, above n 75.
[88] D Nelken, 'The gap problem in the sociology of law' (1981) *Windsor Yearbook of Aceess to Justice* 35–62.
[89] D Nelken, 'Law's Embrace' (2001) 3 *Social and Legal Studies* 444–60.
[90] Teubner, above n 15.

state, the context Ehrlich was originally writing about. Teubner, on the other hand, in developing a highly original autopoietic excursus on global law, explores Ehrlich's relevance in examining the role of law in the international arena in exchanges mainly involving private actors—matters about which Ehrlich said little in his *Grundlegung*. According to Ziegert, Ehrlich is not to be understood primarily as concerned with legal pluralism. Indeed, he uses Luhmannian language to show how different elements of Ehrlich's scheme of thought such as living law and norms for decisions are integrally related. Teubner, on the other hand, takes Ehrlich to be a forerunner in the study of legal pluralism, but gives this a very different meaning when re-examined in the light of the Luhmannian theory of autopoiesis.

Ziegert wants us to accept that Luhmannian insights can help get us to the heart of what Ehrlich was really trying to say. In assessing his interpretation, the question we need to ask ourselves is the relatively straightforward one of whether we find his reading Ehrlich convincing and suggestive. However, with Teubner, it is difficult to know how seriously he wants us to take his argument as an actual interpretation of Ehrlich. Does his use of the term 'Global Bukowina' represent a genuine effort to apply Ehrlich's ideas to the new global context? Or is it no more (and no less) than a playful—and paradoxical—metaphor?[91] After all, if everywhere is now a periphery, where is the centre? (Can there be only periphery?) What, if anything, is there in common between Ehrlich's Bukovina and the world being remodelled by globalisation? Between a province waiting for ethnic nationalism and a world in which state borders lose meaning? On the one hand, Teubner's audacious proposal that Bukovina has now gone global lays a direct challenge to those who say Ehrlich's ideas necessarily relate to specific space and time conditions of a province in the defunct Austro-Hapsburg empire. However, at the same time, the use of this phrase itself perpetuates the misconception that Ehrlich's ideas get their sense from the (relative) lack of state presence in Bukovina. Ehrlich is seen as able to be relevant now (only) because we have a new situation of normative life again being formed *beyond* the reach of state. Yet it seems more faithful to Ehrlich to say that his arguments concerned the possibilities of normative life being formed *outside* of the state, even if not necessarily *beyond* its jurisdiction.

In any case, Teubner is also quite explicit about what he sees as the need to correct and 'develop' Ehrlich's ideas if we are to grasp the new form

---

[91] However, metaphors can be real in their effects. Bukovina in the Americas—the active website for those (overwhelmingly ethnic Germans) nostalgic about their roots in Bukovina—describes features of life there in the past. But whilst it makes no mention of Ehrlich, someone has written in to ask what others think of Teubner's paper on 'Global Bukowina'. See D Nelken, 'An e mail from Global Bukowina' (2007) 3 *International Journal of Law in Context* 103–22. (And the Brazilian Professor in question has since got in touch with me).

of global law beyond the state. This makes it difficult to decide how far Teubner's 'updating' is intended to be true to what Ehrlich might himself have said if asked to theorise *lex mercatoria*. What evidence there is on this point does not go in Teubner's favour.[92] What is more clear is that Teubner finds Ehrlich convincing on some points even if he also sees the need for revisions. Thus he agrees with Ehrlich that the basis of law is in society and not in legal dogmatics—placing Ehrlich's formulation of this truth as the head note of his paper. He also sees merit in the fact that, as he puts it, Ehrlich 'asks where are norms actually produced and treats politics and social on equal footing'.[93] There are also happy parallels in their endeavours. Where Ehrlich's idea of living law, as he says, 'breaks a taboo' that law must be identified with the state, so too does the idea that there can be a *lex mercatoria* independent from all nation states.

However, as with Ziegert, the process of translating Ehrlich's ideas into the theoretical language of Luhmannian autopoietic theory can also make it difficult to know where Ehrlich ends and Luhmann begins. Most important, the source of living law for Teubner is not that hypothesised by Ehrlich. Teubner does not anchor this in the order of associations as such (except in so far as he sees law as 'closely coupled' with economic processes). Rather, he relies on the autopoietic theory of law which takes law to be one of a number of self-referring discursive sub-systems, each constructing their own environment. However, as we noted when discussing Ziegert's recent work, this Luhmannian idea has no real trace in Ehrlich. Nor was Ehrlich, unlike Teubner, trying to explain how law in general or contract law in particular succeeds in keeping the paradoxes of its self- validation latent. If anything, he observed a lack of wider social validity of much state law.

Teubner talks about law being produced 'at the boundary with economic and technological processes'. He tells us that, likewise, according to Ehrlich, 'living law is produced in the periphery of the legal system in close contact with the external social process of rule formation'. It is true that Ehrlich too suggested that economic development has and will transform law from within (the theme taken up later by Karl Renner).[94] However, it is far from obvious that Ehrlich sees the distinction between the centre and the periphery as Teubner does. For example, his definition of 'living law' included lawyers' contracts, which would have been a productive source of law even in imperial Vienna. What is more, the notion of periphery, as employed by Teubner, is ambiguous as between, on the one hand, Ehrlich's

---

[92] Michaels (2005) quotes a little-known paper by Ehrlich concerning the history of private international law from which it seems likely that he would then have denied the status of law to *lex mercatoria*. On the other hand, we do not know what Ehrlich would say now and, on our interpretation, it is that which interests Teubner more than what Ehrlich actually said then.
[93] Teubner, above n 15, 11.
[94] Renner, above n 30.

location in the province of Bukovina on the edges of the Austro-Hapsburg empire and, on the other, everyday life which is *everywhere* peripheral to what goes on in the courts.

Teubner's focus is on the legal regimes created by and for global non-state actors by invisible social networks and invisible professional communities which transcend territorial boundaries. He sees these new forms of global law as growing up in a world characterised by a highly globalised economy and a weakly globalised politics. Even if Ehrlich's own examples were domestic ones, many of the regimes Teubner wishes to analyse do come near to what Ehrlich meant by living law. Transnational contracting, arbitration and the other processes of *lex mercatoria* could be so characterised, as could 'intra organizational regulation in multinational companies'. It would also seem fair to assume that Ehrlich's concept can be applied to 'all forms of rule making by private governments' and 'professional rule production', although it should also be noted that Ehrlich's interest was less in rule making as such and more in the way in which such rule systems are actually applied in practice.

On the other hand, Teubner's example of 'technical standardization' as an instance of living law has a more dubious pedigree. The whole phenomena of so-called 'bureaucratic administrative law'[95] seems far from Ehrlich's concerns, and his account of living law gives little indication that he realised that a form of normativity based on technical standards and conventions would become so important. Even Teubner's example of human rights law is not a straightforward case of living law. Much human rights law is actually promoted or underwritten by state or international law. Even if non-state actors such as NGOs, etc play a crucial activist role, it still seems crucial to recognise the extent to which these associations are making rules for others,[96] not, as in Ehrlich's account, only for their own members. As far as these two key elements of global law are concerned, the idea of living law may obscure more than it reveals about them.

Why then bring Ehrlich into it, given that he had little to say about such transnational legal regimes? Teubner arrives there by a process of elimination. We cannot, he says, understand legal globalisation via political theories, there is no world constitution to 'structurally couple' law and politics: these legal regimes are governed less by international courts or worldwide legislation than by multinational law firms. So Ehrlich's 'living law' is the best candidate for describing how the globalisation of law 'creates a multitude of de-centred law making processes in various sectors of civil society

---

[95] D Nelken, 'Is there a crisis in law and legal ideology?' (1982) *Journal of Law and Society* 177–89.

[96] D Nelken, 'Signaling Conformity: Changing Norms in Japan and China' (2006) 27 *Michigan JIL* 933–72.

Ehrlich's Legacies: Back to the Future in the Sociology of Law? 267

independently of national states'.[97] On the other hand, the way in which Ehrlich himself characterised living law in Bukovina will not as such suffice for understanding these new forms of global living law. Teubner, therefore, draws a strong contrast between the sense of Ehrlich's arguments in their time and place, and the updating of his ideas for today's world.

As against Ehrlich's idea of living law, Teubner advises, law is 'not drawing its strength now from ethnic communities as the old living law was supposed to do'.[98] 'Ehrlich', Teubner goes on, 'was of course romanticizing the law-creating role of customs, habits and practices in small-scale rural communities'. The global world, by contrast, relies on 'cold technical processes not on warm communal bonds'. However, the assumption that Ehrlich is putting forward a thesis of legal pluralism rooted in ethnic communities—even if Teubner is certainly not the only commentator to take such a line—rests on a tendentious interpretation which has poor support in the text itself. This way of reading Ehrlich also displays the genetic fallacy by confusing factors that may have helped give rise to his argument, with the substance and validity of his ideas themselves. In fact, Ehrlich's claims were intended to be potentially universalisable ones, applicable well beyond Bukovina, and had less to do with ethnic differences than with the way in which laws, like norms, are created through the life of 'associations'. This helps to explain why the question of ethnic pluralism was not the main issue for early critics of Ehrlich such as Kelsen, whose objection was more to Ehrlich linking law to the actual normative practices of groups even when these were inconsistent with the Austrian code.

Teubner's revisions go much further, however. For him, the problem with applying Ehrlich's ideas is not merely the non-universability of the contingencies of ethnic pluralism in Bukovina. It is the link between the law and people's social experiences which needs to be broken if we are to understand how law reproduces itself. We must recognise that 'the lifeworld of different groups and communities is not the principal source of global law'. Instead, he argues, we should shift:

> ... from groups and communities to discourses and communicative networks, the proto law of specialized organisational and functional networks nourished not by stores of tradition but from the ongoing self-reproduction of highly specialized and often formally organized and rather narrowly defined global networks of an economic, cultural, academic or technological nature.

---

[97] Teubner, above n 15, xiii.
[98] The formulation of this sentence is somewhat ambiguous and it is therefore not entirely clear whether Teubner himself totally endorses this account of Ehrlich's ideas. Does 'supposed to do' here mean 'as commonly thought'? However, then, if Teubner knows better, why does he makes it seem as if this does represent Ehrlich's views? Or does 'supposed to do' mean what living law 'should' reflect the different laws of ethnic communities? This would be a different claim having less to do with where law comes from than with the need to recognise cultural diversity.

Teubner inserts Ehrlich's ideas into what he (unlike Ziegert) acknowledges to be a new and unfamiliar framework. We must, he argues, replace:

> ... rule, sanction and social control with speech acts, coding transformation of differences and paradox. It is not rules but communicative events that should be our focus and it is the self-organising process of rules that is important in understanding the symbolic reality of legal validity, not the possibility of imposing sanctions.[99]

However, at the same time, he suggests that it is only if we make this move towards autopoiesis theory that we can come to discover how, in some respects, Ehrlich's approach is now *more valid* than it was in the past. As he puts it:

> ... although Eugen Ehrlich's theory turned out to be wrong for the national law of Austria, I believe that it will turn out to be right, both empirically and normatively, for the newly emerging global law.[100]

Once again, however, such striking arguments need to be carefully unpacked. In what sense does the truth of Ehrlich's (many) ideas depend on what happened in the past or on what the future brings? Should scientific claims be judged in the light of historical events? What exactly is Teubner referring to when he asserts that Ehrlich 'turned out' to be 'wrong'? This cannot, for example, include his claims about the centre of gravity of law being in society since Teubner takes this as his starting point. Have Ehrlich's ideas about living law been discredited? Must we really go beyond the boundaries of state law in order to find merit in Ehrlich's theses? When exactly did Ehrlich's theory 'turn out to be wrong'? When the First World War caused the Austrian empire to collapse? Or when he was forced to teach in Rumanian in the last years of his life (before the Nazis and communists then tried to cancel his memory)? Arguably, the rise of ethnic nationalism could actually prove Ehrlich's point about the importance of more local loyalties rather than those to the imperial state (and it is strange for Teubner to call the law of the Austro-Hungarian empire 'the national law of Austria').

What evidence, on the other hand, does Teubner have that Ehrlich will eventually turn out to be right? Even if we choose to look beyond state law, it is not obvious why the growth of *lex mercatoria* proves Ehrlich to be 'right'. It certainly shows that there can be forms of normative ordering that some call law, even though they are not based on state recognition. However, Ehrlich was not mainly concerned with whether normative orderings were (already) actually called law, but with whether scientific observers had reasons to call them law. And there are, of course, with due respect to

---

[99] Teubner, above n 15, 13.
[100] *Ibid* 3.

Teubner, still many who argue that *lex mercatoria* is not really law whatever it is called. Even though Teubner tells us that Ehrlich has been proven right through having 'predicted' the rise of non-state global law, he himself asserts that it is only a question of time before these new forms of global law will be, as he says, 're-politicized' (although admittedly he considers that this will not take place through traditional political institutions, but via 'structural coupling' with specialised discourses). Once this takes place, would this mean that Ehrlich will again have 'turned out 'to be wrong'? Is his a thesis that only works for periods of transition—for interstitial times as well as places?

CONCLUSION: INTERPRETATION AS APPROPRIATION

In this review of Ehrlich's legacies—the way in which his work has influenced and been taken up by later scholars—we have sought to provide examples of inquiries inspired by Ehrlich's ideas as well as efforts to revitalise his work. We have shown the difficulty of maintaining any simple distinction between efforts to place Ehrlich's work in its context and attempts to get it out of its context, and suggested that a degree of 'rewriting' forms an important part of re-contextualising projects whether these be carried out by Pound, Ziegert or Teubner. Once we accept that interpretation is a form of appropriation, it becomes more difficult (although not impossible) to distinguish between the appropriation and misappropriation of a previous writer's ideas.

For the purpose of tracing Ehrlich's legacy, it makes sense to ask first of all how far Teubner is faithful to Ehrlich. However, we should not be surprised if Teubner's account of what is right and wrong about Ehrlich's arguments tells us at least as much about Teubner—and his desire to show the value of the autopoietic approach to law and society—as it does about Ehrlich. Any discussion of Teubner on Ehrlich which is only interested in Ehrlich is therefore going to miss the point of what Teubner is doing. We are dealing with an author who has openly chosen to 'use' Ehrlich as a pretext to introduce a series of papers about non-state law. Therefore, the more pertinent question here, as in other cases of appropriation, is to ask how far Teubner's reading of Ehrlich's work has helped him to throw new light on *lex mercatoria*.

Teubner begins his paper by contrasting a top-down political global order based on American policing (he refers to Clinton's 'humanitarian' peacekeeping) to one constructed by means of an Ehrlich-type bottom-up 'peaceful' legal order. The latter, which he sees as more important, he equates with a range of developments in global non-state law. As it happens, after 9/11 things have 'turned out' differently with respect of the extent of American military engagements than Teubner or anyone else could have anticipated.

However, we can also question whether Global Bukowina really represents the alternative to the imposed Pax Americana that Teubner claims it does. Is *lex mercatoria*, for example, actually emancipated from politics—or is it precisely political by pretending not to be so? It is after all the genius of the common law that it 'appears' to be more geared to bottom-up economic necessities than top-down political projects. Hence the growth of *lex mercatoria* can be seen as helping to promote American ideas about the relationship between state and market and spread ways of doing law which privilege the symbolic capital of their professional elites.[101]

What of the political and practical implications of Teubner's rewriting of Ehrlich? As is not uncommon in his writings, Teubner deliberately blurs the line between describing and advocating.[102] Here he argues that *lex mercatoria* should be legally recognised for what it is, the prototype of non-state law that is inevitably replacing that of the nation state. As against this, Ralf Michaels, for example, has recently insisted that:

> ... instead of moving the state to the periphery of our analyses and thereby ignoring its importance for our problems, we should move it into the center of our analysis, so we can critique its role in globalization.

According to him:

> ... if we want to emancipate non-state law vis-à-vis the state, then it is not enough to look at the requirements on the side of non-state law. We must also look at what is necessary on the side of the state to make such emancipation possible. And we must ask what kind of emancipation this will be.[103]

For Michaels:

> The simple idea that because globalization brings about a plurality of legal orders the state should recognize all these orders as law is either too radical or not radical enough. The idea is too radical if it expects the state to do things that run counter to what the state, as it exists right now, is about. In a nutshell, the state will always react as state to the challenges of globalization, including the challenge from non-state communities and their laws. The idea is not radical enough if it believes that such a change could be brought about without changing the role of the state. In order to overcome the state-focus of conflict of laws, we must, ultimately, overcome the state itself. Ultimately, by acknowledging the right of everyone to make law, we accept that no one has the right to make law anymore. If everyone is able to claim jurisdiction, no one will have a superior position to mediate between conflicting regulations of conflicting communities anymore, at least not from a superior basis.[104]

---

[101] Y Dezalay and B Garth, *Dealing in Virtue* (Chicago, University of Chicago Press, 1996).
[102] D Nelken, 'Beyond the Metaphor of Legal Transplants?: Consequences of Autopoietic Theory for the Study of Cross-Cultural Legal Adaptation' in J Priban and D Nelken (eds), *Law's New Boundaries: The Consequences of Legal Autopoiesis* (Dartmouth, 2001) 265–302.
[103] Michaels, above n 38, 56.
[104] *Ibid* 53.

If Teubner is entitled to appropriate Ehrlich for his purposes, the same applies to those who have in turn been stimulated by Teubner's ideas. Some of these writers have in fact gone on to develop his creative 'reworking' of Ehrlich in unexpected directions. Whilst Teubner himself counterposed Global Bukowina to the idea of a global political government, Thomas Mathiesen, for example, takes Teubner's idea and uses it to chart the recent growth of a global control system, what he describes as a menacing '*lex vigilatoria*' of surveillance removed from the political control of individual nation-states.[105] According to Mathiesen, the signs of this global control without a state may be seen in the ties between, for example, the SIRENE exchange, Eurodac, communication control through retention and tapping of telecommunications traffic data, the spy system Echelon, and so on. Mathiesen's account shares with Teubner's a focus on the way in which legal regimes are becoming increasingly untied or 'de-coupled' (to use Teubner's term) from nation-states, but the idea of imposed international normative order represented here is a far cry from that described by Teubner—or for that matter by Ehrlich.

As we see, Mathiesen cites Teubner on Global Bukowina in order to make an argument that he would probably not recognise. However, other authors offer even more contestable interpretations of Teubner on Ehrlich. In an original discussion of the spread of transgenic technologies through 'timespace', Paul Street draws on the disciplinary resources of critical human geography, post- structuralism and actor network theory. His aim in large part is to show how new developments are challenging the boundaries of existing academic disciplines. Thus he describes modes of ordering that weave together legal and other normative systems through what are made to seem inanimate material technologies. For these technologies to flourish, he argues, a range of interrelationships must occur that cut across social and legal boundaries and mobilise farmers, government departments, texts, individuals, international organisations, corporations, non-governmental organisations, lawyers, as well as the seeds themselves and a host of other 'actants' (as Latour describes them). Law in the form of intellectual property rights plays a special role in bringing together dispersed actors in polymorphic social networks and maintaining the meaning of biotechnologies through time and space so as to enrol farmers into social networks necessary for the purposes of producers.

In the course of developing his argument, Street takes aim at Luhmann, who, he alleges, denies that 'law comes out of the social'. He likewise criticises Teubner for his 'attempt to give law an autonomy beyond society'.[106]

---

[105] T Mathiesen, 'Lex Vigilatoria—Towards a control system without a state?', Essays for civil liberties and democracy, *European Civil Liberties Network* (2005).

[106] P Street, 'Stabilizing flows in the legal field: Illusions of permanence, intellectual property rights and the transnationalisation of law' (2003) 3 *Global Networks* 7–28 at 9.

His case study, he says, shows rather that all law is always social and that there is no 'global law'. Specific companies invent genetically modified seeds, and use text objects, private policing and copyright law with the help of the state so as to enforce their vision of the facts about seeds and the appropriateness of exploiting their property rights. In the end, even (even?) Ehrlich is seen to have got things wrong. Street concludes his article saying that:

> ... only through examining the particular practices and processes can we glimpse the performative power not of law itself, but of those networks that successfully manage to mobilise law. For law to be successful it must in one sense be living law. It must be a law that exists beyond the proclamations and practices of lawyers and the state. But this is not Ehrlich's conception of living law. While it is a law that dominates life itself it is a law that lives within, and a law that leads to convergent habitual behaviour, but only for so long as it continues to be mobilized.[107]

Unlike Teubner, therefore, who tries to anchor his concept of Global Bukowina in Ehrlich's pioneering scholarship, Street prefers to emphasise how new developments require a radical new way of thinking, starting from scratch. It is not entirely clear what Street finds lacking in Ehrlich's approach—his exegesis of what Ehrlich wrote is even more tangential to the real point of his paper than Teubner's use of him. But let us assume, for argument's sake, that Street is right to say that what he is describing does not correspond to what Ehrlich was talking about when he introduced the concept of 'living law'. It would be all too easy to explain this by saying that Ehrlich did not really anticipate the developments described by Street. With due respect to Ziegert and Teubner, we could also wonder why anyone should have expected him to. On the other hand, matters are different if, like them, we are interested not only in what Ehrlich once meant, but also in what Ehrlich means now. In that case, we could argue that his legacy includes all that his work has inspired, including efforts to go beyond him.

---

[107] Ibid 28.

Index

A

'Acephalous', 205
Adat law, 183
  cartoon, 189
  definition of, 183
  tensions with Islam, 184
Adat Law School, *see* Van Vollenhoven, Cornelius
Administrative norms, 164
Aeschylus, 69
  Oresteia, 69–70
Agnon, SY, 68–69
Aktenmenschen, 5
  see also 'Men of Files'
Allen, CK, 86
Anglophone scholarship, 21
Annual Meeting of the German Lawyers' Association, 5
American Legal Realism, 171
Ärgernis, 3
Association of American Law Schools, 41
Ausgleich, 32
  with Hungary, 32
  see also Hapsburg Empire
Austria, 22
  Constitution of 1867, 32
    regarding ethnic groups, 34
      linguistic minorities, 34
  definition of law, 60
  German peasantry in, 67
  no melting pot, 28
  political changes, 30–31
  state sanctions, 62
  see also Hapsburg Empire
Austrian Civil Code, 67
Austrian Liberalism, 31, 32
Austrian 'notable' type, 36
  emergence of, 36
  describes Ehrlich, 37
Austro-Hungarian Empire, 13, 50
  before First World War, 31
    by early 1800s, 32
    Constitutional Law (Diploma) 1860, 31, 32
  compact populations, 33
  'curia', 33
  final years, 76, 80
  'fragmentarian' state, 35
  plural legal conditions of, 13
  need for non-Slavic universities, 26
  regarding ethnography, 23
  see also Habsburg Empire
Autopoiesis theory, 268

B

Barbarism/civilisations dichotomy, 63
  inter-European dimension, 63
  used by Ehrlich, 64–5
Batak, Karo, 187
  inheritance case, 187, 197
'Black letter law', 79
'Black letter legal research', 79
Bobčev, 24, 34, 43
  discovered ancient tribe, 67
  work on Bulgarian customary law, 24
Bogošič, *see* Bogošiš
Bogošiš, 24, 34, 43
  provided 'invaluable material', 43
  work on southern Slavs 24
British Anthropology, *see* Fin-de-siècle British anthropology
Bukovina, 10, 11, 32, 42, 51, 67, 76, 82, 266
  Decree 4091, 46
  'garden theory', 80
  'global', 227
  homo bukovinensis, 46
  integral to empire, 80
  living law in, 267
  mindset of, 29
  no melting pot, 28
  no mention of Ehrlich, 22
  populating tribes of, 232
  real law of, 68
  Reichsrat elections, 34
  Romanians of, 33, 45
    anti-Semitics, 45
    Constituent Assembly of, 45
  'Romanian Lands', 45
  social world of, 27
  understanding daily life in, 16
  see also Teubner, Gunther
Burrow, John, 51

C

Cernovitsi, *see* Czernowitz
Civil Rights Act (1964), 247
Cohen, Jonathan, 246
Cohen, Morris, 240
  criticises Ehrlich, 240

Concept of greater happiness, 59
Constituent Assembly of the Romanians of Bukovina, 45
Constitutional Law (Diploma) of 1860, the, 31
Contracts, 63
  unenforceable, 63
Coombe, Rosemary, 246
Cotterrell, Roger, 11, 15, 154
  encourages us to return to Ehrlich, 239
  perceptions of legal 'insiders' and 'outsiders', 11
'Crisis of reason', 61
  see also Fin de siècle culture
Curia:
  coalesced into, 34
  definition of, 33
Customary Law and Social Associations, see Dniestrzanski
Cyber communities, 251
  law-making by, 251–2
Czernowitz, 10
  birthplace of Ehrlich, 22, 27–28, 51, 76
  propaganda in, 45
  University of, 25, 37, 41, 45, 51, 82
    anti-Semitism, 29
    campaign for, 25–26
    Frank Josef, 26
      authentic Austrian?, 27
      imperial charter for, 26
    historical courses, 29
    transformed into Romanian University of Cernăuți, 46
    see also Tomaszczuk, Constantine

D

Deleuze, Gilles, 10, 55, 70
  Coldness and Cruelty, 50
    role of law in sadism/masochism, 55–56
  Die stillschweigende Willenserklärung, 58
  Die Tatsache des Gewohnheitrechts (The Fact of Customary Law), 40
Dniestrzanski, 43, 67
  Customary Law and Social Associations, 43
Drahomanov, Mykhailo, 33
Durkheim, Emile, 94
  as a functionalist, 255
  'pre-contractual basis of contract', 243–4
  relevance for us today, 239
Dutch East Indies, 13
  complexity of law, 13
  living law in, 178, 182–3
  plans for uniform private law, 193–4

E

Edelman, Lauren, 247
Ehrlich, Eugen:
  age of codification, 37
  anti-statist notion, 60–1
  central theme, 61
  argues for, 39–40
  experience as method/science, 42
  as a cipher, 21–2
  as a 'double marginal', 41–2
  as a functionalist, 255
  attempts to discover life, 66
  captures essence of evolution theory, 226
  characterised as, 16–7
  childhood, typical, 28
  concepts, 11
    'living law', 11, 12, 13, 42, 66–7, 77, 82
      does not correspond to law in action, 195
      seminar for, 41
    legal propositions, 153, 161
    legal norms, 159, 174
      distinguishing from non, 170
    'norms for decisions', 11, 159–61
    of law, 88–93, 127
      dogmatic, 115
      functional analysis, 231
      sociological, 102
    'social associations', 11, 227
      'inner order of', 88–89, 226–31
      lack of discrimination, 89
  contemporaries, 12
  contributions to Free School, 21
  creativity in scientific inquiry, 44
  death of, 46
  defining 'law', 38–39, 98–100
    'as a rule of human conduct', 98–9, 215–6
    dogmatic, 110–12
    how does society create law, 100
    two main functions, 100
  defining 'legal proposition', 161
  defining 'legal relations', 112, 113–4
  defining 'society', 30
  Die stillschweigende Willenserklärung, 58
  discussing social law, 213–4
  disjunction between texts/reality, 67
  dislikes counter-criticisms, 133
    regarding Kelsen, 133–5
  distinctive style, 4
    ambiguous, 135
    multiple interpretations, 6, 8, 9
    social psychology, 7, 8
  'dynamic conception of law', 22
  emphasis on legal norms, 163–4
  empiricism, 42, 145, 150
  'facts of the law' (*Tatsachen des Rechts*), 89, 90, 128, 141
    as 'input', 101
  founded Free Law School, 110
  Fundamental Principles of the Sociology of the Law, 1, 2, 5, 7–8, 12, 43

gets things wrong, 240–1
  when did this happen, 268–9
his alternative 'psychological' criterion, 92
his ethnography, 24, 33–4, 43
  intersecting science/art, 44
  radical proposal, 41–2
his geographic marginality, 80
his legal sociology, 75–6
  alternative fate of, 85
  complex tapestry, 87
  last influence, 83
  'weapon of a radical jurist', 78
holism, 30
judicial decision-making, 109–10, 116–9
  description of legislative cylce, 141–2
  sociology as scientific basis for, 120–1
'Kelsenerie', 146
importance of his work, 15, 77
  'constitutive element', 16
  'dead law', 15
'inner order' of associations, 38
intellectual formation, 23
intellectual outlook, 82
Juristische Logik, 12
  photographs of, 16
legal pluralism, 86–88
  real subtlety of, 88
legal science, 46–7
legal validity/effectiveness, 149
living law, 101
  as 'output', 101–2
obscuring position, 212–3
old law, 67–68
oppressive social practices, 139–140
personal cultural situation, 22, 80–1
pluralism, 29–30,
  was cultivated, 41
primary concern, 83
proposal of 1903, 37
reacts against 'legal science', 42
reception in United States, 41
reception theory, 105
rector in Chernivsti, 34, 81
relevance for contemporary socio-legal
  studies, 13–5
religion, 29
self-consciousness, his, 37, 82
'Seminar in Living Law', 41, 96, 232
scepticism regarding 'free will', 59
'science of law', 97–8
  'art of legislation', 121
separation of powers, 38
shows law's 'blind spots', 261–2
'The State and the Law', 2
  English medieval manor, the, 2
  Roman household, the, 2
  'scientifically untenable', 4
under consideration, 15

universal theory of law, 14
  his vision of, 224–5
'user theory of rights', 41
view of legal evolution, 163
why we obey laws, 58–9
working conditions, 11
Ellickson, Robert, 254
  Order without Law—How Neighbours Settle Disputes, 254, 255
  objections to, 257–8
  superficial reading of Ehrlich, 256
Engels, Frederick, 57
  status/contract, 57
Eppinger, Monica, 10
Empörung, 3
Entrüstung, 3
Ethnographer, 24
  initial job description, 24
  is a translator, 44–5
Ethnography, 23
  as an artifact, 23, 46–7
  as epistemology, 43–4
  as regarded by Ehrlich, 24
  initial purpose, 23
  makes sense of inter-ethnic relations, 35
  see also Franko, Ivan, Hapsburg Empire
Europe, 16
  'living law' in, 16

F

'Facts of the law' (*Tatsachen des Rechts*), 89, 90, 128, 141
  as 'input', 101
Feldman, Eric, 256
  expert on Japanese law, 256–7
Fin-de-siècle British anthropology, 24
  holism of, 30
  1896 Torres Straights expedition, 24
Fin de siècle culture, 10, 11, 68
  crisis of reason, 16, 51, 61
  pessimistic, 70
Franko, Ivan, 25
  'ethnographic' borders, 25
Free Law Movement, 164, 171
'Free School of Law', 37, 41
  Ehrlich's departure from, 40
Friedman, Lawrence, 245
Fuller, Lon, 210
  roots/need for 'legality', 247
Fundamental Principles of the Sociology of Law, 1, 2, 5, 7–8, 12, 56, 110, 113
  anti-formalist conceptions, 68
  conceptual scepticism, 135–141
  free will, 58
  introduction by Roscoe Pound, 158, 260
  legislative norms, 211
  life's priority over law, 142–3

living law, 166
  praise for, 95–6
  'prey to naturalising fallacy', 202, 206
  reception in Japan, 109
  reception in United States, 41
  similarity with *Venus in Furs*, 56
  societal law explained, 114
  three types/sources of law, 128

G

'Gaps' in the code, 37–8, 47
  Ehrlich's 'user theory of rights', 41
  see also Gény, François
Geertz, Clifford, 204
  legal *mixité*, 204
Gefühlstöne, 3
  feelings, 136
    overtones of, 170
Gény, François, 37
  regarding 'gaps' in the Code, 37–8
German BGB, 114
German Historical School, 61
'German Science', 26, 27
  interpretation of, 26
Glasul Bucovinei (Bukovina's Voice), 45
Gobard, Henri, 37
Goodrich, Peter, 57
  courts of love, 57–8
Grundlegung der Soziologie des Rechts, see Fundamental Principles of the Sociology of Law

H

Haar, Ter, 187
  'decision theory', 187
  finding unwritten law, 188
Hapsburg Empire, 22
  emergence of army, civil service, 36
  ethnography, 43
    a descriptive genre in, 43
  last decades of, 30
    era of *Ausgleich*, 30–1
  supranational figure, 37
  use of ethnography, 24
  see also Austro-Hungarian Empire
Hapsburg House, 35
Hayek, Friedrich, 207
Hertogh, Marc, 83
  investigating law in action/legal consciousness, 245
Herzls, Theodor, 25
Historical School of Jurisprudence, 211
  law reflects a specific character, 213–4
Holmes, Oliver W, 95–6
HuMa, 188
  Indonesian cartoon, 188–9, 196
Hurmuzaki, Baron Gheorghe, 26

I

Indonesia, 13
  'living law' in, 13, 177–8, 197
    as dead law, 178–8
    becomes 'lawyers' law', 183–4
    Freie Rechtslehre, 187
    not limited to adat, 186
    with Islamic law, 16
      enforcement of, 184
    'state-Islam-adat', 184
  Supreme Court of, 184
    reconstructed adat laws, 185–6
    went too far, 187
  see also Islamic Law, Van Vollenhoven, Cornelius
Intellectual property law, 246
International Institute for the Sociology of Law, 1
Internet law, 251–4
  see also Cyber communities, 251
  when do norms become law, 254
Interpreting Ehrlich, 242
  how it becomes authoritative, 242–3
Islamic law, 181
  regarded as 'external' law, 181
  see also Indonesia, Van Vollenhoven, Cornelius
Institute (Seminar) for Living Law, 1
Izutaro, Suehiro, 96
  influenced by Ehrlich, 103–4
  judge's dilemma, 105–6
    solution, 107–8
  own living law, 106–7
  radicalised sociological theory, 104–5, 108–9
  regards court decisions as, 107
  'Seminar for the Study of Civil Cases', 108
  sociologist, 103

J

Japan, 16, 153
  'living law' in, 16
  sociology of law, 96
Josef, Emperor Franz, 31, 45
  permitted several traditions, 35
Juridical Society of Vienna, 22
Juristische Logik, 109–110, 135
  contractual agreements, 114
  dogmatic conception, 113
  lawyer's thinking habit, 143–4
Justice Holmes, 23

K

Kafka, Franz, 52, 68
  'In The Penal Colony', 69
Kelsen, Hans, 95, 140, 175, 180, 267

Ehrlich's most famous critic, 12
  controversy with, 96, 129, 239–40
 critique, 129–133, 137, 151
  'intellectual error', 139
  norms for decisions, 160
  possible replies, 133–5, 138, 152
 distinguishes social/scientific law, 12
 empirical evidence, 154
 Pure Theory of Law, 142–3, 147, 154
  validity of legal norms, 148, 149, 153
Klimt, Gustav, 69
 Jurisprudence, 69–71
  links with *Venus in Furs*, 71
  masochist themes, 70–1
Koschorke, Albrecht, 58
Kritischen Ablehnung, 3

L

Lächerlichkeit, 3
Law:
 as a term, 251
 grounded in social practices, 211
 indeterminacy of, 170–1
 may/not coincide with justice, 145
 not necessarily connected to State, 8
 produced by, 84
 social significance of, 8
 sociological definition of, 98–100
 what is, 6, 38–9
 see also Sociology of Law
Law in Brief Encounters, *see* Reisman, Michael
'Law in Cyberspace', 248
Law merchant, 248–9
Legal consciousness, 7, 9, 245
 social perceptions of law, 136
Legal globalisation, 266–7
Legal norms, 159
Legal pluralism, 11
 new forms, 248
 protected/cultivated, 41
Legal propositions, 161
 not a unity, 230
 suitable for larger political entities, 164
Legal sociology, 77
Likhovski, Assaf, 10
 examines 'free will' concept, 10–11
 see also Fin de siécle culture
'Living law' concept, 1, 3, 165–6
 embracing wide range, 254–5
 in a sociological sense, 7
 in Japanese jurisprudence, 103
 in twenty-first century, 234–6
 is the law that survives, 140–1
 legal versus non-legal norms, 3, 7
 'not very useful', 5
 only way to analyse, 7
 three aspects of, 242–60
 versus 'intuitive law', 9

Llewellyn, Karl, 11, 75, 96
 'law jobs', 248
Lüderssen, Klaus, 129
Luhmann, Niklas, 95, 241, 260, 261, 265
 autopoietic social theory, 246
 re-reading Ehrlich, 242
  can help us understand, 264
 scientific observer of law, 262–3

M

MacCormick, Neil, 139
 Searle's Speech Act theory, 139
Maine, Henry, 56, 63
 contract/free will, 56–7, 58, 59
 notions of law, 64–5
Malinowski, Bronislaw, 10
 'no such thing as Austrian', 28
Man's only choice, 59
Masoch, Leopold von, *see* Sacher-Masoch, Leopold von
Masochism, 68
 major cultural theme, 68–71
Mathiesen, Thomas, 271
 '*lex vigilatoria*', 271
Meiji Restoration, 96, 104
 Roman law received during, 105
'Men of Files', 5
 see also Aktenmenschen
'Men of the Senses', 5–6
 see also Mensch der Sinne
Mensch der Sinne, 5–6
 see also 'Men of the Senses', 3
Michaels, Ralf, 249–50, 270
 his juristic perspective, 250
 law merchant, 249
Misconceptions of Adat Law, *see* Van Vollenhoven, Cornelius
Montesquieu, 23
 L'Esprit des Lois, 23
 methods, 42
 use of '*devoir*', 23–4

N

Nelken, David, 14, 173, 175, 178
 difference between Ehrlich/Pound, 195
 reconsidering Ehrlich, 14, 83
  living law, 196
  what is meant by, 237–8
  why study him?, 238–43
 rewriting Ehrlich, 260–9
Neumann, Franz, 89
 reviewing Sociology of Law, 89
Nimaga, Salif, 15
 misleading analogies, 13
Nistor, Ion, 45
 rector of University of Czernowitz, 45–6
 homo bukovinensis, 46

Normative order, 201, 211, 220–1
    always open, 208
    aspirations of, 209
    definition if 201–2
Norms for decisions, 159–60, 164–5, 174
    Entscheidungsnormen, 229–30
    rule of conduct for courts, 162–3
    two sets of, 165

O

'*Opinio necessitatis*', 2, 4
    'behavioural definition', 8
    law versus morals, 7
    new methodology, 5
        'independent science of law', 5, 7
    not taken seriously, 6
    'what is law', 6
Order without Law—How Neighbours Settle Disputes, see Ellickson, Robert

P

Petrazycki, 194
    'intuitive law', 194–5
    'more precise' than Ehrlich, 194
Pistor, Fanny 49–50
Polenklub, 34
    of Polish/Galician, 34
Posner, Eric, 254
    A Theory of Norms, 254
    norms as rules, 256
Postema Gerald, 219
    theory of common law, 219
Pound, Roscoe, 11, 96, 269
    anti-formalism, 171–2
    concern with unmet social needs, 195
    contemporary of Ehrlich, 12
        appreciation for, 166–7
        comparisons with, 13
        kindred spirits, 172–3
    introduced Ehrlich to China, 241
    'law in action', 13, 84–5, 245, 260–1
        linked to 'living law', 157–8
    'Law in Books and Law in Action', 158, 168
        norms and facts, 169–170, 175
    lacking in thought, 84
    non/legal norms, 170
    'not be afraid of legislation', 172
    obscures Ehrlich for us today, 239
    on jurisprudence, 166–7
    promoting Ehrlich, 83
Prodjodikoro, Wirjona, 185–6
    President of Indonesia, 185
Pure Theory of Law, see Kelsen, Hans

R

Rehbinder, Manfred, 1, 6
Reisman, Michael, 254

fleeting relationships, 258–9
Law in Brief Encounters, 254, 258
legal/micro order, 259
Renner, Karl, 35, 81, 246–7, 265
    children exchange (*Kinderwechsel*), 35
Rheinstein, Max, 85n, 245
    characterises Ehrlich, 85n
    hard/sympathetic critic, 240, 241
    regarding generalisations, 247
Roberts, Simon, 205
    'acephalous', 205
    'law' as term, 251
Roman law, 59, 67, 105
    history of contract, 59–60
Romanian National Council, 45
Romanian University of Cernăuți, 46
'Rules of conduct', 104
    distinguished from 'norms for decision', 103–4
Russell, Bertrand, 46

S

Sacher-Masoch, Leopold von, 10, 57, 65, 68
    celebrates loss of will, 59
    contract with lover, 49–50
    interest in the exotic, 64
    shifting identities, 65–6
    Venus in Furs, 10, 50
        anti-formalist conceptions, 68
        based on, 61–2
        border-crossings, 60
        brief outline, 53–6
        can be read as, 68
        'crisis of reason', 61
        exotic, 64
        masochism, 70
            links with *Jurisprudence*, 71
        notion of free will, 57, 61
        role of law in, 54
        to be read with Ehrlich's sociology of law, 52
            similar themes/ideas, 52
        use of contract, 66
Schulz, Bruno, 68
'Science of law', 97
Selznick, Philip, 247
'Seminar for the Study of Civil Cases', see Izutaro, Suehiro
Social associations, 89
Social norms, 63
Sociology of the law, 11, 68, 91
    naturalism/agency in, 211–20
    neglects state omnipotence, 14
    not to replace jurisprudence, 96–7
    perceptions of, 11–12
    replacing jurisprudence, 122
    scientific basis, 119
        for judicial decision-making, 120–1

with jurisprudence, 115, 122–23
   role for, 119
Spencer, Herbert, 14
   committed to scientific methodology, 232
   defining 'proper sphere' of government, 233
   near contemporary of Ehrlich, 14
   important source, 14, 225–6
      for sociological theory, 231–2
   on state power, 233–4
State law, 161
   definition of, 161–2
   inherently non-consensual, 202
   role of, 219
Street, Paul, 251
   criticises Teubner, 271–2
   new developments require new thinking, 272

T

Tacitus, 65
   Germania, 65
Tamanaha, Brian, 251
   state law, 259–60
   use of term 'law', 251
The Discovery of Adat Law, see Van Vollenhoven, Cornelius
The Fact of Customary Law, 40
The Free Finding of Law and Free Legal Science, 41
   reception in United States, 41
The Juristic Logic, see *Juristische Logik*
'The State and the Law', see Ehrlich, Eugen,
Teubner, Gunther, 241, 263, 272
   faithfulness to Ehrlich, 269–70
   global law, 264
   Global Law without a State, 248
   law/not law is the question, 248
   leading interpreter in legal sociology, 262
   lex mercatoria should be recognised, 270
   need to correct/develop Ehrlich, 264–5
   notion of periphery, 265–6
   on Global Bukovina, 242–3, 263, 264, 270–1
   problems with Ehrlich's ideas, 267–9
   'technical standardization', 266
Timasheff, Nicholas, 86
   sympathetic to sociology of law, 86
Tomaszczuk, Constantin, 26, 37
   campaigned for university in Czernowitz, 26
   rector of, 27
   regarding 'German Science', 27
Torres Straights expedition, see Fin-de-siècle British anthropology

U

Ukranians, 34
   rural Ruthenians, 34

United States, 96
   sociology of law, 96
University of Vienna, 22

V

van Klink, Bart, 15
   giving up fact/norm distinction, 12–13
   highly critical review, 12
Van Vollenhoven, Cornelius, 12, 197
   ahead of his time, 195–6
   attention paid to Islamic law, 181–2
   criticised colonial legal policies, 192
      Dutch government, 193–4
   discovered 'living law', 178
   levend recht, 178–9
   founded Adat Law School, 179
      adat law circles, 179–80
      law in its own right, 180–1
   his students, 182–3
   identified social mechanisms, 195
   influential in Indonesia, 13
      cautioned against distinctions, 188
      'common product law', 181
   Misconceptions of Adat Law, 180
   mixed two scientific genres, 194
   'most congenial of contemporaries', 178, 195–6
   similar flaws with Ehrlich, 189–94
   The Discovery of Adat Law, 180
   see also Indonesia, Islamic law
Venus in Furs, see Sacher-Masoch, Leopold von
Vienna, 16
   highest conversion rate to Christianity, 28
   Reichsrat established, 31, 32, 34
   Romanian National Council, 45
   social sciences, 44
   'state law', 16
Vinogradoff, Paul, 85
   writing about Ehrlich, 85–6
Vogl, Stefan, 11, 15
Von Benda-Beckmann, Franz, 13
   characteristics of Indonesian society, 16
Von Benda-Beckmann, Keebet, see Von Benda-Beckmann, Franz

W

Weber, Max, 52, 94
   denounces Ehrlich, 95
   exclusive focus on state law, 225
   relevance for us today, 239
Webber, Jeremy, 13, 15
   'naturalising law', 13–14
Weiler, Bernd, 81
Wittgenstein's theory, 218
   what it means to follow a rule, 218
World War I, 25, 29, 31, 46
   disruptions of, 76, 268

Z

Ziegert, Klaus A., 14, 178, 196–7, 241, 260, 265, 269, 272
   comment on 'living law', 191
   critical of Ehrlich, 189–90
   difference between Ehrlich/legal realists, 195
   forced interpretations, 262
   his new introduction, 261
      re-presenting Ehrlich, 263–4
   legal versus sociological theory, 14